A DARKER ELECTRICITY

THE ORIGINS OF THE

SPIRAL TRIBE
SOUND SYSTEM

MARK ANGELO HARRISON

VELOCITY PRESS

First published by Velocity Press 2023

velocitypress.uk
sp23.org

Printed and bound in Great Britain by Clays Ltd, Elcograf S.p.A.

Cover design
Mark Angelo Harrison

Typesetting
Paul Baillie-Lane
pblpublishing.co.uk

ISBN: 9781913231354

Mark Angelo Harrison was among the founding members and creative energies behind the pioneering free-party sound system Spiral Tribe. Or, as the Crown Prosecutor described him, 'the criminal ringleader' who'd helped mastermind Britain's 'biggest ever illegal rave' at Castlemorton.

In 2011, Mark studied at the Open University, receiving a diploma in creative writing. For twelve years, he managed a permaculture project and two conservation tree nurseries in England, planting over 40,000 native trees.

Working as a writer, photographer and graphic artist, he continues to co-create with several members of the original sound system (now known as SP23), as well as with many other European collectives.

Praise for *A Darker Electricity*:

A fascinating insider account of some of the most remarkable episodes in outlaw rave culture. With a cast of suitably hardcore characters, Mark Angelo Harrison chronicles how Spiral Tribe's determination to stage free parties set them on a collision course with the authorities. **Matthew Collin, author of *Altered State* and *Rave On***

With this beautifully told new book, we finally get to hear the story of Spiral Tribe from the inside, from someone who lived it. An incredible story which leaps from the urban empty spaces to the ancient green lanes of hidden England, moving from deeply personal perspectives to political and cosmological ones. It's an incredible record of an era and movement often misrepresented, as well as a 'connecting of the dots' from that time to the precarious world we now find ourselves in. **Aaron Trinder, filmmaker/creator of** *Free Party: A Folk History*, **a documentary on the origins of the free party movement, Castlemorton and beyond.**

A memorable account of a tempestuous time. *A Darker Electricity* evokes the rebellious mood of an anarchic movement. **Sam Batra, *City Limits/The Wire***

An exhaustive first-hand story of life inside Spiral Tribe, *A Darker Electricity* is a fascinating insight into a pivotal moment in dance music history. **Ed Gillett, author of *Party Lines: Dance Music and the Making of Modern Britain***

Spiral Tribe gave me a purpose beyond just organising parties. It was a family, a mission and a mental trip – with many bumps along the road! **Jeff Catchpole (DJ Jeff23)**

1991. The Spiral Summer of love. After the Avon Free festival we turned our horse-drawn convoy east towards Kent to pick apples in the autumn. All along the route, everywhere we stopped, Spiral Tribe would magically pop up! **Ixindamix**

Spiral Tribe was an improbable adventure. We were swept along on the crest of an exhilarating but dangerous wave. **Debbie Griffith**

The first time I heard the name Spiral Tribe, I was being warned by a friend: 'They're looking for you!' **Simon Carter, Crystal Distortion**

For Zander

There is no single truth. There is no one word that can describe it. But give me some poetry to describe around a point, and I can give you its exact coordinates.

INTRODUCTION

As one of the co-founders and designers of the outlawed Spiral Tribe Sound System, this is my personal memoir of the early nineties free-party scene. Told through my eyes – the eyes of a visual artist. It tells of the circumstances leading to the group's conception, birth and rapid evolution into something much more than just a collection of amps, speakers and cables. A collective, a culture, and later, an international community.

Our movement was rooted in the idea of open access, equality and community participation. As friends, we set out on a journey into a landscape of urban dereliction, abandoned industry and crumbling military bases.

Guerilla-style, we built the people's sound system. Everyone was welcome. Our DIY ethos defied the traditions of cultural production. And our boundless dance floor challenged proprietary claims on social space.

From small squat-scene parties in London to enormous warehouse raves and free festivals. From one little overloaded van to the mighty convoy of matte-black military vehicles that instigated the Teknivals of Europe.

This is the inside story of how the Spiral Tribe Sound System came into being, and how the authorities attempted to crush us – and criminalise an entire culture.

Mark Angelo Harrison, May 2023

FOREWORD

The first time I was exposed to Spiral Tribe was through a television screen in 1992, watching their 'Forward the Revolution' music video. It definitely caught my attention – I felt hypnotised by what I saw. The haunting lyrics, off-key chords, rhythmic repetitive baseline, the strobe light and the spinning black and white spiral backdrop were mesmerising. There was something mysterious about it. Throughout the video, in between layered imagery of microscopic details, floating graphic symbols and flashes of circuit board, was a crew of people singing the lyrics. They were nodding their heads wearing black bomber jackets, dark shades, some with shaved heads, all with a slightly confrontational edge, singing: 'You might stop the party, but you can't stop the future.'

I was just fourteen, craving freedom and already very drawn to anything alternative. I had always been rebellious in nature to authority, rules and any sheep-like way of thinking. I had an unconventional upbringing with my childhood spent growing up in Woodstock, upstate New York, a magnet for creative free-thinking people and where DIY culture was very present. At the time, I didn't feel I related to the kids at school of my age. I was searching for meaning and trying to find the place where I fit in. On viewing the video, I thought to myself: 'Wow, I have never seen anything like this. I need to be part of it in some way.'

Little did I know that fate would lead me that way a year later. At that stage most of my friends were older than me and lived in squats. I started to regularly attend a club night called Whirl-Y-Gig held at the Old Street Town Hall. It was a 'fluffy' night, and a breeding ground for young clubbers and ravers. It was also where I made friends with a slightly older crew including Mutley and Steve, who seemed to know everyone in the building. The night would finish at 12 a.m., and back then there were no other bars or clubs to carry on the night. This was 1993 and the Shoreditch area was completely unrecognisable to the bustling urban circus it has become today.

Anyway, at midnight we felt the night was cut too short and were left in limbo, still buzzing and full of energy. So when Mutley and Steve asked if I wanted to carry on at a Spiral free party in West London, I jumped at the chance. After watching that video and seeing 'In The Area' stickers splattered around the city, the name Spiral Tribe was imprinted in my mind. We called the free party line number from a pay phone to get the address and directions, then we went on our way.

When we arrived, I was aware of the magical but darker energy in the air. It was very different to Whirl-Y-Gig. The music was hard and so were the people. It was also a more mature crowd, which felt more appealing to my fifteen-year-old self. I danced non-stop until the early hours and interacted with every raver in the room. We were all there for the same purpose – to dance and have some temporary escape and release from our weekday lives. The ethos behind these parties were that they were 'free' and always operating a donation-only policy. They were not commercially driven, but were more about rebelling against the over commercialisation of the acid house and club culture that was developing in this country at the time. We were all united through the shared experience and energy of the dance floor. It felt like I had discovered something new and exciting – a deeply underground and hidden world.

I was immediately hooked, and not long after I was 'spiralled', as the saying went. My life soon evolved around the twenty-four-hour parties, going to raves on Saturday night then hanging out in squats all day Sunday and somehow making it to school on a Monday. It didn't take long for me to make friends with all the sound system crews, including the Tribe. Soon after I shaved off my hair and became a 'Spiral Baby'. I looked the part, had the attitude and shared the passion. I wasn't a DJ, producer, backdrop creator or sound system owner. I would sometimes work on the bar or help collect donations on the door. But mainly I was one of the 'vibe providers', which also had its importance. There were of course many other sound systems that I befriended and discovered along the way, but, for me, Spiral Tribe was the spark which lead to the journey of the next decade of my life and shaped me through my formative early adult years. These raves and parties brought thousands of people together through shared values. There was a sense of community that I've never experienced again in the same way.

Even though it was a part of my life until 2003, the free-party scene by 1994 was rapidly evolving and starting to be faced with restrictions and limitations. With thousands of people attending unlicenced free parties and raves via word of mouth, the government was terrified that things were getting out of control, so it put huge pressure on the authorities to focus on clamping down on any gatherings of people where the music was 'predominantly characterised by repetitive beats'. I remember a few parties in London that were aggressively shut down. The police would turn up, beat people up, confiscate equipment and make unprovoked arrests. At the same time there were many anti-criminal justice bill protests that we all attended, to fight for our freedom and protect our right to party.

So why did the UK government clamp down so hard on these free parties? What was the harm? What were they so afraid of? Repetitive beats have been around for thousands of years. Tribal drumming music was used in ceremonies as an expression of energy and emotion, and a way to come together in celebration. The hypnotic drum rhythms connect us to the primal energy of the Earth. Techno music is designed in the same way. The repetitive nature of the sounds can put you in a trance-like state.

As human beings we need moments to let go of our self-awareness, and that can happen through the experience of being on a dance floor. Dance is a way for human beings to express themselves without words. The dance floor is a shared experience, a way for us to feel connected and communicate without speaking. Maybe the idea of the events being 'free' is what frightened the authorities? Perhaps going against capitalism in this way became a political statement.

Reading Mark's book takes you back in time on a magical fractal ride to the early days when the first seeds of Spiral Tribe were planted. It is fascinating to read how it all unfolds. It gives insight into the urban and political landscape of the late 1980's and into the '90s. A reminder of this relevant, pivotal point in history before smart phones and social media. A time lived without the dominance of screens in which we truly existed in the present moment.

I have memories in the early days of hanging out with Mark and having long, inspiring conversations about life and the cosmic connections between things. He also opened up my mind to the 23 enigma. It is no coincidence that I am writing this on 23rd of the month in 2023 before the book is released. Reading through the pages of this book, I felt like a portal had been opened. So many synchronicities took place around me, and I feel as if the Spiral of time has spun. It confirmed to me that everything really is connected.

Seana Gavin

Artist and author of SPIRALLED, published by IDEA

EMBERS IN THE SNOW: NOVEMBER 1993

A few crumpled cigarettes slipped to the dishevelled Mongolian guards would be our ticket into the decommissioning Soviet bases, where, like brooding volcanoes, mountains of military clothing smouldered. On more than one occasion we'd been offered Kalashnikov AK47s, crated in rough pine boxes and wrapped in oiled paper. With our diesel-stained combat fatigues, shaved heads, gaunt features and hungry eyes, we looked like a tribe of desperadoes. We *were* a tribe of desperadoes, but for us, survival in Berlin's sub-zero winter wasn't going to be about guns – it was going to be about big, fluffy Russian hats.

By dawn the wood burner had died and any residual heat had escaped through the thin plastic walls of the caravan. The chill pressed through the rugs and blankets piled on my bed. Huddled under that heap, I was in a dilemma. Should I return to England to fight the multi-million-pound court case being brought by Her Majesty's government against me and my fellow conspirators, or live my life on the run in Europe?

I was already on bail awaiting trial but had escaped the country with the crew and our sound system. Why go back to face the threat of four years in prison? Fight or flight? Or perhaps just stay curled up, freezing to death under a pile of old rugs and blankets?

I crawled out from under the covers and, shaking with cold, got into my quilted Soviet trousers and jacket. Squeezed my feet, with extra pair of socks, into my loose-laced para boots. Put on my fluffy Russian hat and stepped out of the caravan onto the compacted snow of Berlin's city centre – out onto Potsdamer Platz – Berlin's equivalent to London's Piccadilly Circus. At least, that's what it used to be.

●

Fifty years after the event, the city centre was still a war-torn wasteland. Around me lay great tracts of flattened rubble. The few buildings still standing were blackened, broken and shrapnel-pocked. In the final Battle of Berlin, the avenging Red Army had ground Potsdamer Platz to dust.

After the war, the Soviets built the Berlin Wall, dividing East and West. Its route, like a zigzag scar, cut Berlin, and Potsdamer Platz, in two. It had been a prison perimeter as much as a border defence, constructed as two parallel walls – the 100-metre gap between them known, for good reason, as the 'Death Strip'. To keep the machine gunners' lines of sight clear, it had been drenched in weed-killer, and still – four years after the Wall had come down – nothing grew there. To most people it was a no-go zone, a wound still too painful to touch. But to us, a marauding hoard of rag-tag-chancers, it was a no man's land – with free parking.

●

The dawn twilight darkened with the threat of more snow. I pulled up my collar and tried to rub some warmth into my fingers. Stepping over the circle of old beer crates and Jerrycans that we used as seating, I scraped the charred remains of the previous night's campfire together, fanning the embers back into flame. Out of the slush I collected cutlery and dirty plates, left where they'd been dropped after the previous night's meal.

I carefully put a tin can of water in the fire to boil. Living the cold, hungry existence I had been for the last six months meant that no amount of ash in that sooty can, or friction between myself and certain members of the crew, could spoil the luxury of my early morning coffee.

Sipping my drink I looked at our scattered wagon circle: black and silver trucks, tank transporters and fighter jets. Closest to me was the largest of our showman's trailers – our mobile recording studio. Seb and Si, both musicians and producers, usually slept in there, slumped over the mixing desk or computer keyboard. That is, *if* they slept. It wasn't uncommon for the beating heart of Spiral Tribe – the kick drums thudding through the trailer's thickly insulated walls – to beat night and day. And if the showman's studio was the pumping heart of Spiral Tribe, then Seb and Si were a large part of its soul.

Beyond the edges of our camp, I could see the twinkling headlights of the early rush-hour traffic. Beyond that, the nearest standing structures were government buildings – what had once been SS HQ. On the adjoining piece of land, in a couple of bulbous, bug-like trucks, were our neighbours: The Lost Tribe of MiG – a faction of the Mutoid Waste Company that were (and still are) famous for their monolithic scrap-metal sculptures.

The Lost Tribe were already onsite when we'd arrived and had created a garden around their live-in vehicles. The weed-killer-soaked dust meant that a traditional garden was impossible.

But, like dragon's teeth, spent bullets and shrapnel fragments had seeded the poisoned ground – and the artists' imaginations. It wasn't hollyhocks that sprouted from the sterile earth but a jagged crop of metal sculptures – skeletal, cyborg figures.

When we'd first parked up, Joe Rush, sculptor with the Lost Tribe, had welcomed us into the garden. Dressed in dark overalls, with welder's goggles across his forehead, he'd given us some advice: 'Mutate and survive!' And so started a collaboration, at the centre of which were the two MiG-21 fighter jets.

The sleekly muscled, shark-like aircraft had been acquired by the Lost Tribe while beachcombing the debris along the Soviet's high tide line. The plan was to strip the paint from one, back to the polished titanium, then, hidden on a hydraulic arm, it would rise up – the surprise finale of the coming New Year's Eve party. Not a dancing girl pirouetting out of a cake – but the gutted, hung carcass of a military predator.

•

I refilled my coffee can and put it back to boil. When I looked up again, a stranger was approaching. A small man in a dark trench coat, wire-rimmed glasses and a downturned moustache. He smiled and, in perfect English, introduced himself. He was, he said, 'from the government'. If all things were equal, I guessed he'd be a timid man, but in his role as a government employee, he had the quiet confidence of someone who had the full weight of the state behind him.

He brushed the sleet off a beer crate and sat down. My immediate thought was *Here we go again*, certain that I was about to hear the click-click of his briefcase opening as he served me with eviction documents.

I was only half right. Instead, he told me – with some enthusiasm – that now Germany was reunified, they were about to move the capital from Bonn back to Berlin – and that the badlands of Potsdamer Platz, at the very heart of the new capital, were destined to become the most expensive pieces of real estate in the world. Mercedes and Sony, he said, had already drawn up plans for their new skyscraper HQs.

As he spoke, a swirl of snow crossed between us. It picked up ash from the fire and caused a defiant red glow to flicker among the embers. As I watched the glow waver, I realised that the old walls of crude, brutal control may have come down, but new perimeters were under construction, this time, mirror polished.

In the east of the city, anarchists were fighting the capitalists – street by street, house by house, brick by flying brick. Many of the original owners of the occupied properties had been murdered by the Nazis. The communist state nationalised private property. When the Eastern Bloc toppled, the capitalists claimed the territory. But the anarchists had got in there first, and – as the property developers discovered – they'd done a little more than change a few locks.

To avoid escalating the war with the anarchists, the government man wanted to do a deal. If we left Potsdamer Platz peacefully, he would give us an abandoned Soviet base. Message delivered, he politely declined my offer of coffee and left.

It was a tempting proposal. But it didn't simplify my dilemma. Should I return to England to fight the case against us or evade the British authorities and stay in Europe? They wanted to silence us and criminalise the very idea of free festivals and free parties. Fighting the case might be the honourable thing to do. But that would mean walking into their carefully constructed trap. A trap that the Crown Prosecution had now been refining for two years.

If we did the deal with the Germans, we could settle down on an abandoned military base. *Domestic bliss?* I smiled at the thought of red geraniums growing in window boxes under the gun-slits of a Soviet bunker. *I'd be stupid to go back and jeopardise my freedom. But then, if no one defends the cause, the British authorities will win – without a fight.*

The bouncing pulse of a kick drum disturbed my thoughts. Seb and Si were awake and powering up the studio. I threw the dregs of my coffee into the fire. The embers hissed and white steam curled up into the snow that had started to fall. *No, definitely not – not geraniums!*

PART 1

From Fluffy

EXIT SOUTH: MANCHESTER, ENGLAND, SEPTEMBER 1989

Four years before finding myself a fugitive, freezing and half-starved in Berlin, I was in England, packed and ready to leave Manchester – forever. My brother Zander had driven up from London in a tipper truck to help me move.

'Are you sure about this?' I asked him as I dragged a heavy suitcase out of my flat and onto the walkway.

Once Zander's mind is made up, there's no point questioning him, but I was still a little unclear about what he'd suggested – he doesn't like to explain himself once he's set a thought in motion. When he's got a problem to solve, the same intense focus and control that keeps him balanced, split-second to split-second, high up in the tree canopy, blocks out all distractions. He's a strong, practical bloke after having been a tree surgeon all his working life.

He picked up the two heaviest cardboard boxes packed with my sketchbooks and diaries. Out on the walkway, he balanced the boxes on the balustrade and looked over the edge, calculating space.

We were up on the fourth floor of Poynton Close, in the Hulme district of inner-city Manchester. Now demolished, the close had been part of a vast grid of semi-derelict council flats connected to each other by deep stairwells and narrow aerial walkways.

I gave up battling with my suitcase and joined him at the rail. 'Zander, I don't know about this, really. I don't think . . .' I knew whatever I said would make no difference – it was as inevitable as gravity itself. He lifted the first box over the edge and, with a carefully judged shove, dropped it out into the air.

As my worldly possessions fell through space, the finality of my move hit me. I was going to miss my life in Manchester, the friendships, music and memories. Most of which revolved around the dark, rumbling core of the city's cultural centre: The Haçienda. The legendary nightclub was just five minutes walk from my front door.

I'd expected the move to be difficult, especially carrying all my stuff down the eight flights of stairs. I needn't have worried – Zander's plan was in motion. The box finished its four-storey descent, landing in the half-load of leaves and springy brush-wood in the back of his tipper truck.

'Bull's-eye!' His look of absolute concentration was wiped away by a gleeful grin.

Minutes later, the truck was fully loaded. I closed the door on my life in Manchester, and we made a quick exit – south.

BRONDESBURY PARK, NORTH WEST LONDON

Zander slept rough on a railway embankment in Acton, West London. Not because he was down and out but because he liked to sleep under the stars. If he wasn't working up a tree, he'd probably be rock climbing, weight training or kickboxing. All his life, he'd been into nature, often pitting himself against it. As young as nine or ten, he'd spend hours out in the countryside with his bow and arrow or fishing remote stretches of the River Thames. In his early teens, summer or winter, he lived in an ankle-length trench coat: dark green with two rows of brass military buttons – from the pocket of which peeped his white ferret.

With his life-long affinity for the wilds, I wasn't surprised that it took some time to persuade him to share a flat with me.

Brondesbury Park was a quiet leafy area, ten minutes stroll south-west from the Kilburn tube and the lava flow of traffic on Kilburn High Road. The tiny flat we rented was on the second floor of a small modern block – modern in the sense that it was built in the early eighties, out of chocolate-brown bricks, and designed to maximise the developer's profit by minimising the occupant's space.

When we first moved in, Zander got me some casual work with Tree Co, the firm of tree surgeons he was with. After a few months working there as a labourer, I found work at a printers – work that better suited my 'artistic temperament'. Both of us enjoyed London's electronic dance music scene. Every weekend was an adventure, exploring clubs and warehouse parties, usually with some of the other lads from Tree Co.

THE CAUSE OF STORMS: APRIL 1990

On Saturday 31 March, Debbie, a new acquaintance and close neighbour, threw a small party in her ground-floor flat. Some of the people there I'd already met. But not Katia.

I had to raise my voice as Debbie ushered me through the crush at the front door. 'What a lot of people!' I said.

'God knows who half of them are!' she shouted back over her shoulder, briefly fluttering her eyes to heaven. 'It's all a bit more cramped than usual – a great aunt of mine died.'

'Oh,' I stuttered, caught off-guard and not knowing what to say, 'I'm sorry . . .'

'That's okay, she died a while back, but I rescued a load of her stuff – vases, ornaments. I've got twice the furniture I need – and it's not a big flat.'

Music was coming from the downstairs front room, though the corridor and stairs were also crowded. Not with the incoherent drunks common at parties a few years previously, but with people submerged in deep conversation while beaming meaningfully into each other's eyes.

Debbie was slim and had short hair. She worked as a plasterer, painter and decorator, and sometimes nanny. Every time I'd met her, which was always out at parties or clubs, she was running on nervous energy, making sure everyone was all right, that everyone got what they needed and – most importantly – that no annoying DJs played any 'Naff tunes that kill the vibe'.

There was only one thing Debbie liked better than to chat and look after people, and that was to dance. When Debbie danced, she didn't just appear to connect with some other cosmic energy – she actually did.

We pushed our way through the jostling bodies into the candlelit front room. I squeezed past a group of people dressed in loudly patterned surfwear. At about six foot three, with a peaked cap slanted backwards on his head and, on his face – at a recklessly crooked angle – a pair of children's novelty sunglasses, I recognised Hamish, another of Debbie's close circle

6

of friends. In passing, I gave him a high handshake and we exchanged the greeting, 'Awhight-geeza!'

Debbie's new boyfriend, Hubert, aka 'Scallywag', was trampolining on the sofa in a blue tracksuit with white stripes down the sleeves. Mid-bounce, his neat little dreadlocks weightlessly floated around his head like a dark halo. In between fits of giggling, he rapped his own irreverent lyrics over the top of the acid house music that boomed from the home stereo.

'Home-sweet-home!' said Debbie as she spontaneously transformed a shrug of helplessness into a hands-in-the-air dance move, her expression of resignation lighting up in rapture as the bass beat of Alison Limerick's 'Where Love Lives' took hold of everyone in the room.

•

In the morning, a sheet of LSD blotters was being passed around. I noticed that printed on each tiny, perforated square of paper was a red dragon. Already fired by the paper's chemical magic, the dragons appeared to swirl and writhe across the page. I declined the offer. For me there was another, more tempting chemistry occurring at the party.

Sunshine soaked through the bay window and pooled in the room. Everyone dancing danced in liquid light. I squeezed through the crowd, following the current of cool air that came in from the back door of the small, terraced house.

In the overgrown garden, chairs were scattered around the smouldering remains of a campfire. I pulled up the hood on my sweatshirt and sat down. Would the beautiful stranger I'd been dancing with follow me out? Smoke stung my eyes, making me wince. 'I am surprised no one has called the police – or the *pompieri!*' said a woman with a soft Italian accent. When the smoke cleared, there she stood, in jeans and a thick grey sweatshirt, smiling. 'Debbie's neighbours must be very understanding.'

'We are – very!' I offered her a seat.

Introducing herself as 'Katia', she sat down. She told me she was from Avellino in Italy and was now studying at the London School of Printing. Keen to find common ground, I told her I'd recently got a job at a printer. She was intrigued.

'Well, not exactly a *printer*,' I explained. 'There's none of that wet-ink-and-oily-rollers nonsense these days. Now it's all laser copiers and computers . . .' I realised I was babbling. 'So, what are they teaching you at college?'

'Printing,' she said, slowly, to stress the obvious. Then added, 'Typography, photography, DTP.' She shrugged.

'DTP – desktop publishing!' I pounced on the phrase because DTP was the only computer acronym I actually knew (at this time computers were not yet readily available to, or affordable for, the general public). Luckily, before the conversation got any more technical, my attention was drawn to the roof of the house. Someone in a blue-and-black checked shirt with a blond Tin-Tin quiff had emerged out of the attic window. I recognised Tim – Debbie's neighbour from the flat above. He was manhandling a wardrobe onto the parapet.

'What's he up to?' I muttered. Katia looked up.

'They are a *crazy* bunch. How do you know them?' She said the word *crazy* with a special Italian emphasis.

'Uh . . .' I had to pull my attention away from Tim and think about Katia's question. 'Oh, out and about, at parties.'

The wardrobe hit the ground with an almighty crash. Katia jumped, putting her hand on mine. Adrenalin sprang me to my feet and my hand pulled out from under hers.

'You missed!' Katia shouted.

Tim waved at us in exaggerated slow motion as if from the top of a mountain.

'More firewood!' he called through cupped hands, elongating the vowels to stretch the words across the distance between us.

A couple of minutes later, he came down and started piling the shattered pieces of furniture onto the fire. A column of orange flame leapt up. Heat twisted the sky. For a moment we enjoyed the extra warmth, but it quickly became too intense. In the small, overgrown garden there was nowhere to retreat unless we pushed into the hedge, which, like us, was wilting.

'It's a lovely spring morning,' I said. 'We could go for a walk?' Though I'd only moved to London recently, I knew that Hampstead Heath, with views across the city, was only half an hour away from where we were in Kilburn. And even though I'd only just met her, a walk with this beautiful woman seemed like a perfectly sensible way to spend a spring morning.

She gave me an amused yet inquisitive look and said, 'I should be getting home.' I felt the muscles in my face slacken. 'But you could walk me?' she added with a smile.

My blush, I hoped, was hidden by the heat of the fire on my cheeks.

•

What Katia hadn't mentioned was that she lived over Blackfriars Bridge, on the other side of London.

We wound our way through the streets of West Hampstead to the semi-wild parkland of the heath and up the grassy slopes of Parliament Hill. It was still early, and apart from the odd jogger, there was no one else around. Wood pigeons cooed with soft satisfaction; sparrows squabbled in the bushes; a distant aeroplane droned: sounds which, somehow, connected past summers with the promise of all the summers still to come.

On top of the hill, we sat on a bench and looked over the view. Trees, fresh with buds, blossoms and new leaves, latticed the blue-grey city beyond.

I leaned my head back to feel the sun on my throat. Katia jumped up, stood on the bench and shaded her eyes with her hand.

'I think Blackfriars is . . .' I watched her stretch her arm towards the sun's dazzle and point a finger beyond the spindle-topped cylinder of the Post Office Tower. 'Just there.' She curled her finger downward as if to touch the skyline. My eyes moved back from the city to her finger, around the contours of her body and down her legs to the tip of her purple boots. Jumping off the bench, she sat back down with a bump.

'Perhaps,' I said, 'we should've brought a map.'

'No,' she said, moving closer. 'Finding our own way is much more exciting!' Our eyes met. 'I think we should follow our noses!' She peered cross-eyed at the end of hers, then got up and ran down the hill, laughing.

•

We arrived at the busy junction at the bottom of Haverstock Hill. In front of us was the iconic Roundhouse. An immense, circular, windowless building with a gently sloped conical roof.

Victorian, but with a dark futuristic presence, it was built in 1846 to house the newly invented locomotives that would be the muscle at the frontline of the Industrial Revolution.

'It looks empty!' I said as we walked under its shadow. 'You know this place was legendary back in the sixties and seventies – Jimi Hendrix, The Doors, Pink Floyd all played here!' There was a lull in the traffic. 'Be a wicked place for a party.'

We stopped and looked up at the great curved walls as if caught in the building's orbital pull.

'It would be massive!' Katia whispered.

A bus roared past, dragging in its wake all the traffic and background noise of London.

We continued down the High Street through the crowds at Camden Market. On one of the stalls, an enigmatic image grabbed my attention. Just as the dragons on the LSD had appeared to shimmer with life, so too did these abstract patterns. The designs, printed on posters, excited not only my optic nerve but also the air between me and the paper. Together, Katia and I flicked through the racks of prints. Turbulent currents of fern-like spirals pulled in the eye. The forms looked familiar yet strange. They seemed to *explain* something important – not in words, but in shapes.

'What are these?' I asked Katia.

'*Fractals:* computer-generated images. Maps of chaos.'

'Chaos? The Butterfly Effect?' I remembered something I'd read. The disturbance a butterfly makes flapping its wings in Outer Mongolia could cause a storm over here. But these patterns aren't chaotic . . . they're like growth patterns – they're organised.'

'*Si, certo.* More of an *elefante* in the room than a butterfly in Outer Mongolia.'

We forked right down Hampstead Road towards the Post Office Tower. We continued, laughing and joking, into the trendy lanes of Soho and down the Charing Cross Road and out into the expanse of Trafalgar Square.

We stopped. Speechless.

The square was ankle-deep in wreckage. Rubble. Broken glass. Splintered wood and twisted metal. *What could have caused such devastation? A hurricane? An earthquake? A bomb?*

With a sense of dream-like wonder we picked our way across the smouldering scene. I felt as if I was floating. Katia drifted closer to me, hooked her arm through mine and pulled me to her side. We avoided the jagged metal of crumpled street signs and the fire-blackened plastic of melted rubbish bins and gravitated towards the centre of the square and Nelson's Column. Katia pulled away from me and picked up a cardboard placard, its wooden handle snapped short, footprints trodden on its reverse. She spun the placard to face me and raised it above her head.

'No Poll Tax!' she chanted. A flock of pigeons fluttered up over her. It was only when I heard the echo of her voice that I realised how empty and quiet the square was.

She dropped the placard and took my arm.

'Looks like we missed a riot!' I said.

'Who says we missed it?' She kicked a broken bottle from out of her path, sending the pigeons up again.

The pigeons swirled around Nelson's Column before landing. With them, a stillness settled. No traffic. No people. Just us.

She turned to me. We kissed. The world wobbled. But we, tightly embraced, stood steady at its centre.

•

Katia lived in the top-floor flat of a large anonymous building on the busy Blackfriars Road, just south of the river. We sat on her single bed under a large window. She read aloud from the stack of Sunday papers we'd bought. 'Gangs of rioters and looters were rampaging across London's West End last night after Britain's biggest anti-poll tax rally erupted into violence. Police lost control after what had been a peaceful protest degenerated into an evening of chaos.'

After a few minutes of looking through the papers together, Katia got to her feet and went to have a shower.

While she was gone, I spread the papers out on the bed and floor. I tried to reconstruct the riot in a panorama of pictures and words. I read on: '. . . fires, overturned police vans, burnt-out cars and widespread looting . . . 57 police and 75 demonstrators taken to hospital . . . police blame the anarchists.'

The door clicked. Katia came back in, wrapped in a blue towel, her hair dripping. As she walked towards me, she left wet footprints across the paper images of fire and violence.

PRESSING THE BIG GREEN BUTTON

Grove Reprographics had seen the future, and it didn't smell of chemical solvents and printing ink: it smelt of ozone and instant coffee.

I worked in the basement with five or six other people – and the machines. The air conditioning cooled the place and the large desk-sized photocopiers heated it up again. The machines were breathing our air, stripping out the moisture and sucking out the oxygen. Fluorescent lights flickered at the edges of my vision and the blue nylon carpet tiles kept the hairs on the back of my neck permanently bristled with static. But, when I pressed my laser copier's big green button, my physical discomfort evaporated. The high-pitched, twin-tone whine of the digital scanner sent a thrill through me.

The machines, bursting with new computer technology, allowed me to zoom in and out of images, flip colours and distort shapes. Having worked as a graphic designer for years with little more than a pencil, pen and ink, pressing that green button didn't only enable me to do things I'd never been able to do before but also triggered something new within me.

My predecessor had attempted to cheer up the blank white wall in front of my copier by decorating it. There were the usual stock pictures of a Formula One racing car, palm trees silhouetted against a purple sunset, flowers and butterflies, and, looking rather out of place, a spiral ammonite fossil. It was a quiet afternoon, so I decided to have a little play with my machine.

Taking the photograph of the ammonite off the wall, I placed it on the copier glass. The machine's scanner targeted the centre of the spiral with a robotic, twin-tone whine. I zoomed in. Enchanted by the beauty of the spiral's geometry, I zoomed in again, exploring the internal space within the two-dimensional paper. With delight I realised the winding lines also suggested an infinite path beyond the page. Not just in a two-dimensional plane but in an up-and-down, three-dimensional plane. And not only the line but the continuous space between the line. The spiral was connecting everything in all directions, simultaneously. This simple insight into the ammonite's structure and the mathematics of growth felt electric. It was as if my mind had been freed from the confines of linear logic. *Of course, everything is connected – why had I never noticed it before?*

Buzzing with excitement I turned my attention to the picture of the butterflies. Taking it off the wall, I placed it on the glass and zoomed in. Made a copy, then another, this time changing the colours from their natural oranges and browns to cool blues and greens. The intensified magnification and bluer colouring brightened the image. I did another, this time darkening the colouring.

That evening I took the butterfly wings home and laid them out on our glass-topped dining table. The images were both identical, except one was slightly lighter than the other. In pencil, I drew a wave pattern of diminishing yin-yangs across the middle of the darker image. With a scalpel, I then cut the page in half along the swirling lines. Carefully, I glued this doily-like piece back into its original position but on top of the uncut and lighter-coloured twin image. My butterfly's wing was again complete, but now a subtle, transparent wave of fractal energy was blowing through it – causing small eddies of visual turbulence.

•

Katia and Chris, a young lad from Grove Reprographics, were with Zander and me at our Brondesbury Park flat. Neither of them were helping matters by calling out 'left-a-bit-right-a-bit' instructions. I stood on a chair repositioning the wire, which we used as an aerial for our radio. I waved the wire about, searching for the signal. Static fizzed from the hi-fi speakers. When I got the angle right, music filled the room like the warm sunshine streaming in through the glass balcony doors. I pinned the wire into place. A woman DJ chatted – not in the slippery, snake-oiled voice of the legal radio stations but in a normal London accent, excited and unabashed. 'Largin' it big-style to the hardcore massive. Lovin' it, livin' it, this is the sound of the underground!'

With our lifeline to the real world reconnected, I jumped off the chair and dragged it back to the glass-topped table we were all sitting around – all apart from Zander, whose cursing from the kitchen was apparently directed at saucepans that weren't behaving. Katia got up and squinted through the smoke to try and see what he was up to. I went back to explaining my idea.

'So, if you fold it in half, not only is it a butterfly with wings.' I demonstrated by flapping my artwork in front of Katia and Chris. 'But also a cover!'

Katia and Chris looked at each other. Chris decided to get on with rolling the spliff he'd started, leaving Katia to ask, 'Cover for what?'

'Maybe a zine about the stuff we've been talking about – nature's patterns, creativity, the chaos connection,' I said excitedly, though I was unsure myself. Like a word on the tip of my tongue, the precise shape of my idea was just out of reach.

'It's Glastonbury Festival in a week,' said Chris. 'You could write up some of that spiral shit you're always on about.' He flicked his fringe back and sparked up a large, conical spliff. The smoke curled around the sunlight to meet another blue cloud that was drifting in from the kitchen.

'Glastonbury!' I let the butterfly-printed paper float down onto the table. We had a plan. I'd try and find the words and images to express the ideas. Katia said she was up for laying it out on her college computer. Chris was up for helping me print it.

Zander emerged from the kitchen wearing a pair of sunglasses with pink frames and round, dark-green lenses. His long, curly hair stuck out from under a red velvet peaked cap, and his extra-large T-shirt was tight on the muscles of his arms and chest. With a proud smile he lowered a tray of burned toast in the middle of the table. 'How about using that Chief Seattle thing?'

A couple of years earlier, Zander had ridden across the States coast to coast – and back again – on his Harley Davidson. When he returned to England, he brought back a book that had a text attributed to a Native American, Chief Seattle, of the Suquamish and Duwamish tribes. I say attributed because it's now clear that Chief Seattle's legendary words were translated, reinterpreted, added to by environmentalists in the 1970s, and even embellished by a screenwriter for a movie poster. But, perhaps at its core, the words still communicate something of what Chief Seattle actually said.

Zander pulled the book from the shelf, found the passage and handed it to me.

I found the well-thumbed page, cleared my throat and began.

'Where is man without the beasts?

If the beasts were gone, men would die
From a great loneliness of spirit.
For what happens to the beasts,

17

Soon happens to man.
All things are connected.
This we know.
The Earth does not belong to man;
Man belongs to the Earth.
This we know.
All things are connected,
Like the blood which unites one family.
All things are connected.
Whatever befalls the Earth befalls the sons of the Earth.
Man did not weave the web of life,
He is merely a strand in it.'

I put the book down.
'Wicked!' said Katia.
'Wicked!' Said Zander
'Actually,' said Chris, 'Glastonbury isn't in a week – it's in six days.'

•

By Wednesday of that week, the flat was strewn with laser-copied images of the spiral ammonite. I'd spent the previous three days and nights grappling with ideas which, in my mind, were clear and focused, but as soon as I tried to get them down on paper, they'd escape me.

I'd always kept sketchbooks. In Manchester I'd meticulously invented tessellating shapes – positives creating negatives, negatives forming positives. One symmetry generating another. I was intrigued by the feeling that, although it was me who touched pencil to paper, me who positioned the lines, I felt that I was only giving shape to what was already there. The tip of my pencil and the nib of my pen tracing outlines around an invisible mathematics. Inking-in an unseen architecture, discovering some of the geometries that lay hidden above, and below, the surface of the page.

Our rather simple little leaflet was, I suppose, an attempt to find the words to explain the new reality that was unfolding before us. But did the vocabulary, capable of making sense of such things, exist yet? Rationalising the world into a single stream of words was always tricky – whereas when we submerged ourselves in music, everything made perfect sense.

With a few hours left before Katia was due to pick up the work to type out on her college's computer, everything was still unresolved – images and notes were scattered across the table and floor. Nothing was solid. Nothing glued down. Chris had come round, and I was desperate for a second opinion: to know if the threads of chaos I'd been trying to weave together made any sense.

I'd mutated a diagram of the history of evolution which I'd cut from a magazine. At the bottom, the diagram had early globular life forms, then arrows rising up connecting developing species through pictures of trilobites, dinosaurs, mammoths, monkeys and humans. While I'd been cutting the edges of the paper with a steel rule and scalpel, the thin trimmings had naturally sprung into corkscrew curls. These random curls seemed to fit with the notion that *chaos is self-organising* and gave me the idea of replacing the straight arrows with the spiralled strands of white paper. Glued over the top of the diagram the curls gave it a new vitality – twisting threads of DNA connecting all life, across time.

I laid the half-formed pages in front of Chris. The Chief Seattle text, then more of my graphics and words: *The spiral – the primordial, all-connecting symbol, a representation of the asymmetric shape of nature – the turbulence in the fractal flow.*

I then went on to explain to Chris that the spiral *is* a symbol that represents something more than an icon or character. Letters in an alphabet only symbolise sounds – they're not the actual sound. A skull and crossbones can symbolise pirates, but it's not the actual pirates. A spiral is a symbol but not a *symbolic* symbol – it actually *is* what it *is* – not a representation of something else.

'Totally,' said Chris.

•

It was Thursday. 3 a.m. Chris and I were now back in the flat, delirious with excitement after an all-night session photocopying the pamphlets. We sat opposite each other at the glass-topped dining table, catching our breath after having carried the two heavy boxes of newly printed pages up the stairs. The job ahead was to make four thousand folds in the still-warm A4 sheets and to fit the inside pages into the butterfly cover. We got a production line up and running, a spliff on the go and the radio tuned into the local pirate channel. Everything was set: we'd even managed to organise a couple of vehicle passes into Glastonbury.

'I've just had a thought,' I said to Chris. 'What's the date?'

He looked up from folding the pages with pink slit eyes. 'Twenty-first?'

'Solstice! The shortest night of the year. When we were kids,

Zander and I used to hitchhike down to the Stonehenge Free Festival.'

Chris turned and peered through the glass of the balcony doors, past his own reflection and the ghosted room. 'Yep – it's getting light . . .'

I took another wad of butterfly prints out of the box. 'We were total Hawkwind fans. At Stonehenge we'd get wasted, stay up all night and watch the sunrise. For a lot of people it was a spiritual thing. But for me, it was more about making a stand against the authoritarianism we'd grown up with.'

'So how come Stonehenge doesn't happen now?'

'Police violence. The last one in '84 was massive. And I mean – mass-ssive! Like a Wild West boom town. Street after street of tents and wagons all competing for business. Cafs, Indian clothes, incense – like Camden Market, but for drugs. Shed-loads. There were signs up everywhere for acid, puff, lines of Charlie – you name it, it was for sale!'

'Sounds wicked!'

'It felt soulless. It was better when it was makeshift – you didn't feel like a punter. Overrun with dealers it became a hippy shopping mall. I'm up for legalisation – but the dealers were blatantly there to rinse the vibe.'

'Everyone's got to scrape a living.'

'Suppose so, but at the expense of everything else? Anyway, the following year it got stomped on – hard. But as far as I could see, bread-head-hippies had already killed the spirit.'

'Fuck off!' said Chris. 'You can't kill the spirit!'

GLASTONBURY: JUNE 1990

There was a problem.

At dawn, after we'd finished putting the leaflets together, Chris, who lived round the corner at his mum's, had gone home to grab some camping stuff. I'd run myself a hot bath. Though I ached with exhaustion, I felt a deep glow of satisfaction. We'd done it. Our leaflet wasn't advertising anything; it had no religious or political agenda; it was our attempt at mapping and communicating our 'all-connecting' spiral-vibes to the world.

With two thousand leaflets boxed and standing by the front door ready to go, I'd allowed myself the luxury of taking a single copy into the bathroom to read. Having worked as a graphic designer, I knew it was always difficult to view one's own work objectively, especially after it's been in your face for so many days and nights. In an attempt to gauge the finished work – at least that's what I told myself, as I was probably just over-tired – I lay in the bath and tried to imagine myself as a stranger reading our zine.

With wet hands I opened up the coloured cover and began to read out loud. Halfway through I lost my place and had to backtrack. I started at the beginning. Again I lost the thread. Something was wrong. I read the section again – this time in silence.

With a heart-thumping jolt I realised a large chunk of the text was missing. Gone. We'd muffed it. Without that one key passage nothing in the leaflet made sense. Still holding the dampened paper, my hands sank into the bath water. My energy ebbed.

I woke up spitting bathwater. Someone was hammering on the front door. I wrapped myself in a towel and went to answer. Chris stood there with a rucksack on his back, floppy blonde hair brushed, pale face cheery as he babbled excitedly about Glastonbury. In my hand I still clutched the ball of wet paper. I tried to open it up to show him, but the butterfly wings disintegrated and fell to the floor with a soggy splat.

•

And so it was we set off to Glastonbury without the leaflets – and as punters, with Chris, and his mate John, as illegally smuggled punters.

Greg, an old school friend who also worked with Zander's firm, had managed to wangle some dodgy vehicle passes.

As a teenager, seduced by the promise of adventure, Greg had enlisted in the military, but as he'd grown up, he'd discovered he had more of a passion for love and life than being a trained killer. He'd recently bought himself out, let his shaved hair grow into a wild blonde mop, and swapped his combat camo for baggy, psychedelic clothes. He loved the music of The Doors as well as the comic book art of the dope-smoking Fabulous Furry Freak Brothers. Even though the image belongs to another era, I saw in him one of the young Vietnam vets returning to San Francisco in 1968 and placing flowers in the gun barrels of the National Guard. But Greg wasn't all flower power.

We drove down to the festival together in convoy. Zander and I were in the Land Rover, with Chris and John in the back. Greg and his girlfriend Kerry were in the car in front.

Every year thousands of people risked a kicking from security by climbing, tunnelling, or otherwise blagging themselves over, under or through the perimeter fence. As we queued in the bumper-to-bumper traffic feeding into the festival site, we chatted about the irony of having to break into a crowded, enclosed space to escape the controls and conventions of the outside world. We all agreed that what many people perceive as *freedom* often only exists as a contrived and controlled illusion – all part of the stage show.

After a long wait we finally neared the gate. Chris and John ducked out of sight and hid under a pile of bedding. Busy trying to push a broken-down van out of the mud, the security waved us straight through. It was like crossing a border checkpoint choked with fleeing refugees. Cars and vans, their rear suspensions sagging, bulged with people and camping kit.

While we parked up in one of the fields, Greg came over to Zander's open window with his finger to his lips and gave knowing nods towards the back of the Landy. Flushed from the effort of trying to keep a straight face, Greg pretended to be a security guard and demanded to see our tickets. Zander played along.

'Just the two of you in the vehicle?'

'Just two of us.'

'What's in back?'

Zander and I got out and went around to the back with Greg and Kerry. Zander drew out the agony by fumbling with the wrong keys in the lock. After a prolonged few moments, Zander opened the back door – which hadn't been locked in the first place.

'So – just camping stuff is it then?' Greg put a little more boom into his voice for extra effect while he frisked the bedding, patting Chris and John's legs underneath. He then gently took hold of the bottom edge of the duvet that covered the stowaways and snatched it away. John was curled in the foetal position, both fists clasped tight in front of his gritted teeth, his eyes screwed shut. Despite our howls of laughter, it was a few moments before he dared to open them and unclench his body. Chris stayed exactly where he was – fast asleep with a peaceful smile on his face.

•

My crazed week of work had disrupted my sleep pattern. I seemed to be out of sync with the world and everyone else I'd come with. Chris and John – and several other people whose identities were hidden, their faces buried in their pillows – did a lot of sleeping, in my tent. Debbie and her friends were somewhere on site, but it was impossible to find anyone. Mobile phones were still a thing of the near but still-to-arrive future.

•

The arrival of the acid house scene in the late eighties had transformed audiences into participants. At The Hacienda in Manchester, and at some underground parties in London, I'd experienced a real sense of involvement and social equality. Once that equality had been glimpsed, there was no going back to the old rock 'n' roll relationship between performers and audiences. A relationship that – whether intentional or not – reinforced the old power structures of 'us and them'. At the underground clubs and parties, the dance floor was no longer the pit for the worshipping minions. No longer a place to gaze up adoringly at some contrived act strutting about on a pedestal. The dance floor had been reclaimed by the people as a free social space: a place where people felt centred, balanced – together.

•

Despite, or perhaps because of, all the 'entertainment', as I wandered the 600 acres of Glastonbury's razzmatazz, I felt like a bored tourist. Even among the crowds that flowed between fields or pooled with the mud in front of any loud music, I felt the same isolation and anonymity I would while window shopping in any busy city. Probably, after the intense week I'd had, I just needed to rest. Certainly, I was disappointed that things hadn't worked out as planned, but I also felt that the festival was more commercial than it had been in previous years.

More interested in the infrastructure than the performances, I found myself peering around the façade of sideshow glitz, admiring the rows of artic lorries parked behind the scenes; the huge, purring generators; the thick bundles of cabling and, of course, the sound systems. But where was the dance music?

I was about to go back to my tent and evict my snoozing squatters when I came to a little bridge over a wooded stream. The rutted mud track that crossed it led into an area unlike any of the other fields – a shanty town of ramshackle trucks and buses. The Traveller's Field.

There were vintage buses, trailers and trucks, some botched, some cobbled, some cannibalised, into live-in vehicles. Many had sweeping mudguards and running boards, streamlined or jelly-moulded contours, split windscreens and chromium trim. On the grill of a particularly impressive old English truck, its make, *Albion,* was emblazoned in chrome above a radiating rising sun motif.

An overly muscular wrecker, with bulging wheel arches and loops of heavy chain hung from its tow bar, was daubed with the words *Fuck Pig.* There were trucks fitted with window boxes, chicken coops, and one even had a pair of goats living on its back veranda. Whatever the style – quaint-cottage-garden or all-terrain-anarchist – there was something proud and defiantly independent about the atmosphere in the field. An atmosphere that was missing everywhere else. In comparison, the rest of Glastonbury felt as flimsy and contrived as a Hollywood film set, the scenery as thin as the licks of paint and coloured lights that decorated it. But the Traveller's Field was no illusion. The raw, solid, practical mechanics of life-in-a-truck had a powerful magic. There's a romance and allure about the traveller, the Roma, the adventurer. But there was something else too. Something about how all those shapely vintage vehicles had been brought back from the scrapheap of history. Beautifully designed and stoutly engineered, they'd transcended their intended purpose, driven across time into another era, not only as enablers but also as part of the nomadic spirit of an unforeseen, yet inevitable, new current in the British psyche.

It had been drizzling, and crowds of damp festival-goers strolled along the track – the mud on their high-street-bought clothes couldn't disguise the fact that they, like me, were sightseers. It was the wide-eyed look on their well-fed faces that gave them away. In contrast, the travellers – young, old, punk, dread or hippy – wore dark, drab clothes, ingrained with a life spent outdoors or under the bonnets of vehicles. Many had gaunt, weather-beaten faces, hands stained with engine oil and a knowing look lighting their eyes.

Noticing the word "Café" scrawled on a flattered cardboard box propped up against the back wheel of a truck, I decided to get a cup of tea. I stepped out of the main current of people and over a few blackened pots and pans that lay around the ashes of a fire. A pack of wiry little dogs briefly but enthusiastically investigated me as I ducked under the café's tarpaulin canopy. Inside, the small space was crowded with about ten people – travellers and visitors alike. A single small speaker was wired from the truck's cab and hung from one of the rough wooden poles propping up the canvas. From the speaker came the bass-heavy burbling of acid house – and from the crowd, a warm, welcoming feeling.

The woman behind the trestle table bar wore a tweed flat cap, riding jacket, jodhpurs and motorcycle boots. She danced her way towards me.

'All right, lovely, what can I get you?'

'Cuppa tea, please.'

'Milk and sugar?'

'Please.'

'Sorry, ain't got none. You can have it black.'

'Okay . . .'

'Hardcore!' She gave me the thumbs-up and, with a smile, danced off to the steaming tea urn. When she came back, she explained that she never bothered with milk because it soured too quickly, and sugar always got 'borrowed'.

'On the road,' she said, 'you soon find out what's important.' Snapping her fingers to the music, she shimmied off to the other end of the bar to serve a customer who wore a fraying rainbow jumper and a black bowler hat.

As I sipped my drink from a mug with two sharp stumps where the handle had once been, I began to relax. I realised that the manic week leading up to Glastonbury was the culmination of a manic few months. The move from Manchester had been a massive upheaval. Landing in London, and having to reinvent my life, had been tougher than I'd wanted to admit. The passionate new love affair with Katia, the working, and the intense, often all-night, social life, had left me emptied – yet renewed. The shifting reality of the spiral stuff seemed to be about letting go of old yet comforting patterns of belief and exploring the world revealed once the veils of indoctrination had been lifted.

Sipping that hot black tea, I also realised that it didn't matter that our pamphlet had gone wrong – the creative struggle to define those thoughts was, in itself, a rite of passage.

At that moment I heard, or rather felt, a new bassline pulsing through the earth. Someone in the Traveller's Field had just switched on a sound system – a large sound system – and it was playing *dance music!*

I raised my mug to the woman behind the bar, took a last swig, ruffled the ears of one of the little wiry dogs, and went to investigate.

As I moved through the labyrinth of the traveller's camp, the music bounced off the high-sided vehicles, confusing my sense of direction, but the bass, coming up through the ground, guided my feet. As I got closer to the source, more people appeared around me, some already dancing as they too were magnetically pulled in the same direction. I turned a corner and came out onto a track. The pack of dogs shot ahead of me and disappeared amongst the stomping feet of the crowd that was spilling out of the open sides of the already full marquee. Inside was a sound system painted bright yellow, with the word 'Tonka' stencilled on the cabs. I prised myself into the tightening mass of people. *At last*, I thought, as I squeezed my way towards the speaker stacks, *I've arrived at Glastonbury!*

Someone tapped me on the shoulder. I turned and there was Chris, grinning. He leaned close, cupped a hand around my ear and shouted, 'You can't kill the spirit!'

NOTTING HILL CARNIVAL: AUGUST 1990

When Zander and I got back from the festival, the Brondesbury Park flat was a mess.

It had been such a rush to finish the pamphlet that the place was still scattered with cut-up papers and notes. As I tidied up, my thoughts began to settle back into life in London – in a tiny flat. After being outdoors it was disheartening, but the small space, after the grand scale of Glastonbury, pulled things into sharper focus. I brushed the small pieces of paper that were littering the glass-topped table into my hand: fragments of ideas, half sentences and single words – all the debris from the solstice storm that had swept through my life and carried me off to that Traveller's Field. I threw the handful of unnecessary words into the bin. Now I had a new list of priorities and going back to work at Grove Reprographics wasn't on it.

I talked with Katia, Zander and Chris about getting a magazine together. It seemed like a natural progression from our original, but doomed, pamphlet. The creative energy bubbling up around us could, I thought, be directed into a journal that reported on underground events, arts and ideas. Perhaps it was the perfect medium to express words and images – but what about the music?

·

It was hot. Zander and I were sitting round our dining table with the balcony doors open. Now and then, a welcome breeze billowed the long net curtains. We were having a late breakfast of tea and toast. Despite my best efforts, I'd still managed to get blobs of marmalade on the pages of the local newspaper I was thumbing through. A small classified ad caught my eye.

'What do you reckon about this?' I slid the paper across the table to Zander.

'About what?' He half-heartedly glanced at the paper.

'The ad at the bottom: a samba band are looking for a driver for one of the carnival floats.'

'So?'

'Might be a nice little job.'

'If you had a driving licence.'

'I don't mean me – I mean you. Anyway, says they also need a co-driver.'

'A co-driver? What do they need a co-driver for?'

'Navigating?'

'For a street parade?'

'It's massive – biggest carnival in the world.'

'Outside Rio.'

'Well yeah, of course, outside of Rio.' I nodded at the paper that Zander was still ignoring. 'Says here that it's a ten-hour day – so whoever's doing the driving is going to need someone to keep them company, sort out snacks, roll a few spliffs.'

'I hate sitting in traffic.' He moved his tea and picked up the paper. 'How much are they paying?'

'Nothing.'

'Nothing – for sitting in traffic all day!' He shook his head before lifting up the paper to scrutinise the ad.

'It's Carnival and we'd be right in the thick of it, helping out. It would be one of those once-in-a-lifetime experiences!'

Zander put the paper down. 'When is it?'

'Bank holiday weekend.'

He took a sip of tea.

'I'll just give them a bell,' I said, getting up. 'See what they're saying.'

Zander handed me the paper. 'Okay, but just remember sitting in traffic all day is not a once-in-a-lifetime experience for me – I do it every day!'

We got the job.

•

On the morning of the parade, Zander and I jumped in his Land Rover and headed to the top end of Ladbroke Grove. The float – a flatbed truck decorated as a tropical island – was parked outside a warehouse in a small industrial area, round the corner from Grove Reprographics. The warehouse was a modern, plain, brick building, and from out of the open roller shutter doors streamed a crowd of people in winged and petalled costumes.

The colours were shimmering and iridescent. As I got out of the Landy, I felt as if I was stepping into a meadow of giant metallic gauze flowers and dragonflies – with human faces. Many of the people were carrying drums, beaded gourd shakers or jingling tambourines. While Zander parked the Land Rover, I went to find the organiser.

On the patch of grass outside the warehouse, parents were rounding up over-excited kids and trying to get them to hold still long enough to have antennae attached, wings adjusted, and their faces painted. I wandered into the warehouse and spotted a bloke with a clipboard. His hairy white legs, thick socks and walking boots brutally contrasted with his skimpy blue tunic.

'Are you the truck driver?' he asked without introducing himself or saying hello.

'No, I'm the co-driver, my brother Zand . . .'

But the bloke wasn't interested. He thrust a piece of paper at me. 'Here's the route, the keys are in the ignition, we're leaving here eight-thirty – sharp!'

'So, er . . .'

'And tell the driver to take it slowly – we have to keep a tight formation. I'll be on the back. If I bang on the cab roof once, that's stop. If I bang twice, it's go.' He looked at me with the strict intensity of a schoolteacher. 'Do you understand?'

'Er, yes, I . . .'

But he'd turned on his heel, his short tunic whirling up to give me a flash of his tight purple briefs. He strode off, waving pieces of paper at someone else.

Outside I made my way through swarms of feisty little jellyfish-children.

'I got the route, keys are in the ignition,' I said to Zander, who was busy inspecting the truck's wheels.

We climbed up into the cab and sat for a moment surveying our new surroundings.

Already hungry we ate our sandwiches in silence as the float dancers climbed on the back of the truck. We watched in the mirrors as the hundred or so drummers took up their positions to march behind.

I poured Zander a cup of tea from my Thermos.

The bloke with the hairy legs and the clipboard appeared in front of the truck beckoning with both arms as if he were signalling an aeroplane for take-off. Zander started the engine and handed me the Thermos cup, still half full.

With a shudder the truck crawled forward to where the bloke was waving us to stop. Zander wound down his window to talk with him. I could hear him instructing Zander to obey the stop/go signals that he'd bang on the roof. A few minutes later the bloke was gone and up on the back. There were two loud thumps on the cab.

After a pause I said, 'That means go.'

'I know what it means,' said Zander. He mumbled something under his breath that seemed to be directed at the gear stick, and we began to roll.

'Okay,' I said, 'we filter down this road to Ladbroke Grove, where we take our position in the main procession.' I traced my finger around the map. 'Then we follow it down, left into Arundel Gardens, then . . .'

'I know where we're going! And keep that map down, you're blocking the mirror!'

Ahead of us we could see stewards and police manning a

checkpoint. We slowed, and then stopped with a judder. There were a few bumps from the back as people tried to keep their footing on the tropical island. There was a loud single bang on the roof of the cab. Zander cussed under his breath.

A steward came and asked us to wait a minute while the band and float ahead moved down. Drums rumbled in the distance.

'We're on a launch pad,' I said.

Zander laughed, nodded and gave the idling engine a playful rev. There was a particularly loud bang on the roof.

My door opened and a bejewelled hand with long painted nails reached inside.

'*Espera amigo!*' A tall, lithe woman wearing nothing but a thong, a minimal bikini top and a fanned headdress of pink ostrich plumes handed me a small shoulder bag. She was chewing gum, and her sparkling smile and eyes all added to the glitter of the rhinestones and beads that fringed her outfit.

'*Gracias!*' She lightly touched the tips of her painted fingers to her breast and was gone. But not far. Positioning themselves in the space between the front of our truck and the band ahead of us was the woman's dance troop – all in matching costumes.

The parade ahead began to move. There was a rhythmic burst on a whistle, followed by a skipping rhythm on a single drum. Again, the signal on the whistle and all the drums behind us thundered in together. There was a double thump on the cab roof. Zander released the handbrake and, to the rhythm of the samba drums and the wiggle of the dancer's hips, we set off down Ladbroke Grove into the carnival proper.

With both the windows of the truck open, we crept along. The hot August air was spiced with ganja and barbecue smoke.

The deeper we went down the Grove, the louder the music and the denser the huge crowds became. My senses began to merge and amplify. The warm tropical sound of the steel bands rippled in the air. Dub reggae bounced between buildings. Ragga and hip-hop basslines pumped from dark walls of speakers. And underneath it all, the samba drums rolled. The rhythms pushed the dancers on. But no one was in a hurry. Despite our dancers' tireless energy, the pace was set: two steps forward, one step back.

People were dancing on roofs and balconies, waving from windows and crowding the tops of walls. The costumes celebrated life in all its forms. Wings, flowers, scales, horns, fins, fur and feathers. And at the centre of each plumed fan, or burst of coloured petals, was a person – dancing, vibrant and smiling.

Two hours in, and we were only halfway down the Grove.

'I suppose you were right,' I said to Zander.

'About what?'

'About sitting in traffic all day.'

He smiled. 'I'm not complaining!'

'This is how a party should be.' I lifted my hands to view around us. 'Not some cliquey-little-pay-in-vibe.'

Although we were still moving, my door suddenly opened and the dancer climbed back in. I slid over as much as I could, but it was a tight squeeze. Her naked hips pressed against my leg and her pink ostrich feathers tickled my face.

'*Hola*! *Buenos días*!' she said, twinkling. She began to rummage through her stuff and got out a small make-up bag. She slipped off one of her gold strappy shoes and put her bare foot up on the dash. Her toenails were painted gloss red, her bare legs a gold glitter sheen. She pouted and made a purring sound as she examined a burst blister on the back of her heel.

From her make-up bag she took out a small clear plastic bag containing white powder. With the tip of her tongue, she moistened her little finger and dabbed it into the powder, reached over to her ankle and rubbed it into the sore. She held the plastic bag between her teeth while she took a plaster from her handbag.

First aid complete she took out a gold compact mirror. Her leg, with toes wiggling, remained up on the dash. She tipped a little powder onto the mirror, which she held flat on the top of her thigh – the thigh that was pressed hard against mine. I felt nervous about the near nakedness, the close proximity and now the blatant drug use.

I glanced out at the thousands of revellers, jammed shoulder to shoulder in the streets outside. They were having fun. *Was I?* I thought to myself: *This is the one weekend in the year where no grey-suited bureaucrat or uniformed jobsworth is going to be able to interfere with the joy of human nature.* I laughed at myself for being so uptight, and, as I did, my awkwardness evaporated. I turned back to watch her crush the crystals with a credit card.

She looked up into my face. Her dark eyes locked into mine. 'You want?' Her nostrils flared.

To escape her intense stare, I looked back down into her lap. 'Er . . . What is it?'

'Co-caine!' She curled her lips as she said the word.

'No, thanks.' I turned to Zander, 'You wanna line?'

'Nope.' He replied without taking his eyes off the road.

She laughed and went back to making the lines. 'You hold for me.' She handed me the mirror and sniffed the powder through a rolled note. Her eyes closed. Blue glitter sparkled on her long eyelashes. Puckering her nose she gave it a little flick with a finger, then, blinking her eyes open, turned back to me.

'*Muchas gracias querido!*' She squeezed the sides of my mouth together and made kissing noises at me. 'You make same for *mis amigas.*' She released me from her grip, slipped her shoe back on, opened the truck door and slid back onto the street. Leaving me with the mirror, the cocaine and the rolled note. One minute later the door opened again and another woman, with the same sparkling smile and fierce eyes, squeezed in next to me.

•

We got home at about ten that evening. After a couple of bowls of cereal, Zander said, 'Not sure my left leg will ever be the same again.'

'What's wrong?'

'That old truck had a dodgy clutch – that's why we were lurching.' He stretched out his leg and rubbed his calf.

'And I thought it was all the excitement making you swerve.'

'I wasn't swerving! That was lurching – and considering what a pile of total shite that truck was, that was a very smooth drive.'

'Yeah, it was, wicked. But I'm knackered now.'

'You're knackered after being chauffeur driven around London while you racked up lines for the dancing girls?'

'*Co-driver* – clearly a very important job!' I collected our empty cereal bowls and got up from the table. 'You know, I've been thinking – I reckon we could put on our own event.'

'A carnival?'

'No, but some kind of art and music thing. All the effort that went into that fucking Spiral zine – instead of putting energy onto paper, let's do it in real life.' I went through to our little kitchen.

'When you say, "an art and music thing",' Zander called through to me, 'you mean a party, don't you?'

I came back into the dining room. 'Well yeah, I suppose so. Something with that free carnival energy!'

Zander stopped rubbing his leg and looked up. 'Where?'

'We'd need to find somewhere – an empty building, a big empty building.'

'Maybe,' Zander yawned, 'but I've got to get to bed – I got work first thing. And you need to find a new job.'

We said our good nights and I went into the bathroom. While I was brushing my teeth, Zander stuck his head round the door. 'Does this "having a party" idea involve me driving dodgy old trucks?'

With my toothbrush still in my mouth, I shook my head and tried to say, 'No, of course not.' But all I managed to do was grunt and froth toothpaste.

Zander went back into his room and called out, 'Coz if it does, I'm not getting involved.'

DEEP DOWN UNDERGROUND: SEPTEMBER 1990

Partly screened from the road by a thick laurel hedge, the School House was an imposing three-storey building. Though its white stucco walls were discoloured and cracked, it still had an Edwardian grandeur about it. On rising ground, set slightly back from the leafy avenue of Willesden Lane, it looked like a decaying classical temple.

It was a sunny day when Katia and I made the short walk

from the Brondesbury Park flat to Willesden Lane. We walked through the school's ivy-smothered gateway and up the drive, avoiding the thistles that had spiked through the moss-covered asphalt.

'Wow! I wasn't expecting this. Who's this bloke, Stikka?' I asked. Apparently, it was Stikka who'd told Katia about the empty building, but that was all I knew about him. She told me he was a DJ who worked with The Shamen.

We climbed the wide stone steps of the stoop to the porch, which had pillars either side of it. The large front door was locked, and all the ground-floor windows were boarded.

Katia produced a brass key from her jeans and opened the door. 'Quick!' she said, 'Before anyone sees us!'

We stepped inside a wide hallway with high ceilings. Though it was hot outside, the boarded windows enclosed a cool twilight. The air wasn't stale, but the sealed building still had the unmistakable atmosphere of a school: the smell of disinfectant and floor polish had combined with an air of studied hush and the strict expectation of good behaviour. Mischief fluttered inside me, and I'm sure I recognised the same feeling in Katia's cheeky smile as she closed the front door.

'*Fantastico!*' she whispered as we peered into the first empty classroom. Sunshine leaked in around the boards at the window and beams of light pierced the gloom. Treading gently on the polished wood floor, as if we didn't want to disturb the emptiness, we went up to the wall-mounted blackboard. Katia took a piece of chalk and, in two sweeping strokes, drew a large love heart. With the chalk poised, she glanced at me and raised her eyebrows, then initialled an 'M'. She passed the chalk to me. Chalk dust drifted through the beams of light. I initialled a 'K'. She brushed her lips against mine, said, ' Count to ten!' and ran out the room.

Ten seconds later I gave chase. The soles of my trainers squeaked on the polished wood as I jogged through the two other ground-floor classrooms and then out into a huge gymnasium. On one side wooden climbing frames, complete with climbing ropes, were folded flat against the furthest wall. Welcoming the space, I ran with my arms outstretched like a kid pretending to fly. After a couple of extra circuits I trotted back to the entrance hall and sprang up the main staircase, two steps at a time.

On the first floor the windows weren't boarded, and dazzling sunlight burst into the white-painted rooms. Some classrooms were empty, but some had nested desks and children's chairs stacked against the walls. Katia was nowhere to be seen. I continued up another flight to a self-contained flat, which I guessed had originally been the caretaker's. Still no sign of Katia.

I headed back down again, double-checking the rooms and walk-in cupboards. By the time I'd got back down to the twilight of the ground floor, I was treading slowly and softly again. *Where could she be?*

Then, in the last room, at the back of the building, I noticed a small doorway that I'd missed the first time round. The door stood ajar. I stopped, slowly opened it, and found myself looking down a tight, winding staircase into the basement.

As I crept down the wooden stairway, my senses reached out into the half-dark. A narrow shaft, clogged with leaves, drew faint, green daylight down to a grimy basement window. The air smelt damp but clean, like earth after rain. My blood pumped in my ears. The wooden steps creaked under my weight. Somewhere in the shadows, water dripped into water.

'Katia?' I called in a loud whisper.

At the bottom of the steps, I found myself in a large room. A black-and-white checked floor stretched out before me. As my eyes grew accustomed to the low light, I could see other doorways leading into deeper shadow.

I expected Katia to jump out at me at any second. My nervous system was on alert, but there was also something soothing and seductive about being out of bounds in a hidden, secret place – underground.

'Catch-me-if-you-can!' came a giggled whisper.

I followed the trail of words towards the doorway on the left. Tentatively I dipped my toe over the threshold, not quite trusting the darkness.

'Katia?' I heard the uncertainty in my own voice bounce off unseen walls.

'You're getting warm . . .' came the reply from only a few feet away. I turned towards her voice, 'Warmer . . .' she whispered. 'Hot!'

•

To squat such a large building, we were going to need a good, solid crew. Katia and I put the word out.

Zander, Tim (who'd launched the wardrobe off the roof at Debbie's), Greg, Kerry and a couple of their friends were all up for it. Chris was happy to still live round the corner at his mum's but wanted in on the action.

•

When the previous tenants had left the school, they'd removed the company head fuses (the large industrial fuses that bridge the gap between the house's domestic wiring and the high voltage mains supply that comes in off the street). As a result, there was no electricity. Instead, we had candles – lots of candles – stuck singly into bottles or on plates in clusters, the heat of each melting the wax of its neighbour to form glowing palaces buttressed with dribbling wax.

It was our first meal all together. We sat round the huge pine table in the back ground-floor classroom. The table would have easily accommodated fourteen people, and it looked even bigger because we were all sitting on small school chairs, our chins level with the tabletop, our mouths level with our plates.

Earlier in the day we'd had our first visit from the police. A neighbour had called them after seeing Greg, Chris and me precariously balanced on an outside sill, trying to crowbar the eight-by-four boards off one of the ground-floor windows.

There had been no friendly "Ello-ello-ello" about it, just the abrupt screech of the police car's brakes followed by shouted threats of arrest for attempted burglary. Up on the window ledge, the long arm of the law wasn't quite long enough to actually apprehend us. For a moment we tried to reason with the two coppers who, with one hand holding onto their hats, hopped about below us trying to collar our trouser legs. Our perfectly reasonable explanations about what we were up to fell on deaf ears. As far as they were concerned, we'd been caught red-handed – with a crowbar – in the act of breaking and entering. Realising our attempts at diplomacy weren't working, we managed, with just a quick glance between ourselves, to communicate an escape plan. With little more than a long stride, we jumped from the window ledge and back onto the top of the steps, and in through the open front door, which we promptly slammed shut.

Being outmanoeuvred made the cops even more angry. They banged on the door demanding that we open up. We didn't, of course. Instead, we continued protesting our innocence through the letter box. It wasn't until we'd posted them a photocopy of section six of the Criminal Law Act 1977 – our squatters' rights – that they begrudgingly left. Perhaps not happy, but at least wiser after having learned, we hoped, that not all long-haired-dope-smoking-crowbar-wielding-weirdos are bad people. Though I do understand the confusion.

Unable to resist, I poked a hole with a matchstick through a candle's soft skin to release a cascade of hot wax onto the table.

'Did you see that copper's face when you told him we were just doing some DIY?' I asked Greg, who was sitting across the table from me.

'And when you said we've got squatters' rights, and he said, "If you want rights, you're gonna have to pay for them like everybody else!"' Greg played up the outrage in his voice for added comedy effect.

'Pay for them? But everyone, regardless of their financial status, has equal rights.' Kerry tucked her long, blond hair behind her ears as she leaned forward to light a joint in a candle flame.

'But possession is nine-tenths of the law – and we're still here!' said Greg, resting his chin on Kerry's shoulder and nuzzling into her hair.

'So, who is this bloke who gave you the key?' Kerry turned to Katia, then me.

I shrugged. 'I don't know, some DJ character.'

'And what's all this about him wanting to have an illegal party here?' Kerry blew a thin stream of smoke up at the ceiling.

'Does he?' Greg's intense blue eyes widened, but I couldn't tell if he was nicely surprised by the idea or shocked. Whatever it was, he seemed to be asking me.

'I'm not sure.' I deflected the question. 'Katia?'

On the first day we'd visited the building, Katia had mentioned that in exchange for giving us the key, Stikka was interested in having a party. Of course, I loved the idea. The building was perfect – a dream come true. But now other people had moved in with us who might not share my enthusiasm.

Katia waved a hand dismissively. 'He mentioned the possibility.'

'What about all our stuff? Our rooms? This is our home,' said Kerry.

She was right. This wasn't just an empty building anymore. It was a household. But what kind of household? Were we squatting just to create more private space? Everything was in the balance.

'Well, it would be nice to have a little housewarming,' I suggested. 'Perhaps we could do something in the basement – or the gymnasium?'

'Oi, the gym's my bedroom!' said Zander.

'But you've only got a sleeping bag in the corner. Couldn't you just roll it up and stuff it in a cupboard for the evening?' I stood up to pour myself a cup of tea from the huge stainless-steel teapot we'd found in the basement. The conversation was not going the way I'd hoped. Then Chris pointed out that after the day's shenanigans, the police would probably be keeping an eye on us.

'Don't worry about them.' I tried to sound relaxed and confident. 'They're not going to bother us again.'

There was a loud knock on the front door.

We froze.

Then we all leapt up. Chairs scraped. The music went off. Someone was shushing for quiet and someone else was, rather unhelpfully, blowing out the candles. Joints were extinguished and glasses got knocked over as people fumbled to stash their puff.

Another volley of determined knocks boomed along the hallway. Stumbling and bumping into each other in a tangled, slow-motion scramble, Zander, Greg and I got to the front door. Outside we could hear men talking in low voices. I knelt down and eased open the letter box flap a crack.

'What can you see?' whispered Greg.

'Looks like a fucking SWAT team!' I hissed.

'A SWAT team!' Though Greg tried to answer quietly, the incredulity in his voice made it unexpectedly shrill.

'A gang of blokes wearing black security jackets,' I confirmed.

'Let's have a look.' Greg knelt down next to me. As I moved to give him space, I lost my grip on the letter box flap and it snapped shut. Immediately another three heavy blows landed on the door. As if pushed by the force of the sound, Greg and I stood up and took a step back. Undaunted, Zander leaned harder into the door, bracing his weight against it.

'Who is it?' Zander demanded. There was a moment's silence. Then, in an equally defiant tone, came the answer.

'Stikka!'

We all looked at each other with a mixture of surprise and apprehension. We were about to meet the mysterious man himself – our elusive benefactor.

Zander unbolted the door, and Stikka and his crew trooped in: three blokes wearing silky black bomber jackets, their dark hair cropped short. Zander closed the door behind them, and we followed them into the back room.

Stikka sat himself down at the head of the table in the only adult-sized chair. His two friends, whom he introduced as Paul and Paul, stood on either side of him like a pair of bodyguards. Zander, Greg and I sat ourselves at the opposite end of the long table, all of us on the little chairs.

'Cup of tea, anyone?' asked Kerry cheerfully. No one responded.

'There's juice,' suggested Katia as she relit and rearranged the candles on the table.

'Nah,' said Stikka as, hands clasped behind his head, he stretched his legs under the table and pushed himself further into his chair. 'So,' he said, rocking the chair onto its back legs, 'what do you think of the gaff?'

'A bit poky!' joked Greg.

Stikka turned to one Paul, then the other, then back to Greg. A restrained smile flickered across his face, then he leaned forward. 'But it's got potential, don't you think?'

•

After twenty minutes of chatting, no one had mentioned the idea of a party. I was about to bring the subject up when I thought better of it. Perhaps the majority of people in the house were, at that moment, reluctant to throw their doors open to a group of mysterious DJ types and London's nocturnal underworld.

I got up and went round to Stikka's end of the table.

'Want a guided tour?' I asked. 'See what we've done with the place?'

Stikka glanced around the table. Everyone was deep in their own conversations; joints had been relit and the music was back on.

We slipped out of the room and went upstairs. Neither of us had a torch or had thought to bring a candle. But it didn't matter, as we both knew this wasn't going to be about looking at the building – this was going to be about looking at possibilities.

'Still no power then,' Stikka commented as we headed up the second dark stairway to the top of the building.

'No company head fuses,' I replied, holding open the door to the caretaker's flat.

'Reckon I might be able to sort you some.' Stikka went in. I followed and joined him at the window.

'That would be cool. Thanks for letting us know about this place.'

'No problem.' He looked out across the lights of London. 'Nice view.' He turned back to me. 'Now, a little bird told me you might be interested in . . . having a party?' Though it was dark I could see light glittering in his eyes.

'I'm up for it – but the others might need persuading.'

And that was it. The deal was done.

•

Now some people might think I was being irresponsible by doing a deal with some dodgy DJ types who'd just walked in off the street. But though a man of few words, the light I'd seen in Stikka's eyes told me that he too had a passion for the music – and, if eyes really are the windows to the soul, then Stikka's passion burned bright.

There were also other forces at work. Things wanted – *needed* – to be connected. Downstairs, in the deepest part of the basement, was the mains electricity cupboard. In amongst its loops of thick, bitumen-coated cable and blocks of ceramic fuse boxes were a row of four vertical slots, each about six inches long. At either end of each slot were open clasps – sprung brass contacts into which would clip the cylindrical company head fuses. The empty slots waited – primed – crackling with high-voltage potential. The dark, silent basement had stood empty too long. Damp air and cobwebs weren't enough. The void yearned for more.

PAINTING THE NIGHT BLACK

The details of the deal were this: Stikka was going to supply the sound system, lights and music, and I was to supply the artwork, décor, flyers and ticket designs. I was also left to persuade the rest of the household that throwing a party was actually a really good idea.

So as not to upset anyone, I didn't rush things. One day we agreed we'd only use the basement. Another day I negotiated the ground-floor classrooms, then the gymnasium. By the time we came to deciding on the date – Saturday 29 September 1990 – most people liked the idea of a little housewarming. But when it came to talking about how many people we were expecting, Stikka and I vaguely mumbled figures between 150 and 200. Like a pressure gauge registering red, if we mentioned numbers over 200, people started to flap. Stikka and I didn't mention that we'd calculated the area of both the basement and ground-floor rooms. Our scribbled sums filled a page in one of my notebooks. We extrapolated the figures and worked out how many people would actually fit. The four-digit number, which appeared underlined twice at the bottom of the page, was never shown to anyone else – or spoken out loud.

Stikka explained to me that the new anti-acid house law criminalised us, regardless of how good, bad, big or small our party was. So, I figured: *in for a penny, in for a pound.* To my mind, if we got busted, the risk and responsibility would stop at me and Stikka. My housemates would be innocent bystanders, with Stikka and I the evil organisers. The initial reluctance of some of the household wasn't because people didn't want a party: they all wanted it, but without any risk. Stikka and I both understood that without taking a few chances, nothing interesting would happen.

For most people September was still a month away, but to me it was all too close. The atmosphere and look of the venue were going to be a large part of what the event would be. The design and wording on the flyers would also be important – our first point of contact with the outside world.

Most of the people living in the house had proper jobs. Squatters they may have been, but contrary to the view of the local police, they all paid their taxes. Zander and Greg worked at Tree Co, Tim was a sign writer and carpenter, Kerry was a teacher, and Chris (honorary squatter) still worked at Grove

Reprographics. This meant that I was on my own preparing the building a lot of the time.

The first thing that needed to be done was to sort out the basement. With labyrinthine passages and runs of ducting and pipework, it was already atmospheric. But the peeling pastel-green paint reminded me of government institutions. I decided that the darkness in the basement wasn't dark enough.

I lost count of the hours I spent down there painting everything matte black – the days indistinguishable from the nights – my only light, a smoky paraffin lantern. As my sweeping brush strokes cast the spell of darkness, so the smell of damp, the flaky green paint, and the walls themselves, began to disappear.

•

Katia finished her course and went home. Not back to Blackfriars. Back to Avellino, in the mountains above Napoli. We'd never really talked about what her plans were, so it was a shock when she went. I'm still not sure what happened. Whatever it was, everything between us was left unresolved and raw.

The day she left was the day before the flyers needed to be finished. I was back at the flat, staring at, or through, the glass tabletop, a sense of desolation trapped inside me. I pretended to myself that she might come back, but I knew deep down that things would never be the same. I couldn't concentrate. The page in front of me was blank, my pencil blunt.

Chris came round.

'What the fuck's up with you?'

'Katia's gone.'

'Shit.'

'Yeah.'

'How are the flyers going?' He looked over my shoulder at the blank page.

I tapped my pencil against my lower lip. 'I'm going to Italy.'

'We're on countdown now – you can't go to Italy!'

'I can't concentrate, and this . . .' I waved the pencil over the blank page in front of me. 'This all needs to be finished for tomorrow.' I put the pencil down like a child who'd just realised their toy wand had no magical power.

'Then sort it out, geezer!'

I sighed and picked up the pencil again, turned it two or three times in the sharpener, blew the twists of pencil wood off the page and wrote: *DeTension at the Skool House*. Naturally, I spelt Skool with a 'K' and drew every 'S' back-to-front.

•

At dawn, Chris left. He'd stayed up all night with me, encouraging me to see the project through, keeping me focused, making sure I didn't elope. When he'd gone I scrutinised the flyer. A cheeky little figure wearing a dunce's hat danced across a collage of coloured fractal patterns. The hand-painted lettering read, as if scrawled in chalk across a blackboard): *DeTension at the Skool House*. The details, which I'd rubbed down with dry-transfer letters, read: *29-9-90, 11pm – 6am, 183 Willesden Lane NW6. Arrive Early.* I'd credited Stikka's crew as he'd asked me to: *Turbo Sound by Unit One.* And, on his advice, written in bold capitals across the bottom: *INVITATION ONLY*. Apparently, this phrase would help us in the event of a police raid, as the Entertainment Increased Penalties Act of 1990, better known as the Illegal Acid House Act, had recently been made law. Stikka reckoned that the phrase would quell any suspicions that the 10K of Turbo Sound was illegal – acid house, or otherwise – and was, in fact, just your average private party that anyone might throw in their own front room – or basement.

But despite the eye-catching colour, jumping graphics and get-out-of-jail-free clauses, I felt something important was still missing. At dawn I stumbled exhausted into my room and flopped on the bed. As I lay on top of the covers, fully dressed, thoughts of Katia churned through me. Too wired to sleep and still in half a mind to chase after her, I got back up again and went out for an early morning walk.

I had no notion of where I was going, so I just kept walking: up Christchurch Avenue, past the Skool House, along Maygrove Road, past Debbie's house and up to Hampstead Heath.

I sat on the bench on top of Parliament Hill, the same bench Katia and I had sat on the morning we'd met. The morning sun steamed the dew from the grass. The trees were in full leaf, but I still had a clear view across London. Memories swirled around me. The fire in the garden; the gravitational pull of the empty Roundhouse; the fractals on Camden Market; the pigeons circling Nelson's column. Our first kiss.

The hub around which our shared lives had turned had shifted again. Katia's orbit had broken away from mine. I felt completely alone and ached with a hollow grief.

I don't know how long I was there. I watched people come and go. Hand-in-hand couples sauntered up and down the hill. A dad flew a kite while his two little boys jumped up at the string, hoping to get a go. A family arrived and had a picnic. Only when they too had packed up and gone did I realise I'd been sitting there for far too long. But I didn't want to move. I was paralysed with apathy.

I tried to focus on my commitment to the party and what it meant to everyone involved. Katia may have gone, but the Skool House was fast becoming a new hub of contact: a creative community space with a gravitational pull all of its own. Stikka, with that burning passion in his eyes; Chris, who had stayed up all night to encourage me. Other people were getting involved too. Debbie had been coming round to help, arriving in her little red post office van. She'd been eager, wearing her dark overalls, dusty with pink plaster and carrying a canvas bag heavy with tools. Hubert had come too, making decorations from holographic paper while spontaneously bursting into song or rhyming words and phrases borrowed from the conversations around him. And then there was Kirsty, a friend of Tim's. She'd spent many patient hours with me, meticulously cutting molecular shapes out of fluorescent card and glueing them to the walls and ceilings of one of the basement rooms. Tim and Greg helped me make backdrops. We'd spread out sheets of fabric on the gymnasium floor. The three of us on our hands and knees, crawling around between tins and jam jars of fluorescent colours, daubing, smearing and spilling as much paint on ourselves as on the canvasses. The very first backdrop we made said, in giant letters: LEARN THE HARD WAY.

Just as I'd been fitting shapes together over the previous few weeks, so too I'd been playing with words. I wanted to devise a name that represented our creative collaboration – not only the collaboration that there had been between Zander, Katia, Chris and me but everyone who was now putting energy into making the Skool House happen.

While still toying with the idea of producing a magazine, I'd come up with the name *Spiral Eye*. It seemed to say something, but nowhere near enough.

Then sitting on top of Parliament Hill, feeling devastated by Katia's departure, it came to me. The name of our creative community. Our tribe. *Spiral Tribe*. I said the words out loud. I spoke them out across London, and as soon as I had, everything fell into place.

Spiral Tribe. The words weren't just loaded with potential – they were loaded with the genetic code for the entity that was about to be.

ILLEGALLY TAKING POWER

The afternoon of Saturday 29 September, 147 Willesden Lane – The Skool House – stood waiting. Tim, Zander, Chris, Greg and I had taken our mugs of tea outside and were looking up at the front of the building. At our feet was a pile of empty paint cans. Though from the outside nothing had changed, inside we'd transformed the place. The UV paint on some of the backdrops was still wet, but other than that, everything was set.

'So, what time is Stikka bringing the sound system?' asked Greg as he tried to brush dried splats of fluorescent green paint off the blond hairs on his forearm. 'Is this rave paint radioactive?' He rubbed at it a little harder.

'The sound system? Later – this evening.' I replied.

'And the lights?' Asked Chris.

'They're bringing everything in one go, under cover of darkness – switching on at midnight. It's cutting it close, but it's too risky setting up early.' My optimistic tone felt forced.

Tim sucked in a sceptical breath and shook his head. 'That's more than cutting it close. The party's supposed to start at eleven.'

'But if the Old Bill show up when there's only a few people here, they'll nick the equipment and close us down. If the place is rammed, there's less chance they'll storm the building.' When Stikka had explained this to me, it had sounded like a clever strategy, but when I repeated the plan, it sounded risky.

'That's *if* Stikka shows up,' said Zander, peering into his tea.

Chris blew a flop of his hair off his face. 'I thought he was gonna sort the company head fuses. What we gonna do for power?'

Chris had a point: we were still running the building on candles and camping gas.

'All we can do is wait,' I said, trying to shrug off the doubts. But there was no hiding the uncertainty in my voice. 'Well,' I said as decisively as I could, 'I've got stuff to do.' I drained my cup, went up the porch steps, and stepped back into the building.

After the weeks of work there really was nothing left to do, but I grabbed a redundant broom standing in the hallway. It proved to be a useful prop in the act of killing time. As I pushed it ahead of me across the polished parquet flooring, I felt slightly guilty. Not for ducking out of answering everyone's perfectly reasonable questions. Or for printing a thousand more tickets than I'd told them I had. Nor because I hadn't mentioned the other sound system – instead of the one rig in the basement, there was going to be another, an outfit called Sugarlump, upstairs.

No. As I idly pushed the broom from room to room, it wasn't these things that made me feel guilty. Surprisingly the feeling came from the opposite direction. I'd promised everyone something fantastic. But the whole idea had been dreamt up out of thin air. It was all a creative invention, a vision, with no more substance than a few words and shapes scrawled on a flyer. An empty building. A glint in the eye. A hope.

Would the hope hold good?

Finding little more than a few offcuts of fluorescent cardboard, a stray drawing pin and a nicotine-stained roach on the floor, I still went through the motions of sweeping down the basement steps.

In the room with the black-and-white checked floor, we'd pasted op-art wallpaper to the ceiling. Chris and I (we still had our contacts in the trade) had, late one night, printed the paper ourselves on a huge A0 plan photocopier. The idea was that the optically twisted design of black-and-white check – under the intensity of the strobe – would cause a blizzard of geometric patterning to play on the retinas of the dancers. Stikka liked the idea and had promised to include, along with all the other equipment, a smoke machine and 500-watt Terra Strobe.

Of course he's coming, I reassured myself again as I pushed the broom through a small pile of brick dust below the long rectangular hole we'd knocked in the wall to create the DJ booth. I swept the growing collection of debris through another doorway into The Underground Laboratory – the room Kirsty and I had decorated with fluorescent molecular shapes – then out into the adjoining boiler room. Large ventilation grills in the walls let slatted beams of daylight in. In between the vents was a doorway that led outside, up a short flight of concrete steps, to the back of the building. This was to be the entrance, hidden between outbuildings and well out of sight of the road. With a final push of the broom, I shunted the sweepings under the maze of pipework that surrounded the boiler. The broom knocked the metal, sending a deep bass-note vibration into the foundations.

Nothing left to do, not a speck of dust to sweep. Everything was spick and span. The space pristine in its emptiness. Nothing to do but wait. The resonating bass note hung in the air, along with the smell of new paint and an aching anticipation.

As I turned to go back upstairs, I passed the empty company head fuse box. I was sure I could sense a dark electricity seeping out into the room. The hairs on the back of my neck stood on end. My spine tingled. *Of course Stikka was coming – how could he resist?* I left my doubts with the sweepings under the boiler and went back upstairs.

•

It had just got dark. The Skool House was quiet, the atmosphere subdued. My housemates were elsewhere in the building, relaxing in their rooms after a long day getting the place ready. We had packed down and cleared our communal kitchen space and pulled the large table to one end to make a bar. All the little chairs had been stacked away and locked into a small room by the front door. Chris and I sat on the bar, dangling our legs. He was practising his smoke rings.

'What was that?' I asked in an urgent whisper.

'What was what?' Chris was concentrating on holding the spliff upright, trying to keep an inch of ash balanced at its tip. Without flicking it, he slowly passed it towards me.

'I thought I heard something. Do you want an ashtray?' I slipped off the table to get him one of the many saucers that had candles burning in them.

Chris cocked his head to listen. His hand wavered. The ash toppled to the floor. There was a thud. Chris and I looked at each other. There was another, followed by another. Vehicle doors slamming outside. Voices coming round the back of the building. Zander and Greg burst into the room.

'Did you hear that?' they asked in chorus.

We all made a beeline for the basement. In the rush the candle I was carrying blew out, but we confidently moved down into the darkness and felt our way through to the boiler room and the cellar door.

We stood in silence in the dark for a moment. From outside, torch beams slanted through the ventilation grills. I didn't recognise any of the low voices but could hear them grunting with effort.

Light swept back and forth over the door. 'This is it,' said someone. 'You sure this is going to fit?'

'That's what she asked me last night!' said someone else. There was a burst of laughter that immediately got shushed to a snigger.

'Easy,' said the first voice, 'watch the steps!'

From around the building came the sound of casters crunching the asphalt.

'Knock-knock. Open up!' said a voice on the other side of the door.

I slid the bolts. Two men and a bass bin almost tumbled into the small room. Immediately behind them came another two with another speaker, and another, and another. Everyone and everything were silhouetted against the dazzle of torches. In the sweeping beams, all I could see were flashes of black boots, silky black bomber jackets and bald heads. Amp racks, flight cases and crated equipment poured in.

Zander and I were keen to get outside and help unload, but it was difficult moving against the current. When we finally managed to squeeze out, we found Stikka and one of the Pauls dragging a generator around the corner of the building. The weight of its oily bulk dug it into the asphalt, and gravel locked its wheels. The physical effort of shifting its dead weight turned our breathing into a hiss of curses. After a struggle we managed to manhandle it into an outbuilding. As if the generator were some untamed beast, Stikka shut the outhouse door and leaned his back against it.

Someone cursed. I guessed that they'd skinned their knuckles trying to manoeuvre a bulky box into the building. Zander jumped to their aid and was immediately swept away by the flow.

I wiped sweat from my brow with my forearm. 'Wouldn't it have been easier just to switch on the leccy?'

Stikka was also still catching his breath. 'If the Old Bill show, the first thing they'll do is arrest us for illegally taking power. If we supply our own, it gives them one less excuse to pull the plug.' He pushed himself away from the door. 'Where's Mr Craig?'

'Here,' came a disembodied voice from the darkness. A tall man appeared from the gloom. He was carrying a large spool wound with cable.

'The gennie's in here.' Stikka tapped the outhouse door.

Mr Craig put down the cable, opened the door and shone a pencil beam of light at it. The shadowy flow of people carrying equipment continued to squeeze past us.

'Stikka?' enquired a stocky man with both arms wrapped around what I guessed was another speaker.

'Yes, mate.'

'It's Olly Sugarlump. Where do you want us?'

'First floor, front classroom. Paul is on the door, so he'll show you what's what.' Stikka started to walk away towards the front of the building.

Mr Sugarlump disappeared down the steps.

'Let's get those vans unloaded and gone,' Stikka said to the other Paul.

'Do you want a hand?' I asked, but he was already round the corner.

'You can help me. Here.' Mr Craig handed me his torch. I held it while, like an explosives expert laying the firing wire, he unwound the cable from the generator into the house.

Like chunky black bracelets, Mr Craig wore two reels of black gaffer tape on his left arm. He deftly threaded wires and connectors up in the ceiling through the basement pipework, taping sockets at strategic intervals. When we got to the checkered room there were no more pipes to sling the cables from, though we still needed to get power across into the DJ booth on the opposite wall.

'Got any nails?' he asked. I dug into my sweatshirt pouch pocket, which sagged under the weight of a staple gun, screwdriver and a spray-paint can. I proudly produced a handful of nails. He hammered them above the door frames to create cradles to carry the cables and then nailed up a couple of brackets.

'What are they for?' I asked.

'Got a Terra Strobe and smoke machine to go in there – should look wicked with all this mental op-art!'

The DJ booth was actually a large canteen kitchen lined with stainless steel work surfaces, now full of consuls, mixing desks, keyboards and, taking centre stage in the middle of the long slot-like window we'd knocked through the wall, was the twin Technics decks. Both the canteen and the black-and-white room were crowded with piles of black boxes and metal-edged flight cases. Everyone, apart from me and my housemates, wore black. The light from their baton-like metal torches bounced off the stainless-steel surfaces, throwing busy shadows across the walls.

When Mr Craig had suspended the rope of cables across the room to the DJ booth, he handed them over to a lively, stout, bald Scot who wore a black Shamen T-shirt.

'Hey, are you Mark?' he asked.

'That's me.'

'Nice venue, loving the artwork!'

'Thanks.'

'Mr. Mann – sound engineer.' He warmly shook my hand. 'Could I ask a wee favour?'

'No prob.'

'With this amount of sound stacked so close, we'll have a problem with feedback interfering with the decks. Any chance you could borrow a couple of paving slabs from outside?'

'Paving slabs?' I was intrigued.

Mr. Mann smiled. He could tell I was dead impressed with

his mysterious know-how. 'We put them under each deck. The concrete'll deaden the vibration, so it dinnae come up through the table. Keeps the needle on the record.' He affectionately slapped one of the large stacks of Turbo Sound speakers. 'When these bairns power up, anything that's not nailed down is gonnae be blown away!'

Looking into the throat of one of the speakers was like looking into the intake of a jet engine. From the centre of each dark recess protruded what I can only describe as the nose cone of a black missile. 'Killa,' I whispered, then, realising I was gawping, closed my mouth. 'I'm on it!' I said and immediately set off in search of the crowbar and a pair of unsuspecting pavement slabs.

POWER SURGES

Mr Mann and I finished sliding the two paving slabs into position in the centre of the DJ consul.

'Connecting power!' came a call along the dark corridor from the direction of the boiler room.

With a flash of his torch, Mr Mann looked at the power junction box that he'd rigged up to dangle from the ceiling.

'Just checking everything's off, dinnae wantear blow the hoose doown.' Mr Mann seemed to be talking to himself but suddenly looked at me, the low torch beam enhancing his demonic grin. 'Well, maybe not just yet!' He crouched down and checked the amp rack.

Satisfied that everything was off and protected against power surges, he stood up and boomed through the slot-like window, 'Connecting power!'

Someone else relayed the call up the stairs and I could hear it repeated through the classrooms above.

'There's the generator.' If he hadn't pointed it out, I probably wouldn't have noticed the distant growl of the engine starting. 'Won't be long before we can warm things up.' He rubbed his large hands together with relish.

'How we doing for time?' I asked.

'Must be near enough eleven. Are those not the first of our guests?' A huddle of five or six people had wandered into the middle of the empty dance floor.

'If we're all done here,' I said, 'I'm going to see how they're doing on the door.'

'Aye, we're almost done.'

I left him flicking switches on banks of equipment. To get out of the room I had to duck between the splayed legs of a step ladder which spanned the doorway.

'You all right up there?' I asked Mr Craig, who was carefully positioning a strobe.

He had his torch in his mouth but the grunt he made sounded positive.

•

In the candlelit boiler room, we'd installed a desk to represent the ticket office. We'd decided to charge a three pound entry fee. A fair and affordable price which we hoped would cover our costs.

Standing around the outside door were a group of crew members sharing a spliff. Though they were actually DJs and musicians, they looked like a firm of dodgy doormen. DJ Paul (yes, this Paul was a DJ while the other Paul was a student film-maker) sat behind the desk on a little chair, idly testing out the rubber stamp and ink pad. Illegible purple words dotted the desktop in front of him. With his other hand he riffled a small stack of pound coins which chinked together. Clearly DJ Paul was ready, and we, in theory, were open for business.

'How's it going, Paul?' I noticed some of my credit card-sized flyers on the desk.

He looked at his watch. 'Cool. It's eleven ten and they're beginning to drift in.' He picked up one of the plastic laminated flyers and flexed it between his inky thumb and forefinger. 'These flyers work well. I reckon things'll get busy tonight.'

'It's all coming together, just hope more people show, but whatever happens, I reckon we all work well as a team ...'

At that moment Stikka strode in through the blokes standing round the door, wiping his hands on an oily rag. He threw the rag behind Paul, took the flyer from him and sat on the edge of the desk.

'I see you managed to sneak your thing in.' With an oil-stained finger he tapped the tiny Spiral Tribe logo in the bottom corner of the flyer. It was the same motif that Greg, Tim and I had stencilled in the corner of all the backdrops we'd painted.

'Sneak?' I smiled, uncertain of how else to react. I looked at DJ Paul, who shrugged. 'I was just saying to Paul how well we all work together. If we pull this one off, who knows what else we could do?'

There was a pause. Stikka nodded. 'Yeah, you've done a good job. The building looks pukka – the flyers too.'

'Thanks.' I looked at DJ Paul, who gave me an inky thumbs up.

'I got a few of these.' Stikka put the flyer down and reached inside his black bomber. He handed me a white cylinder, with each end sealed with a metal cap. It was a large electrical fuse about six inches long. Embossed on the ceramic body were numbers and electrical symbols that looked like hieroglyphs. The cartridge shape and weight of the object gave it added power – it felt loaded, dangerous, like a detonator.

'The company head fuses.' I gently bounced the weight of it in both hands. 'Where'd you get them?'

Stikka didn't answer, instead holding out his hand to take it back. 'I'm going to stash them somewhere safe. You don't want to be caught in possession of these motherfuckers.'

I gave it one last bounce, then handed it back.

Stikka stood up, tossed the fuse high enough to give it a little double flip, caught it, and slipped it back into his inside pocket. 'We can't take any chances. Tonight, we'll just use the gennie.'

'How about some proper light in here?' asked DJ Paul.

Stikka zipped up his jacket and started to walk into the next room. 'The cable's live, so talk to Mr Craig.' As he said this, Mr Craig clattered through the doorway with the aluminium step ladder. At the same moment a large group of punters arrived.

While Mr Craig taped a pink gel over a desk lamp, DJ Paul started taking money and stamping the backs of people's hands. I recognised one of the girls in the queue. A tall, dark girl with long, plaited dreads: Harmony.

Harmony lived a couple of minutes walk away on Chatsworth Road. We'd met at a rave in Camden Palace. We'd exchanged phone numbers. She was wearing a tightly ribbed top and bell-bottom jeans, which were heavily embroidered with flower-power motifs. The gap between her top and low-slung hipsters showed off her narrow waist and tightly curved hips.

'Hello, Mark.' She gave me a kiss. Though only a peck, as her soft lips pressed onto my cheek, I got an overpowering urge to slide my hands around the curve of her waist and give her a hug. I managed to resist and my hands dangled at my sides, tingling with the thought.

DJ Paul coughed. 'That'll be three pounds, please.'

I felt awkward. Uncertain about what to say to him. My costs had been minimal – just the paint, brushes and fire-proof fabric – but Stikka's crew had hired in equipment.

Harmony cast her long lashes downward and began sliding her fingers into the tight pocket of her jeans.

I found the words I was looking for. 'Actually, Harmony's my guest – my special guest.'

She flashed me a smile. 'Thanks, Mark, that's very sweet of you.' She held out her hand to be stamped. When she turned to follow her friends into the party, she stopped and said, 'By the way, you've got a smudge of paint on your cheek.'

I wiped my hand across the side of my face.

'The other cheek.' She giggled and went into the building.

•

Mr Craig had finished installing lights throughout the basement. In the checked room, a mist of smoke hovered at waist height and a strobe intermittently fired with an electrical pop. Each flash imprinted op-art check on my retinas. *Chris is going to love this*, I thought. Through the imprinted lattice and layers of mist from the smoke machine, the long slot of the DJ booth glowed red. I peered inside to see Mr Mann and his crew, who were now wearing headphones, adjusting dials and mixing-desk sliders. But there was still no sound. In fact, they looked as if they were studying the silence. As in a submarine. Standing by. On red alert.

I was upstairs when it happened. In the bar, which, by midnight, was packed. All of the thousand people we'd invited had turned up – and then some more. Projectors decorated the walls and high ceiling with swirling patterns of coloured light. Zander and I had to put our heads together to hear each other over the excited chatter. Everyone was charged with the anticipation of the sound systems powering up. I was worried. But not about the lack of music.

'I must look a mess. I haven't had time to change.' I showed Zander my paint-smudged hands. It wasn't just my hands – paint was all over my hooded sweatshirt, jeans and black baseball cap.

'No more of a mess than usual,' he grinned.

A line of five or six people, each holding the shirt tails of the person in front, squeezed past us on their way to the bar. They appeared to be dancing a conga – not to music but to some internally shared rhythm. They were all smiles, big glistening eyes and their faces sparkling with beads of sweat. Zander and I pressed closer together to let them pass.

Zander continued, 'Don't worry about it. Rave organisers are always covered in paint – you can spot them a mile off, glowing under the UV!'

'An occupational hazard, I guess, and a dead giveaway if we get busted!' I laughed.

'There's no escape – this crime scene's going to have your fingerprints all over it!'

It was then that a smooth, purring shudder ran up through the foundations of the building. Mr Mann had fired up the sound system. A cheer went through the house as the bassline of Joey Beltram's 'Energy Flash' pumped through the floor.

Though I'd been a main instigator at the core of the organisation, the Skool House was now infinitely more expansive than the sum of its parts. Like a ship leaving the dock, the Turbosound engines in the basement floated the building free of all material constraints. Moments earlier, the narrow stairway to the basement had been all too familiar. Now, each step down took me deeper into an underground reservoir of elemental energy. The strobe fired bursts of intense light into an impenetrable fog. Space existed somewhere in the flicker between the pitch-black void and the snow-blinding flash. The misty silhouettes of hundreds of dancers emerged from the fog, with movements that both reached out to explore and define the emerging reality – the new reality that each and every person there was now bringing into being.

I flowed through the crowds and through the mix. A flux of dance-energy, pumping bass and intimate joy. In the labyrinth, Mr Craig had programmed rope-lights to chase intense bursts of blue down and around the corridors. In the UV Laboratory, things were a little calmer. The near-invisible ultraviolet light soaked into the darkness but activated the fluorescent molecular structures. They appeared to drift free in space with a magical luminosity. Again, I was struck by a sense of extra perception. I'd spent weeks at the coal face: painting, cutting and glueing. I was in on the illusion. But this was no illusion. This was a glimpse of what was possible when a group came together to celebrate community.

Back upstairs Zander and I both took a crate of oranges from behind the bar and went off in opposite directions to hand them out. I offered one to Debbie, who I found sipping water from a plastic bottle in between wiggling to the beats coming up through the soles of her feet. She pointed to her mouthful of water and shook her head, swallowed, then with a gasp said, 'Top tune!' She gave me a big smile and, still moving to the music, slipped through the bobbing crowd towards the basement door.

After offering fruit around the gymnasium – carrying the box on my head and feeling like I was wearing a tropical carnival hat – I found Harmony, looking very slinky, dancing in the Sugarlump room.

I offered her an orange. She refused and asked if I could take her out to get some fresh air. Rather than pushing through all the crowds down in the basement, we walked together along the hallway towards the front door. Apologising as we stepped over people sitting on the floor. By the time we'd got to the door, I'd given out the last of the fruit.

Our household committee had decorated a note with hearts and flowers and pinned it to the inside of the door. It read: "Emergency Exit Only! Please Please Please Keep Shut!!!"

Harmony and I slipped outside into the cool night air. I looked back to see a group sitting in a circle, holding up their oranges and studying them with smiling expressions of beguiled delight.

'It's nice to know our efforts are appreciated,' I said as the door clicked shut behind me. Squeezing between the cars on the forecourt, we made our way around the side of the building to the playground. The music pulsed through the walls and rays of coloured light pierced a section of glass roof at the back. We sat on the mossy asphalt and chatted about the spirituality of rave music and parties. I was happy to have some close company after feeling lost without Katia. Harmony moved closer, her mouth an inch from mine. I puckered my lips and half closed my eyes. The lights from the party caused little stars of colour to twinkle between my lashes. Sparks of pink and green – and blue. Blue lights strobing in the misty September air.

She said softly, 'My faith is very important to me. You know I don't take drugs – and won't have sex outside marriage.'

Blue? I opened my eyes. The house was silhouetted against a backdrop of blue flashing lights.

'Fuck!' I stood up. 'The police!'

MAKING THE CALL

A group of four or five lads had got through the encircling police cordon. They'd hopped garden hedges, jumped fences, sprinted and crawled across lawns. The crew were trying to shut and bolt the back door, but there were too many people crowding in, including me and Harmony.

'Please, keep it moving folks!' urged a big bloke in a black bomber. Harmony and I were in the thick of the crush when he finally managed to squeeze the door shut and lock it tight behind us.

'I'll catch up with you later,' I called after Harmony, but I wasn't sure if she'd heard me above the music, which suddenly sounded a lot louder. I watched her disappear into the crowd, then I went over to DJ Paul, who was clearing his desk. Even though the small room was lit with the warm pink glow of the gel-covered desk lamp, he looked pale. He'd hidden the rubber stamp, pad and money, and, with his sleeve, was trying to rub away the blur of words he'd printed all over the desktop.

'Indelible!' He showed me his ink-stained hands and looked at me with resignation. He straightened up and tucked the small chair under the table – as if leaving the crime scene neat and tidy would bode well when pleading for a lenient sentence.

'How many are out there?' he asked, trying to rub ink from his fingers.

'I didn't see. I was out the back.'

'Shitloads,' said a bloke with twigs and leaves tangled in his long curly hair. 'They've blocked both ends of Willesden Lane.'

'Not a good sign.' DJ Paul shook his head, his expression somewhere between a wry smile and a pained wince.

'All the best parties are road blocked, matie! Legging it through those coppers has got me proper buzzed up. Fuckin' love it!' To demonstrate his enthusiasm the bloke lifted his right hand level with the top of his head and, as if trying to cool burnt fingers, gave it a vigorous shake. Keeping his hand up, he punched the air in time to the music and bounced off towards the dance floor.

I turned back to Paul. 'Do you think we should . . .' I hesitated, uncertain if what I was about to ask might in some way be sacrilegious. 'Would it help if we turned the music down a little bit?'

'We might be able to negotiate something,'

'Negotiate?'

'As far as the police know, this is just another private party – must be thousands across London tonight. So long as they don't get into the building, we hold all the aces.' DJ Paul nodded, but his expression looked doubtful.

'Shit!' I suddenly had a horrible thought. A vision of the front door and the wispy-thin fragility of the hearts and flowers decorating the sign: "Please Please Please Keep Shut!!!" 'Is anyone guarding the front door?' It was a rhetorical question that I addressed to the ceiling. In my mind I could clearly see the smiling, spangly-eyed ravers I'd given fruit to, opening the door and welcoming in an army of goose-stepping, orange-squashing policemen.

I didn't wait for Paul to answer. I pressed through the dancers to get upstairs as fast as I could. By the time I'd got to the bar, I could sense all was not well. An unsettled wave of body language spread through the crowd from the direction of the main hallway. It was the body language of people trying to look unphased as they patted down their own pockets, desperately trying to remember what they'd done with their stash. In the hall the crowd had completely thinned, leaving just an avenue of those ravers who were so engaged in caressing the invisible shapes made by the music that they either hadn't noticed what was going on or were beyond caring.

At the end of the swaying avenue the front door stood wide open – and through it advanced a squad of five or six policemen. Perhaps not the goose-stepping army I'd imagined, but they were strutting, chins up, eyes shadowed by cap peaks, mouths downcast, thin-lipped and grim, with hands clasped behind their backs and their chests puffed up so hard it looked like their tightly buttoned jackets were about to burst.

I froze. The police were upon me.

'Is there a problem, officer?' I asked the particularly severe-looking leader of the pack. He pushed past me without answering. For a moment the feeling of having been snubbed jostled for position with a sense of relief. The relief won over, and I fell in behind and followed them into the building. As if a corrosive chemical was seeping through the party, so the crowd in front of them dissolved. The alarm had been raised and the music in the Sugarlump room dropped in volume, shortly followed by the basement – but nobody stopped dancing.

As we moved through the building, unknown to the police, their escort grew. Ahead of them, like invisible outriders, members of the household quietly warned unsuspecting ravers of the dark cloud that was drifting their way. Stikka appeared on the right flank and Mr Craig on the left. Behind, more crew and concerned guests followed with me.

After a full tour of the party, our entourage arrived back in the hall. The chief took two steps up the staircase and turned to address the crowd.

'This party is over. Turn the music off. Pack up and go home.'

'This is our home!' called someone I didn't recognise. Even if they didn't actually live with us, their sentiment was well meant and caused other non-residents to proclaim that the Skool House was their home too – material, spiritual or otherwise.

'Clear the building now,' said the chief copper, raising his voice to be heard over the growing voice of solidarity. 'Or we *will* make arrests!'

I caught Stikka's eye. He had the same dark glint that had so impressed me the first night I'd met him. It could only mean one thing. He gave me a single nod – I understood.

'Okay everybody, you heard what the nice policeman said.'

Stikka held his hands up as if surrendering, or perhaps appealing for calm. He moved through the crowd towards me. As he passed, he quietly said, 'Tell everyone to look like they're leaving – we just need to get the Old Bill out the building.' I passed the message on, and the whisper rippled through the crowd.

After a few minutes the music went off. People did a great job of looking as if they were about to drift, dejected and disappointed, home to cold lonely beds.

In the lull I decided to try and talk with the chief. A perfect opportunity, I thought, to learn about the implementation of the law from the horse's mouth.

'We're not causing any trouble. Couldn't you let the party carry on?'

He glared at me. 'The party is over!'

'Is it the music? We can turn it down.'

'The party is over!' He stiffened.

'But it's a private party – it says so on the invitation.' I knew I was pushing my luck, but as the firm's resident artist and publicist, I was keen to find out exactly how much legal weight Stikka's notion of having the words *Invitation Only* on the flyer actually had. From the look of contempt the copper gave me, I was expecting him to have me bludgeoned, handcuffed and thrown into the back of a police van. Instead, he reached into his pocket and pulled out one of my flyers.

He flexed the flyer at me. 'There is no question that this party was professionally promoted.' He looked around, scanning the scene with narrowed eyes. 'I can see that this is a well-organised and illegal acid house party.' He sounded, and looked, like a robot reporting back what its visual sensors were detecting. 'And as such, you are committing a criminal offence.'

For a second, I wanted to explain: *No, this isn't a professional job, not a criminal offence, just me and my mates. I cobbled the flyers together, stayed up all night, struggling to get them finished in time – even though my girlfriend had left me and I was heartbroken . . .* Luckily, I managed to keep my mouth shut. But then I had a sudden urge to thank him for thinking we'd all done such a good job, even if that meant accepting the dark mantle of being an organised criminal gang. Before I gushed myself into a prison cell, I regained my sanity and realised I'd learned an important lesson. Once a government has outlawed something – no matter how creative, positive, or community spirited that thing might be – there is no such thing as taking the credit, only taking the blame.

I walked away from him looking as downtrodden and defeated as I could. The copper rounded up his men and began to leave. I waited a few moments to let them get down the porch steps. I held back. Counted to ten. Then crept to the door. I peeped out to watch them walk back up the road. Hardly daring to breathe, I very, very gently closed the door.

•

Yes! Yes! Yes! What a doddle! The party was still packed. No one had left – everyone had understood the whispered message: 'Hold tight, London!'

I'd just got back downstairs to the DJ booth bursting with the good news when, without warning, the house plunged into darkness.

Lighters, matches, candles and torches all flickered into life.

I groped my way through to the boiler room to find out what was going on. In the darkness, I recognised Stikka's voice.

'They've taken the gennie! The bastards have taken the fucking gennie!'

'All right, Mark?' Zander was standing next to me.

'Yeah, well . . . no. For a minute there I thought we were all sorted.'

Stikka pushed past us, still cursing under his breath.

'I reckon Stikka might need a hand,' I said. Zander and I followed him down the basement corridor that led to the room with the company head fuse box. He rummaged in the dark for a moment, passed me his torch and asked me to shine it into the metal cabinet that housed the four ominously gaping slots. He rolled up his sleeves, took one of the large fuses, being careful not to touch the metal caps at each end, and then paused. He was staring into the jaws of death. One wrong move and he would be electrocuted. He blew out a long, steady breath. Then, with a single push – blue-green sparks spat as metal touched metal – he clipped the fuse into the live mains feed. His hand clear, he let out another long breath and took a step back. After repeating the manoeuvre another three times, he casually dusted off his hands and, without a word, swept out of the room. Zander and I gave chase.

First stop was the DJ booth. Stikka, Mr Craig and Mr Mann rerouted a few cables, but still no power. Stikka headed back out across the dance floor, which was packed with people, each keeping the faith by holding up a flame. Someone started humming, 'Ohmmm', and one by one the whole building joined in – the air, the walls, our bodies resonated with the sound. Zander and I hurried after Stikka. We were heading up to another fuse box on the first-floor landing, but as we came to the hallway, I saw that the front door was open again. A girl I didn't recognise was standing out on the porch making a phone call. With a mind to ask her to get back inside and shut the door, I headed over, but as I approached, I overheard her conversation.

'Basically, yeah, the police have cut the power. Would you be up for lending us your gennie?'

I looked over her shoulder and out onto the road. There was no sign of the police. The girl holding the chunky black mobile turned and smiled – a huge dazzling smile, probably not intended for me but for whoever was delivering the news over the airwaves.

'Wicked, totally sorted, thanks Rudi!' The girl looked at me again and gave another smile and the thumbs up.

Zander tapped me on the shoulder, 'You've got the torch,' he reminded me. I gestured to the girl to close the door after she'd finished, and I followed Zander back inside.

We found Stikka positioning a chair under the fuse box on the first-floor landing. I handed him his torch. He climbed up and peered inside. He pulled out one of the white ceramic fuse housings as if it were a Lego brick.

'No fuses,' he mumbled, then turned to us. 'Got any nails?'

'As it happens.' I reached into my sweatshirt pocket and passed him up a handful. He sorted through them. The ones he wanted he held tight in his lips, and the rest he passed back. He flipped the large mains switch to the off position.

The stairs had filled with an audience – their faces turned up at Stikka as he balanced on the chair, their eyes wide with expectation. Stikka took a nail from his mouth and was about to press it into the fuse housing when a girl in the crowd called up to him: 'Are you sure that's a good idea?'

Stikka's shoulders sagged, and he turned to face her. He spat the nails into his hand.

'Good idea?' he yelled. 'It's a fuck of a better idea than you interrupting me when I'm standing up here trying to get the power back on!' He turned back to the fuse box, regained his composure, put a nail into each of the fuse clips, then pressed the blocks back into the fuse board – and flicked the mains switch.

The lights came on. We all blinked, as much with surprise as with the sudden brightness. Stikka jumped down off the chair and got patted, hugged and kissed by everyone as he made his way back down the stairs.

Both sound systems boomed back to life and the house erupted with waves of exhilaration. A new energy flooded into us all – the energy of celebration. The intervention of the police and their attempt at breaking up the party had made the event even more special. The threat of oppression had, as is so often the case, made the bond between everyone stronger.

With the party back in full swing I went to see if I could find the mysterious girl who'd been organising the back-up gennie. That kind of on-the-caseness needed to be congratulated.

ABSOLUTE ZERO

What the Land Rover lacked in acceleration, Zander made up for in high revs and tight cornering. He turned down the stereo but still had to shout to be heard over the noise of the engine and the tools sliding about in the back.

'You know, all this area used to be woodland?'

I didn't need to answer; the landscape said it all. As we crossed the Scrubs Lane Bridge, all I could see was an expanse of railway sidings that stretched to a distant industrial skyline. Zander turned the music back up – breakbeats skipping over a dark, rumbling bassline.

'What's this tape?' I'd not heard anything like it before.

'Danny made it for us.' Zander took his eyes off the road for a second to give me a grin.

'It's wicked!' I had to brace myself against the dashboard to resist the G-force of the right-hand turn into Du Cane Road. 'Do you reckon he'd be up for playing a set?'

'Why don't you ask him?'

We were on our way to Tree Co in Acton, West London, where Zander had managed to wangle me a few days' casual work. Like Zander, Danny was one of the fifteen or so people that worked for the firm as climbers.

Du Cane Road took us past Wormwood Scrubs Prison. The traffic slowed as we approached the main gate. I looked up at the windowless towers that stood sentinel on either side of the great door. A chill ran through me. The traffic cleared and we accelerated away.

'Yeah, this music has got attitude – could be the perfect theme music.'

'Theme music for what?' Zander yelled as we took another tight corner.

'Real life!' I yelled back.

•

80

Tree Co's premises were set back in a small yard below an over-grown railway embankment. In amongst the tightly parked pickup and tipper trucks was a 1930s, flat-roofed, yellow-brick industrial building no bigger than a two-bedroom house. Upstairs was the office, downstairs a cobble-floored stable which was used as a kit room.

The smell from the cold metal of the machinery and the damp brickwork mingled with the smell of cut grass, resin and petrol vapour. Zander put his chainsaw on the oil-stained workbench. He ran the sharpening file at just the right angle over each cutter-tooth of the chain. He worked to a rhythm: two long, rasping strokes, metal on metal, then moved on to the next link. As he worked, he told me cautionary tales about blokes who, roped high into trees, had cut themselves with chainsaws and bled to death before they could be lowered down. Of blokes who'd survived falls through glass roofs, only to break legs slipping off the back of their trucks. And then there was the ever-constant peril of the ground crew feeding the dangling end of a climber's rope into the cogged jaws of the wood-chipping machine.

'You're in a cheery mood this morning!' interrupted Kane as he ducked through the curtain of ropes and harnesses that hung from the kit room rafters. Kane was tall, broad and had short, dark hair. Like Zander and I, his work clothes had taken on the hue of bark – weather-beaten, scuffed and ingrained with the sap of London.

Zander looked up but didn't stop what he was doing. 'The Monday morning reality check.'

'Blinding party! When's the next one?' Kane put his chain-saw on the bench.

'Thought we'd all pile round your gaff next time!' replied Zander, handing the sharpening file to Kane and picking up a spanner.

'I wish, mate! Danny, he'd be up for it – wouldn't you, Danny?'

Danny was coming through the wooden garage doors. 'What's that?'

'Party round yours.'

'Anytime – slight problem with space.' Danny held the curtain of ropes open with one hand, a steaming mug of tea in the other.

'Maybe next time you'd be up for playing?' Danny smiled shyly at my suggestion and shook his head. Despite his blond-hair-and-blue-eyed good looks, he was a quiet, modest bloke.

'Go on Danny, you've got some top tunes and a wicked set,' said Kane.

'I don't know.' Danny took a sip of tea. 'Most weekends I go night fishing.'

'Fishing?' I'd somehow imagined Danny would be more of a man-about-town.

'Yeah, just me, the water, the stars. It's so peaceful.'

Kane looked at me and Zander and gave a little shrug.

After hitching up the chipper onto the tipper truck's towbar, I slung my bag and jacket into the crew cab of one of the vans. The drivers were revving the engines, impatient to get on the road. Danny was loading his climbing gear onto the back of another truck.

As he walked past, I said, 'Perhaps we should have a chat sometime about you playing, if you're up for it.'

'Yeah, maybe – what you got in mind?'

•

Rose Farm was the secret HQ of Debbie's close circle of friends. It was owned by Heather, who was in a relationship with Debbie's brother, Mickey. Heather had four children, three of whom were in their late teens or early twenties. The whole family loved music – preferably electronic and loud. Though not a particularly big house, Rose Farm did have two large rooms knocked into one, the kitchen and the dance floor, which at one end had a table set up with decks, mixer and a small rig – and lots of space. It was the perfect after-party set-up.

On this particular Sunday afternoon, we'd been up all night and were still enjoying ourselves. While Mickey played some seriously fluffy tunes, Debbie, along with Greg and Kerry, and six or seven other people danced about in the billows of smoke that Vince (a workmate of mine and Chris's from Grove Reprographics) was spraying at them from a portable smoke machine.

Sitting around the table was Heather, Tim, Zander, Chris, Hubert, Tony (the friend who had first introduced Zander and me to Debbie and the Rose Farm posse), Roger (or, as we called him, DJ Hush-Hush), Kirsty, Paul Brash (not to be confused with any of the other Pauls) and sitting opposite me, Hamish – the six-foot-three geezer who wore baggy, brightly coloured clothes and skewed kid's sunglasses.

Hamish had asked me to explain exactly what Spiral Tribe was all about. I was still wondering myself but tried to simplify my chaotic notions into something that made more sense. Making something simple is a complicated business, especially after a sleepless night.

Hamish had a pushy charm, a certain barrow-boyishness. Having a conversation with him was sometimes like haggling with a market trader: it could be fun, but when he felt things weren't going his way, he knew he might still swing the deal by talking louder than anyone else. His latest enterprise was selling the baggy surfwear he was so fond of. He was certainly a good advert for it: you couldn't miss him on the dance floor, and it wasn't only his height and large frame – he had some killer dance moves too.

'What is Spiral Tribe?' I repeated to myself. I looked around the room as if searching for the words in the dense fog that Vince had filled the room with. As the mist thinned, silhouetted figures emerged, dancing against the solid blocks of sunlight that pushed through the open windows. Vince, along with his smoke machine, had drifted out of the French widows. The colours of the flowers – oranges, reds, pinks, purples – soaked into the mist that he enthusiastically sprayed around the garden.

'This . . . this is Spiral Tribe. All of us. Everyone together. All tribes.

'*Feel-the-vibe-with-Spiral-Tribe!*' rapped Hubert.

'And what does Spiral Tribe do?' asked Hamish.

'Frees up empty spaces and brings people together.'

'*Feel-the-bass-in-outer-space!*' Hubert echoed.

'Why don't we put on another party?' I suggested, eyebrows raised to everyone round the table.

'Where?' Hamish's question sounded like a challenge.

'Anywhere! Where do you want a party?'

'*Here-there-everywhere!*'

In a whoosh of smoke, Vince came in from the garden and

the kitchen began to fog again. Mickey mixed in Tuff Little Unit's tune, 'Join The Future' – a tune with a bassline and beat that suited the searching movements of the dancers disappearing back and forth in the smoke.

Hubert got up and vanished into the white cloud.

'Where do you think we should have one?' I asked Hamish. He shrugged. 'Hubert, got any ideas about where to have the next party?' I called. There was no reply. 'Hubert?'

He popped up next to me. '*I-have-joined-the-future-and-I-am-I-am-in-Amsterdam!*' he laughed, disappearing back into the smoke.

'Amsterdam! What's wrong with Shepherd's Bush, or Acton?' I protested.

'*I-am-I-am-in-Amsterdam!*' he insisted.

'Okay, fuck it, Amsterdam – why not?'

'Amsterdam! Have you got contacts there?' Hamish asked, suddenly eager.

'No.'

'You're not serious!' said Heather. 'Why not do something closer to home?'

'How you going to organise a party over there with no contacts, no venue, no sound system?' Hamish's voice was getting louder with each point he listed.

Of course he was right, except that he hadn't mentioned the biggest hurdle – no money. But the gauntlet was down and I'd picked it up. We'd got the most important ingredients – creative talent, ideas, DJs, artists – and let's not forget our rapper from the future!

'*Come-alive-with-Spiral-Tribe!*' came Hubert's voice from the mist.

●

I hadn't got a venue in Amsterdam, but I had one in mind. Months earlier, on a previous visit to the Netherlands, Zander and I had found ourselves at a squat party. It was in a huge concrete warehouse on the end of one of the runways at Amsterdam airport. There was only a handful of people there, and the tiny sound system had been dwarfed by the echoing chasm around it. I hadn't met the people who lived there or had any contact with them since. I didn't have an address, only a vague memory of how to find the place. I had nothing. Absolutely nothing. I had to start somewhere, so I gave the nothingness – and the future event – a name: 'Absolute Zero'.

●

When I'd asked for a cup of tea, I hadn't expected what the waitress put in front of me. I gently tugged the small anchor chain attached to the perforated stainless-steel infuser, which caused golden-red clouds to swirl in the tall cylindrical glass of hot water. This was no soggy brown teabag bunged in a mug – this was tea Amsterdam style.

Reflected pink and green neon highlighted the edges of the polished aluminium café chairs and tables. It was mid-morning and the coffee shop had just opened. The place was empty, apart from me and the girl behind the counter who was stacking cups and polishing glasses.

I picked up my pen, tapped it against my lower lip, then put the pen down again. I watched a tram blur yellow in the condensation that trickled down the large plate glass window, then, with a sigh, picked the pen back up. Everything depended on the letter of introduction I was still trying to write. I'd done numerous drafts on the ferry over from England, but I was still struggling. I reread what I'd written.

"A message from Spiral Tribe.

I come from a community of squatters in London. We are artists, designers, musicians and DJs who have connected together to demonstrate through our work the power of creative energy using all communicative channels available.

At the moment, we are combining music and dance with visual imagery.

Simultaneously using electrical technology, new and experimental music mixed with dance music, live musicians, live sampling, and rapping, we create a new dimension to music. Coupled with our powerful visual imagery and lighting effects we strive to create a totally new environment for the senses and the soul, an environment built and engineered by all involved for the single purpose of showing others that new or undiscovered ways of perceiving and living life can and do exist.

This self-made reality is only one aspect of many, or a tiny fragment of the whole, but in our experience, once one new angle has been revealed, the psychological barriers crumble to open forgotten doors.

We make music that has not been corrupted by political, advertising or commercial messages. We make new sounds with words of freedom.

Things are moving fast – this is the age of change, but traditions of exploitation and profit run deep in our culture.

Today millions of people go hungry, military conflict and

arms sales escalate. Racism, ignorance and greed prevail, destroying the world. All that is wrong is symptomatic of insecurity and fear of the unknown, anxieties that are mercilessly reinforced by the profit culture.

We seek to undermine these negative aspects by introducing an element of balance achieved with creative input.

We believe that once one has experienced the unleashed power of creative thought, a suppressed sense of personal identity and freedom of being is rediscovered. This wider sense of awareness and balance contributes to the chain of events that will help to forward the evolution of life and civilisation and so help to change the world."

Rereading this now, it sounds breathlessly evangelical. Probably because I was breathlessly evangelical – filled with the excitement and fervour of realisation and discovery. The world was tittering on the brink of transformation, but I was still struggling with how to pronounce the Dutch name of the place I was looking for. I took the crumpled piece of paper out of my wallet and smoothed it out on the table. In pencil I'd written '*Rykshemelvaartsdienst*'. I got up and went over to the counter to see if I could enlist the help of the waitress.

'Excuse me, could you tell me how to get to *Ryk-shem-el-va-arts-die-nst?*'

The girl stopped what she was doing just long enough for the blank look she threw me to sink in and make me feel even more self-conscious. '*Ryk-she-mel-vaarts-dienst?*' I fumbled with the piece of paper as if adjusting its angle slightly might help unjumble the letters. '*Ryks-hem-elva-arts-dien-st?*'

She put the glass she'd been polishing up on a shelf, put her hands on her hips and gave me the stare again – less blank – but more indifferent. With a tremendous effort of will she took the two steps towards the counter and held out her hand. I passed her the piece of paper, embarrassed about how scruffy it looked.

'Ahhh! *Rykshemelvaartsdienst!*' she smiled. 'Sure, I know this place. It's a community of artists on Oude Haagseweg.'

'A community of artists? Is it far from here?'

'Not so far, maybe thirty minutes. Take the number two tram. Ask for the *eindpunt*.

'Eindpunt?'

'In English it means *the end of the line.*'

THE PROPOSITION

Holland, as everyone knows, is flat, but the tram stop at *the end of the line* somehow felt flatter than anywhere else I'd ever been. And there was also something unsettling about the new and apparently unused roads. The tarmac was freshly pressed, the road markings newly painted, all squeaky clean, like some toy version of the real thing. There were canals and waterways – too straight to be picturesque. No buildings, no cars, no people, only tidily mown verges and lines of neat little trees.

The wide grey sky was just as featureless – and strangely bright. The few remaining leaves on the trees glowed an intense, almost artificial, golden yellow. But there was nothing unreal about the cold: as soon as I stepped from the tram my lips began to chap.

I didn't recognise the area. The last time I'd visited had been late at night, in a taxi. I consulted my precious scrap of paper. The waitress had sketched me out a map. I put my faith in her directions – crossed Sloterweg, then went right down Anderlechtlaan. Ahead of me I could see the E19 Autobahn, which marked the outer orbital of Amsterdam. As I walked, I turned up the collar of my leather jacket, but it didn't help. *Next time I must remember a hat, and scarf, and gloves, and woolly socks, and long johns.*

As I emerged from under the Autobahn flyover, the rip and rush of the high-speed traffic above turned to a deafening shriek. A passenger jet, so low that its underbelly blotted out the sky, came in on its final approach. I covered my ears and watched the roaring bulk float down behind the trees ahead of me. Clearly, I was heading in the right direction.

When I got to Oude Haagseweg I turned onto a section of older road. Weeds cracked the asphalt and woodland closed in on either side to form a leafless tunnel. After a few hundred metres I came to a clearing. A collection of utilitarian buildings – which I guessed were ex-military, or perhaps part of the airport before its modernisation – were dotted about under the trees. I passed several old vehicles. Most looked road worthy, but one car, daubed in rainbows of paint, was a crumpled wreck. Behind the smashed windscreen and under its sprung bonnet sat broody chickens on their nests.

Through the trees I recognised the warehouse: a vast, windowless, cast-concrete block of a building. This was my holy grail, the temple that stood at the centre of my imagination. I hurried across the glade.

At the base of the building's steps was a rusty scrap metal sculpture. A humanoid figure built of cogged machinery parts, ribbed black plastic tubing and a shrivelled gas mask as a face. Dark ivy grew up between its legs. A robin landed on the figure's nozzle-like nose, cocked its head and looked me up and down. I paused a moment and looked around. There was no one about, so I carried on up the steps. The great riveted-metal door stood open.

I stepped over the threshold. Avenues of pillars disappeared into the shadows. It was bigger, colder and darker than I'd remembered. It was beautiful.

My echoing footsteps gave shape to the void. I walked out into the centre, where a patch of grey filtered down from a single large skylight. Here the floor was made of glass bricks, perhaps to illuminate a basement. Walking on the glass felt like moving across the surface of a deep pool that had frozen over. I imagined watery green lights and projections positioned far below – an effect that would enhance the sense of depth. The endless rows of concrete pillars also had great potential. Excitedly I fumbled for my camera. I needed to document every aspect of the building, start taking measurements, make notes and sketches. I looked out into the darkness. The décor had to *celebrate the space* in all its industrial, utilitarian glory. After all, warehouse parties are *warehouse* parties.

Caught up in the creative possibilities, I'd forgotten that I was an uninvited guest. An intruder. An intruder who was making some huge and unreasonable assumptions. I put my camera back in my pocket. I didn't want to get caught nosing around. My excitement turned to uncertainty. Standing on the black glass floor I suddenly felt exposed, watched. I turned around. Silhouetted in the doorway behind me stood a figure.

Walking back towards the door I felt apprehensive, even a little scared. *What if this person's a psycho?* Whoever it was, they were tall, broad and blocking the only way out.

'*Goede middag, wat doe jij hier?*' I didn't understand each word, but I got the gist – who the hell are you?

'Hi, I was er . . . just admiring this wonderful building. I visited before, a while back. I don't think we met. I'm Mark. ' I held out my hand. There was a pause.

'You're English?'

'Yes, just arrived on the ferry.' I made small up-and-down undulations with my hand. 'And the tram.' I made side-to-side snaking motions.

'And you are here to see who?'

'Er, well . . . do you live here?' There was another pause. My hovering hand lost energy and sank back to my side. 'I understand there's a community of artists living here. I'm interested in working on a project – I have a proposition.'

'You are . . . an artist?'

'From England.' I nodded.

He snatched my hand and shook it. 'Martin,' he smiled. 'Come, I must show you my work.'

•

Martin's studio was located in a stall in an old stable block. It would have been a dark, damp place but he'd rigged up a street lamp bulb, which, he told me, he'd salvaged from the recent road-building works. When he switched it on, it burned with the light and heat of a small sun.

I didn't really like his art, but I still shot a whole reel of film.

I couldn't resist his poses: chin held high, arms thrust towards his smeared canvases and sculptures made of tangled wire and driftwood. As soon as he'd shown me one item, he flung it aside and pulled out another. After I'd seen his entire collection, he made us some strong black coffee on a camping gas stove. I sat on what looked like a sack of sand while he perched on a paint-splattered sawhorse.

'Sure, I will talk to the others about your concept. Maybe they will like it. But after the last party here, we decided not to do any more.' He waved a copy of my new leaflet. 'Maybe this will help change their minds.'

•

That morning, before I'd set out on my tram journey, I'd visited a photocopy shop. I hadn't liked the letter I'd been writing, as it was too long and over the top. Instead, I decided to present my idea in a four-page leaflet. I decorated it with my graphics: a naked cartoon character that looked as if it were made out of splatted jelly and some swirling spirals that looked a little like swirly number sixes. On the counter of the photocopy shop I'd painstakingly handwritten my new text – in block capitals. Looking at a surviving copy of the booklet now, it's a bit loud – and why I decided to print it on purple and yellow paper is anyone's guess. But as I handed over the small stack of pamphlets to Martin, I was pleased with them – even proud. It was my very best possible effort, and that, I hoped, would be enough to swing the deal.

'Come back on Wednesday evening at seven,' said Martin. 'That's when we have our meetings. You can talk to everyone then.'

As I got up to leave, I noticed that the sack I'd been sitting on had leaked some of its contents – fine grains of dazzling light.

'What's this?' I asked.

'Ah, this I also got from the highway builders. It's what they mix into the white paint for the road markings. It's reflective.'

'Wow!'

'Here, you must take some.' He found an empty jam jar and filled it with the micro-beads of light.

'Thanks, this stuff will look wicked on backdrops!'

We shook hands and I walked out into the evening.

•

As I headed back towards the tram stop, I felt frustrated. I was going to have to wait another three days – three days of uncertainty.

Sitting on the warm tram, gazing past the reflections on the windows, I tried to quell my impatience and growing nervousness. Meeting Martin had been a good result, I reassured myself. But other problems were stacking up. Finding the venue was only one piece of the jigsaw. With no money, where exactly was I going to find a sound system? And how was I going to publicise the event without the authorities closing it down? I needed local contacts – underground contacts.

UNDERGROUND CONTACTS

Underground contacts, empty warehouses and massive sound systems were one thing. Surviving Amsterdam's freezing climate was another. No doubt, that night, I would have been shivering in my sleeping bag in a corner of Martin's studio if it hadn't been for the generosity of a complete stranger – at least, a stranger to me.

Though the split between Katia and I was painfully unreconcilable, we did occasionally speak on the phone. I'd mentioned that I was going to Amsterdam, and she gave me the address of a friend of hers. And so it was, with my rucksack on my back, I turned up on Marcia's doorstep.

Originally German, Marcia, who I guess was in her late thirties, had made her home in Holland. Her apartment was at the very top of one of Amsterdam's tall, narrow buildings, close to the city centre. The living room was divided in two by a zigzag folding door. She showed me into the half that looked out over the main street and canal. I dumped my rucksack next to a large potted palm. A grey tabby cat, who was curled up on a white sheepskin rug, lazily opened one eye.

'This is beautiful, thank you.'

'You are very welcome – stay as long as you need. And please, make yourself at home.' She handed me a key.

•

On Monday I was up early and thumbing through Marcia's phone book, scribbling down the addresses of Amsterdam's record shops. A good place to meet people in the underground music scene – or so I thought. Out on the cold streets it was a different story. After visiting five or six shops I began to lose my enthusiasm. It turned out that each had its own DJs and organised their own commercial club nights. Amsterdam is not a big city, and the last thing any of them wanted was some young upstart organising a large event that would pull hundreds of their punters out of the weekend club circuit. My frustration grew and my feet began to ache. *What was I thinking, leaving England and coming to Holland with nothing, nothing but a gut feeling? Follow the vibe, just follow the vibe,* I told myself. What else could I do?

I had visited the last record shop on my list and was wearily trudging the cobbled streets of the red-light district when I heard a tune. A tune I didn't recognise. The sound lured me down a narrow side street. It was coming from a coffee shop which was brightly lit with white and pink neon. The double glass doors were wide open. The music beckoned. I hesitated. On a chrome bar stool sat a bloke with short, cropped hair. At his feet was a large pit bull. Behind the white marble bar was a busty young woman wearing a black PVC-laced bodice. I wasn't sure what I was more nervous about, the dog or the girl. Just as I was about to step over the threshold, I decided that this wasn't really my kind of place. I turned to leave, but the dark bassline turned me full circle and pulled me in. I sat a few stools along from the bloke with the dog.

'*Hi, wat wil je?*' asked the girl as she wiped away something invisible from the bar top in front of me.

'Hi, coffee please.' I consciously ignored her breasts bulging from the top of her bodice. 'And er . . . could you tell me the

96

name of this tune?' She smiled but gave me a quizzical look. 'The music, who's it by?'

The aroma of freshly ground coffee blended beautifully with the resinous smell of weed smoke which was drifting over from my neighbour. I glanced across at him. He was looking at me with dark, unsmiling eyes. So was his dog.

'Mr. And Mrs Dale . . . "It's you" . . . Free House Mix,' the girl read from the cassette tape cover.

The bloke with the dog slid along to the stool next to me. 'This is a very good tune!' He had a Dutch slant to his voice, but his accent wasn't European. 'You have good taste in music!'

'Thanks, I just followed the bassline down the street.'

'It is good when the music moves you.' He passed me the spliff. Though it was probably a bad idea, I didn't want to seem ungracious, so I took it. 'You on holiday?' His eyes were blood-shot but intense.

'Just some business.'

'What's your business, man?'

I was slightly taken aback by his directness, but it was impossible to ignore. 'At the moment . . . at the moment, I'm looking for a sound system.'

'A sound system? What kind of sound system you looking for?'

'What do you mean?'

'Big? Small?' He tilted a hand back and forth.

'Big,' I said with a nod of satisfaction.

'Big?'

'Very big.' I smiled – the grass seemed to be working.

'Hey, you making a dance party?' His guess surprised me, and it must have shown because he suddenly laughed and slapped me on the shoulder.

'Maybe.' I grinned – the grass was definitely working.

'What you mean maybe?' His smile evaporated.

I gave the spliff back. 'Well, there's a group of us in England who want to come over and play.'

'You DJ?' His dark look lifted.

'I guess I'm a scout, and I do the promotion, the graphics, the décor, that kind of stuff.'

'That's good! That's very good!' He took a long pull on the spliff and called out something to the girl behind the counter.

'Do you DJ?' I asked him.

'No, but I put on dance parties.'

'You serious?'

'Yah, serious man. Me and my friend we put on big parties.' He puffed up his chest.

'Big parties? Do you have venue?'

'Ah! This is always the problem here. The police, they don't like these things.'

'It's the same in England.'

'In Suriname it's okay – you want to party, you party. Here the police they always want to control.'

'Suriname?'

'Brazil is here.' He stabbed a finger onto the counter. 'Suriname is here.' He slid his finger up an inch. 'And you – you are from London?'

'Yeah, London – it's okay.'

'London's good. I'd like to visit one day. So, my friend, what is your name?'

'Mark.'

'Hesley.' We shook hands. He held my hand and my gaze.

'I've been talking to the record shops in town, but they don't want a dance party here.'

'Hey man, it's all bullshit with these racist people. You talk to me – the Department of Underground!'

'The Department of Underground?'

'That's right, man. The Department of Underground.' He released my hand and presented me with a clenched fist. I clenched mine and lightly punched his. He laughed again and gave my shoulder another slap.

The waitress put two small glasses on the bar in front of us.

'What's this?' I asked.

'Schnapps – drink!' He picked up his glass.

'Well, here's to the Department of Underground!'

'And here's to . . . what do you call your parties?' he asked.

'Spiral Tribe.'

'Spiral . . . Tribe?' He narrowed his eyes. 'It's a good name!'

•

Walking into the first bar that was playing good music in the red-light district of Amsterdam, and making deals with strangers with pit bull terriers, was not how I normally operated. Actually, that's not true. I had no norm. And if my short track record was anything to go by, then that's exactly how I did things.

Though Hesley was clearly someone you didn't want to mess with, he had a directness about him, and, like Stikka, a passion for the music. He was keen to introduce me to his business partner, so we arranged to meet again the following Thursday – the day after I'd get an answer from the artists with the beautiful concrete warehouse.

'It's the devil's work!'

The bloke had jumped up from his chair and was waving one of my leaflets about. On his shaved head he wore a beret, and on his shoulder he carried a large ghetto blaster. 'Look at these spirals – what do you think they mean?' He flashed me a glassy stare. 'Look, it is six-six-six!'

I made a move to stand up and answer him, to make my case to the group of fifteen people that sat around in a circle in the warehouse basement. A large man with dreadlocks beat me to it.

'Daaf, please sit down.'

Daaf continued to hold my gaze, a twinkle of mischief in his eye. He switched on the ghetto blaster. Acid music gurgled into the room. With a long lanky stride, he went back to his seat opposite me and sat down, pouting.

'Daaf? The music, please?' the big bloke asked. Reluctantly Daaf obliged, then blew me a kiss. 'We have decided,' the big bloke continued, 'that we don't want any more dance parties here. For us, this kind of thing is not interesting.' He sat back down.

The news came as a blow. I felt stunned. It was all over.

I was about to get up and leave when I realised everyone was looking at me expectantly. I guessed they wanted me to respond. I stood up.

'Hi, everyone. I'm Mark . . .' I resisted the urge to give everyone a little wave. 'Sorry, I don't speak Dutch. I hope you've had a chance to look at the information.' I gave Martin a nod, but he was staring at the floor. Everyone else looked cheerless – apart from Daaf, who was stretching his long arms and legs and enjoying a fit of loud yawning. 'Can I ask what it was about the last party that made you decide not to have any more?'

'Sure.' The big bloke remained seated. 'The sound was terrible, we were all kept awake for nothing, no people came. It was not what we like here.'

I remembered the tiny little sound system and dispirited group of dancers half-heartedly wobbling about. If the residents here had a problem with that meek little gathering, there was no way they were going to agree with what I had in mind. I needed their agreement – everything depended on it. Backed into a corner, I was going to have to fight my way out, albeit nice and gently.

I tried to find some common ground. 'Like yourselves, we are a group of artists, musicians, and DJs.' It was probably too late to redefine what my proposition was, but I thought it was a good idea to tone down the loud music aspect of the event. 'We have just done two "installations" in an old school building in London. We now want to collaborate with other artists who understand that creative space is what is missing in mainstream society. Mainstream society is a grid of interlocking business interests. Anything outside the grid is underground – and free! Something to be celebrated! These opportunities are few and far between. Now, what I am proposing may be a bit bigger than the last . . . '

'How much bigger?' the bloke with the dreadlocks interrupted.

'Oh, well, I'd say . . . quite a lot bigger. Maybe fill the place.'

'And the sound?'

'Well, yes, of course, we would need a *good* sound system.'

There was some discussion in Dutch between the big bloke and those sitting near him.

'He is the devil!' The finger Daaf was pointing at me remained perfectly still while the rest of his body squirmed.

'I'm sorry,' said the big bloke – and as he spoke, I sank, deflated, into my chair – 'but if you can promise to fill the building and will have a good sound system, then yes, we would like you and your friends to come and play your party. Maybe in February?'

It took a moment for the information to sink in. *Did I hear it right?* I stood back up. For a moment I was speechless. A grin spread across my face. 'Well . . . thank you! Thank you – that's wicked!

Daaf switched the gurgling music back on and started to body-pop – apparently ecstatic about the decision.

Before the meeting continued with other business, I said more thank yous and endless promises that they wouldn't regret their decision. Martin walked to the door with me.

'So, what made everyone change their minds?' I asked him.

'At first they were worried that the party would be small and with bad sound, but now they know you want a big party they are happy. You look surprised?'

'Er . . . no, no, not really,' I lied. 'Before I go, do you mind if I take some photos of the space?'

Martin gestured towards the stairs. 'Please, our space is your space!'

I was so excited that it was difficult to hold my camera steady. I took pictures from the centre of the warehouse, turning a full 360 degrees. Then I made sketches and plans. I took measurements and scribbled them in my notebook. The look and feel of what I wanted to do was coming together. I liked the idea of the under-lit glass floor. Along the blank walls I pictured continuous backdrops depicting my splatted jelly character doing cartwheels and back-flips. But when it came to the colonnades of concrete pillars, I was stuck. I wanted to enhance them – make more of them without covering them up or disguising them.

After an hour or so I left to catch the tram back into town. *I had a venue – a beautiful, big venue bursting with creative potential!* I was so happy that I skipped along the avenue, laughing out loud and firing off my camera at the crescent moon.

•

The next morning, I took my films to be developed, paying extra to have them done in an hour. I waited in a coffee shop sipping black tea from a glass and sketching ideas about how to decorate the pillars. Nothing worked. Anything hung between them would look like washing hung out to dry. Ideas to construct Atlas-type figures supporting the roof were too elaborate – great if I could spend a few months building them, and had the materials and resources, but that was sadly not the case. I finished my drink and went to pick up the photographs.

In among the grey, underexposed pictures – in such a large space, my small flash had done little more than show the distant warehouse walls as faded banks of mist – there were two or three dazzling gems: the pictures I'd randomly fired off at the moon. The surprise was that it wasn't the moonlight that illuminated them but the bare branches overhead. The flash had bounced back off the branches to create what looked like great stabs of lightning. It occurred to me that the trees took years to grow, while lightning lasted just a fraction of a second – but both were the same energetic shape.

My problem about what to do with the pillars was solved. I would paint branches in UV, wire them to fan out from the tops of the columns and, with the same UV paint, continue the branching lightning down and around the pillar. The effect – in directional, strobing UV light – would be of avenues of lightning trees.

I had the concept: Absolute Zero. The logo artwork: the splatted acrobatic dancer. The décor: the electric forest. Things were going well. Next up was the meeting with Hesley – and his business partner.

•

Even though it was daylight, the address where we'd arranged to meet was difficult to find. I walked past the building a few times before I decided that the plain black door must be it. I buzzed the intercom and waited. No answer. I knocked with the ball of my fist. After a minute or two, a spyhole slid open, then snapped shut. Bolts were drawn. The door swung open and a girl with radiant blonde hair showed me inside. It took my eyes a few seconds to adjust to the low light and deep red décor. I had to watch my feet as I followed the girl down the steep basement steps. Chairs were up on tables while another girl swept the floors. On a small, raised stage area a bloke boisterously played with three dogs – all pit bulls. Hesley and another man were lounging in a stall. As I approached, the man stood up and introduced himself as Richard.

Richard was tall and broad, with a mop of black curly hair. He didn't smile. I pulled up a chair, but he ushered me into the stall to sit between him and Hesley.

'So, you want to make a dance party in Amsterdam?'

'Yeah, if I can get the right people together.'

'Hesley tells me you've been having some trouble with the record shops.'

'I wouldn't say trouble – it's just they've got their own thing going on. It's difficult for me coming over here not knowing anyone.'

'Sure, I understand.'

'Are you from Suriname too?'

'Suriname? No. All over – here and there. I was in New York before.'

'New York? DJing?'

'Yeah, I DJed – it's a good city for music.'

'And now you and Hesley run parties together?'

'Yeah, we've done a few things. So, tell me more about what you need here in Amsterdam.' Richard motioned to the girl who'd shown me in. *'Hey, Biertjes graag!'* He turned to me. 'You want a beer?'

'Thanks. Well, I need to find someone to collaborate with. I've got DJs, artists, and a wicked venue.' As I said this, I noticed the largest of the three dogs got bored of being teased with the rubber bone and trotted towards our table.

'You have a venue here – in Amsterdam?' Richard fixed me with his dark-rimmed eyes. The dog muscled its way up onto the seat between Hesley and me. Hesley slapped him affectionately round the head a few times.

'Yeah, a wicked venue,' I said as the dog turned its attention to me. 'Just outside . . .' The dog pushed his way onto my lap and lay his head on my shoulder, his huge jaws against my throat. My voice involuntarily wavered. 'The airport . . . a warehouse . . . no neighbours.'

Richard looked at Hesley. The girl brought the beers over.

'For sure you have this venue?'

'Sure.' It was difficult to speak with the weight of the dog on my chest.

'This could be interesting. So, what do you propose?'

I tried to politely push the dog away. His neck was as thick as my torso, and he didn't want to budge. 'Can we let the dog go and play?'

'Hey! He likes you!' said Hesley.

'He's a very nice dog!' I managed to say. 'Can I just get him to . . .' I was pinned down my pure muscle.

Hesley called the dog to him, and I tried to regain my composure.

I laughed with relief, though I pretended to myself and anyone else who might be interested that I was laughing about the beast's lovable nature. 'If you, that is, The Department of Underground, can supply the sound system, lights and distribute the publicity.' I pulled out a folder in which I had laminated A4 photographs of the décor at the Skool House, examples of the tickets and also the sketches I'd done of the new venue. 'I can supply the DJs, the artwork, the décor, and the venue.'

Richard looked through the folder in silence. When he was done, he slid it over to Hesley. 'I think we can do business. You want another beer?'

'That would be nice,' I said as cold sweat trickled down my back.

OUT INTO THE EVERYWHERE

'This yours, sir?' asked the customs officer at Harwich, barely able to conceal his delight at finding Martin's jar of glistening white powder. I'd completely forgotten about it, stashed away in the bottom of my rucksack, along with my dirty underwear.

'It's paint powder,' I said, 'reflective paint powder.'

He looked me up and down. I could read his mind: *A dishevelled young man with long hair and ripped jeans carrying half a kilo of crystalline white powder in his luggage. It's a text-book case!*

'Artist are we, sir?' he said with a sneer.

'Yes, actually.' I felt my cheeks colour.

'And what was the purpose of your visit to Amsterdam?'

'To organise a . . . ' I searched for the right word. 'A multi-media arts event.'

'Multimedia?' His eyes narrowed.

'Yeah – art, music, projections . . . dance,' I said with a sweet smile.

'And reflective paint?'

'Yeah, lots of reflective paint!' I grinned.

Whatever tests he ran on the powder didn't take long, and a few minutes later he begrudgingly told me I was free to go. And so it was that I smuggled my notebook overflowing with illegal acid house plans back into England.

•

I spoke to Danny at Tree Co. 'The venue is in the bag. The sound system, the lights, the publicity – all sorted! What you saying, Danny?'

He bit his bottom lip.

'There's loads of canals,' I continued,' lakes, rivers, the whole place is below sea level. It's practically crawling with fish!'

His eyes lit up. 'I'll pack my fishing kit. Shall I bring a few tunes?' He gave me a wink.

Stikka and Charlie Hall were also keen.

•

Some parts of London look pristine: brass work polished, streets swept, potholes filled, broken windows repaired. Harlesden wasn't one of those places. It sat on top of the big railway junctions of Willesden and Old Oak Common, just above the huge industrial estate of Park Royal.

Number 20 Station Road was a semi-detached house. Detached being the operative word, as the house appeared to be breaking away from its neighbour. The front doors of each property stood side by side, but an ominous crack between them widened as it ran up the front of the building.

One morning, after dancing all night at Egg – Charlie Hall's club night – a load of us piled round to the Station Road house. As we went through the front door, I nervously glanced up at the crack and then down at my feet. The thought had crossed my mind that the weight of us all crossing the threshold might be enough to snap the last few unbroken bricks and send the crack zigzagging down through the foundations and out along the garden path. That didn't happen, but still, as we made our way along the gloomy hallway and up the narrow stairs to Zarrena's room, there were far more real hazards: all the floorboards were dangerously uneven or loose – that is, the floorboards that were still there.

In Zarrena's room were Charlie Hall (DJ), Addie (philosophy student), Ian (who worked in a café), Zander, and Zarrena (who was probably still at school). We were lounging around on a double mattress on the floor, chatting and drinking tea.

I explained my plan to Charlie.

'Absolute Zero?' Charlie adjusted the earflaps on his blue Laplander hat.

'Normal zero is just the number water freezes at. Absolute Zero is the lowest. It's proper zero, where things really start,' I enthused.

'Or stop.' Charlie raised an eyebrow, then gave me one of his twinkly smiles. 'No, I like the idea, geezer – Absolute Zero. I reckon I might come along and help you liven things up!'

While we'd been talking there'd been a whole lot of noise coming from one of the rooms on the opposite side of the landing – from a large hole into the next house. What had sounded like a load of furniture being dragged about turned into the dull thud of a kick drum. The sound tightened up into fast rolls and symbols crashes. Disjointed chords jangled from electric guitars. After a few minutes the drum rolls stopped and the oscillating squelch of a Roland 303 – the acid machine – liquefied the air.

Later that morning, when Zander and I left, we popped our heads through the hole. Two scruffy blokes were bashing about on guitars. Sitting between them, cross-legged, with the little silver 303 in his lap, was a young guy in a bright orange jacket. He was making fine adjustments to the bubbling acid machine.

'Hello!' I shouted. The noise almost drowned out my voice, but the bloke in the orange jacket looked up with the wide-eyed delirium of a child playing with a new toy. Zander and I gave him a little wave, and he gave us a big grin back.

As we went out the front door I glanced up. 'I'm sure that crack has got bigger.' I looked down at the path. No fissures gapped at our feet, but rosettes of stunted weeds, which had pushed through the concrete, crazed the ground with light-ning-forked patterns. 'It's amazing how nature just keeps on pushing through.'

As we turned out of the garden gate and onto the busy road, the burbling sound of the acid machine oozed from the crack in the building and, despite the smoky growl of the traffic, fol-lowed us up the street.

•

It was a few weeks later that we properly met the bloke with the 303. His name was Seb. He was nineteen and a music stu-dent. He'd come to the Skool House parties and, ever since, had been inspired to experiment with the acid sound. It turned out that the day Zander and I had put our heads through the hole in the wall was the very first day he'd managed to get a 303 and start those experiments. Well, when I say properly met him, I mean we tripped over each other while running around blindfolded in the dark – on top of Parliament Hill.

*

I'm not sure whose idea it was but somehow a bunch of us: Seb and Ian (from Station Road), Automanic Josh (a DJ and close friend of Charlie's), Hubert, Greg, Chris, Zander and I were standing on top of Parliament Hill on Hampstead Heath in the middle of the night, with a large square of blue plastic tarpaulin wrapped around us. Someone said, 'Hey, I got a load of red dragon acid – want some?'

We were there for hours, tobogganing down the snowless grassy slopes, some sitting on the tarp while the others dragged them along. When we'd got bored of that game we ended up in a little gaggle with the tarp over our heads. With just our legs sticking out we ran around blindly, like a blue octopus possessed by Ouija board spirits. Amazingly we missed running into any trees or plunging into the lakes, but we did sustain multiple, but minor, bruises when we crashed into the iron railings that surrounded Boudica's burial mound, which legend holds to be the grave of Boudica. The warrior queen who fought the Romans.

•

Before I'd gone on my reccy to Amsterdam, we'd moved out of the Skool House. Our numbers had swollen, not only with friends who were in need of housing but also with people who thrived in the atmosphere of our creative community.

Simone was one such person – the girl who, after the police raid at the Skool House, had been trying to radio in another generator. She was nineteen and wore black, with her straight, shoulder length hair dyed red. Not ginger red. Deep red. She also happened to work at a disco equipment hire shop.

At this moment, our community was still a loose-knit group of friends. There was no *Spiral Tribe* – at least not as a tangible, physical entity. Spiral Tribe were the words that pulled us together in cosmic discussions and creative events. After each of the two Skool House parties the Spiral had unwound and returned back to the realm of ideas. Unwound it may have been, but each time it re-materialised it became more tangible, and for longer.

When we left the Skool House we moved a couple of miles south to an empty building which overlooked a small triangular park called Tamplin Mews.

Number 53 Chippenham Road was a large, three-storey – four if you count the rubble-filled basement – Regency house on the end of a short terrace. Though in a state of semi-dilapidation it still had a sense of grandeur about it, which is more than you could say for its immediate neighbour, which was a roofless, floorless shell.

All the buildings in the area were painted white. Not quite the icing sugar white of richer areas, but more weathered, grey, cracked and crumbling – and still white enough to add a little sparkle to the neighbourhood. All except number 53, which was dark green, so we called it the Green House.

Though the Green House was big, an endless flow of friends – and the nameless individuals that forever haunt the sofas of squat-land – meant that, on any night of the week, the place was bursting at the seams.

•

It probably wasn't the most sensible place to sit, but there I was, in the middle of the floor in the communal sitting room, my sketches and plans of the Amsterdam warehouse spread out around me. It was late afternoon, but people were still milling about getting breakfast. Debbie and Simone were sitting together on a sofa with busted springs, passing my photographs between themselves.

'Hmm,' mused Debbie, 'it's a huge building.' She passed the handful of photos back to me. 'How on Earth are we going to decorate it?'

'I don't think it needs much,' I replied. 'I like the raw industrial look.'

Simone agreed. 'You just need to get the lighting right – it'd be wicked!'

'Yeah, I was thinking about something like this.' I passed her the last photo.

'Lightning?' asked Simone, handing it to Debbie.

'Trees?' said Debbie. 'Branches!'

I stood and held my arms up, spreading my fingers to give my interpretation of a concrete pillar impersonating a tree. 'I thought we could paint a load of branches in UV and wire them on top of the columns, like a forest of lightning trees – it'd look pukka under strobes. Can you get UV strobes?' I sat back down.

'When is this all supposed to be happening?' asked Debbie.

'The twenty-third of Feb,' I said.

'I'm not sure. I've got a plastering job to finish, and anyway, I can't afford it.' Debbie closed her eyes and shook her head.

Simone beamed her huge smile. 'But we don't need money, do we?' She opened both her hands in front of her as if to reveal the simplicity of the plan. 'This would be all expenses paid, wouldn't it?' She shrugged and looked at me.

'Of course. We'd be the Spiral crew,' I nodded.

'I'm totally up for that. How about you, Debbie?'

'Well . . .' Debbie frowned and crossed her arms. 'I need to get that job finished.'

'Come on, Debbie – what you saying?' Simone ladled on the charm.

Debbie uncrossed her arms. 'How long would we be away?'

'I reckon three days max.' I began tidying up the papers around me.

Debbie flopped back into the sofa. 'Okay, I'll come,' she smiled, clearly relieved that she'd granted herself the time off.

'Sorted!' said Simone. 'I love it when a plan comes together!'

•

Due to the overcrowding at the Green House, a group of us opened up another boarded-up, three-storey building on the opposite side of the little park: 74 Walterton Road.

The Walterton Road posse included Debbie and me (Debbie and Hubert were no longer an item. Debbie and I now shared an upstairs room together). Debbie's sister Tracey (who was training to be a bus driver) and her boyfriend Karl (aka DJ Karl K), who were in the top-floor room next to us. Simone had the room on the middle floor and Hubert had the downstairs front room.

Although the rooms at number 74 were a lot smaller than those in the Green House, Debbie and I gave over what little wall space we had to painting backdrops. We pinned up large sheets of fabric, sketched out the designs in pencil, then painted them in fluorescent colours. After each new backdrop was finished, it was taken down and a fresh sheet would go up.

In this way, all the walls became printed with multiple layers of our spiral designs that had soaked through the fabric.

Painting spirals was like meditating on a mandala. The more time we spent doing it, the deeper we became submerged in the spiral. Visitors to the house would often get drawn in too, and we'd all happily while away the days and nights focused on our work. One friend in particular helped with the backdrops – his name was Camden.

One morning Debbie and I came downstairs to the kitchen to find the floor, cooker, fridge and sink all knitted together with entwined fluorescent brushstrokes. The trail of paint left the kitchen and went down the hall towards the front door.

'Camden must have run out of fabric last night.,' said Debbie, swirling a finger in the still-damp paint on the fridge door.

'He wasn't here yesterday. Perhaps it was that other bloke?' I rinsed the paint off the kettle. 'What was his name?'

'I dunno, I thought he was your friend.' Debbie wiped paint off the seat of a chair and sat at the table.

'Whoever he was, he's done a good job.'

'All this creativity – it's taking on a life of its own!' Debbie made space on the table by sliding a cluster of paint-stained jam jars to one side. 'And now it's escaped out the front door, into the nuss.'

'The *nuss*?' I flicked the switch on the kettle.

'Yeah,' she said, 'you know – the everywhere-*nuss*.'

•

In the weeks leading up to the party in Amsterdam, I returned to Holland with Danny and Kane to finalise things with Hes-

ley and Richard. Then, back in England, I got on with designing the artwork: tickets, flyers and posters. Chris and I printed
them up and posted them to Holland.

On 21 February, Debbie, Simone and I – our hair now cropped
bonehead short – set sail on the night ferry to Amsterdam.

A FUNNY NUMBER: AMSTERDAM, FEBRUARY 1991

It was the day before the party, and I was up a tree outside the
gate to the airport squat. I was trying to cut some branches to
decorate the warehouse pillars. Sounds straightforward, but it
had already taken me half an hour to find a tree that I could
get up and had branches of the right shape and size. The glowing UV grove I'd envisaged wasn't going to work with great
bulky logs or thin wispy twigs. Everything had to be in propor-
tion. Plus, I hadn't accounted for the slippery green algae that
coated all the trees and made climbing messy and treacherous.

Clipped to my belt was my Japanese pruning saw. I carefully
slid out the curved blade, ready to make my first cut.

•

'What on Earth happened to you?' asked Debbie as, scratched
and bruised, I unshouldered a bundle of branches onto the
warehouse floor. 'And why are you bright green?'

'How are the lads,' I asked, gesturing to the other side of
the warehouse where Hesley and a couple of his mates were

wrestling the dismembered limbs of a shop mannequin from their pack of pit bulls.

'Laid back,' said Debbie, 'but they did bring us these halogen work lamps.'

In a pool of orange light, Debbie, Simone and I got to work wiping the algae off the branches. Then we scrubbed white paint into every fork and twist of each branch. The final coat would be fluorescent yellow, but it needed a white undercoat to work properly. Another thing I hadn't taken into account was just how vast a surface area branches and all the little twiggy bits have. It took hours. And hours. And then once all the white was done, they'd all have to be redone in a topcoat of UV yellow. There were other complications too. It was 22 February, midwinter, in an unheated warehouse. It was not only so cold that our fingers hurt but it was also preventing the white emulsion from drying properly. On the tin, it said: 'Drying time four to six hours under *normal conditions.*'

Debbie and Simone were exhausted. They'd arranged to stay at an acquaintance of Simone's in the city. Though they didn't want to go, I knew it would be hours before the decorations were finished. I reassured them that I'd grab some sleep when the job was done, and so they rushed off to catch the last tram back into town.

I'd hardly slept the previous night in England because of all the last-minute preparations. So, I felt like weeping when, at eleven thirty, I realised I wasn't even halfway through the stacks of branches that still needed painting. Hesley and his mates weren't much help. Well, I'm sure if they weren't wearing their super-cool-bad-boy clothes they would have mucked in. As it was, Hesley kept the vibe alive by fuelling his monstrous ghetto blaster with ultra-sultry house tunes while the others stoked large cone-spliffs with strong Dutch Skunk. And then there were the pit bulls, all of whom gave great balletic performances while they ripped the mannequin's body parts to pieces.

•

I was so tired, so cold – and yet, so excited. There we were, on the eve of a momentous event. As midnight approached, my excitement grew.

At first I put it down to the sense of occasion, enhanced by the wicked tunes, powerful weed and boisterous company. But my excitement kept on getting stronger. As midnight grew closer, so the feeling increased. I was in a state of rapture, and it was all about the approach of midnight. *But why midnight?* I kept asking myself.

'Hesley?'

'You want to know the time – again?'

'It's important.' I put my paintbrush down and rubbed my fingers, which were sore with cold and tacky paint.

'Okay, it's nearly midnight! You want me to count down?' He remained serious.

I shrugged. 'Yeah . . .'

'Eh!' Hesley called to the other lads. 'Countdown! *Vijf, vier, drie, twee, een* . . . Absolute Zero!' Hesley and the lads cheered and the dogs barked. I tried to cheer but felt strangely removed from the situation, as if I was watching the whole scene from outside my body. But what a feeling. Pure joy pulsed through me. It was like I'd had a taste of the world's best Ecstasy. But I was completely straight, apart from being delirious with hunger, cold, fatigue – and maybe the skunk.

Hesley continued. 'Today's the day, my friend! Spiral Tribe and Department of Underground make big party history! Today is the day, the big two three!'

Then it hit me. It wasn't the countdown to midnight; it was the countdown to the 23rd. Not the date – the number. Don't ask me what strange signal was pumping through my body at that moment, but the number 23 had triggered something profound.

What exactly does the random and apparently significant arrival of the number 23 have to do with anything? Well, at that moment – trading shoulder slaps with the boys and throwing plastic body parts for the dogs – I was asking myself the same question. But in all the blissful uncertainty, one thing was apparent: the number 23 was not an *answer*. Not the result of a mathematical problem. Not a religious icon. Not a political symbol. In fact, it was an antidote to that kind of polarised cause-and-effect way of thinking. The number 23 is just itself. And as any physicist will tell you, everything in this wildly oscillating universe has its own particular vibration.

NO KNIPPERLICHT

Miraculously, by ten o'clock the next morning all the branches were painted, cut to size and ready to be wired up around the top of each of the pillars. They were even almost dry. Actually, there was nothing miraculous about it. I'd stayed up all night to finish the job. Three of Martin's disembodied streetlights were positioned on the floor and, to try and speed up the drying process, I'd stacked the painted branches in their hot orange glare. A forest of shadows tangled the concrete space.

I was up a step ladder attaching the first branch when Richard showed up.

'Hallo!' he said as he walked underneath me.

'Hi. Richard, I was wondering . . .' But he already had his back to me as he continued to walk towards Hesley and his crew, who were lounging on an old sofa, their dogs curled at their feet looking uncharacteristically cute.

I'd wanted to ask Richard about the lighting I'd ordered – without the right lights the décor wouldn't give the desired effect.

I wrapped the first strand of wire around the top of the pillar and, with a pair of pliers, twisted the two ends tight. Then I climbed down the ladder to double-check everything with Richard.

The street lamps on the floor stretched my shadow ahead of me as I walked over to where the guys were locked into a heated discussion in Dutch. I loitered a moment, waiting for the right moment to ask my question. If the moment came, I never found out, as Debbie and Simone arrived and called to me from the opposite corner of the building. I left the lads to it and walked back towards Debbie and Simone.

'So, what needs to be done?' asked Debbie, looking up at the rather lonely single branch jutting out from the pillar.

I spread both hands out towards the light-bathed stacks of florescent yellow branches.

'You had any sleep?' asked Debbie. 'You look rough!'

I closed one eye.

'Here, we brought some breakfast,' said Simone, rummaging in a supermarket carrier bag.

We sat on some wooden packing cases and, among the bloodless gore of savaged mannequin's limbs, had a picnic. We were ravenously hungry and sat in silence while we devoured slices of white bread, squares of rubbery cheese, and chunks of chocolate. All washed down with what Debbie had guessed from the picture on the carton was fresh juice but turned out to be strawberry-flavoured sour cream.

Richard, Hesley and the lads wandered over, trailed by a line of very tired dogs.

'Okay,' said Richard, 'we must go now and get things ready.' He smoothed his fingers through the wet-look ringlets of his hair. 'We will be back later. Everything alright with you guys?'

With our mouths full, Debbie, Simone and I all nodded.

Richard continued. 'If we are not back in time, there are some people coming. The sound is arriving and also the beer.' He started to walk away, followed by the others. Hesley gave us a little salute as he left, but the dogs sat fixated by the packet of cheese. Hesley growled at them, and they reluctantly trotted out after him.

Suddenly I remembered I wanted to ask about the lights. I wiped pink cream from my lips and called after them.

'The man with the sound, he brings everything,' Richard answered over his shoulder.

•

When he arrived that afternoon, the man with the sound – sporting tight leather trousers, a mullet haircut and a huge moustache – didn't know what I was talking about. Probably because he didn't speak English. The more I tried to explain exactly what was required, the more annoyed he got. The more annoyed he got, the more frustrated I became. Luckily the tension was alleviated when, completely unexpectedly, the Rose Farm posse showed up with Greg and Kerry. Zander, Chris, Tim and Tracey among them. Though most of them quickly disappeared to find the nearest coffee shop, Zander, Tim, Tracey and a couple of others stayed behind to help. With the extra hands on deck, we made good progress getting the UV trees constructed. We also helped the sound man unload his staging, amp racks and speakers. After that he seemed to cheer up, and even attempted a little English. Actually, just one word. *No*.

I'd gone off to find Martin in his studio. I decided to ask him for the Dutch words for UV strobe. He'd carefully written them out for me, and I hurried back to the warehouse to present the translation to the sound man.

'*No* ultraviolet-stroboscoop, *no* flitslicht, *no* knipperlicht!' he frothed at me.

If earlier that morning someone had told me how despairing the words *no knipperlicht* would make me feel, I wouldn't have believed them.

But I was too busy to let the disappointment slow me down. As soon as we'd put up the staging and stacked the speakers into two fat columns, the beer man arrived – in an articulated truck. Worryingly, both he and his mate also sported overtight trousers and spiked mullets.

When Richard had mentioned that they were going to have a bar, I hadn't quite grasped the scale of what he'd planned. I watched in admiration as one of the draymen skilfully backed the huge truck next to one of the warehouse loading bay doors. Once docked, they wheeled out pallet trucks of metal trestles, which they bolted together to construct the bar. The stage and sound system were large – as they should be – but both were dwarfed by the bar that began to take shape, stretching as it did the entire length of one of the warehouse walls. The draymen then trolleyed out the metal kegs, clamped beer pumps to the bar top, connected pipes to the barrels and then, clipboard in hand, came to find me.

'Please to sign here,' said the stouter of the two as he passed me the documentation. I scribbled my name with a flourish.

'Happy party, guys!' he said and, pulling a pained look, gyrated his hips while he fingered an imaginary guitar. I handed him back the clipboard and smiled politely.

As the truck pulled away, I wondered if it had been such a good idea to put my name on the paperwork. It was too late to do anything about it, but if anything did go wrong, I'd be responsible for any unpaid bills, and looking at the huge number of kegs stacked behind the bar, it would be massive. I wondered where Richard and Hesley were. It was getting late.

'Hey, Mark, where'd you want this?' called Tracey, waving the last fluorescent branch at me.

'Perhaps in that gap above you. We also still need to finish off painting the lightning zigzagging down the pillars.' I picked up a tub of fluorescent yellow and went over to her. In jagged brushstrokes, I spiralled the energy of the glowing tree canopies down the pillars towards the dance floor. An hour later and the effect was complete. Instead of an avenue of concrete pillars, we were standing in an enchanted glade.

It was late afternoon when Richard and Hesley showed up again. They'd brought a takeaway pizza for us. Debbie, Simone and I perched on the packing cases again and hungrily devoured the cold, soggy dough and stringy cheese. They'd also brought their bar staff: a group of nine or ten young women dressed in black-and-white waitress garb, their hair scraped back in buns. Debbie, Simone and I were in dark overalls, streaked with paint, looking pretty androgynous with our shaved heads. The entourage of girls walked past us in a cloud of chemical fragrance and completely blanked our greetings of *Hello* and *Hiya*.

'So what are you wearing to the ball tonight, Cinderella?' Simone asked Debbie.

'Oh, you know, I thought a slinky little black number and high heels.' she replied deadpan. 'How about you?'

'I thought I'd come in fancy dress.'

'As?' Debbie dabbed a finger on the crumbs still left in the empty pizza box.

'Oh, I don't know – maybe a painter and decorator?' Simone smiled. 'What about you, Mark? Got your glad rags on underneath those scruffs?'

'Nothing but my tutu!' I raised my eyebrows. All I actually had were the clothes I had on. And even if the clothes under my overalls had escaped the paint blotches, which they hadn't, they were still stained with green algae and ragged from my earlier antics up the tree.

'It's a glamorous life!' said Debbie. 'Anyone got a rollie?'

WAITING IN THE COLD

Though the warehouse was one vast, cold concrete slot, by midnight it was a steaming sweatbox. Among the thousands of Dutch ravers that jostled for space, there was a fashion for multicoloured tinsel wigs and skin-tight Lycra. Lime-green belly-tops, lemon-yellow leggings and cerise-pink leotards. I also met people from Italy, Germany, Belgium, France and, of course, England, but none of them shared the same taste in rave wear as the Dutch – unless you count Hamish, who was busting his moves in big, baggy, black-and-white checked trousers, with a matching peaked cap.

Mastermixer Zoefff (aka Richard) played a set of up-tempo house.

As soon as Charlie got on the decks, Camden, who had helped paint the backdrops back in England, jumped on stage and – samba-style – blew a whistle while wagging an instructing finger at the heaving crowd below.

Sadly, Stikka had pulled out because of some last-minute commitment working with the Shamen, but he'd sent over a mate of his instead: DJ Para.

But, for me, the highlight of the night was Danny. After he'd played, I met him as he came down off stage.

'That was one wicked set, Danny!' I shouted as we walked away from the speakers.

'Thanks.' He wiped sweat off his forehead. 'I think it went pretty well.'

'Fucking blinding, mate!' I ducked to avoid being whipped by a girl's long hair while she thrashed her head from side to side.

'Bit of a problem with the monitors early on, but it all got sorted.'

'Didn't notice,' I said as we stopped in a relatively uncrowded space. 'Top set! Pure darkness!'

'Glad you think so,' he smiled. 'Deeper, darker basslines – that's where we're heading!'

•

At some point in the evening I wandered downstairs to where the Dutch squatters had set up their own coffee shop. It was a chill-out zone with candles on the bar, low tables and hay bales as seats. Well, it would have been a chill-out zone, except they were playing high-treble, discordant punk. Behind the bar, in the shadows, I glimpsed a wiry figure writhing disjointedly and out of time with the music. Even in the shadows I recognised the silhouette and the intense twinkle of the eyes. It was Daaf playing the music. The big bloke with the dreadlocks was working the bar.

'Hey,' he nodded, 'good party?'

'Very cool, thanks. Things going well down here?'

'It's good. A different space. Different music.' He gestured with his eyes back towards Daaf and smiled.

'Yeah, very cosy.' I looked around and spotted Zander and Chris sitting on bales in the corner.

'You want a drink?' he asked.

'Any water?'

'Sure.'

'A big glass, please.'

The room was crowded and it was a squeeze to get over to the corner where Zander and Chris were sitting. I sank down next to them with my back against the wall and closed my eyes. Just taking the weight off my feet was bliss.

'You okay?' I heard Zander ask.

I opened my eyes and realised I'd snatched a second of sleep. 'Hanging on in there – totally wrecked though!' I mumbled.

'Rushing your tits off?' laughed Chris.

'Actually, no.' I shook my head, more to wake myself up than in denial. 'I've been up too long. Far too long.' I sat up and took a big gulp of water. 'Remind me next time we do a party not to stay up the night before painting sticks!'

'Looks good though,' said Chris. 'The sound's good, and everything's worked out wicked.'

'Shame about the lights not being right.' I shook my head. 'But yeah, it's all come together. We've got a good solid crew. None of this would have been possible without everyone doing their bit.'

'So, what about the Dutch crew?' Chris got out his Rizlas.

'How do you mean?'

'What's the arrangement with them?' He fumbled in his pocket for his weed.

'The squatters?'

'No, the blokes running the door and the bar – do you get a cut?'

I looked at Zander.

Zander had fronted all the money to get us over from England, and we still had to see Richard and Hesley about getting paid back.

'Well, not exactly . . .' I took another sip of water. 'It was never meant to be a money-making scheme.' I set my water down on the table and watched the candlelight bead in the condensation on the glass. 'I'd kind of imagined it would be more like the Skool House. I didn't realise the bar would be so massive.'

'So you don't get anything for putting on the party?'

'Expenses.'

'Expenses?' Chris looked up from the spliff he was rolling.

'Yeah, expenses.'

'And the other crew make all the money?'

'Well, they are hiring in all the sound system, the lights.'

'The wrong lights!' Zander reminded me.

'Okay, the wrong lights – that was just miscommunication.'

'Like the massive bar and all the money we're not going to make?' Chris continued.

'Well, maybe . . . I guess I thought the whole thing would pay for itself.' I took a deep breath. 'Isn't it just the vibe that's important? The connections between people? Isn't it money that's broken those connections?' I was searching for what I was trying to say. But Chris was right – I hadn't thought any of it through.

'You know what I reckon?' said Zander.

I turned to Zander and raised a weary eyebrow. I braced myself for one of his harsh-realities-of-life lectures. 'What?'

He looked preoccupied and serious. 'I reckon we need our own sound system.'

●

In the morning the party started to wind down, and by nine most people had drifted away, their bodies exhausted but their spirits shining bright. The sound system was being packed down and the bar staff were sweeping up the thousands of crushed plastic beer glasses that littered the floor. Zander and I were looking for Richard and Hesley, but we couldn't find them anywhere.

'Alright, geezers!' Charlie popped up from nowhere, looking remarkably fresh-faced and cheerful. 'I'm just off now – going to visit a mate in town.' He shouldered his record bag, and Zander and I walked outside with him. 'Top buzz geezers!' he said as we each gave him a hug.

'Cheers for everything, Charlie. See you back in London. Safe trip!'

'Yeah, be good to do this again sometime.' He adjusted his hat – this time a bright orange ski hat which didn't have a pompom, though it looked like it needed one – and headed towards the gate. 'Laters!' he called back over his shoulder.

Zander and I waved him off, then turned back up the steps. But when we tried to get back inside, we were stopped by security.

Being told you can't enter your own party by the security employed by your partners sends a bad signal, especially when there's money still owing.

Neither Zander nor I wanted to think the worst. But where were Richard and Hesley? *Were they inside adding up the takings? Were they cutting us out? Were they even still in the area? Perhaps the security were holding us back while they made their escape?*

As the minutes passed, so too did our hopes of seeing any money.

After twenty minutes of standing in the cold, Zander had had enough.

'Fuck this!' he hissed as he stepped back into the open doorway.

The five or six security blokes who'd been standing around the ticket desk chatting all jumped towards him. As soon as Zander was over the threshold the largest of them moved into his path. He put both his hands up against his own huge chest in a strong gesture of *stop!* But Zander kept on walking. The bloke's big hands absorbed the full weight of Zander's entrance. Then, like compressed buffers on a railway locomotive, the guard gently bounced Zander back out the door. The guard didn't say anything, only shook his head slowly.

'Jobsworth!' Zander looked him flat in the eye. But the bloke just folded his arms and stood firm.

'Hey, Zand. Let's just try and chill.' I gripped his shoulder for a moment.

'What the fuck are they playing at? They know we're crew' Zander turned to me but still kept an eye on the guard.

'Who knows. I'm sure everything's going to be fine.' But that wasn't what I was thinking. I feared the worst, though I knew we needed to keep the situation as calm as possible. A situation that was about to explode at any moment.

Zander has an unshakable sense of justice. If he, or anyone he cares for, is threatened or victimised, he will step forward and challenge that threat. Without question and regardless of the odds.

Finally, after a very tense hour of waiting in the cold, Richard appeared with an entourage of girls. He beckoned us inside the doorway and, on the ticket desk, counted out a pile of cash. He handed it to Zander, who counted it through and nodded.

'Thanks, man – thanks for making it happen.' Richard shook Zander's hand and slapped him on the back. 'And here's a little extra. Was a good party, no?' He handed Zander another fat wedge of notes. 'So long! Was good to do business with you guys. We must do it again sometime.' He shook my hand and, surrounded by his girls and security, left.

A TOP GEEZER, BUT

'You're not going to believe this!' said Simone as she burst into the kitchen of Walterton Road, slapping snowflakes off the arms of her black bomber jacket.

'What?' said Debbie, looking startled.

'No, everything's fine.' Simone put a hand on Debbie's shoulder. 'In fact, everything's fucking pukka!' She then went on to explain that a mate of hers was moving to Spain to run a beach bar. He had a sound system that he wanted to sell. 'A totally wicked 5K sound system. With all the amps and the bits and the bobs – and a van!'

Debbie sat down.

I bit a knuckle.

'How much?' I asked.

'Four grand,' said Simone, 'but it's worth loads more. He wants it to go to a good home.'

'Four grand?' Debbie was rolling herself a cigarette and shaking her head. 'That's an awful lot of money.'

'No, honestly Debbie, that's cheap. He's a totally safe geezer and he's doing us a massive favour!'

'I'm not sure.' Debbie tucked her rollie behind her ear. 'It might be cheap but how are we going to afford four grand?'

Simone looked at Debbie. Debbie looked at me. I looked at Simone.

'I'll go and get Zander,' said Simone, and hurried over to the Green House.

While Simone was gone, Debbie paced up and down the small kitchen trying to light the impossibly tight cigarette she'd rolled.

I wasn't physically bouncing around the room, but I had loads of questions bouncing around my head. Not even questions but annoying little fragments of what-ifs and maybes. Before I could get to the end of one train of thought, another would pop up and push to the front of the queue.

Who is this bloke? How big is a wicked little 5K? What kind of van?

When we heard the front door open, Debbie froze, and I jumped up and took over the job of pacing. We could hear Simone and Zander's voices as they came up the stairs.

Of course Zander would be up for it. It was him who'd first mentioned the idea in Amsterdam. But that was before we'd had the grief with Richard's security and the long wait for the money. Though it had all worked out well, it had brought home the precarious and dangerous nature of the game. Zander had already gambled a large chunk of money – money that he could barely afford – on my chaotic, high-risk, zero-profit scheme.

Simone breezed into the kitchen flushed with excitement and bursting with smiles. Behind her was an equally flushed Zander, but his smile was more introverted – perhaps he was trying not to look too enthusiastic. Whatever he was doing, he couldn't hide the fact that he liked the idea, at least in theory.

And what exactly was the plan? Well, there wasn't one beyond *let's get a sound system.* But that afternoon the four of us sat around the tiny kitchen table ping-ponging ideas back and forth.

Zander was up for fronting the cash, but it needed to be paid back. We thought we could do some paid gigs, hire the equipment out, do some – fairly-priced – pay-parties. We ran through all the permutations of how we could set up, run and pay for the system. With Simone's guidance – what with her working in a disco equipment hire shop – we all agreed that the best way forward was to do a little bit of everything, and that way we'd be sure to earn the money back.

At that moment none of us, apart from Simone, knew how to wire up and run a rig, but we decided that once we'd learned the trade we might even be able to earn a living out of doing the thing we loved most. And once the rig was paid off, we'd be able to concentrate on the music, the artwork, the décor – the vibe. Once the rig was paid off, all things were possible. We could even put on our own events – for free.

'Hang on a minute,' said Zander. 'We need to know more about what's on offer before we start making all these plans.'

'Yeah, we need to speak with this bloke – what's his name?' I asked, turning to Simone.

'Ben,' she said.

'And have you actually heard this rig Simone?' asked Debbie. There was a moment's pause.

'Okay-okay!' Simone got up from the table. 'So we need to go and check it out.'

Zander jangled the keys of his Land Rover.

•

Zander and Simone had gone to meet Ben. Waiting for them to get back was too much to bear. Debbie and I went upstairs to the room at the top of the house to try and kill time finishing off some painting. Our mattress leaned up against one of the walls to give more space, the floor crowded with jam jars of fluorescent colours. Behind the door, taped tightly across the wall, was our latest backdrop – a new design. It depicted a large, pink, flower-shaped splat on a fluorescent yellow background. But it wasn't the flower that was new. What was new was at the flower's centre – a large, silver, number 23.

Our impatience for Zander and Simone to get back made it difficult to concentrate. When it stopped snowing, we went to the local shop to get teabags. On the way back we decided to pop into the Green House to say hello. We were crunching through the snow along Elgin Avenue. Just before the junction of Chippenham Road, Debbie said, 'Isn't that the empty place that Greg mentioned?'

I looked up at the boarded shop front.

'Hmm, could be. Might be worth a look later.'

We turned the corner onto Chippenham Road and crossed to the Green House.

Greg and Chris were in the sitting room on the first floor, their eyes pink, tear-stained slits. They were both sighing and moaning with relief as they managed to surface from a long and breathless fit of giggling. *Furry Freak Brothers* comics were strewn across the coffee table in front of them and a blue fog of weed smoke hung in the room.

Greg, who was skimming through *The Adventures of Fat Freddy's Cat*, held up a hand to call for quiet – then both he and Chris recited together: 'Wait till he puts on his stereo headphones!' They both rolled backwards into the spongy sofa and endured another minute of painful, gasping spasms.

'Right,' said Debbie, 'these two pot-heads look like they need a cuppa.'

A few minutes later Debbie came in with a tray of steaming mugs.

After a few deep breaths and slurps of tea, Greg and Chris were able to sit up straight again. I asked Greg about the empty building he'd found just round the corner on Elgin Avenue.

'I Had a peep.' he said, wiping a tear off his cheek, 'Round the back there's a short drop over a wall to the basement and the back door's just hanging off.'

'Did you take a look inside?' I asked.

'Couldn't see much but it's a big basement room – and the walls are all mirrored.'

'Mirrored?' asked Debbie.

'Yeah, guess it used to be a disco.'

'Boogie on down!' Debbie did a little wiggle.

'Up for another peep?' I asked.

'Can't tonight, Kerry and I got plans'. Greg did a smoochy little move and grinned.

'I'll come,' said Chris, trying to heave himself out of the sofa again.

'It'll be better after dark,' I said.

'What time?' Chris sank back into the flaky beige leatherette.

'When the pubs close?' I suggested. 'There'll be more people about then.'

'*More* people?' Chris looked puzzled.

'We don't want to leave it too late. If the streets are empty and quiet, we'll look conspicuous. I reckon dark but busy is best.'

Chris nodded sceptically.

'Right,' said Debbie, 'if you lads have finished your plotting and planning, I'm going back to finish off that painting.' She got up to go.

'What are you working on at the moment?' Greg asked.

'A backdrop,' she described a rectangle in the air with her finger, 'with the number twenty-three in a kind of flower-power splat-thing.' She quickly traced the shape of the flower in the invisible rectangle.

'Why the number twenty-three?' asked Greg.

'God knows!' said Debbie, picking up her tobacco. 'Mark's gone all cosmic on us again and suddenly it keeps magically appearing everywhere.'

'Have I? Does it?' I laughed.

'No!' Greg was incredulous. 'I was reading an article in a book this morning about the number twenty-three!'

'Are you coming or what?' Debbie made her way to the door.

I took a swig of my tea and got up. 'Hang on. See you at ... eleven-*ish*?' I asked Chris.

'That is so weird.' Greg still had a look of astonishment on his face. 'I'll dig the article out for you – it's worth a read!'

'Eleven-ish,' said Chris, narrowing his already slit eyes. 'That's twenty-three hundred hours!'

'Der-der-der-der . . . Der-der-der-der . . .' Greg rolled his eyes and wiggled his fingertips as he sang the opening bars from *The Twilight Zone*.

•

Later that afternoon Zander and Simone got back to Walterton Road.

They were clearly conspiring to keep Debbie and me in suspense.

'Tell us!' laughed Debbie, threatening Simone's nose with a paint-laden brush.

Simone momentarily squeezed her lips together but couldn't hold it in. 'It's fucking pukka!' She waved her hands about while she jumped from foot to foot.

Zander stood silently behind her but was unable to restrain his grin.

'The only thing is,' said Simone, 'it's in storage and Ben hasn't got the space to set it up. I mean it's a fair old size: two huge bass bins, two mids, and tops, and the monitors, and a wicked amp rack, and . . .'

'So, what you're saying is you don't know if it's any good?' asked Debbie.

'Well, no, I'm sure it's fine – and Ben's a top geezer.' Simone turned back to Zander for confirmation. He nodded.

'So Ben's a top geezer, but the rig is too big to set up, and you still don't know if it works?' Debbie had a point.

Simone bit the corner of her lower lip, a thing she did when she was about to lose patience. 'Look, all I'm saying is, we need to find a space big enough to set it up! Ben will come and give us a demonstration.' Her hands criss-crossed as she pointed to each of us. 'Then *we* can all decide.'

There was a moment's quiet.

'Well,' I said, suddenly feeling very cheery, 'in that case we may have the perfect place.'

THE COLOUR OF BLOOD

As planned the previous evening, Chris and I, along with Zander, snuck over the back wall of the building. It was in a terraced row of rundown shops with no residential neighbours. Greg was right: the basement had been some kind of disco. Twenty minutes after getting in, we'd changed all the locks and, from that moment on, we were the proud new proprietors of our very own nightclub.

•

It was a dull Sunday afternoon. The sludgy snow from the previous day had refrozen and was icy underfoot. I was shivering, even though I wore multiple layers of tatty wool jumpers under my sweatshirt; its large floppy hood would have covered my eyes, but the peak of my baseball cap kept it up off my face.

'What?' I asked Vince after I caught him giving me a one-eye-brow-raised look.

'Nice hoody.'

I laughed. 'It's a work of art!'

'Is it pink?'

'That was an unfortunate encounter with a red T-shirt in the wash.' I held up an arm to show off daubs of fluorescent yellow. 'Whereas this was from painting the trees in Amsterdam.' Then I tugged at the black mottling on the forearm. 'And this was from painting the Skool House basement. It's all part of a rich history!'

Vince smiled and nodded. He, of course, was looking dangerously cool. He only ever wore black. Expensive, silky, black tracksuits were his favourite, which he wore with the quiet, self-assured poise of a kickboxer. His dress sense reminded me of the iconic image of Tommie Smith giving the gloved, black-power salute on the Olympic podium in 1968. It wasn't just Vince's athletic build, close-cropped hair and neatly trimmed beard that reminded me of this image – it was the gloves. Vince always wore thin, black leather gloves.

We arrived at the front of the building and the steel security door, which looked like one of the bulkhead doors you might find on a submarine – but without the faucet handle.

'This is the one,' I said.

'Is it locked?' Vince gave me a quizzical look.

'Locked tight!' I smiled as I produced two gleaming brass keys.

'Nice! How'd you get those?'

'These doors might look impenetrable from the outside, but if you get in round the back, it's easy to swap out the locks.' I turned the first key. 'They're just your standard five-lever Chubbs.' I turned the second.

'One of the world's richest cities and all these locked empties – something's not right.' With an accusing, gloved finger, Vince tapped the steel.

With a hollow groan the door swung open. We stepped inside and I locked the door behind us. We turned on our torches to see down the narrow corridor that ran into the building.

'Watch out, there's a few floorboards missing,' I whispered. Not that I needed to whisper, but somehow it felt right while creeping around in the dark. 'It's dusty but easy enough to sort out. It's cleaner in here.'

At the end of the corridor was the main staircase up into the rest of the building. To our right was a doorway into a large room that looked as if it had been a shop. I stepped inside the shop space and turned to face Vince, who was shining his torch up the stairs.

'What's up there?' he asked.

'It's totally trashed. Rubble, damp, piles of crusty pigeon shit.'

'Shame,' said Vince following me into the shop. 'But this is nice.'

'We thought we'd use this as the bar.' I spun my torch around to show a low false ceiling, grubby white walls and dark carpet tiles.

'Up this end?' Vince waved his torch towards the back of the room.

'Yeah, I reckon. But come and check this out.' I walked to the front of the room where, on the right, there was a doorway that led to the top of the basement stairs.

The previous occupier had painted the walls and bannisters of the stairwell red. Red can be a cheerful colour, but this wasn't that kind of red. This kind of red made my heart beat faster. It was the colour of blood. And the high gloss finish made it look wet. As I walked down the stairs I felt as if I were walking into an open wound.

At the bottom of the stairs our torch lights bounced about the room in kaleidoscopic beams. Every wall and pillar in the basement was mirrored, each wall endlessly reflecting its opposite. I went over to the far side of the dance floor where there was a DJ booth. It had clear perspex screens around a desk which was purpose-built for decks.

'So when are you getting the sound system?' asked Vince as he played his light from mirror to mirror.

'Friday. Ben, the bloke who's selling it, is bringing it down just before he goes off to Spain.' I stepped out of the kiosk and followed Vince, who was wandering between two mirrored pillars, towards the back of the building.

'Male *and* female toilets.' Vince looked impressed as he swung open the door and scanned them with his torch.

'And they work,' I said. 'We found the stopcock in the street and got the water on.'

'And that's the back door?' He turned to a door beyond the toilets.

'Yeah, we only had to repair the emergency exit bar. Guess we need to keep that unlocked in case people have to get out quick. I wouldn't want to be stuck down here if there was any kind of problem.'

Vince frowned and shook his head. 'Without an emergency exit this place would be a death trap.' He pushed the bar up and the door swung open. Snow-brightened daylight hurt my eyes. 'So this is where you got in?' He smiled at the trail of footprints across the yard.

'It's a bit of a drop this side, but on street level it was an easy jump up.'

Vince closed the door and turned to me, "Okay, I'll help you out.'

'Nice one, Vince!'

'No worries. I grew up round here. I know all the local faces. Most of them are good kids, a bit boisterous maybe, but good kids.' Vince's words reassured me and soothed the slight anxiety I'd felt spreading between my shoulder blades. He turned away and looked out into the dark basement. 'But there are some ...'

I waited for him to finish, but he started to walk back towards the middle of the room. 'Some what?' I felt the anxiety tighten in my shoulders again.

'Don't worry,' he said quietly, 'I'll have words.'

I hesitated, then walked out onto the dance floor. Vince was doing a slow 360-degree turn, his torch beam taking in the full measure of the space. 'Thanks, Vince.' I was grateful, but the tension in my shoulders hadn't gone away.

'No problem. I've got a mate who lives locally, Mr P. He DJs, MCs, and he'll give us a hand on the door. With the three of us, things should be cool. You'll be helping out on the door too, right?' He stopped, and his torch beam momentarily dazzled me.

'Yeah.' I blinked and he continued to turn, the beam swinging away. 'Of course – no problem.'

'Definitely, if you're taking money on the door?'

'We need to raise the dosh to buy the rig – that's if it's as good as Simone reckons.'

'What are you going to charge?' he asked, still turning, his torch beam bouncing between mirrors.

'Well, at the Skool House it was three quid.'

'Why three?'

'Just enough to cover the costs – to make it happen.'

'How about five?' he suggested.

I shrugged.

He continued. 'Five's affordable. Believe me, people would be happy to pay a fiver to come here. And it's an easier number to deal with on the door. Not so much messing about with shrapnel. Three is fiddly, know what I mean? Especially when you're under pressure.'

I nodded to myself in the dark, remembering the heavy bucketloads of change at the Skool House and the problems it had caused for DJ Paul when the police burst in.

'A five-pound note keeps the transaction neat and tidy.' he said, 'Whatever you decide, if we're taking money then we're going to need a minimum of three handy blokes to work the door: one to keep the queue off the street, one to take the money, and one to watch the others' backs. You don't want to be on your own when everyone knows you're the one carrying the cash.'

'No.' I rubbed the knotted muscles in my left shoulder. 'I suppose not.'

'It'll get busy. People will be well happy to see this place open again. Back in the day, this was a Caribbean shebeen.'

'Not a disco?' I was happy to change the subject from thoughts of money, security and personal safety.

Vince laughed. 'More your roots culture, and before that, your rude boys.' He started back up the stairs.

'So this place has got some real history.' I stopped and looked around, imagining the place full of rude boys skanking in the smoke, in dark sunglasses and stingy-brim trilbies.

'Yeah, real history.' Vince continued talking as he went up the steps. 'None of that kings-and-queens-bullshit. Real people.'

I paused at the bottom of the stairs and shone my torch into the infinitely reflected tunnel of mirrors, the beam disappearing into the glassy green depths. The history I'd learned at school had been the history of rulers: their victories, their champions, their empires. Stories that were taught to me as if they were the definitive reality: the measure against which the present is calibrated and plans for the future made. I'd been born into a construct that only echoed tradition. But whose construct was it?

•

That week we set to work. Paul Brash (not to be confused with any of the other Pauls) got the power on. Mickey (Debbie's brother) and Chris (with rollers tied to broom handles) whitewashed the ceiling and walls of the bar room. Hamish and Tim built the bar out of scrap wood and an old kitchen worktop that we'd liberated from a skip. Simone and Zander had scavenged a load of corrugated cardboard boxes, which they flattened to soundproof the front of the building. A foot of cardboard tightly packed behind wooden stud frames is a quick and effective way of insulating windows and thin walls. Debbie, Camden and I painted backdrops and decorated the bar with psychedelic, long-lashed, eye-shaped plankton motifs. I'm not sure what plankton with long eyelashes had to do with anything, but the frieze of wiggling lifeforms cheered the place up. People from Rose Farm and the Green House dropped by every day and mucked in, as did Vince and his mate Mr P, and by Thursday we had the venue in full working order.

•

Friday Night. 11 p.m. With a squeak of brakes, Ben's old *Financial Times* newspaper delivery van bumped up onto the pavement outside. Vince, Mr P and I were waiting in the dark corridor behind the security door. It was unlocked, but, not wanting to break cover till the last possible moment, I held it closed. We heard the roller-shutter door on the back of the van open and the heavy thud of stuff being shifted about in the back. Simone had explained that the van came with the deal and was the perfect undercover vehicle. In the early hours the residential streets of London were empty and quiet. Anything that moved could arouse suspicion, but newspaper delivery vans made their rounds throughout the night. Who'd suspect such a van, especially one that was painted in the livery of one of the establishment's most well-respected newspapers?

I swung the steel door open. A shadowy line of people carrying large speaker cabs came towards me. Zander, wheeling a big black bass bin, was the first inside.

FIRST NIGHT NERVES

It was a tight squeeze getting the bass bins down the long dark corridor. I helped Zander get the one he was manhandling through the doorway into the bar room, taking care not to get my fingers crushed between it and the door frame. Behind us, I could hear the bump and scrap of another coming in, and Mr P cussing under his breath.

Simone had managed to get a deal from Rudi (her boss at the disco hire shop) and so we had a small selection of basic lights: UVs upstairs, a Moonbeam (a clunky device which spun while projecting beams of colour) downstairs, a White Lightning strobe, and, of course, a Monster Mist smoke machine.

The ultraviolet light activated the florescent plankton designs we'd painted on the walls in the bar, making them glow brilliant pink, yellow and orange. Mickey, wearing a black porkpie hat dotted with tell-tale droplets of white paint, and Tracey, whose jacket hadn't escaped unsmeared, were behind the bar unloading a sack barrow stacked with slabs of fruit juice cartons.

'You want a hand with that, lads?' asked Karl K.

'We're all right, cheers,' said Zander, 'but they'll need a hand with the amp rack – it's one heavy bastard.'

Paul Brash, an old friend of Debbie's, was at the bar, his silver tool case open in front of him.

'How's it going?' I asked.

'All good, geezer.'

'Thanks for sorting the leccy. Any problems?' I asked.

'Nah, it was a piece of piss with the company head fuses from the Skool House. Once I'd got them in, I just had to flip the trips.'

I got out the way to let Hamish and Mr P bring their bass bin through the doorway.

Hamish always had a pallor to his completion, but the ultra-violet light made him look more translucent than usual. Only the white squares on his black-and-white checked clothes glowed, giving him the appearance of an electric blue harlequin.

'You got your tunes with you?' Hamish asked Mr P as they let their bass bin come to rest for a moment. Mr P's dark skin was invisible in the UV, though his silky green bomber jacket shone with metallic iridescence.

'They're back at mine, but I'm only two minutes away. Tell

you what, I'm gonna need a mic.' He called out, 'Anyone got a mic?'

'I gotta mic,' said Hubert as he came through the door with his arms wrapped around a monitor speaker.

I left Mr P and Hubert having a friendly but rather lively discussion about which of them was going to MC first. I caught up with Zander, who'd wheeled the bass bin to the top of the basement stairs.

'Two's up?' said Zander.

The steep stairwell was brimming with strobing fog. 'Someone's got a bit overexcited with the smoke machine,' I said as I took up position a few steps down. Waist deep in mist, I turned to face the bass bin and took hold of the leading edge as Zander tilted it back.

'Okay?' asked Zander.

'Okay!' I said between gritted teeth as I took the full weight and took a step backwards down the stairs. Halfway down I was fully submerged in the smoke. I couldn't see the cab in front of my face and each step was an act of faith.

My right foot searched for the next step down.

At the bottom of the stairs I lowered my end of the cab and helped steady it as Zander tipped his end forward.

I still couldn't see anything in the pulsing whiteout.

Hamish called from the top of the stairs. 'You lot, sort it out – we can't see a fucking thing!'

With arms outstretched I headed to the wall and felt my way to the back of the building and the fire exit. I pushed up the bar. Cold night air surged through the basement and the smoke began to clear. Behind me I could hear the bumps and cussing as the others brought the rest of the rig down the stairs.

Next, I headed back towards the hiss of the unattended smoke machine, which I found in the DJ booth. I turned it and the strobe off and turned on the house lights.

In the middle of the dance floor, in the last remnants of drifting fog, was a sight to behold. A group of shadowy figures around a heap of monolithic black blocks. Black blocks that had the presence of standing stones in the mist. I knew then that, even though I'd not heard it working, the Spiral Tribe Sound System had arrived.

•

Simone introduced me to Ben. He was a quiet bloke with fair, sun-streaked hair, a suntan and a shy smile that was embellished with a gold front tooth. Under his direction we made two stacks of speakers, one on either side of the dance floor. Zander and Simone were to be Ben's apprentices for the evening, but I was also intrigued to know how it all worked. I watched as the three of them crouched around the back of the amp rack and began to plug in cables.

'We better get back to the door,' said Vince over my shoulder. 'We got to make sure people don't queue out on the street and give the game away.'

'Yeah, you're right.' I dragged myself away from Ben's tutorial and went upstairs with Vince and Mr P.

Through the steel door we could hear a noisy group had already gathered outside. We turned off our Maglite torches so that no tell-tale beams would escape into the street. Vince peered through the spyhole before he unlocked the door and slipped out.

'Local kids,' he said a minute later as he came back in and locked the door behind him. 'I told them to come back at midnight.'

Vince turned his torch back on and propped it up against the wall. Its narrow beam lit layers of peeling wallpaper and a high ceiling with gaping holes in the plasterwork. In the dim light Mr P's metallic green bomber jacket shimmered as he swayed and rolled his shoulders to the tune he was quietly humming. 'So how we working this?' he said, slapping his hands together.

'The way I see it is we need people off the street,' said Vince. 'We've got the length of this corridor.' He nodded at Mr P. 'So if you or me are on the door getting people in, then Mark can take the money down the other end in front of the bar room door. But one of us needs to ride shotgun with the money – that way we've got all angles covered.'

'Sounds like a plan,' said Mr P, who'd incorporated his nods of agreement into his dance moves. His positive nod then became a negative shake. 'I can't be up here all night, though, coz I've got my set to play – and I'll be MCing.'

'Maybe one of the other boys will come up and do a shift?' Vince looked at me.

'Yeah, no prob,' I said. 'I'm sure the others will be up for a stint.'

'So who else we got playing?' asked Mr P.

'There's a few,' I replied. 'Not just tonight but tomorrow too. We got you. We got Mickey. Stikka. Danny. Karl. Hush-Hush. Ben said that a DJ mate of his, LTJ Bukem, is also coming. And Hubert, MC Scallywag.'

A thin rhythmic hiss floated up through the loose floorboards. The sound thickened up into a steady midrange beat, then faded in and out as if someone was tuning in a radio.

'Sounds like things are just about to . . .' I was cut short.

I'm sure it wasn't only me taken by surprise when the bass kicked in. It felt as if the floorboards jumped up an inch and plaster dust sifted down from the ceiling. Mr P whooped, clapped his hands above his head and began to rotate his hips. Vince, cool as ever, raised an eyebrow and adjusted the cuffs on each of his black leather gloves.

There was a metallic tap on the front door.

'Let's get the party started!' said Mr P as he peeped through the spyhole. Just before opening the door, he turned to me and said, 'Remember, working the door is all show. Play it cool and play it easy. Okay?'

'Okay,' I replied.

Vince grabbed his torch and we went further down the corridor to stand sentinel on the bar room door. Mr P swung the security door open.

'Keep-it-moving-just-keep-it-mov-ing!' Mr P sang in time to the bass which throbbed through the building. A line of people filed in off the street, filling the corridor. 'Welcome-la-dies-n-gents,' he called, fitting his words to the rhythm of the music. He closed the door. 'Welcome-to-Spiral-Tribe-n-leave-ya-troubles-outside!'

Vince was also on form. 'Fives in ladies and gents. Get-cha readies ready!'

I had to hold my torch up as if I was a human lamp post so that people trying to pay had enough light to see. Flurries of notes and awkward handfuls of coins were counted out and given to me.

Once our guests had paid, they squeezed passed me. Vince, who stood just behind me, let them through the second door.

The corridor emptied and Mr P opened up the front door again. Another ten or fifteen people were hurried in.

'Fives in, please. Have your readies ready!' I followed Vince's lead and tried to sound as if I'd said it all a thousand times before. More money was thrust at me.

Separating and smoothing the crumpled notes was difficult with the heavy metal Maglite in one hand. I tried to tuck it under my armpit to keep both hands free, but it kept slipping, making my job more difficult than it should have been.

After twenty minutes my tracksuit top, sweatshirt and jeans were tight with bulges of cash. Giving change became difficult because I couldn't easily slide my hands into my overfull pockets.

In a momentary lull, before Mr P let more people in, I leaned over to Vince and said, 'I gotta sort some of this cash out.'

Vince opened the bar room door. 'I'll find Zander so he can hold some. Can you manage for a couple of minutes?'

'Wouldn't it be easier if you looked after it?'

Vince hesitated. 'Best to keep it away from the door, just in case anyone tries anything. We don't want all our eggs in one basket.' He disappeared into the bar.

What he said made sense. But knowing that everyone through the door would recognise me as the only egg in the basket, regardless of how much cash I was actually carrying, made me feel uneasy.

The metal security door opened and another twenty or so people piled in. They were a feisty bunch.

'Hang on, hang on!' I tried to keep my voice calm and light-hearted, though I had to physically block the corridor with my body to stop them barging their way in and, at the same time, try and conceal the conspicuous wad of notes I still had in my hand.

'Aye, big man – dis your club?' asked the pale-faced ginger kid at the front of the crush.

'Er, well, actually, no . . .'

'Say what?' He spoke loudly to be sure all his crew could hear him.

'No.'

'So who's da don? Lemme chat wid da man.'

'There is no don, we're . . . we're a collective.' As the words left my mouth I regretted them, thinking that I'd have saved myself a whole load of trouble if I'd just invented the name of some super-sinister underworld boss.

'A co-llec-tive? So who like owns dis place?'

'We're squatting.' I knew my answers were only complicating the situation, but the words just fell out of my mouth.

'Squat-ting? What, you isn't s'pose to even be here?' The bloke shrieked in disbelief. His friends whooped and laughed.

I was outnumbered and had my back against the door. I was surprised to hear myself say, 'Babylon shut it down. We opened it up.'

Mr P called from the other end of the crowded corridor, 'Every-ting cool down there, bro?' The easy, relaxed tone of his voice was reassuring and reminded me of what he'd said earlier: *play it cool and play it easy.*

'All cool, Mr P!' My words glowed with as much confidence as I could muster. I turned my attention back to the group in front of me. 'Okay.' I said, 'We don't play by Babylon's rules. We don't bow down to no don or no man. This place is for the people. What we're asking for is a donation to help pay for the sound and lights. You wanna come in? Then talk to me.'

There was a moment's pause then the bloke said, 'Me an ma crew we grew up dis end. You get me? And you is taxing us top dollar? Know what I'm sayin?'

'Okay. Tell you what I'll do. How many of you are there?'

'Five.' He held up his hand with splayed fingers to reinforce the number.

'Give me twenty.'

'Twenty?'

'Twenty – all in.'

'You know that!' He handed me a twenty and, after counting in his four friends, gave me a high-five handshake. 'Safe bro, safe.'

I took the money from the rest of the people queuing and the corridor emptied. Vince came back with Zander.

'Any problems?' asked Vince.

'Nothing that a little maths couldn't sort out. Hey Zand, you up for taking care of some of this cash?'

'How much?'

'Too much,' I laughed.

'Mr P?' called Vince.

'Yay bro!'

'Can you hold the door a minute while we sort out this business?'

'You got it.'

Mr P kept the front door shut and Vince stood guard on the bar room door. I unloaded my pockets and handed scruffy wads of cash to Zander.

'We're doing all right then,' said Zander, tucking handfuls of money into the inside pockets of his jacket.

'Better than I ever imagined,' I said. 'If this keeps up, we'll have enough to pay for the system soon as.' I paused a second. 'That is if we're going with Ben's deal?'

'Course we are!' he said, grinning.

'Spiral Tribe comes alive!' I laughed as I patted all my pockets to check for more money.

'All done?' asked Zander.

'Er . . . hang on.' I discovered another wedge in my back pocket. 'Tell you what, let me keep some fivers for change.' I shuffled through the dog-eared stack.

'We got a queue backing up the street,' called Mr P.

'Nearly done!' I shoved a heap of money at Zander and stuffed what I needed back into my pocket.

Zander adjusted his jacket. 'Do I look okay?' he asked.

'Like the Michelin man!' I said, slapping him on the back.

'You geezers sorted yet?' called Mr P. 'We gotta get this lot off the street.'

'All sorted, Mr P!'

Vince opened the bar room door and Zander went back into the party. The front door swung open and another load of people squashed in.

It turned out that everyone from Walterton Road, the Green House and Rose Farm were too busy enjoying themselves to want to do a shift on the door. I'd hoped it would have been more of a collective effort. Zander was keen to help but agreed that, as he was holding all the money, he needed to disassociate himself from the door. Secrecy was our only security.

PREDATORS

The first night was a great success. The sound system was far better than any of us could have hoped for. We hadn't made all the money we needed, but Zander fronted the extra and Ben was paid in cash: used notes, small denominations. Not, as it happens, neatly packed into a black suitcase, but stuffed into a sticky, cardboard carton that had once contained Mr Kipling Bakewell Tarts, the ones with the glacé cherries on top.

Saturday night was equally good. Perhaps there was a touch more feistiness on the door, but nothing a little relaxed negotiation couldn't sort out. Vince and Mr P were the masters of charm and working with them taught me that a nice easy attitude was what kept things calm. The only problem with working the door all night was that I didn't get a chance to join in the party – but getting nutted and dancing till dawn wasn't going to be what earned us the rig. If all-night shifts, standing in a cold corridor and haggling with gangs of energetic youngsters was what was needed to get a sound system, then that's what it would have to be.

After two nights on the trot, at about eight on Sunday morning, we switched off and people drifted out into the cold dawn. We manhandled the speakers back up the basement stairs and loaded the van. I jumped into the passenger seat next to Zander, expecting a thirty-second drive around the corner to unload at the Green House.

But that wasn't to be. Ever security conscious, Zander drove away from the Spiral Shebeen in the opposite direction from home. He wove through the back streets and then parked up in a random spot.

'That should have thrown any snoops off our scent,' he said an hour later as we pulled up and parked outside the Green House.

'What snoops?' I was tired and irritable.

'We can't take any chances.' He was right, but all the ducking and diving on top of the intensity of working the door was sapping what little energy I still had left.

He opened his door and jumped out. 'Do you want to open up my room and get a few bods down here to help unload?' He chucked me a bunch of keys, which, tired as I was, I made a grab at – but missed the catch. With an exhausted sigh I reached down into the footwell and picked them up. When I sat back up, a woman with long, black hair and dressed in blue denims with cowboy boots appeared on the pavement in front of me. She seemed to be waiting for someone. I thought nothing of it, although it did strike me as odd that she seemed to be mumbling to herself – but perhaps she was mouthing the words of her favourite song.

I jumped out of the cab, adjusted my cap to my preferred upwardly-skewed angle, walked past the woman, who was now tight-lipped and avoided my gaze, and made my way up the steps to the Green House front door. Halfway up, I heard a sound behind me. A familiar sound, but one which I couldn't quite place. It was just a split-second burst – a gritty, electronic, white-noise fizz. I turned round at the top of the steps. The woman was nowhere to be seen.

The Green House was a fortress. The stoop steps spanned a long drop down to the basement. The basement itself was impenetrable because it was choked floor to ceiling with rubble. The basement and ground-floor windows had panels of steel mesh bolted over them: all part of the local council's bomb-proof armour against homeless people.

Zander lived on the ground floor in the front room – on the left, next to the front door. He'd installed another steel security door over the existing doorway – 'Just to be on the safe side.' Together with Greg, Chris and the others, we unloaded the rig and carefully stacked it in his room.

After we'd finished, Greg asked us if we wanted a cuppa.

I yawned. 'I really need my bed.'

'Me too,' said Zander, unrolling his sleeping bag in the gap between the speakers, then throwing a pillow into the lower opening of one of the bass bins. He lay down on his back and tucked his head inside the speaker.

'Luxury!' he said with a satisfied sigh.

Greg and I tiptoed out the room.

•

Everything was fine – till Thursday.

I was over at the Green House having a relaxing chat over a cup of tea with Greg and Zander. We were in the communal sitting room. I'd sagged into the broken sofa. Kerry was offering around a selection of cakes. As was often the case, some enterprising member of the household had had a rummage in a skip round the back of one of the supermarkets and liberated two large plastic sacks of food. Everything was edible, having only just passed its sell-by date. I was on my third chocolate mini roll.

The front door downstairs slammed shut and someone ran up the stairs. Geoff, one of the blokes who lived in the Green House, burst into the room. He stood in the middle of the room, panting and wildly pointing behind himself.

'I was . . . I was round at me mates.' He gasped for breath. 'Just 'aving a smoke. Just sittin' there. Then bam! The front door's kicked in. A gang of blokes steams in, all masked up, swinging baseball bats.' Geoff arms flayed the air as if he were fighting an invisible foe.

Kerry moved over to Greg and sat on his lap. Greg's mouth was open, as was mine, a half-finished mini roll poised in front of my face.

Zander jumped to his feet. 'Where was this?' he asked.

'Just a few doors down – Rory's gaff . . . they fuckin' steamed the place, man!'

'You okay?' Kerry asked.

Geoff looked as if he was staring straight through the wall, back down the street, into the house where it had all just happened. He pushed a splayed hand across the top of his forehead as if he was running his fingers through his hair, though he had a skinhead.

'Just steamed the place!' He swung an arm in front of himself in a gesture meant to include everything as far as the eye could see. Then he shook his head and dropped his arms limply to his sides.

'Come and sit down, Geoff. I'll make you a cup of tea.' As Kerry got up, she tussled Greg's hair. Greg closed his mouth.

'Did they rob you?' Greg asked.

'They were smashing the place up – going wild.'

'Were you hurt?' I lowered my cake and put it on the corner of the comic-strewn coffee table.

Geoff lifted both his arms and looked from one to the other as if checking they were still there.

'I'll make that tea.' Kerry moved towards the pink Indian

print bedspread that was nailed across the hole in the wall that served as the kitchen door.

'Your cheek looks a bit swollen,' I said.

He touched it and suddenly laughed. 'Is it? That's nothing, man! You should have seen the other blokes!'

'What, Rory's mates?'

'No! The twats that steamed in.'

'Soon as I heard that front door come through, I grabbed a shovel – a garden spade – it was just there, propped against the kitchen wall. I didn't think, I just grabbed it.' Geoff's eyes gleamed. 'Telling ya, a garden spade tops a baseball bat any day! They steamed in thinking we was some bunch of pussy motherfuckers. Man did they get a surprise!'

Kerry, who had frozen in the kitchen doorway, moved back towards Greg.

'So you saw them off?' asked Zander, coming to sit next to me on the sofa.

'Fucking battered 'em!' Geoff's fists clenched and he did a boxer's shuffle.

'And they didn't manage to rob any of you?' asked Greg.

'Rob us? No way!'

'So it all turned out okay in the end.' Kerry smiled reassuringly. 'So long as you're not hurt.' She began to move back towards the kitchen.

'Well . . . yes and no.'

'You didn't kill them, did you?' asked Greg, who sounded surprised by the sincerity of his own question.

'Should've!' Geoff laughed. 'But nah, they all legged it.'

'What's the problem then?' asked Zander, leaning forward to finish off my cake.

Geoff bit his lower lip and looked at us each in turn.

'It's what they were shouting when they burst in.' He paused. 'They wanted to know where the Spiral Tribe Sound System was!'

RESPECT

On Saturday night, Vince and I ambled round to Elgin Avenue. We were careful with our body language – no lurking, no skulking, no sideways glances. We casually chatted, letting the conversation carry us around the corner from Chippenham Road onto Elgin Avenue. At the crossroads we slowed to a halt but continued talking.

'The most unusual job?' I turned to face Vince. Over his shoulder I had a clear view of the doorway of the shebeen and west along Elgin Avenue. My breath steamed in the cold air. 'Working on the Grove with you and Chris was interesting. Getting paid to experiment with all that new technology, that was cool. I suppose if I hadn't zoomed into that spiral I'd still be working there!' I laughed. 'But feeding branches to Rosie was pretty good too!'

'Rosie?' Vince was facing me and had a clear view along Elgin in the other direction.

'Rosie the rhino. All clear your way?'

'All clear this way. Rosie the rhino?'

We resumed our stroll towards the steel door.

'Working at Tree Co,' I continued. 'If, after a job, we had a truck full of nice leafy branches, we'd give the zoo a bell. They'd open up the back gates and we'd drive in and feed the elephants and rhinos.' I slipped the keys into the door and the locks turned with a double clunk. The door groaned open. 'Normally they only got dry hay and pellets, so they were always very happy to get a taste of greenery – a taste of freedom.' We stepped inside and I locked the door behind us. 'Wild animals being confined behind all that concrete – it's out of order'.

Neither Vince nor I bothered turning on our torches. We waited in the dark, close to the cold steel door. Our misting breath swirled in a beam of orange streetlight that cut through a crack at the edge of the doorframe. We didn't talk. We just listened to the street outside.

Above the background rumble of evening traffic, a car impatiently revved at the lights. A group of giggling girls tittered past on heels. A distant siren rose and fell.

Then we heard it. The familiar squeak of the paper delivery van's brakes. The bump as it mounted the pavement and came to a stop. I unlocked the door and the crew rolled in the rig. It was a slick manoeuvre. If you'd blinked, you'd have missed it.

Even though it was our busiest night so far, it was cold working the door. To keep warm, Vince, Mr P and I were jigging about in time to the music that pumped through the building.

'You all right for a minute?' I asked Vince. 'I gotta go to the gents.'

'Yeah-yeah, no worries.'

I went into the wet tropical heat of the bar room. In the ultraviolet glow I had to carefully step between people who were sitting in groups sharing bottles of water and giving each other shoulder massages.

The dance floor was packed. In the DJ booth – through the mist of weed smoke and fog from the smoke machine – I recognised Ben's mate, DJ LTJ Bukem. Every cut, stab and spinback he made had the crowd punching the air.

It was sweltering, the mirrors running with condensation. I made my way towards the back of the building and the toilets.

I found Zander by the fire exit, his money-puffed jacket zipped up to his chin.

'It's a fucking sauna in here – you must be boiling!'

He gave me a *you're-not-wrong-there* look, then told me that he was guarding the fire exit as a gang of lads had piled in over the wall and someone had let them in.

'Any trouble?' I asked.

'Nah, they just disappeared into the crowd.' he shrugged. 'But it was good to get a blast of fresh air!'

Zander was hot, uncomfortable and potentially vulnerable. I had a plan. The place was full, so we could stop letting people in. That would mean Zander didn't need to be the banker anymore. I could let him out of the fire escape, then he could nip over the wall and stash the cash back at the house. I'd close the door after him and make sure that no one followed. Once everything was stashed, he could come back to the party through the front door and enjoy himself – without that jacket.

'Okay, let's do it!' He said and pushed open the fire door. 'See you in ten minutes!'

Back upstairs, with Vince and Mr P, just as we'd decided to start a one-out-one-in policy, there was a tap at the door.

'Just one last lot?' I suggested.

Mr P peered through the spyhole, then opened the door. 'Good evening, good people. Come along in. We have a full house pumping and we're locking down the groove tonight!'

A group of people squashed in, paid and went through to the party. The corridor was empty again.

'Tell you what, if we're leaving it at that, I'm gonna go and get a boogie in before I play my set.' Mr P raised his arms above his head and, rotating his hips, shimmied away along the corridor.

'Guess I'll take a break too,' said Vince. 'If you're cool for twenty minutes?' He stretched his arms back over the top of his head, his gloved fingers interlocked.

'Yeah, of course. I'll hang here. Zander's back in a minute, so he'll do a stint with me.'

Vince followed Mr P into the party.

There was a gentle tap at the door. *Perhaps it's Zander?* I peered through the spyhole. No, it was a group of guys. I opened up to tell them they'd have to wait till some people left.

Now, I'm six-foot tall. And maybe I'm slim, but not skinny. The five or six blokes in front of me were way taller, with pumped muscles bulging under their tracksuits.

There was a half-beat pause of silence before I said, 'Er, sorry, we're fffff . . .' The bloke at the front of the group wrapped his arms around me, squashing the breath from my lungs. He picked me up and carried me all the way down the corridor. At the bar room door, he held me up against the opposite wall – my feet clear of the ground. The rest of the blokes filed through into the bar. When the last one was in, the bloke lowered me back down. Then, without a word, he followed his mates inside.

'Fives in, please,' I squeaked as he closed the bar room door behind him.

I guess I was in a state of shock. Well, maybe not shock, maybe surprise and confusion. I wasn't sure what had just happened. They hadn't demanded any money and, despite their aggressive attitude, had left me unhurt.

The front door was still wide open, so I hurried back and had a quick glance up and down the road for Zander. No one. I pulled the door shut and locked it, which felt counterintuitive. I leaned my back against the cold steel.

I decided that the best course of action was to stay calm and stay put. I needed to be by the door to let Zander in – chasing after Vince and Mr P wasn't going to solve anything. My mind was racing. *If the blokes were going to rob us, then they would have had a go at me. Or perhaps they were looking for Zander? What if they were after the rig? Perhaps this was the same gang that Geoff had seen off? But who would try and snatch a sound system from a packed club? Nutters, that's who – big muscly nutters.* Nothing made sense.

'Fuck-fuck-fuck!' I paced up and down in the dark. *Just stay calm and wait for Zander.*

But it wasn't Zander who appeared next. Vince burst into the corridor from the bar. He leapt along the corridor towards me.

'There's a bit of a situation downstairs.' He unlocked the front door. 'Some fool is flashing a gun. I'll be back in five!'

'What?'

'Nothing I can't handle. I just need . . .' He paused and looked me in the eye. 'I just need to sort something.'

'Vince?'

'Don't worry about it. I'll be straight back.' And he was gone, sprinting down the road.

I felt trapped. Trapped behind the locked steel door. Trapped by responsibility. Uncertainty and powerlessness tightened around me.

The bar room door opened. I expected the big blokes. Back

to turn me upside-down and gut me for the loose change in my pockets. But it wasn't them. My torch beam caught the mass of blond ringlets of Celia and the Brylcreemed slick of her boyfriend's hair. They were friends of Simone's from a squat off the Holloway Road.

'Off already?' I asked in my best imitation of cheerful.

'Yeah, gotta get back. Good party – thanks for the invite,' said Celia, all smiles.

I let them out and waved them off. I lingered out on the pavement. It was good to be outside. The open door seemed to let some of the pressure escape. I rolled my shoulders and took a few deep breaths of icy air. I watched Celia and her boyfriend wander down the avenue. Something moved beyond them, weaving between the pools of shadow under the sodium streetlamps. A figure. It was Vince, running at full tilt. Seconds later he arrived inside the door, his hands on his knees as he caught his breath.

'Close the door! Close the door!' He stood up. 'Stay here!' He forced out a long, controlled breath. 'I'm going to sort things out . . . don't move. I need you on the door . . . If it kicks off, we'll need to get people out.' He went down the corridor and into the party.

What the fuck? The more I thought about it, the more it troubled me. Events were out of my control and out of reasoning. Time stagnated into heavy, unmoving minutes. Claustrophobia smothered me. I was scared.

By the front door I stood between any situation downstairs and the world outside. I had an overpowering urge to hide – or to simply open the door and run away. But I held my ground, fingers on the key, ready to blow the safety valve.

The bar room door opened. Vince swaggered calmly towards me.

'What was that all about?' My voice faltered.

'It's all taken care of.'

'What is?'

'I just made it clear we're the crew running things here. Don't worry, there won't be any trouble.'

'But . . . How can you be sure?'

He paused. 'Let's just say we've earned their respect.' He adjusted the cuffs of his gloves.

UNDERNEATH THE OUTLAW IMAGE

Even though there were no further incidents that night, I was very glad when morning came and we switched the music off. But even as we carried the rig out into the fresh, sunlit morning and loaded the van, a feeling of claustrophobia followed me into the street.

Zander was back to help pack down. It turned out that, after he'd gone to the house to stash the money, he'd stayed for a cup of tea – and a bit of breakfast.

After we'd finished loading the speakers, I leaned against the side of the van to soak up a little of the low morning sun. Zander joined me.

'You all right?' he asked.

'Yeah, glad that's over. It all went a bit wobbly after you left.' I told him about the door being steamed.

'You weren't hurt?'

'No, just weirded me out.' I shook my head and laughed, as much at the image of my feet dangling when I'd been squashed against the wall as with relief that morning had come and I was still alive.

'So was there any more trouble?'

'No, Vince had words.' I heard the thud and cuss of people negotiating the corridor with more equipment. 'I'll tell you about it later.'

'But no one was hurt?'

'No, he was very . . . diplomatic.'

Back inside the building, as I swept crushed paper cups off the empty dance floor, I thought about the night's events. *Had a situation been defused, or was this the first of many stand-offs over territory? Peace had prevailed. But for how long?* I felt the problem (like Rory's house getting steamed by the masked gang) would probably be recurrent. We'd be forever defending our claim, not just to the space but also to our equipment and the money we were making.

Holding down an urban territory was doable – we had (perhaps unwittingly) already staked our first claim – but was that the way forward? Were we drifting into a feuding loop of muscle and money? Just another gang that, underneath the outlaw image, has the same aspirations as the politicians profiting from boarding up the affordable housing in the area. The politics of enclosure.

To my mind, we were on a different path – one of social inclusion. Not about control, but not *out* of control. Always in flux, each twist and turn unpredictably branching into unexplored spaces.

After we'd unloaded the rig, we had an impromptu get-to-gether at the Green House. Debbie, Simone, Zander and I were in the room we used as a kitchen.

Though no one was after a profit, DJs needed new tunes, so we sorted them with some cash. We also wanted to see Vince and Mr P right, as well as spend a little on replenishing our stocks of paint and fireproof backdrop fabric.

Although the kitchen was cluttered with heaps of used plates and saucepans, it was a little quieter and less crowded than the sitting room next door. We had, of course, set up the decks and the monitors. Not at full whack, but loud enough to keep everyone at the after-party dancing.

'You know,' I said, perching on the corner of the kitchen table and putting out a hand to steady a column of dirty crockery. 'I've got a bad feeling about doing another weekend there.'

'Everything went so well!' said Simone. 'The system sounded pukka!'

'Except when that really annoying DJ played that off-the-vibe fluff,' said Debbie. 'I hope we didn't pay him!'

'I don't have a problem with paying the DJs and what have you,' said Zander, folding his arms across his chest, 'but we still need to buy our own decks and mixer.'

Simone squeezed her hands into tight fists. 'And we're so close!'

'I'm just not sure about doing another weekend there.' I shook my head and the tower of plates next to me wobbled. 'Last night it came this close' I pinched my thumb and fore-finger together. 'This close to kicking off.'

'Okay, okay,' said Simone, 'so let's sleep on it.'

As I left the Green House, Greg, Kerry and Hubert were out on the small balcony above the porch. Hubert was singing his own words to the music that escaped out the windows. His neat dreadlocks bobbed back and forth in time to the beat. Greg was singing discordant harmonies and parodying some rock star, possibly Robert Plant. With each burst of gibberish, Greg thrashed his blond mop about. Kerry, in between them both in a rainbow-striped, knitted hat, looked like a mischievous pixie as she tried to conceal a hookah pipe behind her back. Greg, when he wasn't sucking smoke through the pipe's long tube, pretended it was a microphone.

They waved and smiled. I waved back, then pulled my hood up against the cold afternoon and made the two-minute walk over to Walterton Road.

As I pulled the duvet up around my ears and relaxed into my pillow, I let go of my worries. I had to. If I hadn't, I wouldn't have been able to sleep. But if I'd know what sleep would bring, I would have done anything to avoid it.

WARNING SIGNS

Debbie was sleeping peacefully next to me. Sunlight soaked through the yellow sheet we'd pinned over the window. I was cold with sweat, trembling and scared. Scared that perhaps I'd woken into another looping nightmare. I got up, had a coffee and a shower. The sense of unease was difficult to shake off. A trip to my favourite shop – the scenery materials supplier,

Brodie and Middleton on Drury Lane – would, I was sure, sort me out.

When I'd been at Grove Reprographics, I'd also worked on and off at one of their other branches in London's Seven Dials, the area between Soho and Covent Garden. I loved the place – not *for* its expensive boutiques and trendy bars but *despite* them. There's an incorruptible energy in the area, regardless of the polished gloss and sterile chrome of the storefronts.

I made my way from Covent Garden tube station, down James Street and cut the corner of Covent Garden. Drury Lane might be legendary in the pantheon of nursery rhymes, but in the world of bricks and mortar, it's little more than a narrow back street that runs behind the Theatre Royal. Brodie and Middleton is a small shop that appears to be embedded in the back wall of the theatre. The little bell above the door was still tinkling when a large man, who, apart from the navy-blue French beret, looked like a Māori rugby player, emerged from the back room and asked if he could help.

Distracted by the profusion of artists' materials stacked floor to ceiling in pigeon-hole shelving, I looked around with hungry eyes. There were rolls of fabrics: canvasses, linens, calicos, gauzes. Brushes of every style, from precise sable points to wide course stippling and graining brushes. Cans of varnish and primer. Reels of tape, tubs of glue, and tubes and tins of paints in every imaginable colour.

'Hi, I'm after fluorescent powder paint – pink, yellow, green, orange. And does it come in blue?'

'Indeed it does, sir.' His dark eyes glittered.

'And do you sell metallic powder?'

'What colour?'

'What colours have you got?'

'Old Gold, Green Gold, Red Gold, Bright Bronze, Antique Bronze, Copper, Gun Metal, Silver Grey, Brilliant Silver . . .'

•

I left the shop loaded with two heavy bags, one full of clear plastic bags of pure, dazzling colour, the other with metres of carefully folded white calico.

Though excited to get back home to continue painting, as I walked towards Covent Garden tube station, I found myself momentarily pausing to look at the Theatre Royal's coat of arms. The royal crest, a lion and a unicorn on either side of a shield.

I remembered what Vince said about the history of kings and queens versus the history of real people. Rulers manipulating history and the spaces we inhabit. Born into the realm. Eager in our innocence to adapt to the world we find. We search for reference points, landmarks to navigate by and stars to guide us. New generations look at the statues, palaces and skyscrapers and fall under their fairy-tale spell. Flesh and blood, our stories die with us – usually untold. Carved stone and cast metal live on, passing their version of history to the next naïve generation. It's a cute trick. Fooling so many to believe in the lineage that the monuments promote. It's a theatre that depends on a passive audience.

•

On the train back to Westbourne Park I admired the graffiti that burst like flowers over every vertical surface. Why the courts impose prison sentences on kids caught decorating the lifeless urban wastes was suddenly less of a mystery to me. Public space and everything in it – including the entire visual bandwidth – has been appropriated by the authorities and their business partners. A blank wall can be rented to an advertiser, but it's a crime if someone paints on it freely. Advertisers have bought not only the wall space but also the right, protected by law, to invade our personal visual space – our optic nerves poisoned with corrosive messages of anxiety and envy. Yet anyone who disrupts the oppressive silence of a blank wall with an energetic outburst of abstract scrawl is criminalised.

At that moment I decided it would be a good idea to design a Spiral Tribe tag. Perhaps not a spiral – something a little feistier.

As the train thundered down the underground tunnels, my thoughts turned from ideas for designs to the coming weekend. I wasn't sure whether it was a memory of the claustrophobia I'd experienced or a flashback to the nightmares, but from somewhere deep within me, a shadow began to grow. I tried to ignore it, focusing my attention back to ideas for some spiral graffiti. But the shadow darkened, and with it came a raw and aggressive fear. I took deep, measured breaths. The train rocked and lurched out of the tunnel and into the daylight. The claustrophobia eased, but I noticed that the man-made landscape of low girder bridges, pylons and concrete pillars were particularly grey. Even the graffiti was colourless. With disbelief I realised that my vision had switched into black and white. All colour had drained from my world. I blinked and rubbed my eyes. I reached down and picked up the carrier bag of paints that was nested between my feet. I peered inside. All the brilliant pigments were the colour of ash.

The sense of panic had given way to gob-smacked surprise. I found myself marvelling at the strangeness of what was happening to me.

The train pulled out of Royal Oak. The next stop was West-bourne Park, my stop. That gave me some comfort, but when I arrived, things took a turn for the worse. Stepping out of the train and heading towards the exit stairs I noticed a single flash of red while everything else in vision remained mute grey. My curiosity pulled me past the exit and further down the platform to investigate. My eyes strained to the end of the platform. A few steps closer and the violent smear of red came into focus. It was a metal sign. It was a simple warning. In bold white letters on a red enamel ground was written one word: *Danger.*

The walk back to the house from the station wasn't easy. Everywhere I looked I was assaulted by red warning signs. In the normal multicoloured world these signs are camouflaged, but in my super-sensitive state, the fearful colour jumped out at me.

•

'How did it go?' asked Debbie, looking up from the fabric she had tightly pinned to the wall.

I dropped the heavy bags by the door. 'I've gone colour blind.' I flopped onto the bed.'

'What?'

'I can only see in black and white, except for the warnings.'

'What warnings?'

'Red danger signs – that's all I can see.'

'Are you tripping?'

'No, it's all about the red – the red of the shebeen. I knew it as soon as I saw the red stairwell. It's a bleeding wound. We mustn't do another weekend there – something really bad is going to happen.'

'You need to rest. Come on, get yourself comfortable.' Debbie put down her paintbrushes and plumped up a pillow for me.

I kicked off my trainers and tugged my sweatshirt over my head. Debbie pulled the duvet over me.

'Come on, calm down, relax. If you're still suffering tomorrow, you can go to the doctor.'

'Doctor?' I knew there was nothing *wrong* with me, and that this was some deep-level communication between me and the outside world. But if I tried to explain that to a doctor, I'd get locked up.

Whether what was happing to me was coming from within my subconscious, or from some other-dimensional guardian angel with a dark sense of humour, was irrelevant. What was important was the message. A message I couldn't ignore.

'Shall I make you a cup of tea?' asked Debbie.

'No, thanks. I think I just need to sleep.' The thought that my condition was not an affliction but a guiding force helped me to relax.

'I'll be over here finishing this,' said Debbie. 'Do you like it?'

I peered at the large square of white fabric. On it were some words roughed out in pencil encircling a globe. '*Travelling Nation*,' I read out loud. 'That's it! That's what it's all about. Spiral Tribe isn't about holding territory. That's where the danger lies. We are messengers! We need to keep moving!'

'Glad you like it! Did you manage to buy any fluorescent blue – preferably before you went colour blind?'

'You tell me.' I managed a smile.

Debbie stepped over her jars of paint and picked up the bag. 'Wow! Beautiful!' She reached in and pulled out one of the polythene sacks of powder. 'It's electric!'

•

I don't know how long I slept, but when I woke up, Debbie was putting the finishing touches to her backdrop. The words *Travelling Nation* were now painted in green around the electric blue sphere of planet Earth. My colour vision was back. I threw off the duvet and leapt out of bed, sending a jam jar of liquid silver flying.

'Mark!'

'Sorry.'

'It's all over your clothes.'

I picked up my sweatshirt and admired the silver globules. 'Liquid metal – totally techno!'

'How are you feeling this morning?'

'Morning?' I looked at the window.

'You've been asleep all night.' Debbie rinsed her brushes in a jar of clean water.

'How do I feel? Totally up for it!'

'Up for what?'

'Everything!' I pulled the silver-splattered sweatshirt over my head.

'And this weekend?'

My head re-emerged through the neck hole and popped into the hood. 'Why not?' I jumped up. 'Let's get the last of the money together, get the mixer, get the decks and get out of here! Spiral Tribe travels the nation!'

Debbie shook her head. 'Vince was round earlier, but he didn't want to wake you. Something about security trying to break into the shebeen. He left you a note downstairs.'

I grabbed my trainers and hurried out the room.

•

Mark,
Security guards forcing door of 55. Gone to see what can be done.
Vince. 9.20 am Tuesday.

•

Rubbing sleep out of my eyes, I ran out the house and round to 55 Elgin Avenue. What we didn't know at the time was that Shirley Porter, leader of our local council and heiress to the Tesco supermarket empire, was running an illegal property scam. Pushing poorer people out of the area, sealing all the empty properties, and then selling them on to her wealthy friends. When the scam was discovered, Porter was found guilty and ordered to pay costs of £43.3 million – she fled the country.

•

Later that day I wrote an account of what happened in one of my notebooks:

Tue March 26th. 'Sitex' (Void Property Protection Contrac-
tors) are forcing the locks at 55. These boys are eager. Crowbars
and sledgehammers can't get them in fast enough. Muscle and

hardware are supervised – at a safe distance – by Westmin-
ster Council's administrative wimp, who, as each blow falls,
flinches behind his clipboard.

   By 6pm they're gone, but doors, windows and skylights have
all been secured with steel. It looks like a bank vault. And so it
should: this week I read in the paper that each secured build-
ing costs the taxpayer £4,160.00 per year. A complete waste of
money – as by 7pm we were back in the building.

Vince and I had been watching the council workers, and
when they drove away, we – dressed in liberated 'London
Underground' orange hi-vis vests – undid all their hard work
and reopened the building.

TIME TO SKEDADDLE

Friday night. At 10.30 our *Financial Times* delivery van
bumped up onto the pavement. Zander parked it a little further down from the front door as there was a car parked in the
space we normally used.

   I opened the steel door as Zander wheeled the first bass bin
towards me. Mickey and Chris were lowering the next speaker
from the van to the ground. When I went out to meet them,
I noticed a woman standing a few feet away. There was something familiar about her. Long black hair, denim jacket, cowboy boots. I tried to place her. She seemed to be whispering to
herself. As I approached, she hurried away.

   'Hang on, Zand,' I said as I passed him, 'something's not
right.' I caught up with the woman on the corner of Elgin

and Chippenham. She stopped, turned, and looked me in the face. It was the same woman I'd seen two weeks ago hanging around outside the Green House. She had a fierceness in her eyes – the look of a cornered animal.

'Police!' she shouted as if the word would conjure a perspex riot shield between us.

In a gesture of calm I raised both my hands. I was puzzled. What was a plainclothes policewoman doing alone outside 55? But before I could ask, there was a screech of tyres and the thud of car doors. I turned to look at Zander. He'd clocked what was happening and pushed the bass bin towards 55. I ran over to help him. Two uniformed coppers legged it to the steel door. They were between us and our bolthole. We were cut off.

'Hold it right there!' one of them shouted.

We'd run out of space, and short of crushing the blokes against the steel door, Zander and I had no option but to stop.

A police van jerked to a halt across the road. The doors flew open and out swarmed another load of coppers. But instead of rushing us, they stood about straightening their helmets. A middle-aged sergeant pushed through them and strode over. He took off his flat hat, smoothed his fingers through his thick grey hair and said, 'Not tonight, lads – and take this with you.' He looked at the bass bin as if it were littering the street.

Zander and I stood there for a second. Then I blurted, 'But we haven't done anything wrong!'

The sergeant shook his head and sighed.

'Listen, lads. It's not happening here. If I were you, I'd go and find somewhere else.' He nodded slowly as if giving us a piece of good practical advice. Advice he'd only give once.

There was no further discussion. Mickey and Chris had

already reloaded the other speaker. Zander and I wheeled ours back to the van and jumped in. Time to skedaddle.

Back at the Green House we regrouped, including Vince and the others who'd made their escape from the shebeen over the back wall. I'd broken the news about the police to everyone who'd congregated there, including Heather and the Rose Farm posse.

'What's the problem?' asked Heather as she waved an unlit cigarette about in one hand and a glass of fizzy wine in the other. 'Let's take the party up to the farm!' It wasn't the first time, nor would it be the last, that Heather's hospitality saved the day.

•

After our brush with the law, Zander kept the rig under lock and key in the Green House and we kept our heads down for a few weeks. Actually, that's not entirely true. Zander and the Green House posse kept their heads down, while the Walterton Road posse – me, Karl K, Tracey, Hubert, Simone, Debbie and any number of visitors – went wild.

It had been an intense three weeks: working hard to buy the rig, dealing with all-comers on the door, and not to mention my freaky blood-red visions. We'd escaped any serious entanglements with gangsters, the police and, more importantly for me, the claustrophobia of the shebeen. All in all, we had reason to celebrate. But our plan to earn enough money to buy our own decks and mixer had been thwarted.

One thing was becoming clear: the Spiral Tribe Sound System was going to be an independent entity. The decks were crucial. Desperate times required desperate measures. Simone wrote to her nan.

A week later, Simone unpacked the brand-new Technics SL-1200s in the large empty room next to the kitchen at Walterton Road. Upstairs, Karl K had his own decks set up and mixed day and night. We managed to persuade Zander, who remained stubbornly sensible, to let us use just one amp and the monitor speakers. Walterton Road now had two sets of decks and two floors of sound.

THE FACTORY

In Hammersmith, West London, tucked behind the King Street shops, was a derelict factory building. It was a surprise to find such a vast complex of abandoned space standing wide open, only a stone's throw from the busy high street.

One afternoon, Debbie, Simone, Zander and I squeezed through the slit in the chain-link fence, doing our best to ignore the dog that was barking at our heels. Parked on the cracked concrete forecourt were several traveller's caravans. Behind them, on the far side of the forecourt, were a couple of twin vintage trucks. A bloke in goggles and dark overalls was working on one of them, orange sparks spraying from a disc cutter.

'Nice little vehicles,' said Zander.

'Love the 1950s curves.' Debbie held her hand out level with her eye as if to caress the lines. 'What are they?'

Zander thought for a moment. 'Look like Austin K9s, an ex-military four-by-four.'

I stopped to admire them. 'They'd get the rig in and out of anywhere.'

'Not exactly undercover though, are they?' said Debbie.

'Perhaps not undercover,' said Simone, 'but unstoppable.'

'If you can get the spare parts,' said Zander.

We entered the main building through a large rectangular opening which was curtained with thick, clear plastic strips. Inside we found ourselves in a vast single space. Whatever machines had been bolted to the blue-painted factory floor were long gone, but the footprint of each was still outlined in bare, unpainted concrete. A line of high widows ran around the top of the back wall, all broken. Gingerly we picked our way across the shards of broken glass. The dog stayed outside but was still barking. The sound bounced off the walls of the cavernous room and echoed around other empty spaces deeper within the factory complex.

'Watch out for live cables!' said Zander as we avoided a tangle of trunking and bent pipework that dangled from the high ceiling.

I shook my head. 'Doubt there's any power.'

Zander scowled at the ends of the bare cables and then at me. 'But walking into that lot isn't the way to find out!'

'I can't understand why anyone would want to vandalise such a beautiful place,' said Debbie.

'Looks like someone's been weighing in the cables and the pipework,' said Zander.

'And what about all this pigeon shit?' Debbie screwed up her face.

'We can sweep it up.' I kicked at the speckled crust on the concrete floor.

'You don't want to fuck about with that,' said Zander. 'The dust can give you some very nasty lung diseases.'

'Maybe we should take a look at some of the other rooms?' suggested Simone.

We went deeper into the building and climbed a narrow, white-tiled stairwell. On each landing two doorways – one left, one right – led into factory spaces as big as the one downstairs. In all the rooms the cables and pipes had been ripped from the ceilings, walls and floors. Most of the windows were smashed, and pigeons fluttered from one bent metal perch to another.

'It's crazy that such fantastic spaces aren't being used,' said Debbie. 'Imagine what you could do with all this.' She turned full circle, 'I suppose the property developers are just going to demolish the place.'

'Looks like they already have,' said Simone, shaking her head. 'There's no way we can clean all this up for Saturday – shall we check out the next floor?'

We went up another level, but every room lay in ruins. After five flights we began to lose interest.

'Looks like there's one more to go,' said Zander, starting up another flight.

'Oh, gawd!' moaned Debbie. Simone and I waited with her as Zander disappeared around the corner of the stairwell.

'Come and check this!' he called.

We followed him up. At the top was a normal-sized doorway, but instead of a hinged door it had a steel roller-shutter.

'It probably goes out onto the roof,' said Debbie.

'Let's take a look.' Zander bent down and got hold of the bottom edge of the door. He strained. The door stayed shut.

'It's locked,' said Debbie, 'let's get out of here.'

'Hang on,' said Zander. 'Mark, give us a hand.' I crouched down and got my fingers into the gap under the door. 'One-two-three-hup!' It moved an inch. 'One-two-three-hup!' With a dry metallic screech, it slid another few inches. 'And-one-two-three-hup!' The shuttering rolled open.

We stepped into a room, not as large as on the lower levels, but still with the capacity for a thousand people. It was pristine, with no damage or pigeon shit – just cobwebs and dust. Continuous windows ran around three of the four walls, and large rectangular skylights let the afternoon sunshine flood the space.

'Well, this is more like it!' said Debbie as she twirled across the wooden parquet floor.

At the other end of the room there was an opening into a small office. Across the entrance was a counter – the perfect bar or DJ booth. On the opposite wall, in between the windows, was a frosted-glass door. In it was a key. I unlocked it and we stepped out onto a flat roof.

'A warehouse loft *with* a rooftop garden,' said Simone. 'We are so in the fucking area!'

We walked to the parapet, leaned against the wall and looked out across London.

'This really is something,' said Debbie, shading her eyes from the sun.

I turned back towards the room. With its walls of windows and flat roof, it looked like the observation deck of a ship. 'Hey, look at that!' I pointed to a tall flagpole. 'We could hoist a Jolly Roger – or better still, stick up a pirate radio transmitter.'

'We haven't got a Jolly Roger or a transmitter,' said Zander.

'Even if we did,' said Debbie, 'waving a flag from the rooftops and beaming pirate radio signals would just bring it on top!'

'And pumping five thousand watts of bassline over the rooftops won't?' said Zander.

'This site is so big that no one will ever know we're here,' said Simone.

Still gazing up at the top of the flagpole, I imagined a black-and-white flag fluttering high above the building. It wasn't a Jolly Roger. It was something new. Something enigmatic that gave me a tantalising glimpse of itself, then escaped me.

We went back into the building to look for Sally, the woman who'd invited us to have a room at the squat party that the travellers were organising in the factory.

We found her downstairs. A tall woman who wore skimpy, tight black clothes, ripped fishnets and black DM boots. With a can of lager in one hand, she was supervising a group of punks unloading scaffolding planks from a flatbed truck.

'Well, what do you think?' she shouted over the sound of the wood being dropped into place on the scaffolding base of the stage.

'We like the room right at the top,' I replied, 'if that's okay?'

'You go wherever you like, my love – not exactly short of space, are we! It's a bit of a trek up there though. Are you sure you don't want to be closer to the action?'

'No, we're happy up in the crow's nest!'

She laughed. 'So you've got everything you need?'

'Yeah, but is there any leccy in the building?'

'Nah, it's all off, so best bring a gennie.'

'I'm sure that's sortable.' I looked at Simone, and she gave a reassuring nod.

'You'd be welcome to run off ours, but what with the band's PA and lights, we're going to be short on juice ourselves.'

'No worries, we can get a gennie easy enough.'

'But still,' said Zander, 'we'll check there's no live wires dangling anywhere.' He nodded towards a section of tangled pipework and cabling that twisted down from the ceiling like a motionless tornado.

'You go ahead, my love, but my lads have already made it safe.'

'What bands are playing tonight?' asked Debbie.

'We've got a fantastic live line-up – 2000 DS, Community Charge, RDF, all confirmed. And then there's you lot, with your bleeps and bang-bang-bang. It's gonna be one hell of a gig!' She took a swig of beer. 'So when will you set up?'

'Saturday morning, I reckon?' I looked at the others, who made agreeable faces. 'It won't take us long to decorate, rig the lights and connect the system.'

'See you Saturday then. Now I gotta get back to work.' She drained her can. 'Oh, and have you got a copy of this?' She rummaged in a shoulder bag and handed me a photocopied A4 sheet. It was a calendar of the year's free festivals. The artwork was interesting. A plan of Stonehenge, as seen from above, inside the outline of a Mandelbrot set.

I folded the list and slipped it into my back pocket. We said our goodbyes and Sally went back to telling the punks what to do.

The dog guarding the hole in the fence recognised us and didn't bark, but as we squeezed through the slit in the chain-link fence, he took the opportunity to nuzzle and lick us.

'What do you mean you can't see any problems?' said Debbie as she stepped back onto the street, holding her dog-licked hands at a safe distance away from the rest of her body. 'I counted a hundred and ninety-two.'

'A hundred and ninety-two?' I was puzzled.

'A hundred and ninety-two steps to get the system up.' She raised her eyebrows and gave me a tight-lipped smile.

•

Debbie was wrong. But also right. It turned out it wasn't the sound system that was difficult to get up the six flights of stairs. Although having said that, it wasn't exactly easy – but we managed. The real nightmare was the gennie.

The gennie we'd hoped to get through Simone's contact wasn't available, so we had to find another. It was all a bit last minute, but on Saturday morning, when I made the phone call to the hire shop, I was thinking, *power – and plenty of it.*

'10 KVA should do it,' said the bloke on the other end of the line.

'Wicked!' I said. 'We'll be over this afternoon to pick it up.'

'We close at noon on Saturdays,' he said.

'Hang on.' I covered the mouthpiece and turned to Zander, who was in the phone box with me. 'Can we collect it this morning?' Zander nodded, and I uncovered the mouthpiece. 'No problem, someone will be over right away.'

'Better make it quick coz I've only one left, and if it goes, it's gone.'

•

That afternoon, Vince, Camden, Tracey, Paul Brash, Hubert, Hamish, Mickey and a whole load of other people came to help tidy and decorate our new industrial penthouse. With the door opened out onto the roof, the air was fresh, and people were in and out of the sunshine admiring the view.

Inside, Vince was up and down a step ladder wiring star-shaped decorations from the ceiling pipework. Camden was pasting giant black-and-white spiral photocopies on the walls, and Debbie and I were hanging backdrops. Simone was looking increasingly frustrated with the coils of cables she was trying to match with their corresponding sockets in the amp rack. Ben had gone to live in Spain, and so it was now down to her to remember which bit went where.

Zander arrived with Sean, his close friend, workmate and sparring partner. Not only did Sean look like a world champion kickboxer – with his broken nose, chiselled features, military haircut and powerful V-shaped torso – he actually was a world champion kickboxer.

'We've got the gennie downstairs in the Land Rover,' said Zander. 'We're going to need a good few hands to bring it up – it's a chunky fucker.'

Chunky fucker was an understatement.

It was a vintage beast, the size of a car engine, though it looked as if it was designed to run on steam. It was bolted onto a steel trolley with small wheels, and on the front end it had a T-bar handle. Although there were seven of us to lift it out of the Land Rover, we all strained to lower it gently onto the ground without mishap. We'd decided, after the experience of the police confiscating the gennie at the Skool House, that we'd take the gennie up onto the roof. But that was going to prove more than a little tricky.

Because the axles were near enough the same width as the stairwell, we couldn't get either side of the machine. The only place we could get any purchase was either behind it or at the front, pulling on the T-bar. The difficulty was that the T-bar handle was only wide enough to fit the grip of two people, and the space behind was limited by the narrowness of the stairs.

Sean and Zander, being the strongest blokes on the firm, took hold of the T-bar and pulled. Paul Brash, Mickey, Hubert, Vince and I crammed in at the back to push. Having five of us squeezed together at the back was a bad idea. We were in each other's way and, consequently, only two or three of us were actually taking the strain at any one time. Above us, Zander and Sean were holding a lot of the weight and trying to keep their footing on the steep tiled stairs. I'd seen both Zander and Sean push themselves working out with weights at Tree Co, but nothing compared to the effort that twisted their faces now.

'One-two-three-heeeave! And . . . one-two-three-heeeave!' Spitting a rhythm from behind gritted teeth, Zander kept us working as a team.

The weight was at the very limit of what was humanly possible, and by the time we were halfway up the first flight we were getting into difficulty. It was almost as much effort holding the gennie fast as it was trying to move it. Going back down was impossible – one slip and the machine might run away and crush us.

My left arm was wrapped into the metal railings of the steel bannister, my hand gripping the rail, my right arm and shoulder tucked into the black oily metal of the diesel engine. I was a human chock, my body blocking the weight. Hubert was over and above me, and Paul's arms were under us both.

'One-two-three-heeeave! And . . . one-two-three-heeeave!' We all joined in Zander's mantra.

Paul slipped.

The gennie rocked back, the weight feeling as if it was tearing my ligaments.

'Oil!' shouted Paul. 'It's leaking oil!'

I felt my foot slide. 'Shit!' I gripped the railing harder. The gennie dug deeper into my body. We managed to hold it firm against the pull of gravity and the physical pain. My heart was thumping in my ears, but somewhere far below us I could hear the echoing bark of the dog.

Paul got back into position. We had no option but to press on.

'One-two-three-heeeave!'

'Hey, you lot!' came Chris's voice from the floor below us. 'Guess what?'

'One-two-three-heeeave! And ... one-two-three-heeeave!'

'Guess who's arrived?'

'For fuck's sake, Chris!' Zander broke his rhythm and the gennie's weight sagged back into my bones.

'Sorry. Just thought you'd be interested.'

'What?' shouted Zander.

'The police are here.'

That did it. We connected with our inner superpowers and managed a final drive to get the gennie up onto the first-floor landing. We stood around it, painfully gasping and rubbing bruised muscles.

'Hey,' said Chris as he climbed the stairs. 'You better be careful, there's loads of oil here.'

'We know,' I said in an urgent whisper. 'So where are the police?'

Chris registered the need to keep quiet and waited till he'd joined us on the landing before answering.

'They're talking to what's-her-name,' he whispered, 'the punk woman. Their chief's telling her to pack down their PA and dismantle the stage.'

'So they're inside the building?' asked Zander.

'Yeah, downstairs!'

'How many?' asked Vince, thoughtfully stroking his beard.

'Difficult to say – a fair few, maybe twenty.'

'Fuck!' hissed Zander.

'But they don't know we're here.' I held up a single finger to make the point.

There was a moment's pause while the penny dropped.

'So let's get this gennie up!' said Zander.

'It's all right for you hard bastards,' said Paul, 'but there's five more flights and that one nearly killed me.'

'How about leaving it here?' suggested Hubert. 'We could stash it under some rubbish?'

I was reluctant. 'Yeah, but if they do find it, we're totally scuppered.'

'I've got an idea,' whispered Zander, a smile flickering in his eyes. We all moved a little closer. 'I've got a block and tackle in my Landy. If we can get it, we could rig it at the top of each flight and float this fucker up. Problem is getting to my Landy without the Old Bill seeing.'

'Where you parked?' asked Chris.

'This street behind.' Zander gestured over his shoulder.

'I know a way,' said Chris. 'A service door out the back of the boiler room.'

'Service door?' I'd missed that in my earlier explorations.

Chris flicked his floppy blonde fringe out of his eyes. 'Well actually, it's a small, round metal door – more of an escape hatch.'

'Escape hatch?' I smiled.

'It opens out into the street behind.'

'Show me,' said Zander.

'On a mission!' Chris started down the stairs, and Zander followed.

The rest of us wheeled the gennie inside one of the first-floor doorways. It was no protection against the police if they bothered to look, but it would at least keep us out of sight if they happened to glance up the stairwell. Mickey went to warn everyone upstairs to keep the noise down and not to show themselves over the parapet.

The rest of us waited in silence. I felt like a kid playing hide and seek, certain that the cops would appear at any moment, but also holding on to a blind and irrational faith that we had the power of invisibility.

Ten minutes later, Zander and Chris were back with the block of pulleys and rope.

'They're fucking everywhere!' said Chris, adrenaline making it difficult for him to control his whisper. 'Searching the building, nicking people – and equipment!'

Though going back into the stairwell felt counterintuitive, we couldn't hang about and wait for the cops to find us.

As quietly as we could, we wheeled the gennie into position at the bottom of the second flight. Zander rigged the block and tackle to the top of the second-floor bannister railings, then came back to secure the rope to the gennie's T-bar handle. Chris positioned himself behind as lookout. Zander and Sean went to the front of the gennie to steady it. The rest of us, like a tug-o-war team, got hold of the rope.

In a loud whisper, Zander put us on starter's orders. 'And . . .

one-two-three-heave!'

The dead weight of the solid metal was now as light as air. The only tricky part was when the gennie reached the top of its pull, just short of its anchor point, so we still had to lift it up over the last few steps, but it was a doddle compared to what we'd done before. Once the gennie was safely on the next landing, Zander unhitched the block and fastened it to the top of the next flight. In this way we made good progress.

Halfway up the last flight we thought we were home and dry. Then I caught sight of Chris frantically waving both his hands to get our attention. He held a finger to his mouth and pointed downstairs. We froze.

At the bottom of the stairs, we heard heavy footfalls, deep voices and the unmistakable sound of two-way radios. I tightened my grip on the rope and bit my lip. The footfalls and voices disappeared as the coppers left the stairs and went to investigate the rooms on the first floor. From above us, Zander nodded. As we resumed our pull, the ropes creaked under tension.

We'd just got the gennie to the anchor point when we heard the voices coming back into the stairwell. We listened to them advancing up another flight. A few moments later they were gone again and searching the second floor. We didn't need to speak – we knew this was our cue. We grappled the gennie up over the last few steps. Zander unhitched the ropes and we wheeled it into the top room. Debbie, Simone and the others were standing around the door, pulling faces of disbelief and mouthing words of silent jubilation. But it wasn't over yet. Zander snuck back out onto the landing to check the cops weren't within earshot, then quickly came back in and pulled down the roller-shutter door. He then jammed a batten of wood into the narrow gap between the door and the metal groove in the frame. If the cops tried to open it, with a little bit of luck, the wood might hold.

WHISKERS ON KITTENS

We reckoned we only had a few minutes before the squad of police searching the building got up to the top floor. Just in case the door didn't hold, we moved the speakers and gennie – as quietly and quickly as we could – into the small side room and covered them with an old tarp. It wasn't perfect, but it did mean, at least to the casual observer, there was nothing immediately in view. Then we all went out onto the roof. I locked the frosted-glass door behind us, and we sat down, out of sight, behind the parapet.

'Nice here, innit,' said Paul, breaking the silence.

'That all depends on how long we have to wait,' replied Debbie.

'We can out-wait the boys in blue – any time. We're the hardcore massive.'

'If you say so, Paul.'

'Especially these hardcore geezers.' He nodded towards Zander and Sean. 'I wouldn't want to tangle with them. Hard bastards.'

'Just ignore him,' said Debbie to Sean, who was looking puzzled, then turned away from Paul and raised her eyebrows at me. 'Are we just going to sit here and hope the police don't find us?' She searched her pouch of tobacco for some Rizla.

'Got any better ideas?' I asked.

'Maybe.' Camden got up. 'We could at least see what they're up to.'

'Oi! Don't break the skyline!' Zander made a slapping-thin-air gesture.

'Sorry!' Camden bent double and went over to a group of large ventilation ducts that came up the side of the building.

Staying half-crouched, I went with him. We peered through a gap.

'You can see the main entrance,' he said quietly as he pushed his wire-rimmed glasses further up the bridge of his nose. Below we could see two parked police cars.

'Oh, yeah,' I whispered as I leaned in closer. 'At least we'll know when they go.'

'*If* they go.'

'It's Saturday – it won't be long before a pub kicks off somewhere in London.'

Camden turned to me. 'What I don't understand is why they even bother with us.'

'Orders from above, I suppose.'

'I think they're just bored.'

'Maybe that too.'

•

About half an hour later we were all jostling for a view between the air ducts to watch the police get back into their vehicles and leave. The roller-shutter door had held fast – either that or the cops hadn't been bothered to climb all six flights of oily stairs. But even though they hadn't found us, they weren't going to be a complete pushover and, just in case, had left one of their number standing out on the street guarding the hole in the chain-link fence.

'Whotcha reckon?' I asked the squash of people surrounding me.

'None of the travellers have gone,' said Chris, 'and there's what's-her-name!'

Beer can in hand, Sally strode past the caravans on the forecourt to where the young copper was at the fence. She began to wildly gesticulate with both hands. Beer splashed to the ground. The copper shrugged his shoulders and shook his head. Then Sally shouted something at him, which set the dog off. Sally stormed back towards the building. The dog trotted behind her, but every few steps ran back towards the policeman, barked at him, then scampered after Sally.

I unlocked the glass door and Zander, Chris and I were the first to creep back into the building.

Chris volunteered to go and find out what was happening downstairs.

'Whatever you do,' said Zander in a loud whisper as he carefully pushed up the roller shutter, 'don't let that copper see you!'

'Don't worry, they saw me earlier – they probably think I'm some lost-it-nutter.' He pushed his tongue behind his lower lip to make it jut out and, walking like a zombie, went out onto the landing.

'Nah,' said Zander, 'you were a more convincing nutter when you pulled that other face.'

Chris straightened up and turned to Zander. 'What other face?'

'That's the one.'

'Fuck off, you cunt,' said Chris, carefully avoiding the oil as he went down the stairs.

•

'You want the good news or the bad news?' asked Chris, breathless from the long climb back.

Debbie and I were taping backdrops to the wall. 'Shall we start with the bad?' I suggested.

'The downstairs PA has gone, and the gig's been cancelled.'

'And the good news?' Debbie tore a length of gaffer tape from the reel.

'The travellers haven't been evicted and they're totally up for us doing the party.'

'What about that copper on the gate?' I asked.

'He's got orders to stop people who don't live on-site coming in.'

'Isn't that bad news?' asked Debbie, her face still turned to the wall as she concentrated on sticking a corner of the pink fluorescence fabric down.

'No, that's good,' said Chris with a smirk.

'How's that?' Debbie looked up.

'They don't know about the secret hatch round the back.'

•

That afternoon we finished decorating the room and scrubbing the oil off the stairs. Although all the stage PA had gone, the stud-encrusted punks managed to keep their gennie. As daylight faded, they set up a small domestic record player in the big space downstairs. They positioned it just behind the plastic strip curtain with the speakers turned towards the copper guarding the entrance. First up was Julie Andrews with the theme from *The Sound of Music*. It was a nice touch but seemed to make our guard nervous. Twenty minutes later he was joined by reinforcements – two police vans which blocked the road outside. Why they didn't raid the building again and stomp on the cheeky little record player was a mystery. Perhaps it was because the dark, cavernous, derelict factory, echoing with 'raindrops on roses and whiskers on kittens, bright copper kettles and warm woollen mittens', was simply too weird for them to get their heads around. Whatever the reason, the music acted as both a sign of defiance and an effective diversion, keeping the police's attention at the front of the building.

A couple of the punk lads helped hook up strings of blue chaser lights along the route to the back door. At first there wasn't enough length of cable to wind all the way along the route – in and out of a maze of stud-walled offices. Zander and Sean got on the case and, using their kickboxing skills, blazed a more direct trail through any inconvenient plasterboard walls.

'What've you been up to?' I asked Zander when he came back upstairs.

'Putting up fairy lights,' he said as he brushed plaster dust off his shoulders.

•

Night fell. At the front of the building the police were turning everyone away. Meanwhile, we snuck out the back and – mingling with the drifting crowds – redirected them to the opposite side of the building, to the small, round metal door. Rusted and riveted, low in the blank brickwork of a dark side street, no one would have suspected that it was an escape hatch. A way out of the drunken and aggressive reality of a normal Saturday night and into a world of friendship and music.

Once inside, our guests followed the rope of light-chasers along the tunnel of holes that had been bashed through the office walls. At the bottom of our stairwell the rope-lights continued, entwined around the bannister rail, spiralling up to the top of the building.

We had a mixed crowd: some faces I recognised from the shebeen, local kids, acidheads, and punks that had come for the bands. The sound system was sweet, the music a mix of acid, house, techno and breakbeat. Something for everyone, including the punks who energetically moshed all night.

In the morning we opened the glass door and took the party out onto the rooftop. We were passing around the photocopied calendar of festivals that Sally had given us. Among the bikers' rallies, protests and free festivals advertised, there was a walk marking the sixth anniversary of the Battle of the Beanfield – the name given to the brutal attack by police on the men, women and children travelling to the 1985 summer solstice Stonehenge festival with the Peace Convoy. There was also a short article about how some of the attacked travellers had sued the police for wrongful arrest, assault and criminal damage. The travellers had won their case, but the judge awarded them less than a thousand pounds each – and refused to award them any legal costs.

'So what's all this about police at the Beanfield covering up their numbers?' asked Debbie, passing the festival list to Vince.

'Wouldn't surprise me,' he said, handing the list to me without looking at it.

'Nah, that's illegal,' I said. 'They're obliged to have their numbers visible – it's the law.'

'If you don't mind me saying so, mate,' said one of the punk lads who was sitting up on the parapet swinging his legs and drinking cider. He jumped down and sidled over to me, offering me a go on the crumpled plastic bottle.

'No, thanks.'

'Suit yourself.' He passed it to Debbie and sat down next to me.

'Don't take offence like.' He put an arm around my shoulders and leaned into my face, his breath smelling of tobacco and alcohol. 'But you don't know what the fuck you're talking about.' He gave me a squeeze and turned to Debbie. 'Got any baccy, love? I think I might have a blim.' He released his grip on me and started patting the pockets of his paint-daubed leather jacket. 'If you lot are thinking of doing any of those free festies, then fair play – the scene is in a right sorry state after those fascists stuck the boot in.' His head lolled in the direction of the party. 'This music is what it needs. You get this Spiral-whatsit to Stonehenge and, you never know, you might just change the world!' he laughed, showing more black gaps than teeth.

'Sounds like a plan,' said Simone.

He nudged me with his elbow. 'But watch ya backs, coz whether you believe me or not, those cunts with no numbers won't be far behind.'

DISBELIEF

The small rig – made up of one amp and two monitor speakers – was set up in the room next to the kitchen at Walterton Road. It was up and running, at various volumes, most of the time. The house soon became a social hotspot and attracted lots of new visitors. There were a few local kids, including Joe, a lad of seventeen who lived round the corner with his mum on Shirland Road. There was a bunch of Italian girls who made regular trips over from their East London art studio. Seb, the music student who was experimenting with the Roland 303. And, of course, the police, who kicked the door down once or twice. Apart from those minor interruptions, everyone else got on really well. Most of the time.

Though everyone at Walterton Road and the Green House were close friends, the short two-minute walk between the houses had begun to widen slightly.

Fuelled by rapidly evolving styles of techno and British breakbeat, gallons of day-glo paint, two sets of Techniques decks and sheets of high-quality LSD, the non-stop Spiral party took a hold at Walterton Road. And, after Debbie, Simone and I'd painted 'Round and round the spiral spins, it never stops – just mixes in' on the kitchen ceiling, we decided it was time to go and check out a free festival – without the rig – to see what was what.

The next one on Sally's magic list was on the last weekend of May, on Chipping Sodbury Common – about two hours out of London. But by the time we'd decided to go, it was already nearly over. Luckily a bloke called Dennis said he had a car, a full tank of petrol, and would gladly run us out there for a quick daytime reccy.

Zander, Debbie, Simone and I jumped in and escaped west down the M4. Dennis had his window wound down, his foot on the floor and the radio on full whack. Signal from our preferred pirate stations faded in and out, and it was my job as co-driver to navigate and scan the radio frequencies for the best music. But the further from London we got, the fainter the music became – until there was nothing. Tearing down the motorway we didn't want to listen to the bland sound of commercial pop or the oppressive mainstream news, as it would only spoil our buzz, so Dennis and I took it in turns to twiddle the tuner between squelchy sounds of electronic interference, fizzing radio static and fragmented words and music. Dennis, with his baseball cap firmly turned backwards on his head, right arm out the window and hand slapping the top of the roof, added his own spontaneous lyrics in his deep, growly voice – punctuated with little yelps of 'Hardcore!'

Simone joined in with a 'Come-on-let's-av-ya!' as we overtook all but the fastest-moving traffic.

'This is our turning!' I shouted over the roaring hiss of the radio's white noise.

Dennis slung the wheel over to the left and, with a squeal of rubber, veered off the motorway and up towards a roundabout.

The force of the turn had flung me against the passenger door and I'd lost my place on the map. I turned it around and tried to regain my bearings before we ran out of road.

'Left!' I shouted.

We found ourselves on a straight but narrow B-road, crossing open country, heading, I hoped, towards Chipping Sodbury.

Ahead there was a blind rise in the road. Dennis kept his foot down. My hands, still clutching the concertinaed map, automatically braced my body against the dash. Dennis turned to me, laughing.

'Wotcha saying, geezer? Don't you trust my driving?' He kept his face turned towards me.

'Only when you've got your eyes on the road!'

He let out a self-satisfied laugh and turned back just as we approached the lip of the rise.

'What the!' Dennis braked. I closed my eyes and my arms stiffened. The tires bit. We slid. Our bodies pressed painfully into our seat belts, then rocked back in our seats. We'd stopped – a few feet short of a police roadblock.

'Fuck!' said Dennis.

There were several police in uniform in the road. One still had his hand up. If he'd had any fear of being mown down, he didn't show it, but he didn't look happy.

At the side of the road more police were coming out of a couple of Portacabins. The copper in front of the car lowered his arm and started walking towards us.

Dennis, while hurriedly rummaging inside the front of his trousers, made strange little gasping noises like he'd bet his life savings on a horse and it was now neck and neck in the last furlong.

'Debbie!' he shouted over his shoulder as he freed something from his trousers. 'Fucking sort this lot out!' He threw a bundle wrapped in a black plastic bin liner onto Debbie's lap.

I stared at Dennis. 'What the fuck's that!'

'Es!' Dennis spat drops of saliva at the windscreen as he tried to contain his panic.

I looked back at Debbie. She was white, frozen with fear. The bundle, the size of a fat paperback book, was on her lap.

The first copper reached the front of the car. Others started to close in.

'What the hell am I supposed to do with that!' Debbie had sparked back to life.

'Just ... just ... put it down your top!' Dennis's face twisted and reddened.

'It's not going to fit!'

I still had the map in my hands. I opened it up to try and obscure the view of the approaching policemen. But it was no good, we were surrounded.

The copper at the front was at Dennis' open window. Dennis leaned out and made some cringing gestures.

Behind me I could hear the rustle of the plastic bag.

'Good afternoon, officer. What seems to be the problem?' Dennis' voice sounded brittle.

My window darkened as another copper came to my door. I lowered the map and wound the window down. I tried a smile. Bad idea. It felt false, and worse, it felt guilty. The copper glared at me.

'Get out of the car. All of you! Out of the car!'

I opened the door. As I got out, two more policemen came out of the Portacabin. They were pulling on green surgical gloves. That meant only one thing: strip searches. My mind was racing, but everything else was in slow motion. *Just act natural, just act natural, be polite – at least Debbie's safe coz there are no women officers to search her. Everything's going to be fine.*

When I saw the two women officers follow the blokes out, also wearing the rubber gloves, I felt the blood drain from my head, and chest, and legs. My head swam. This was it. Debbie was doomed. I felt sick.

We were led into the Portacabins. Boys in one, girls in the other. Our names and addresses were taken. Our clothes were removed and searched, and we were made to bend over and flash our arseholes. But none of that mattered – what mattered was that these moments were Debbie's last moments of freedom. *How many pills must be in that bundle? Five hundred, a thousand, five thousand? What the fuck is Dennis playing at? And just throwing them at Debbie like that! Fuck!*

With my search over and dressed again, I was allowed to go back outside. Dennis and Zander, who'd been before me, were waiting outside the door, police on either side of them. Dennis was cracking jokes. Zander was quiet.

Simone came out of the women's cabin, biting her lip. I wanted to ask her what was happening, but this wasn't the moment to speak. I stared at the ground, fighting the dizziness and listening to the coppers searching the car, taking details, writing stuff down.

Minutes passed. The women's cabin opened again and out came one of the WPCs, pulling off her gloves. I avoided her cold gaze, knowing she'd be able to read me.

Then Debbie appeared in the doorway, eyes downcast.

The coppers said some more stuff at us, but I couldn't concentrate on the words. Dennis made another joke. Then we were told we could all go.

Go?

I just stood there. We all did. Confused.

'Go on – git!' one of the coppers ordered.

I glanced at Debbie for some clue as to what had happened.

Her eyes remained downcast and unreadable. We drifted towards the car in a surreal, half-dream state. The coppers that had searched the car were still standing around it. All the doors were wide open. As I approached my side, I looked into the foot well of the back seat. There, clear as day, was the black plastic bundle sitting there. Unseen. I pulled my eyes away and tried not to react – or think. *Don't blow it now, we're nearly there – don't let them read your mind.*

We all got in. Dennis started the car, and with a nervous lurch and a squeak of tyres we drove away.

The remaining five-minute journey up to the festival was sullen. All apart from Dennis, who was loudly babbling about something – but I wasn't listening. I was still reeling, now with relief and disbelief. Relief that the package had not been found and Debbie was safe, but also disbelief at what Dennis had done.

THE AVON FREE FESTIVAL: MAY 1991

Against the skyline the festival looked like a nomadic citadel. The walls were high-sided vehicles, the roofs were tented spires and, flying high above it all, was a forest of tattered flags.

The car bumped off the road and onto the short, grazed turf of the common. We left Dennis sorting through his big bag of drugs and headed across the grass towards the music. The festival was winding down, but it was by no means over. We passed several patches of anaemic grass where tents had been pitched, but it was still a large site, crowded with old trucks and buses; some arranged in sociable circles, others with tarpaulins stretched between them to make covered courtyards. Though not everyone was so well organised, especially those who'd arrived in cars. We passed one car overflowing with sleeping ravers, who huddled together to keep warm and had disappeared into their big, baggy sweatshirts, hoods pulled down over their eyes, sleeves dangling over their hands. Another car looked as if it had crash-landed with all four doors left wide open, apparently abandoned by its occupants in the rush to get onto the dance floor. We walked together slowly, still shocked by the incident with Dennis.

'You okay?' asked Simone, putting her arm round Debbie.

'I'm fine.'

'What the fuck does he think he's playing at?' I said.

'Don't worry about it,' said Debbie, who was still walking with her eyes downcast. She looked up and managed a smile. 'No harm done.'

'What I can't understand,' said Simone, 'is that he's usually such a safe bloke – totally on the vibe.'

I shook my head. 'Except when the pressure's on! No way can we have people like him doing dodgy shit like that.'

'You mean dealing?' asked Debbie.

'I'm up for legalisation, but doing your own private business and then, when it comes on top, jeopardising innocent people – fuck!'

'Maybe,' Zander suggested, 'we should have a policy of no dealers on the firm?'

'Tricky when so many people depend on knocking out a few bits-n-bobs,' said Simone.

'A pact then?' I suggested. 'Between the four of us?'

'That's a bit unnecessary,' said Debbie.

'Why?'

'Well, obviously I've absolutely no intention of ever selling any drugs whatsoever! Anyone else got plans to start a Spiral Tribe cartel?'

'It just gives the police an extra excuse,' said Simone.

We all looked at Zander. 'I've already got a job, thanks!'

'What about you then?' Debbie looked at me.

Zander answered her. 'He'd be a rubbish drug dealer!'

I scowled at him. 'No, I wouldn't!'

'Yeah, you would – you'd give them all away!'

I had to agree.

As we approached the music, we managed to shake off the bad vibes. I took a deep breath, smelling wood smoke and campfire cooking. It sparked memories of my teenage summers in the seventies and eighties spent at the Stonehenge Free Festival. Each step I took across the springy turf towards the music opened up my senses.

We soon found the source of the music: a circle of old trucks where fifty or sixty people were locked into the basslines of acid house. To one side of the circle a patchwork of tarpaulins had been roped from the side of the vehicles. Above them, coloured gauze had been made into sail-like flags, and, up on the roofs of the trucks, people were dancing against the afternoon sky.

Debbie and Simone headed straight for the speakers. Zander and I hung around on the opposite side of the dance floor, next to a short section of scaffold tower which had been decorated with the same coloured gauze as the flags. We both shifted our weight from foot to foot as we began to slowly melt into the music.

'Hello, Harrison brothers!' It was Kirsty, the girl who'd helped me decorate the basement at the Skool House. Her little pointed woollen hat, with tassels dangling from the earflaps, made her look even more impish than usual. 'Fancy meeting you here!'

'Yeah, you know,' I said, pushing up the peak of my baseball cap, 'we just happened to be passing – saw all the roadblocks and thought, *Ello, this looks like fun.*'

Kirsty's smile evaporated. 'Yeah, that was heavy – did you get searched?'

'Heavy's not the word,' said Zander, crossing his arms over his chest.

'Bit of a nightmare,' I said, 'but it's all sorted now. Well, no, it's not at all sorted, but we're all fine. So, what are you up to?'

Kirsty's face lit up again. 'I've been thinking I might go and see if I can get a go on the mic,' she giggled, turning towards the sound system. 'I'm feeling a really amazing energy here.' She turned back towards us. 'Really connected.'

'I didn't know you MCed.' I pushed my hands into my back pockets.

'No, I don't – never done it before,' she laughed. 'But I can feel this mad energy coming up through me.' She held her splayed fingers in front of her as if she were caressing an electrified football.

At that moment Stikka ambled over from the crowd. He nodded at each of us in turn. 'Nice little set-up they've got going here.'

'Haven't seen you for a while, Stikka – how's it going?'

'Isn't it fantastic!' said Kirsty, grinning and throwing her invisible ball into the air. 'Right, I'm off to give it a go.' She wiggled her fingers at us and strode off across the dance floor.

'All good,' said Stikka watching Kirsty go. 'What's she up to?'

'I don't think she knows yet,' said Zander.

Kirsty disappeared under the patchwork canopy.

'Do you know this crew?' I asked Stikka.

'Yeah, DiY. From Nottingham. Been doing this stuff for a while. Good people.'

'Nice sound.' I nodded.

'Bit fluffy.' Zander's arms were still folded.

'Check that bass,' said Stikka.

'And the vocal,' I said. 'Trippy stuff.' An ethereal vocal was coming in over the tune. 'Hang on.' I pulled down the peak of my cap to shade my eyes and squinted in the direction of the system. 'That's Kirsty!'

Microphone in hand and smiling brightly, Kirsty strolled out of the tent singing the sweetest, pitch-perfect scat harmonies.

The three of us stood there riveted, watching as she got into the swing of things and started to dance. After a few minutes, Stikka turned to me and Zander. He had the same dark sparkle in his eyes that he'd had the first night I'd met him at the Skool House.

He opened his hands to include not just Kirsty and the dance floor but the whole festival. 'This is where we should be – this is what we should be doing!'

I lifted my fist towards his and we punched them firmly together.

The building where Lucia and her Italian friends had their studios was a four-storey Victorian factory building with a huge, glass-covered courtyard at its centre. After one visit, we were sold on the idea of throwing a party there. A tour launch party. One final bash in London before the summer solstice – before Stonehenge Free Festival.

I got to work on the décor and flyers. In recognition of our pirate status, I painted a series of large boards with stylised skulls and crossed bones – the base layer of each was in a different fluorescent colour and the top layers were an intricate tattoo-like black lattice, which added to the tribal look. My favourite was a black and yellow character emblazoned with stylised sparks and lightning bolts, not only in homage to the electricity that pulsed through the circuitry of our sound system but also because of the sense that techno connected into the future. I'd read somewhere that lightning simultaneously strikes up as well as down. The best electronic dance music also had something of that quality. A good tune connects with the future, or more accurately, the future flashes down the musical pathway and the current connects with you.

I'd taken Stikka's advice about putting the words 'Invitation Only' on the Skool House flyers in an attempt to hold the law at bay. It hadn't worked. But other rave organisers were advertising their events as music video shoots. *Gotta be worth a try,* I thought. To this end the Italian girls billed themselves as a film company – and, who knows, maybe they were – and we billed ourselves as the sound system. The finished black-and-white flyer read:

Magic Moment Film Co.
Spiral Tribe Sound System
Invite you to dance in a new music video and tour launch party
Top DJs, PAs, and performances
This event is to be filmed, all rights belong to MM Film Co and
Spiral Tribe
Sat. 15.6.1991 Midnight and beyond
556 Cable Street Studios E1
Admit one.

It all sounded totally kosher to me.

What I hadn't noticed about the flyer, even though I'd designed it from scratch, was the significance of the strange little face that formed the central piece of artwork. It was symmetrical, not just left to right but also top to bottom. The skull-like grin of the teeth reflected above as a crown or plumed headdress.

•

From the outside the grey brick Cable Street building looked like a factory built as a fortress.

Keeping a close eye on the wing mirrors, Zander inched our van through the arched gateway under the entrance tower. The arch didn't have a portcullis, though it looked like it should. As I pushed the heavy oak doors shut behind us, iron bolts dragged along a semi-circular groove worn in the cobbles.

Inside was a huge courtyard with a glass roof. Balconies ran around each of the three floors that overlooked the courtyard and, along one side, at ground level, a raised loading dock provided the perfect dance podium.

It was just after eight o'clock in the evening and there was another hour of daylight left, being, as it was, only six days to the solstice and the shortest night of the year. I recognised Lucia and her Italian friends, but there were perhaps ten or twelve other people helping to shift piles of timber, scrap metal and sacks of plaster out of the courtyard. I guessed the helpers were artists who shared studio space in the building. Certainly they shared the same taste in hats, as they all wore silver Gatsby-style caps.

'You like my hat?' Lucia asked me as she lowered her face and touched the peak. Crystalline rainbows sparked under the surface of the holographic plastic.

'Totally techno!' I said. 'Where'd you get it?'

Lucia kept her face down but raised her eyes to look at me. She smiled and reached for my hand. 'Come, I'll show you.'

She led me up the stairs and along one of the walkways towards a group who were having drinks on the balcony, some of them wearing holographic suits. I smiled and said hello as we squeezed through them and into a brightly lit workshop. It smelt of vinyl and spirit-based glue and was crowded with people in various states of undress.

Lucia introduced me as 'Spiral Mark' to the designer, Mer.

Mer was a dark-haired young woman with twinkling eyes and red lipstick. She was dressing a bloke in one of the silver outfits. She nodded hello but couldn't speak because she held a row of dressmaker's pins between her lips.

I looked around while she finished adjusting the hems on the bloke's trousers. The room was small but appeared bigger due to the large, full-length mirrors on the walls. The people dressing were almost disappearing into the suits as if they were dissolving into the iridescent light. Mer stood up and looked her model up and down, adjusted his collar and said, 'That's you done, my love', then turned to me.

'I like your designs,' I said, shaking her hand, 'very futuristic.'

'Well, in that case – welcome to the future!' she smiled.

'I've never seen anything like this.' I smoothed my fingers over the surface of the fabric that was still on a roll.

'Cybernetic skin, and it's not just for show – hologram technology is going to be big. Very big.' Her eyes shone.

'I'm sure they'll sell well.'

'The clothes? They're the tip of the iceberg. Holographic printing is where it's going. Credit cards, IDs, banknotes – imagine the demand.'

I tried to imagine but needed help. 'How do you mean?'

'Security. An authenticating hologram on every credit card, every banknote. The contracts will be massive.'

I'd never been able to grasp the selling-me-debt concept of credit cards and, as for authenticating the illusion of money with another optical illusion, well, I could appreciate the irony but knew the idea would never catch on. 'What a good idea,' I lied, 'but these hats – now they're totally pukka!'

'Ah,' she laughed, 'my hats!'

'Blinding.'

'Really? Are you, by any chance, after one?'

'Well, I'm not sure I could afford . . .'

'No, I'm not sure you could!' she smiled. 'Tell you what I'll do, seeing as you're with the sound system, if you can answer my little quiz, I'll give you one – with my love.' She lightly touched a finger to her lips while she thought. 'Okay, I'm thinking of a dragon.' She raised an eyebrow. 'Tell me, what colour is it?'

The Celtic LSD dragons danced in my mind. 'Red,' I replied without hesitation.

'Very good!' She looked me up and down and gave me an approving nod. 'Very good indeed!' She walked over to a large cardboard box and pulled out a hat.

'Did I win?'

'Sorry, it's not quite *that* easy. Let's make it a little harder, shall we?' She went over to a large mirror. 'Come here.'

I did as I was told. She took me by the shoulders and turned me to face the mirror, put a hat on my shaved head, adjusted the peak, then turned me back round to face her.

'Okay, let's try again. In my mind I have an image of a dragon. What colour is it?'

I thought for a moment. No colour came to mind. 'Green,' I guessed.

'Wrong!' She shook her head. 'It was red again!' She pinched my cheek.

'But I got one out of two right,' I protested.

'No, two out of two. You are, in fact, a lucky winner.'

I looked at her blankly.

'If you'd have said red,' she explained, 'I'd have known you were cheating.'

'What?'

She flicked my peak. 'These hats give the wearer total psychic protection.' She smiled. 'Suits you. Now, if you don't mind, I need to finish these fittings – and haven't you got a party to organise?'

Back downstairs I found Zander crouching behind the amp rack, frowning at the coils of cable that surrounded him.

'Bet you don't know what I'm thinking,' I said.

'What?' He stood up, holding a tangled bundle of coloured wires.

'I bet you don't know what I'm thinking!' I gave him a wide-eyed stare.

'You want to know,' he said slowly, 'if that hat makes you look like a total dickhead.'

'Fuck!' I said, pulling it off to look inside. 'It must have sprung a leak!' I put it back on.

'You want to give me a hand with these cables?'

After a few moments of untangling the colour-coded wires, I asked him, 'You know how the government is always trying to stop solstice and kill the scene?'

'Yeah?'

'Well, I'm wondering where we stand legally.'

'When have you ever worried about whether something was legal?' He turned away to continue sorting the cables.

'Take the new acid house law and the Public Order Act, they're all about money or disorder and violence. If we're doing free festivals and the peace and love thing, then none of those laws apply, right?'

'Yeah, maybe, and anyway,' he said, pulling a purple cable free of the knotted heap, the acid house law is out of date.'

'How do you mean?'

He stood up, pulled another silver hat from his jacket pocket, and put it on. 'Because we play *techno!*'

I laughed. 'Where'd you get yours?'

'Anna-Marie. She's invited me to go to Spain with her.'

'Who?'

'Anna-Marie, Lucia's mate, to visit her folks in Barcelona.'

'But she's Italian!'

'Shows how much you know.'

'So, are you going?'

'Yeah, next week.'

'But it's Stonehenge.'

'After Stonehenge.'

'Okay.' I picked up the purple cable and asked him what I should do with it.

He scratched his head. Simone came over.

'Thank you!' she said as she plucked the cable from my hands and plugged it into the amp rack.

•

The party went well, though the guests were not quite the same lively mix that we'd had over in West London. At the Cable Street studios, it was more of a self-conscious arty-media crowd. Despite the wild silver suits that half the guests were wearing, the edginess and sense of belonging which had been so apparent at our other parties was missing.

The police put in a brief appearance, but when I showed them the flyer they were satisfied that the party was a legitimate music video shoot. Which was good – but it did leave me a little cold. Why should an event organised by a music video company be allowed, no questions asked, but if I'd billed the exact same party, with the exact same music, without the pretence of a video shoot, we could face criminal charges? Clearly the law favoured the entertainment and leisure industry and discriminated against spontaneous community events. Though our scam had worked, portraying ourselves as something we weren't didn't feel right. We were Spiral Tribe. We didn't need permission to exist. We didn't need the authority's stamp of approval to be real. We didn't need authentication – holographic or otherwise.

SUMMER SOLSTICE 1991

Greg may have bought himself out of the military to grow his blond crop into long golden curls, but he still had contacts.

'I know where I can get a tent – not a marquee but big enough to house the system, just in case the weather turns nasty.'

'What colour is it?' asked Debbie.

'NATO green.'

'Very undercover!' she said approvingly.

And it was: a brand-new, NATO green, military frame tent the size of a double garage. It could be pitched without the ends, making it open on two sides. This was the perfect space to install the amp rack, a couple of trestles, the decks, a whole load of DJs and their mates. The speaker stacks didn't fit, but they could be covered with tarpaulin and finished off with another of Greg's military gems: camouflage netting.

'This isn't *Underground*,' said Hamish as we loaded the great tangles of camouflage netting into the van. 'This is *Undergrowth*!'

•

The Summer Solstice of 1991 fell on 21 June, which was a Friday. After the experience we'd had with the police surrounding

Chipping Sodbury Common, we thought it best to get there early – ahead of any police cordon.

On Thursday our inconspicuous convoy of three set off, heading west again. Debbie driving her little red post office van, Zander driving our *Financial Times* truck with me and Simone in the cab, and any number of people in the back, lying in a nest of cushions and bedding on top of the speakers. And Hamish, sometimes ahead and sometimes behind, in a borrowed white transit van. Stikka had arranged to meet us there.

The area of Salisbury Plain around Stonehenge is an open piece of rolling countryside. All across the exposed landscape are ancient burial mounds and long barrows, which give the place a sacred and solemn atmosphere. Though the famous stone circle is, in itself, a marvel of prehistoric engineering, there is something gloomy about the place, even oppressive. If the stone circle was built as a temple, it's hard to imagine it was a temple to celebrate light and life. All the more reason to go and cheer the place up.

But as we approached the area, things weren't looking good. Police roadblocks had already shut off the surrounding access roads. We couldn't hang about in the danger zone, so Zander drove past. We pulled up in a layby and Simone made some phone calls on our new mobile phone – a black, plastic brick with a three-inch aerial.

'Longstock – hundreds of people are gathering on a drove in Longstock!' Simone said, scrabbling for the map.

An hour later we were driving up the country road towards the drove.

'Up here, somewhere, should be on the left.' Simone lifted up the map and squinted at the detail.

'Can't see the mirror!' Zander objected.

'Sorry, Zander, but I'm just trying to get us there!' Simone lowered the map back onto her lap.

'Shit!' Zander hissed. 'Old Bill!'

A police van and two cars blocked the entrance to the track on the left. We drove past, Zander and me casually adjusting the peaks of our silver hats downward.

'What now?' I asked.

Simone lifted the map back up. 'There's no other way in unless we turn around. There's a farm track that looks like it might join up with the top end of the drove.'

'Mirror!' said Zander.

'For fuck's sake!' Simone crumpled the map onto her lap.

'So where do you want me to go?' asked Zander.

'If you'd let me look at the map, I could tell you – Je-sus!' Simone lifted the map again. 'Okay, turn around here.'

'Have we still got Debbie?' I tried to catch a glimpse in the mirror.

'Yeah,' said Zander, 'but I'm not sure about Hamish.'

Ten minutes later we were driving down a concrete farm track.

'Right, here,' said Simone.

'Here?' asked Zander.

'Yes! Here!' We bumped onto a grassy track that ran between fields of green wheat. 'Now this should bring us to the top of the drove.'

'Fuck it!' Zander snarled.

My heart sank. Fifty metres ahead of us was a closed farm gate, and standing in front of it, arms crossed, was a solitary copper. Debbie was right behind us, but Hamish hadn't reappeared.

'We could ram the fence.' Zander revved the engine a little harder.

'No, no, slow down and stay calm,' said Simone. 'Let me do the talking.'

Simone slid her window open as we came to a stop, and the copper, who looked no older than eighteen, came over.

'Sorry,' he said, shaking his head, arms still crossed, 'the track is closed.'

'Oh, hello officer.' Simone's attempt to sound surprised to see a lone policeman in the middle of a field didn't sound convincing, 'The problem is, you see, that we live here, onsite, with our families. We just popped out this morning to get some shopping, and now we need to get back to our kids, who are all alone – and extremely hungry.'

'What's in the back of the van?'

Someone in the back was singing. There was a heavy thud and giggling.

'Oh, just more children – we've got a few.' Simone turned to me and Zander. We both nodded enthusiastically.

The copper shook his head and started to say something but took off his helmet and scratched his head instead. He sighed and looked at us each in turn. We all looked back expectantly.

He glanced around. 'If my boss ever finds out about this, I'm in serious trouble!' He left the side of the van and opened the gate.

As we passed him, he smiled and said, 'Have a good party!'

•

The rough no man's land on either side of the drove was dotted with the occasional gorse bush and wind-stunted hawthorn. Zander drove slowly, trying to avoid the deepest ruts.

Ahead of us, on a wide curve of the track, a group of traveller's trucks came into view. I volunteered to get out and scout the area for a suitably flat spot. Zander and Debbie parked up while I walked ahead along the ancient road.

The ruts, which cut down through the turf into the stony ground, felt charged with all the journeys of those who'd passed along the route before.

I looked back at our blue newspaper truck and Debbie's little red post office van. *Delivery vans*, I thought, *and here we are, delivering music. Not just any music – new music. How many travelling musicians have, across the ages, trodden this exact same path?* Walking in that ancient landscape, I felt as if I shared the eyes, and excitement, of my ancestors – not only past ancestors but also those who would make the journey long after I'd gone.

As I came around a thick patch of gorse, I got a clear view along the drove. On either side were buses, trucks and trailers from every period in history going back to the 1950s. Abruptly rectangular 1970s buses, curvy coaches, squat military trucks, wood-panelled horseboxes, and further down I could see a collection of bow-top gypsy wagons, the tethered horses grazing beside them. Kids and dogs chased each other between the different camps, and blue wood smoke drifted in the air.

In the elbow of the curve, I found a large area – not exactly flat, but as good as it was going to get.

•

After a couple of hours we had the new NATO tent up. The sound system was unloaded and the speakers positioned either side of the gently sloping, rabbit-nibbled, springy-turfed dance floor. The music wasn't on – but the gennie was. Debbie was sorting out a crew kitchen area in the back of the tent – well, actually, it was less of a kitchen and more of an electric kettle, a box of teabags and some mugs, all neatly laid out on the lid of the decks' flight case.

Zander passed me a couple of red plastic cans of petrol from out the back of the van. He grabbed a clear plastic water bottle that had been cut to make an improvised funnel.

'What we doing with this lot?' he asked, slapping out a short drum-roll on the large cardboard box full of the flapjacks that Debbie, Simone and I had made the previous night.

'Living off them?' I suggested. 'In fact, chuck us a couple.'

Zander took out a handful of the film-wrapped bars and passed them to me. I tucked them into my bomber jacket pocket.

'Is this all the food we've got?' he asked, unwrapping one.

'Unless you brought anything else?'

'I'm already sick of them.' He took a bite. 'They're way too sweet.'

'Survival rations,' I said. 'Full of natural goodness!'

'Not sure how good they are,' he said with a mouthful, 'when most of the goodness gets stuck to your teeth.'

'Hamish said he was going to bring some supplies – wonder what's happened to him.'

Zander jumped down out of the truck. 'He knows the score. He's probably lying low somewhere, waiting for an opportunity to sneak in after dark.'

With the petrol and funnel we went round the back of the tent to where the gennie was in a gap in the hedge.

Over the relentless engine noise Zander lectured me about how dangerous it was to fill a generator while it was running. 'One drop of petrol on the hot exhaust – and boom!' He was so focused on telling me how it shouldn't be done that he ignored all his own advice. He held the funnel, I poured, and the gennie – hot exhaust and all – purred away appreciatively.

'I reckon we were the last people through that cordon,' I said, tightening the cap on the petrol can. 'That copper letting us through was a one-off miracle.' I wiped my petrol-covered hands onto my jeans and stood up. At that moment I heard a high-revving engine. Zander and I peered through the gap in the hedge. There, in the middle of the next field, was a white van, slipping and sliding in the mud. On the other side of the field, against the skyline, was a group of five or six coppers on foot, trying to give chase. The mud was clogging their boots and slowing them down to a moonwalk. All of them, except one.

The engine screamed. The wheels spun. Mud kicked into the air.

'What's going on?' asked Debbie, who'd come over with her cup of tea.

'Isn't that . . . Hamish?' I could hardly believe my eyes.

Simone came over. 'Come on, H!' she shouted.

I stuck my fingers in my mouth and let out a long piercing whistle.

People from the camp ran over to the hedge to see what all the commotion was about.

The copper was closing in on the van but, to avoid being pelted with mud from the rear wheels, had to approach on a wider circle. I glanced nervously along our edge of the field. Everyone was whistling and cheering like spectators at a friendly football match. But as the copper gained on the vehicle, I could see that the mood might flip. The image of a Celtic army ready to charge came to mind.

Just as the copper got level with the cab, the wheels took grip. The van lurched forward. It wildly zigzagged, pelting the copper with mud as it careered towards us.

Zander grabbed my arm. 'Quick! The gennie!'

It took a second for me to realise what he meant. 'Shit! The gennie!'

'Give him space,' Zander shouted as he and I pushed through the people and made for the petrol cans. 'He's heading for this gap!'

The crowd pulled back. Zander dragged the gennie. I grabbed the petrol cans. The sound of the screaming engine was upon us. I flung the cans aside and turned to see the van crash through the hedge and, with a crunch of metal, come to a stop on the spot where the gennie had been.

Still rocking on its springs, the mud-splattered van door opened and out stepped the huge figure of Hamish. Dressed in his loudly patterned baggy clothes, he took off his star-shaped sunglasses and pushed back the peak of his cap.

'In the fucking area!' he laughed, wiping his forehead with the back of his hand. He put the glasses back on. 'Right, who's gonna give us a hand unloading the merchandise?'

'Merchandise?' I glanced towards the gap in the hedge to see the mud-covered copper trudging back across the field towards his mates. 'What kind of merchandise?'

'I hope you brought more teabags,' said Debbie.

'And some proper food,' said Zander, making a point of sucking his teeth.

Hamish held up the van keys and jingled them. 'Teabags? Do I look like the kind of geezer who'd run untold roadblocks to smuggle teabags!' He walked round the back of the van. We eagerly followed.

Grinning proudly, Hamish opened the back doors. Stacked in amongst trestle tables, assorted cushions and rolls of bedding were large plastic jars and Tupperware boxes full of confectionery.

'Sweets?' Zander sounded close to tears.

Hamish didn't notice our exchange of glances as he launched into barrow-boy mode. 'Not just any old sweets.' He opened up a Tupperware box to show us the coloured sachets inside. 'Space Dust!' He opened up another. 'Jelly Dummies!'

Zander's face contorted. 'Jelly Dummies?'

'The ravers love 'em!' Hamish shook a sweet jar full of chemically coloured balls.' And these make your tongue go blue!'

•

As soon as the music was on, we had a tight group of perhaps a hundred dancers exploring the acoustic sweet spots in front of the speakers. We had a great crew of DJs with us – Stikka, Charlie Hall, Automanic, Hush-Hush, Karl K, Mickey – with Hubert and Kirsty on the mic. Stikka was playing that afternoon, though you couldn't see him in the shadow under the apex of the tent.

With the traveller's military trucks around us, the camouflage netting and the monolithic black speaker stacks, the sound system had the look of a guerrilla outpost – except that our fluorescent backdrops and pennant flags, decorated with spirals and the electrified grinning pirate skulls, added a surreal cartoon twist to the scene.

I'd just finished unfurling the last flag when Debbie came over and, so as to be heard over the music, leaned close to my ear. 'We've got a problem.'

'What kind of problem?' I stepped back to watch the pink and blue flag catch the breeze above the tent.

She came close again and cupped a hand around her mouth. 'Drug dealers – moving in!'

'Drug dealers? What kind of drugs?'

She leaned in close again and said in a loud whisper, 'LSD.'

'Oh, okay.'

'No, it's not the LSD that's the problem, it's *the moving in*.'

'What?'

'Into the bass bins.'

'Drug dealers in the bass bins?'

Debbie smiled and shook her head as if she had trouble believing it herself. 'Come and see for yourself.'

When we got to the other side of the dance floor, a bloke in a tweed flat cap was crawling around on the ground pegging out a small plastic tarpaulin he'd tied to the front of the speaker stack. Through the open door-flap of his makeshift tent, I could see he'd laid out two sleeping bags, the tops of which disappeared inside the bottom of the booming bass bin.

I tapped him on the shoulder. He looked up at me. He was in his late twenties, with a boyish face and mischievous smile. I raised a hand in greeting, then gestured that we move away from the speakers so we could hear each other talk. He followed me and Debbie round the back of the stack.

He took my hand and shook it. 'Awright, geezer – Tweedie. Was just having a word with Debz here.' He smiled at Debbie. 'She was saying she was going to ask you about me and my girl squatting your gaff.'

'Well,' I said, 'you won't get much sleep.'

'We ain't come all the way down from Lambeth to sleep!' He gave us a wink. 'But, I mean, if I'm in the way, you just tell me to shove off, it really ain't a problem.'

I looked at Debbie. She laughed. 'So long as you don't muffle the music!'

'Me? Muffle the music? Debz, please!'

'Okay.' I gave a shrug. 'But no campfires!'

He laughed. 'No worries, and er . . . ' He rummaged in his back pocket and brought out a polythene bag. 'Can I give you a trip? Lovely clean acid.' He opened up the bag and pulled out a sheet of white blotting paper.

'What are they?' I asked.

'Oms,' he said. 'Purple Oms, as it happens.'

'That might be a plan.' I raised my eyebrows at Debbie. 'Are you up for a bit of solstice acid?'

She stuck out her tongue to show me a tiny square of paper printed with a purple Sanskrit glyph. 'Way ahead of you!'

'In that case, yeah, thanks. But I haven't got any money.'

'Money? Geezer! What the fuck has *anything* got to do with money? But I tell you what, you haven't got any food, have you? I'm near enough starved.'

I reached into the pocket of my bomber. 'As it happens – flapjacks.' I brought out a handful. 'Homemade and very nutritious.'

'Flapjacks – now there's a blinding idea!' He carefully tore one of the tiny, perforated squares off the sheet, stuck out his tongue and nodded at me to mirror him. He put the blotter on the tip of my tongue.

'Lifesaver!' he said. 'And er … any time you wanna trade, you know where to find me.'

I nodded appreciatively and swallowed.

•

With the NATO tent fully loaded with DJs sitting on their record boxes, eagerly waiting to play, and the rig pumping good vibes into the early evening crowd, I went down the track to see the horses.

Our end of the drove was furthest from the main entrance, the one which had already been blocked by the police vehicles when we'd first arrived. I wound my way through the chaotically parked trucks and buses, passed DiY in their mishmash of tents, awnings and pink gauze flags. They too had a heaving dance floor, the crowd deeply submerged in slow, laid-back house music.

The further down the track I went, the more I became aware of the magnetic pull of the horse-drawn camp. When I arrived, there was nobody around apart from a small terrier who sat in the doorway of one of the wagons and pretended to be asleep. The intricately painted bow-tops and peacefully grazing horses were both surreal and, at the same time, intensely hyper-real. I felt as if I was buzzing between a scene from the past and an insight into the future. Continuing my walk down the drove, I went to look at the main entrance.

There were about fifteen cops standing across the bottom of

the track and several vans blocking the road behind them. But between them and me, between the festival and the outside world, was a huge brown puddle. It spanned the entire width of the drove, its muddy edges imprinted with tire tracks. And sitting in it, laughing, splashing and making mud pies, were four, very small, naked children. Their mums were standing close at hand, apparently not enjoying the moment.

Coming up to the shoreline of what to the little kids must have been a lake, I was shocked to realise that the police – including their puffed-up boss, who was strutting up and down – were hurling abuse at the women.

'Look at the state of your kids!'

'Living in filth!'

'It's disgusting!'

'You're a disgrace!'

The women were clearly disturbed by the relentless insults but did their best to ignore them. The kids were too busy having fun to take any notice. I stood there aghast. What kind of deprived, sterile childhoods did these coppers have? There is something so pure and elemental about playing in a big, beautiful puddle. I know, as kids, me and Zander made the most of every puddle we came across, big or small – and this was a corker! It's what puddles are for. It's what being a child is about. It's one of the single best connections we have as children with the Earth.

Behind the women stood an enormous ex-military truck. It was clearly four-wheel drive, its rounded snout and hunched wheel arches giving it the character of a monstrous pit bull. It was just sitting there, keeping an eye on the jeering coppers and their flimsy little roadblock.

The kids ran off chasing each other with mud pies, and the mums followed. The cops shuffled about, then drifted back to their vans. The monster truck stood calmly by. A huge sculptural beast, built as a military transporter, but whose reincarnation as a guardian of this other-dimensional world would never have been guessed by its military owners or manufacturers. To know that you had to be standing on this side of the police line. This side of the muddy puddle. The fun side.

•

Communities all around the world celebrate the solstice. Regardless of local belief systems, everyone that participates is aware, even if it's only for a few moments, of the greater whole of our beloved planet and its spin around our local star. Yes, it's cosmic – but in a very down to Earth way.

That night our dance floor moved as a super-organism. Locked into the heartbeat of the sound system. Everybody was an integral and vital part. Conscious of the spinning planet and our ride around the sun.

Finding Stonehenge ringed with police roadblocks on that first day had made me angry. But having been displaced by the authorities to find a haven on that ancient roadway made a new kind of sense. Stonehenge, it now seemed clear, was built to lay claim to a geographical, astrological and spiritual territory. A temple to the trickery of the priesthoods, the brutality of the military and the power of the wealthy. Stonehenge was a monument to hierarchical power and control. Stonehenge? They could keep it. We'd escaped its dark gravity and were now flowing with other currents.

•

At dawn, thin layers of mist drifted low over the wet grass of the fields into the sunken drove and across our dance floor. Overnight orbits had shifted. Overnight we'd moved away from the notion of 'home'. Overnight we'd become nomads.

STONEY CROSS: JUNE 1991

Nomads or not, when it was time to leave, we had to fix the van. The 'F' and 'I' from the van's livery had peeled off to leave us with the word 'Nancial', which had become her pet name. That wasn't the problem – the battery was flat. Luckily the lads from DiY gave us a jump start and we trundled down the drove towards the main exit – and the police.

Ahead of us the mighty pit bull truck made its exit in style. Taking the great puddle at speed, it threw up a muddy wave that got the lines of sneering cops running for cover and swamped their white vans. Following one by one, our vehicles also took the plunge. We were back on the open road.

Next on the list of free festivals was Stoney Cross. It was just half an hour's drive south from where we were. Simone and Debbie volunteered to shoot ahead in Debbie's post office van to scout the place. We'd decided that it was smarter to reccy the area first, without risking the rig, in case there were any roadblocks or nasty rubber-gloved surprises.

A couple of hours later, Debbie and Simone returned to the layby where they'd left us, all smiles and super excited.

'It's amazing! Wild horses! In a forest! Magical!' said Debbie.

'An airbase! Abandoned! No cops!' said Simone.

We jumped back in our vehicles and gave chase to Debbie's van.

The New Forest is 300 square kilometres of heath and woodland on the Wiltshire–Hampshire border. Stoney Cross is a flat plateau in the centre of the forest. The spot that Debbie and Simone had found was right on the edge of the old airfield. A large circle, perhaps twenty metres across, of the most beautiful springy turf, with a low grassy bank all around the outer edge. I guess it had once been a stand for the planes, or a turning circle. Whatever its history, it now formed the most luxurious outdoor dance floor, and to make it even better, it stood on the edge of a steep drop that fell away into a thickly wooded valley.

There was nobody else there. Only us and the wild horses. Which was strange because, as it was so close to the festival site we'd just left, we'd expected at least some others to come. This made us a little nervous at first, so we didn't immediately set up. But after a few hours we got bored of waiting and put the tent up. A couple of lads we'd recently met, Billy and Tom, lashed a simple pyramid of timber together to hang up our single strobe, UV strip and smoke machine. That done, we fired up the rig. As soon as we did, the horse-drawn convoy of six wagons appeared on the horizon and pulled up onsite. Across the afternoon more traveller vehicles arrived. After dark the ravers came, and by midnight we had a full dance floor.

Around the campfire we met a young crew from Winchester who had a bag of White Dove Ecstasy pills, which they shared freely with everyone there. The Doves were particularly strong and had a very nice optical effect. Seb, minus his 303 but still in his orange coat, and I had one each and got into a deep conversation about music and geometry as we walked around the perfect circle and explored the edges of the woodland.

The geometry highjacked our conversation as the Doves overlaid everything with interlacing techno patterns. *Maybe it was the music generating the techno patterns? Or was it the people on the dance floor?* Whatever it was, it got us hugely enthusiastic as we explored ideas of frequency, rhythm and harmony. We came to the bottom of the slope and paused. There was silence, only broken by the screech of a distant night bird. In our enthusiasm we'd scrambled down the edges of the valley into the woodland below. It hadn't occurred to us that we were walking in complete darkness because of the glow of the techno patterns and the amplified starlight that hammered down through the leaves. In that silent pause we both seemed to be on exactly the same wavelength.

'You know what we should do?' said Seb.

And I answered, 'Make our own music! A Spiral Tribe record!' It was the single most obvious thing in the whole entire universe.

The silence deepened as the profundity of our shared insight sunk in.

Seb laughed. 'Damn, now we're lost!'

'Nah, we just need to walk back up the hill,' I replied, stumbling over a root and bumping into a tree.

It took us a few more minutes of scrambling through the tangle of neon until we heard the music again and got our bearings. When we arrived back at the dance floor, DJ Kaos Ray was playing a set of twisting acid, and it was clear that the swirling centre of the dance floor was indeed the source of the techno patterns.

The fact that none of us had any money, studio equipment or knew anything about making records didn't matter. What mattered was the clarity of the vision, which was made all the more vivid by the new connection between Seb and me. It was clear from that moment an important friendship had begun.

The party went on uninterrupted until Monday. It was a good run. Mainly because we were miles from anywhere and not disturbing anyone. But that's not what the cops thought. They'd arrived in small numbers, one car sitting there watching. But as we began to pack up, more arrived. By the time we had Nancial loaded there were five or six nosing around, including a sergeant who spoke with me. He seemed more curious than openly hostile.

I asked him why they bothered coming to harass us, and he replied, 'We've had a complaint.'

'Seriously? Out here?'

'From over twelve miles away.'

'From over twelve miles away?' I could see that he too didn't really believe what he was saying.

He offered a possible explanation. 'A lot of people don't like travellers. They might have seen you were here, perhaps walking their dog, and complained when they got home. Just because they phoned from twelve miles away doesn't mean they could hear the music.' He smiled wearily. Now, get this lot cleared up – and go!'

Again, Nancial wouldn't start. Clearly the problem we'd had leaving the drove was more than a flat battery.

'The alternator?' Kaos Ray suggested as he turned the key

in the dead ignition again and again – and again. More police arrived. Debbie pulled out an RAC card. Simone pulled out the brick phone. Twenty minutes later, complete with flashing amber lights, a recovery low-loader winched Nancial onto its back.

We were away, leaving the perfect circle as perfect as we'd found it. The police were left wandering about. Some chatting, some enjoying the sunshine. I noticed the sergeant standing alone on the furthest edge of the circle, hands on hips, looking out over the forest. I supposed he was pondering the truth of the spurious complaint – or perhaps he was just admiring the view.

THE DEVIL'S PUNCH BOWL: JULY 1991

The crew from Winchester had invited us to come and do a party with them the following weekend in a spot they called The Devil's Punchbowl. After we got a new alternator fitted, we were happy to oblige, especially as they told us that the spot was 'crop-circle-central!' It was a beautiful journey across an undulating landscape of green wheat and golden barley fields. And as we neared the secret location, more and more crop circles became visible on the hillsides.

We all enjoyed speculating about extra-terrestrials, but we had no serious belief that the designs were made by UFOs or any other inexplicable phenomenon. But what I'd always found interesting was what motivated the creators of these vast shapes. Is it just to prank the public? Is it a form of artistic expression? Or is it a combination of the two? Perhaps an urge to conjure a mystery with elemental geometry? For me, the very ambiguous nature of the works and their geometric form fitted perfectly with my own sensibilities. I often asked myself: *Is mathematics a language or a structure? Or a language that describes a structure – and if so, what is that invisible structure without the language to describe it?*

We arrived late in the afternoon. The Punchbowl was a large, shallow depression in the expanse of open fields. Simone expertly navigated us down a bumpy farm track to its centre, where a building had once stood. There was nothing left of it above ground apart from a rectangular scar where the walls had once been. Deep foundations had shielded the area from the farmer's plough and given us a perfectly flat, grassy dance floor. A solid island in a gently rolling sea of barley.

It was a small party. Just us and our new friends from Winchester. And their big bag of Love Doves.

After a beautiful night of darkness and stars, with little touches of strobe, the sun rose as a huge Egyptian disc above the ripening fields. In rhythm with the summer breeze, crop circles swirled through the oceans of techno gold.

•

'We need to go back to London,' said Simone as we loaded up the rig that evening.

'I could do with some clean clothes,' agreed Kaos Ray, 'and I got boxes of blinding tunes at home.' He affectionately slapped the top of his record box. 'This is just the tip of the iceberg!'

Debbie, who was still dancing even though the music had been off for a while, joined in. 'We need to get Zander!'

'And Joe.' Simone added. 'Just a quick in and out mission.'

Since solstice we'd lost track of time. It had all been a euphoric flow of dance music and happy people. When we got back, London felt stagnant. Familiar streets that only a few weeks ago I would have felt at home in now felt strangely empty – despite the people.

We pulled up outside the Green House. Simone ran up the steps to see if she could find Joe and Zander. I opened up the roller-shutter door on the back of Nancial to let the passengers out. We'd made it pretty comfortable in the back with foam mattresses and duvets on top of the sound system. Everyone got out to stretch. I was still standing at the back of the van arranging the empty petrol cans when I looked up to see Stikka coming out of the Green House.

'Awright?' I smiled as he approached.

'Nah!' he scowled.

I was confused. And the confusion deepened when I noticed that we had an audience. Every single window of the three-storey Green House was now open, and from each window – plus the balcony and the steps up to the front door – the residents were watching. Their faces sullen, yet expectant. Clearly, they all knew something that I didn't.

'What's the problem?' I asked.

'What's the problem?' Stikka growled. 'Where the fuck have you been?'

'Been?' I was at a loss to understand.

Stikka stood there, looked around at the spectators, then turned back to me. He picked up a large pillow-sized wedge of yellow foam from the back of the van, lifted it as if he was going to start a pillow fight, then changed his mind. He pushed it towards me to hold, then reached into the back of the van and pulled out the tent, which was tightly stowed in its green canvas bag.

'The tent! You fucked off with the tent.' He dropped its heavy weight onto the road and dragged it back towards the steps. The group gathered there helped him carry it up the steps and into the house. The front door closed. The people at each window turned away. I was left standing there holding the piece of yellow plastic foam. It was a surreal moment.

The Green House door opened again, and Simone came out.

'What the fuck was that all about?' I asked.

'Oh, the usual.'

I stood there bewildered.

She added, 'They all think we've totally lost the plot on acid and have no idea what we're doing.'

'What's that got to do with anything?'

'Fucked if I know!' she said, busying herself with coiling a cable that was dangling out the back. 'Anyway, who needs a tent – we've got the sky!'

I smiled.

She continued, 'Zander's not back yet. Let's find Joe – and get out of this town!'

•

Zander was still in Spain. He too was also having a surreal moment. He later told us that he'd been eyeing up an empty villa that he thought might be nice to squat. Eager to show off his climbing skills to the girls he was with, he'd scaled the high walls and dropped down into the courtyard – only to be attacked by two Dobermans. Luckily, he escaped unhurt. He later found out that the house was Salvador Dali's – now a museum.

Joe, on the other hand, was at his mum's round the corner.

DEVON: JULY 1991

After Debbie and I had grabbed our paints and brushes from Walterton Road, we all headed west again. Deep west. Towards Croyde, Devon. It was Paul Brash's suggestion. He was something of a diver and knew the area as a mecca for surfers. If we wanted ravers, Croyde, Paul reassured us, was the place.

Near Croyde, on the north coast of Devon, we found an isolated beach with a great little park up in the dunes. Charlie Hall had driven down with Automanic Josh from London in his old-school VW bubble bus. Paul Brash was there in his VW T3 camper. And then there was our little convoy of battered delivery vans.

While we'd been in London, Kaos Ray had managed to grab a load more of his records. He had a monster collection and a passion to match.

Despite the ever-present desire to organise a party, we decided to take a break and chill out for the weekend. That afternoon, Charlie and Josh had to get back to London for another gig, so we said our goodbyes. As the sun set, Kaos Ray volunteered to cook us all a special dinner.

'Rice and chilli,' he said, 'with extra spice?'

A little after dark, I went around the side of Paul's van where

Kaos was minding the pots bubbling on the gas cooker. He was sitting on one of his many cubed record boxes, busily shuffling through the sleeves.

'Sorting your next set?' I asked.

'Nah, I had some real classic acid at home, and I stashed it inside one of these sleeves for safekeeping.'

'Acid-acid? Or *acid*-acid?' I asked.

He looked up from the box with a big grin. '*Acid*-acid! From a few years back, I saved it for a special occasion. Here we go!' His eyes lit up as he held out a handful of small, cling-film-wrapped squares. 'These are the bollocks! Pink-Floyd-The-Walls!'

'Bloody Hell, they're . . . legendary!'

'Totally!'

'But they're strong – I mean crazy strong, right?'

'I reckon around 500 mics.' His smile got bigger.

'Gosh.'

'But they're a few years old now...'

'But still . . . 500 mics.'

'Yeah, maybe I should just put a little bit in.'

'In?'

'The chilli.'

'Why not,' I shrugged, 'but hang on, everyone's starving – better check they're all up for it.'

Of course they were.

The chilli was delicious – the best food we'd had in weeks. Kaos Ray scraped the last of it from the pan, and we finished it all. Debbie filled the kettle and put it on the gas. It was very cosy sitting around chatting in our little encampment, nestled in the dunes. After an hour or so I could feel the acid:

brighter colours, a strong sense of connection and camaraderie. I guessed Kaos Ray had been right: the blotters hadn't lasted well and weren't so strong. At least that's what I thought, until I nipped around the back of the vans to have a piss.

It was a beautiful night. The darkness felt comforting. Safe. The air was clean, freshened by the sound of the sea. The wind rattled the clumps of dune grass and I could even hear the grains of sand blowing across the dune's rippled surface, giving visible form to some of the currents that shape the coastline. The stars. *So bright – so . . . wild!* It was an epic piss. Then, halfway through, a skeleton wearing a very fancy ostrich-plumed headdress sprang up out of the sand and snapped its teeth in my face. I jumped back in shock. My heart pounding. My leg wet.

As suddenly as it had appeared, it disappeared back into the sand. I tried to control my breathing and suppress the panic. I reassured myself: *it's the acid, just the acid – but fuck . . . it's strong!* This calmed me a little, and with no sign of lurking skeletons I stepped forward and resumed my business. As soon as I was in mid-flow, it happened again. A snarling, snapping skeleton. Right in my face. My fear reflex kicked me backwards again. *It's the acid, just the acid . . . but hang on, what's this all about? The fucker is trying to scare me. It's winding me up!* My fear flipped and I began laughing.

As is often the case with strong acid, the oscillations between terror and elation are so fast that there's no time to stay scared. As soon as I remembered this, I was in on the joke. Then all the clumps of dune grass around me became headdresses, and an army of jack-in-the-box skeletal warriors popped up and down, in and out of the sand, gnashing their teeth.

The grimace and fanned headdresses were becoming a theme. I'd first noticed it on the tour launch flyer I'd designed for our Cable Street party. A design where I was not consciously creating a grinning face crowned with plumes, but a reversible face that remained the same when turned upside down. More a case of tracing the geometry rather than trying to create a particular character.

I zipped myself up and peered around the back of the van at the others sitting in the pool of yellow light outside Paul's camper van.

'How much acid did you put in that chilli?' I called to Kaos Ray.

'All of it!' he replied, his normally pale freckled face now animated with squirming tattoos.

We didn't really need to wash up, at least not at that exact moment. But I think, for me, it was more a test of will. Each of us took our plates down to the sea. To get there we had to negotiate the rock pools that were exposed at low tide. Paul Brash had a powerful new diving torch, the bright beam of which now appeared dangerously solid. The sea was a mix of metallic black liquid and monstrous eels. I rinsed my plate as best I could, considering the circumstances.

'Tea, anyone? Debbie asked from somewhere in the slithering darkness. I ducked as Paul's solid column of light swept around and bumped her on the head. Her face popped and twisted into a million versions of an angelic alien-imp. I declined her offer, thinking that I preferred the company of the writhing sea rather than watching my friends sipping tea as they melted, sprouted and blossomed into demonic flower fairies.

Instead, Paul Brash and I ran away along the beach, throwing his rubberised diving torch into rock pools. And I don't mean we plopped it in and watched it sink. I mean we took it in turns to hurl it, spinning, as high as possible into the night sky. Its intense beam creating spoked wheels of gold that whirled up into deepest space. Spectacular as this was, the real surprise was the splashdown. As soon as the torch returned to Earth and plunged into a rock pool, its light became trapped under the surface and illuminated the glassy colours of the aquatic world. Filigrees of crimson and emerald green. Semi-transparent red anemones. Spiney orange urchins. Grey and purple crabs. Pink starfish and weedy bunches of blue-violet mussels striped with iridescent mother-of-pearl. But it wasn't only the dazzling pools of colour that delighted us. The trapped light flowed freely into all the pools that were interconnected. So wherever the torch landed, jewel-like archipelagos of treasure would suddenly switch on all around us.

•

The following weekend, the police got wind of our plans to have a party in an overgrown quarry. They weren't aggressive, just adamant it wasn't happening. They blocked the roads and, when we left, followed us in a Land Rover up onto the high, wide and wild spaces of Exmoor.

On Sunday morning at first light we got tired of being followed and pulled up in a spot where there was nothing but us, an empty horizon and a huge dawn sky. We rolled the speakers out, plugged in – and played. They parked up and watched but made no attempt to stop us.

After the all-night drive, there were probably only about fifty die-hard party people still with us. But that didn't matter. We were dancing on top of the world, hands reaching up into the stratosphere. The police remained Earthbound and just sat in their Land Rover looking bored. But their presence was still a niggling reminder that the chain of command they worked under claims all territories. Even the uninhabited wilds.

We didn't care. Like the kids in the puddle, we were too busy appreciating the joy of life to give a fuck about how the old dysfunctional power structures were wasting their time watching us.

LLYN TEGID: JULY 1991

The following weekend we travelled 200 miles north to the next festival on the magic list. The Happy Daze free festival, near Llyn Tegid in Wales, or Lake Bala as the English like to call it.

The site was in a flat-bottomed valley, on meadowland, divided by ancient hedgerows that had matured to full-grown trees. The fields had recently been mown for hay. In the late July sunshine, the ground was dry and golden, in contrast with the lush greenery of the hills on either side. The lake was further down the valley, and in the distance we could see the foothills and mountains of Snowdonia.

When we arrived on Saturday there were already hundreds of traveller's vehicles and tents sprinkled across the fields. Old military trucks, coaches, decommissioned ambulances, caravans and lots of cars that clearly belonged to people that didn't normally live on the road. The trees and tarped awnings created much-needed shade, but most people were all-out bare-shouldered and burnt in the hot sun. Kids and dogs ran around kicking up dust. Music, of one sort or another, blared from all directions. But there was nothing with a bassline.

The atmosphere on site was one of friendship and solidarity. I often hear stories, only ever second or third hand, of friction between 'travellers' and 'ravers'. I never once witnessed it. Labelling one section of the same group as *different* is a dangerous trap. People might enjoy carelessly gossiping, but even that can be weaponised in the campaign of divide and rule.

The thing that struck me about all the festivals I went to as a teenager, and the more recent raves, was what they had in common. Openness. Sharing and the sense of community. There were occasional moments of arseholes being arseholes, but that happens in any large movement and doesn't mean it's representative of the entire group. Of course, you're going to get someone appointing themselves as an arbiter of who, or what, is worthy, who or what is in or out, but these complaints are very often from individuals who are still under the spell of the old hierarchical institutions. They may reject the old establishment's claim on territory, but they, perhaps without realising it, are then laying their own territorial claim on the alternative. It's the exact same mindset.

•

After a beautiful party on Saturday night, the morning was hot and sunny. Hamish got a little petrol generator running and plugged in the hair clippers. Whenever the clippers were out, a queue formed. Hamish's mood was for something a little more creative than just a bonehead. Justin and Sanchia, new friends we'd met over the weekend, were both treated to a rather unique style of mohican. Not centred on the top of the head – more skewed to one side. Not of parallel width – fatter in the middle and tapered at both ends. Not high and spiky – but chopped-n-low. Sanchia looked at the finished result in the wing mirror of the truck.

'It looks like you've slapped a kipper on my head!'

And so the summer of silly haircuts began, with the lop-sided 'kipper-cut' being particularly popular.

TORPEDO TOWN: AUGUST 1991

The first weekend of August was Torpedo Town. The festival had its roots in a peace camp that was set up in 1982 to protest against GEC-Marconi starting construction of a research and development building for the production of Spearfish and Stingray anti-submarine torpedoes. The camp did manage to slow the construction of the building but not prevent it. So, in 1984, an annual protest festival was organised. The name Torpedo Town stuck, as did its anti-war ethos.

The site for that year's festival was Ministry of Defence land near Liphook, on the Hampshire–Surrey border. Again, Debbie and Simone had gone ahead in the post office van to reccy the site.

'It's pukka!' was their official report back.

When we arrived with the rig, the site was already crowded,

though it was difficult to know how many hundreds, or even thousands, of people were there, as the area was overgrown with birch, sycamore and pine. DiY, Sweat and Stikka with the Fundamental crew were also there.

Debbie and Simone had scouted out a large, flat clearing. Underfoot was mossy tarmac and gravel. Parked along the edges of the space were two buses, one with an awning roped off its roof to form 'The Brainstorm café', run by a bloke called Rob Universe. It was decorated with full-size figures constructed of rolled paper tubes painted in fluorescent colours. A few metres further around the glade was the other old bus. Daubed all along its side, in large letters, were the words 'Free Party People!'

While Simone got the rig on, Debbie and I unpacked the backdrops. When I say *unpacked*, I mean un-scrunched them from the back of the truck where somebody had been using them as bedding. A souvenir hunter had stolen all our flags at Llyn Tegid. It was a bit dispiriting as a huge amount of time and care had gone into painting them. Luckily, we still had heaps of camouflage netting. We untangled it as best we could and draped it over the speaker stacks. Instantly we had that dangerous guerrilla-camp look, which was in contrast to our few surviving fluorescent backdrops. Debbie and I smoothed them out on the ground, looked around at the tall trees, looked back down at the large, coloured sheets, then back up at the trees. As we stood there scratching our heads, a tall chap with long dreads came over and introduced himself as 'Mr Free-Party-People, from the bus next door'.

After a friendly chat, it was confirmed: he had a huge coil of rope that he'd stretch across the diameter of the clearing, and on it he'd attach all our backdrops, plus his equally fluorescent 'Free Party People' banners. We handed ours over, and within the hour he had them all flying high across the vast new dance floor.

On a mission to replace the missing flags, Debbie and I rummaged through the piles of bedding that had accumulated in the back of the truck. Anything we deemed 'surplus to requirements' was sacrificed for the greater cause. Once we'd found what we needed, we cut up the fabric and taped it onto our outdoor easel – the side of the tuck.

The edges of the new flags were ragged, but we decided that the raw look was part of the style. That style being: frontline flags that had seen some seriously hardcore action – when in reality they were all chopped out of a threadbare duvet cover with a pair of blunt scissors. The only paint we had was fluorescent powder paint and the metallic silver I'd bought in Drury Lane.

We still only had one UV striplight, a Moonflower and one strobe, all of which were generous long-term rentals from Rudi. So far, these had been more than enough, especially as nature was providing us with plenty of fiery sunsets, clear night skies and misty blue dawns.

With our limited resources, I thought it would be interesting to maximise the optical effect of both the strobe and UV strip. The idea was to use fluorescent paint as the background colour and silver for the main motif. In this way, at night, when the strobe flicked off, the silver paint appeared black against the bright UV-active background. When the strobe flashed on, the silver reflected the intense strobe light and became the brightest part of the design, while the glowing background colour remained more or less constant. The tonal shift from black to brilliant silver was dramatic.

My mood was for circles and semicircles connected with straight lines. They were infinitely modular and variable, so we just started painting and allowed them to grow. The shapes they made resonated with the enigmatic images that were illegally popping up all over Britain – and I don't just mean the crop circles. They also had some semblance to the geometric patterns that only showed themselves with the use of outlawed psychedelics.

'Looks like we've invented an alien language,' I said to Debbie when we stopped for a cup of tea.

'We have,' she said. 'It's called *Technoglyphic*.'

To my knowledge that was the first coining of the word and its variant, *Technoglyph* – a single motif or character – and the word immediately entered the Spiral lexicon.

Debbie's ability to create words, and give shape to the shapeless, did not end there. She was also going to come up with a monumental word which, when spoken out loud or written down, would invoke a wild and powerful spirit. A spirit that would sweep around the world. But that didn't happen at Torpedo Town – that happened later.

While we silently painted, we moved to the music. It was a meditative process. I thought about the Technoglyphs, crop circles, printed circuit boards and psychedelic geometric patterns. I loved the shared symbolism. Just as the shape of the spiral didn't require any explanation, so our Technoglyphs didn't require the linear logic of language to function. The Technoglyphs invited the observer to make their own connections, their own synaptic sparks.

If on Friday there'd been hundreds of people hidden from view in the forest, by Saturday afternoon there were thousands, all out in the open – and many of them on our dance floor. Our biggest crowd yet.

Simone, Debbie and I were minding Hamish's bar while he'd gone to dance. The bar was his new venture, having given up on the Candy Store idea. Breaking through police lines and crash-landing van loads of Jelly Dummies into the solstice party was spectacular but not hugely lucrative. Being a walking advert for his loudly patterned rave wear may or may not have been an entrepreneurial success, but as a dance floor power-house, Hamish was second to none.

Debbie, Simone and I each had a sticky carton of squash in hand – a perk for minding the bar. The three of us looked out across the scene. Our big spiral banners flew high above the crowd. Out in the sea of people, towering above every-one else, Hamish had found the system's sweet spot. His body was locked into the music, and with big, generous moves, he showed the whole world exactly where the groove was.

'Not bad for just 5K of sound,' said Simone before slurping the last of her juice through its little bent straw.

Debbie and I nodded our agreement in time to the music. What we were witnessing wasn't only our small rig's techni-cal capability but also the moment we first glimpsed the full potential of Spiral Tribe's pulling power. At solstice we'd real-ised we were happiest 'on the road'. At Torpedo Town we saw which road we were on.

With a slurp Debbie drained her carton. 'Right, I'm off for a dance! Coming, Simone?'

They launched themselves off into the swell of bodies towards Hamish. I finished my drink and turned back to the bar.

Standing right behind me, in full uniform – including a pointy helmet – was a copper. It was an awkward moment. I didn't know how long he'd been standing there. *What had he seen? What had he heard?* We were clearly selling cans of beer without a licence, which, in Britain, was often used by police to immediately close down events and make arrests. But the expression on his face was relaxed and friendly. He was even, very discreetly, allowing his body to sway with the music. His relaxed demeanour appeared to be infectious as he was drawing no hostility or heckling from the crowd.

With nothing to lose, I decided the best course of action was to say hello.

He smiled and said, 'This is wild!'

I agreed but was suspicious – not necessarily because he was probably spying on us, but because he genuinely seemed to be enjoying himself. It was weird.

We got into some small talk, but I needed to know. 'You haven't got a problem with us – with this?' I purposefully gestured away from the bar towards the general throng.

'This?' He loosened his shoulders with a rhythmic wiggle. 'This is great!' It was then that I noticed that the badge on his helmet was a little different than regular police.

'So you're Military Police?' I asked.

'Yep.' He raised an eyebrow and smiled.

'And you don't mind this . . . *lawlessness?*' I laughed as he was now gyrating his hips.

'Cheers the place up!'

'And you're getting paid to party?'

He smiled. 'Oh, if only you knew!' He wagged a telling finger at me, and just before he turned to leave, he did an impression of Groucho Marx smoking and flicking ash. I watched him walk away. I tried to process what he meant by this cryptic mime. Then after a couple of steps, as if he could feel me trying to figure him out, he turned back to me, grinning and again flicking ash off his invisible . . . *cigar? spliff?* He seemed to know exactly what I was thinking and nodded knowingly, then disappeared into the crowd, laughing.

CHELTENHAM: AUGUST 1991

The site of our next party was in a remote part of the Cotswolds, in a recently harvested wheat field, with large stacks of straw bales making perfect dance podiums. Kids in floppy hats and baggy clothes showed off their moves as if translating the music into hand signals – communicating the groove far and wide in a rave version of semaphore.

On the Sunday, the local TV news reported 1,500 ravers had attended. The police responded by blocking us in and giving us the ultimatum: 'Pack up and leave, or get arrested.'

We turned off, tidied up and loaded the rig. As soon as that was done, the police arrested us and everyone else that had stayed behind to help. Thirty people in total.

At the police station we were all locked up. After we'd each been separately interviewed by CID detectives – about the apparent disappearance of a generator from a licensed 'pop concert' in the nearby town of Cheltenham – they let us go, saying, 'It was good to chat with some nice people rather than the same old local rogues.'

The same old local rogues may well have been *old*, but their age had obviously taught them some cunning. They'd got clean away with a stolen gennie while we, in the naivety of our youth, had been put under mass arrest and locked up all day for nothing more than dancing.

PART 2

To Tough

ARUNDEL: AUGUST 1991

Droves, stone circles, burial mounds and hill forts are some of the archaeological remains that visibly shape the British countryside. The atmosphere of many of these places is mysterious and magical. And that magic is not lessened when one delves into their archaeology and science.

The South Downs is a long range of chalk and flint hills on the south coast. They stretch 87 miles (140 km) from St Catherine's Hill in Winchester to Beachy Head, near Eastbourne. The south side of the Downs is one of the most densely populated areas of Britain, with many large towns and cities squashed between its steep slopes and the sea. On top, the terrain rolls with deep folds, secret blind valleys and high vantage points. Look north and you look over England. Look south and you're looking out over the English Channel. If you take the high ground, as the chieftains of the past did, you could take control of the landscape and its resources. But if you find the right wrinkle in the hills, you could have a huge party and no one would know.

We arrived at the next festival site on the list, Cissbury Ring Hillfort, late on Thursday, pulled up in the visitor's carpark and got some sleep. Early on Friday morning, just as we were waking up, Martin arrived.

Martin was a torchbearer, carrying the eternal flame and spirit of the free festivals. He was the author, printer and distributor of the festival list. The flame he'd been so carefully tending was starting to burn bright again – but perhaps not in the way he'd imagined.

He was a shy, quiet guy with thinning hair, an olive-green combat jacket and multiple shoulder bags, which I presumed were full of photocopies of festival information. We'd met him in passing a couple of times before, once at the solstice festival and once at Torpedo Town. On both occasions he didn't take us particularly seriously, or he didn't like dance music – or perhaps both. But he was too polite to be explicitly rude. He simply smiled and went quiet when we jumped about proclaiming, 'Techno is the sound of the future! Techno will unite the world! Techno will save the planet!'

That seemed to have changed at Cissbury. He now clearly understood that we walked our talk and, whether we would actually succeed with our rather ambitious agenda, our intentions were good. We were anti-authoritarian. We were audacious. We showed up – and we didn't back down.

He had a plan. At least he had half a plan. The carpark we'd slept in was in full view of the hillfort, which was a popular tourist destination, and the road. With our small number of vehicles, if the cops did show up – highly likely as the site was next on the list – it would be easy for them to stop the festival before it even got going. He suggested that we should leave the carpark and hide out at a meeting point ten miles west. That way we could get a bigger group of vehicles together and take the site en masse.

We spread our map out on the bonnet of Debbie's van and he showed us the place he had in mind. We jumped in the vehicles and set off west along the Downs.

•

It was already afternoon, and the clock was ticking. At Llyn Tegid, Justin had decided to travel with us in his old bus, or as we now called it, The Techno Bus. Justin's bus wasn't the only new vehicle in our convoy, as we were also beginning to accumulate other ravers who'd latched on to the fact that we were the sound system. As we headed west the convoy grew, and we began to worry we'd attract the attention of any passing patrols.

We soon found the off-road parking area that Martin had suggested, on Bury Hill. But it was still in clear view of the main road. Despite this, we pulled up. It was getting late, and the longer we hung about in the open, the riskier things became.

Martin had not got back to us with the second half of his plan. We took out the map again and discussed alternative sites. Big Reggie, who had joined us at solstice, Hamish, Steve, Zander, Simone, Debbie and I all crowded around the map on Debbie's bonnet, tracing fingers over deeply contoured valleys, hill forts and old farm tracks – but it was difficult to choose, especially with so many of us getting excited about this or that place.

'No-no–NO! Simone's voice managed to break through our over-excited babble. There was silence, apart from Simone's fingernail tapping on the map.

'Look – here. It's in the middle of nowhere, in a forest, easy access, plenty of parking, nice and flat.'

We all squeezed in to see exactly where her finger was, but Simone turned and took a few steps.

'Look at this place! It's perfect!

We turned and watched Simone walk across the parking area towards a large picnic site, complete with wooden benches and tables. There it was, staring us all in the face.

The grassy area along the edge of the forest was long and wide and curved away from the main road. We drove as far down as we could and started rolling the speaker cabs out the back of the truck. Halfway through setting up, a chap in a leather cowboy hat came over and asked if we'd like to use the back of his car transporter truck as a stage. He had it in the carpark and would be happy to drive it over. It had a big flatbed platform with vertical side bars that were the perfect height and position to hold a canvas roof. Zander, being a climber, knew all the necessary knots to lash and tighten a large tarpaulin up the back and over the top, leaving the stage front open. For a spontaneous stage, thrown together in twenty minutes, it was very professional.

Even though the picnic site was on top of the Downs, surrounded by forest and with no neighbours, it was a quick and easy drive to some of Britain's most densely populated towns, the nearest being clustered all along the south coast – from Southhampton and Portsmouth in the west to Worthing and Brighton in the east. And just one hour south of London. This meant, of course, that of all the picnics held on that particular weekend, Spiral Tribe's was probably the biggest and liveliest on the entire planet – though *lively* is probably an understatement.

The Friday night was huge, with an atmosphere of pure joy and celebration. An atmosphere that, as the night sky turned to a deep-blue dawn, only got better. As the sun rolled up into the clear sky, the crowd's energy blossomed. The dance floor grew into the edges of the forest and further back into the carpark. Everybody seemed to be sharing the same rising euphoria. Rather than getting exhausted, the longer we danced the more energy we generated. The vibe kept rising higher and

higher. And just when we thought it couldn't get any better –
that tune came on.

To call it an anthem would do it a disservice. An anthem
gets everyone up and moving, hands in the air, whoops and
cheers. This tune did that – and more. It went deeper, and that
was just the sub-bass.

The intro is a low growl that oscillates upward into an alien
chatter. Then the monstrous sub-bass starts to breathe rhyth-
mically. The sound of circling seagulls is incongruous and
disorientating. Absurdist vocal samples recite: *The doors are
where the windows should be – and windows are where the doors
should be.* These elements map out a surreal and disturbing
soundscape. Then, with a comical burst, skipping breakbeats
and impish bleeps jump into the action. It's a classic, not only
because of its arrangement and atmosphere but also because
it was so perfectly in tune with the zeitgeist of that moment.
The undercurrents of uncertainty and confusion vanquished by
a defiant spirit that is both fearless and playful. A spirit that
takes joy in dancing towards the unknown. The track is: 'No
Idea' by Earth Leakage Trip.

It was another bright, sunny day. Large hornets buzzed
overhead as they made their way in and out of the forest. They
were completely non-aggressive and didn't bother anyone.
Even more remarkable was that no one in the crowd bothered
the hornets, and a live-and-let-live attitude prevailed.

I was chatting to Steve Watson, who had also recently
joined the crew. He presented me with a pair of blue mirrored
sunglasses that he'd found on the floor. I put them on. Though
metallic blue on the outside they made everything orange.

'Totally techno! Cheers, Steve!'

'No worries, man, thought they'd go well with your holographic hat!' He climbed back up onto the top of the truck that he and the Bovingdon posse were dancing on. Debbie came over, shaking her head.

'Some off-the-vibe DJ is trying to get on the decks!'

I looked towards the stage. Karl K had the crowd tuned into his set after captivating them with Earth Leakage Trip. MC Scallywag was on the mic, his raps boosting the good vibes. But lurking behind, I could make out another figure.

'Who's he?'

Debbie put her hands on her hips. 'I've no idea, and quite honestly, I can't be bothered with these macho-diva types. They're so fucking annoying. Nice shades!'

'Thanks.' I took them off and gave them a polish with the bottom edge of my T-shirt.

'Okay, let's go and play Rave Police.' I put the glasses back on and adjusted the peak of my silver hat.

Standing around the back and blocking the step up onto the stage was a large group of young lads dressed in loudly branded sportswear. They eyed us suspiciously as we pushed through them with smiles and nods.

The guy on stage was wearing the same style of clothes as the other lads. Karl was visibly annoyed with him but remained cool and focused on his set. School teacher style, I peered over the top of my sunglasses, caught the bloke's eye and beckoned him over by pointing my index finger down to the spot in front of me. He gave me a blank stare and swaggered over, shrugging his shoulders and lifting his palms as if doing so might be enough to shoo me away. He stepped up close to me and scrunched up his face.

'You got a problem?' he asked, clearly playing the tough guy for the benefit of his friends. Not that they could hear him, but to make up for that he rolled his shoulders and made big, floppy arm movements.

I gave him my infinitely patient smile and leaned closer to his ear. 'Do you want to play?' He wasn't expecting that and took half a step back. I took out my DJ list.

'What style are you playing?' I asked as I uncapped my Biro. He shrugged again, but this time in a more thoughtful way. I looked at him expectantly.

'Well, err . . . I guess I'm playin' mainly hardcore, but with like a darker thing goin' on. Like ya man.' He gestured backwards with his head.

'Karl K – Mr Karl K,' I prompted.

'Yeah, like yah man, Mr Karl K.'

I looked through the pages of my list. 'Well, the next slot we have is . . .' I turned the page, 'This time tomorrow.'

'Tomorrow?'

'Yeah, tomorrow. Midday. Shall I put you on the list?'

'Err, yah man, sweet. Midday.'

At that moment a ruckus broke out amongst his crew with much yelping and flapping. A spliff got hit, creating a shower of sparks.

Someone was shrieking, 'Bees, man! Killer bees!'

Our DJ friend's swaggering body language stiffened as a large hornet bounced above us on the tight canvas ceiling. He grabbed his records and, with his crew flapping thin air, made a quick exit.

Whether Karl had seen what had occurred, or whether it was just coincidence, as Debbie and I left the stage an electrical buzzing of bees and a growling bassline came through the speakers. The crowd went wild. It was another of Karl's classics: 'The Bee' by The Scientist.

That afternoon was a solid soundtrack of ominous sub-bass tones, skipping breakbeats and alien bleeps. Added to this were surreal samples and the rhythmic chat of MC Scallywag. What we weren't expecting was Big Reggie, at key moments, to burst into song.

Big Reggie was big, broad and bold. He could have been the archetypal sound-system guy with a don't-mess-with-me fire in his eyes. So to hear such angelic harmonies resonate up from within his barrel chest was a complete surprise. His skill allowed him to perfectly place improvised vocals, adding another level of euphoria to the upper edges of the mix.

●

On Saturday night we had two halogen work lamps up on stage, positioned so that their warm glow bounced off the white canvas roof and Zander's ropes. This added to the impression that the stage was a ship rocking across a rolling ocean. An ocean that was swelling as more and more people arrived. At the helm, Big Reggie on the mic and Mickey on the decks.

I was on stage, in the wings, still on the job of managing the endless stream of DJs who were keen to play. The rig was sounding gorgeous, and the crowd were appreciating every detail of every beat and bleep.

Then the mood changed. It was not the music. It was a turbulence out in the crowd. A palpable ripple of fear. I went over to Big Reggie. We had both sensed it. I picked up one of the halogen lamps and turned it out over the dance floor towards the carpark. Another silent wave of fear rolled through the crowd. People were moving away from something unseen. I held the light's position, but whatever was happening was beyond the furthest edge of the dance floor. Then we saw a flicker of flames in the carpark. *A car on fire?* It got worse.

Someone from the crowd came around the side and called up, 'There's been a stabbing in the carpark!'

We decided it would be a bad idea to turn the music off completely. Instead, Reggie, mic in hand, went and had words with Mickey to keep it mellow. Reggie spoke over the music, keeping everyone calm.

'Listen up, people. We have some trouble at the back there. Move forward, we have plenty of space along the sides. Move away till we get this sorted. Listen up at the back. Spiral-Tribe-is-on-the-vibe! Don't bring your problems here!'

The flames in the carpark had taken hold, and behind them we could see the blue flashing lights of the approaching emergency services.

Reggie was on the case. 'Okay, people, we have a fire crew coming in. Let's give them space. Nice-n-easy.'

At that moment I noticed, through the metal-mesh floor, someone covered in blood under the truck. I repositioned the lamp on the desk so as to continue floodlighting the crowd and went to investigate. At the back of the stage, I shone my torch underneath. There was a man crouching in between the wheel struts. He was bloodied and bruised. In his hand was a baseball bat.

'You okay?' I called to him.

He nodded. I shone my torch over his body, trying to check

for wounds. He appeared to have cuts on his arms and head, but nothing too deep. He was alert and energetic, so I assumed he wasn't seriously injured.

'What's going on?' I asked, though it was already clear he was somehow involved in the trouble and wanted to hide. He didn't answer, just shook his head and pulled the baseball bat tighter towards himself.

'Do you need a paramedic?'

He shook his head.

I went to get him some water. I had no idea if he was an attacker or a victim, perhaps both. All I could be sure about at that moment was he needed assistance and was in fear of further injury. When I got back, he was sitting backstage with Sanchia, who was a trained nurse. She was cleaning him up and checking him over. He was visibly in shock but had no stab wounds.

Despite the violence and the waves of fear that had swept through the crowd, Big Reggie not only kept the situation calm, but once the fire brigade and ambulance had left, he managed to fix the ruptured atmosphere and, with Mickey playing, brought the good ship Spiral back on course. On the mic, at the end of Mickey's set, Reggie gave a shout-out to the crowd.

'Let's hear it for the man keepin' the spiral vibes alive – DJ Mickey Meltdown!' Mickey's new DJ name stuck.

The next morning Big Reggie, Mickey and I were chatting about the night's events when a group of four men wearing suits appeared backstage flashing police ID. They were CID. We went over to meet them.

The chief was a plumpish bloke and looked hot in his crumpled suit, sweat-stained white shirt and crooked tie. I guessed he too had been up all night. As we approached, he said, 'Reggie? I'm looking for Reggie.'

Without hesitation, Reggie stepped forward. The chief held out a hand. 'Reggie, I just want to thank you – personally.' Reggie shook his hand. The chief continued, 'You really handled that well last night – it made all the difference. Thank you, thank you so much.'

Reggie mumbled something like, 'Anyone would have done the same.'

As an observer standing a little back from the scene, I was struck by the intensity of the chief's gratitude. It was a telling moment. It wasn't a copper and an outlaw looking each other in the eye. It was two people. The other plainclothes officers standing around also seemed to be respectful of the moment. They weren't there on a surveillance mission. They really were there to express their gratitude.

As they were leaving, the chief turned and called back, 'By the way, even with the trouble here, over the weekend we had a big drop in violence in Portsmouth and Southampton – and that's saying something!'

•

Sunday. And another glorious day. Rather than having unsettled the crowd, the horrors of the night had somehow consolidated everybody. The crowd was no longer 'The Crowd'. The crowd was now 'The Community'.

That afternoon I was dealing with the usual scenario: big posses of DJs and their crews all getting pushy to play. With the continuous practice I'd had over the weekend, my diplomatic skills were getting sharper. What I found ironic was that many DJs would complain about the other DJs having overblown egos. It was almost the opening line of all the timetabling negotiations. Each crew complained about the others. I would explain that Spiral Tribe were 'The People's Sound System', happy to share our resources with them – and everybody else – but that took some mutual respect and understanding. My attitude was: if ego is the energy that drives a person to spend every waking hour searching for and collecting tunes, practising and refining their skills day-in-day-out; travelling miles to search out the party; avoiding police roadblocks to lug heavy boxes of vinyl through rough terrain; get up on stage in front of so many and give us their best possible performance – then I recognised and respected that effort.

After successfully slotting another two DJs into a near-bursting list, I was approached by a heavily built bloke with dark, straight, shoulder-length hair – not as tall as me, but wider. He quietly introduced himself and a couple of his friends. He explained that they really appreciated what we were doing, bringing people together, especially as the neighbourhoods they came from were rough and full of gang rivalries. He said the violence of the night had been over an unpaid drugs debt and they shouldn't have brought their quarrel to our party. He apologised, then disappeared back into the crowd.

I found Zander tightening some of the cords securing the stage canopy.

'How's it going?'

'Pretty good,' he said, pulling down hard on a rope and tying it off, 'considering the carnage.'

'No fatalities, I hope?'

'It was touch and go. When it kicked off, I went over to the carpark. The ravers were standing around the burning car like it was a campfire! I moved them all away in case the tank went up. Idiots!'

'Fuck!'

'Clueless! Though I learned something new.'

'Oh yeah?'

'There was another bloke injured. Stabbed. He was on the ground, bleeding. Two of his mates were trying to help him – this was before the ambulance arrived. A woman copper turned up and showed them how to take a plastic bag, stick two fingers in it, then slide it into the wound. It stopped the bleeding.' He tested the tension on the rope he'd tightened by giving it a twang.

While we were chatting, Debbie and Simone came over with a couple of other girls who said they were with the horse-drawn travellers. Debbie introduced them as Ixy and Ness. It was them and their crew who'd been at the solstice party and Stoney Cross with their wagons. When they'd left Stoney Cross, they'd started a long and slow journey across the south of England, headed east towards Kent to get some work picking apples. It was purely by chance that they had been passing along a lane nearby the picnic site and heard our music.

They had a plan.

Ixy explained, 'I can't believe you lot aren't collecting donations!'

Debbie and Simone looked at Zander and me. She continued, 'If you like, me and Ness will sort it for you?'

We didn't know Ixy or Ness, but their enthusiasm immediately won us over.

'Yeah?' asked Ixy impatiently.

'Yeah!' we all agreed.

And so, the two of them set off into the crowds with a couple of buckets and returned at intervals with heaps of coins, even a few notes.

Money, or the lack of it, was always a problem. As a group, we shared what resources we had and de-commodified community transactions. But too often that depended on personal sacrifice. We didn't have all the answers, but we were searching.

Hamish was working to achieve some solvency by selling drinks, but for all its good intentions it didn't really solve the problem because, without a clearly defined collective economic structure, even a small enterprise can just mirror the bigger extractive system. And at that moment we were simply too inexperienced to even give that question any real thought.

We could do occasional pay-in events, as we had done at the shebeen to raise the money to buy the rig. But there was perhaps another, more interesting way we could gain economic autonomy. It would be a bold move and take a huge amount of planning and focus. If successful, it would give us the potential to own the means of our own production. That vision, though, was still just an embryonic idea. The dials on the vault doors of destiny were still in spin.

Meanwhile Ixy and Ness' idea of donations was a godsend, creating a collectively shared pool of money that we could at least spend on the basic life-support necessities such as food for the crew and fuel for the gennie.

DAVIDSTOW AIRBASE: AUGUST–SEPTEMBER 1991

Two hundred miles is a long way to drive on the off-chance there might be a festival, and, as we were beginning to find out, Martin's list contained as much wishful thinking as it did solid fact. Of course, I fully understood the tactic. His list was not so much a guide to where things actually were but more a plan that inspired and focused intention towards a still-to-exist moment. It's a magical effect – such is the power of art and communication.

This time I rode passenger in the cab of the truck Hamish had hired. Zander was in the back, as his Land Rover was off the road for repairs. Also with him were our ever-expanding crew, the sound system, a stack of sticky fruit juice cartons in slabs, a load of warm beers, various old fridges, and a gaping hole in the front corner of the fibreglass roof where somebody, who shall remain nameless, hadn't noticed the height restrictions picking up the supplies at the cash and carry.

Hamish turned off the ignition and the truck shuddered to a halt. We both sat there, staring past the drops of rain that had begun to dot the windscreen.

Hamish broke the silence. 'Davidstow Airbase,' he read aloud from the note scribbled on a ripped Rizla packet that he rotated in his large oil-stained fingers. 'Bodmin Moor, Cornwall.'

We looked at each other. Then out again at the endless landscape of rock and tufted marsh grass. With no trees or buildings to give scale to the moorland, distances fell away over the horizon. Though we were parked on the flat, with level views over the old concrete runways, I felt a pang of vertigo, as if at any moment we might fall off the planet into the darkening sky.

'Well, I suppose this must be it,' he said with a note of resignation. The truck flexed in the wind.

On our journey west we'd crossed Dartmoor – another great wind-sculpted expanse of wilderness that dipped down into the Tamar Valley and then up again onto Bodmin moor. Landscapes where the scars of human activity were still visible. Deforestation, industrial ruins, abandoned quarries and mines. Mines for the metals that marked steps in the development of tools and technology.

As the sky darkened, the dots of rain on the windscreen got bigger. The wind gusted and rocked the cab on its springs.

•

That evening the wind dropped and a hush descended on the world. We decided we'd set up in the morning, so we played cards by candlelight on the Techno Bus. We spoke together quietly as if not to disturb the stillness of the air. Exhausted by the long drive and the intensity of the previous weekend, I went to get an early night.

Debbie and I shared the back of her small van, which was barely big enough for us both and only just big enough for me to lie in. Simone always made herself a camp under the trucks and everyone else crashed in the back of the truck or on the Techno Bus. It wasn't unusual in the morning to find people curled around the embers of last night's fire.

I stepped out of the bus and looked up at the moon. It was only three days from full. High and bright. Away from the light pollution of roads and towns the moor was pitch black. The night was still and silent, but the sky was alive with stars. In daylight the airbase's concrete runways and turning circles were just crumbling relics of the last war. But now, illuminated by the moon, they were the silver circuitry of a great Technoglyphic design. No longer runways for warplanes, but magical moonlit paths, asking to be explored. An invitation I couldn't refuse.

I walked towards the moon, enjoying the unearthly glow of the concrete and the vastness of the night sky. As our vehicles dropped out of sight behind me, I stopped in my tracks. Ahead of me was another encampment. A ring of trucks parked around the edges of one of the concrete turning circles. They must have arrived unnoticed while we were sheltering from the weather. The runway I was walking headed straight into the new circle, but on either side, as if guarding the entrance, were two large trucks. In the silvery light their polished chrome grills and split windscreens gave them the appearance of sentinels, grimacing with frozen snarls.

Cautiously I passed between them, and then stepped into the wagon circle's arena. There was no one around. But facing me was a large, open-sided truck, stacked to the roof with speakers which faced into the circle. I could hear the muffled purr of a gennie somewhere in the distance and realised that all the power was on. The system was warming up. Waiting.

The acoustics were strange, as if a microphone was absorbing the night and playing it back at full volume. As I crossed the circle to the centre, I stepped softly, self-conscious of even the smallest sounds I made – the grit under my boots, my breath.

Standing in the middle, with all that shadowy hardware focused on me, made the hairs on the back of my neck stand on end. I felt as if I'd been led into a place where familiar things could be reimagined, reconnected and redefined. It was a vision of a possible future.

I jogged back the way I'd come, my shadow running underfoot, my mind running wild with curiosity about who these new people might be.

I burst back into the candlelit stillness of the Techno Bus. 'We've got company!'

•

The following day was a Friday. 23 August. The sky was blue. The sun was hot. We got to work. Hamish's big hire truck was curtain-sided, so with no more effort than sliding the curtain around, we transformed it into a stage. Our dance floor was also a concrete turning circle, but in theory there was the whole moor to dance on. Just 500 metres away was a large lake. And to the left of that, in the distance, a series of tors – monolithic rock formations.

Across the day, party people began to roll in. Cars, vans, trucks and buses, but there was no activity from our new neighbours. The truck, which the night before had been loaded with the mighty sound system, was closed, with no clue of what was inside. If it wasn't for the collection of vintage trucks and traditional showman's trailers, which were even more impressive in the daylight, I would have thought that the moonlit portal I'd stood in had been a dream.

By the afternoon the party at our camp was in full swing, with numbers growing as the sun set over the moor. But still, no sign of life within the ring of vintage trucks. Wild rumours began to circulate. They were a biker gang. Fugitives. On the run for despicable crimes. I'm not sure where these stories came from, but clearly our neighbours had a legendary reputation. There was one thing that we could be sure of. And that was their name. They called themselves 'The Normals'.

The circus colours of their large towing vehicles and the traditional style of their showman's trailers emphasised the irony in their name. And knowing what I knew – that hidden behind their funfair façade was a monster sound system – added to the magnetism of their presence. Clearly, The Normals relished the fact that they were anything but normal.

It was Debbie and Simone who made first contact. They'd gone over that evening and come back with the news that they'd met Gastro, The Normals' sound guy. Eager to hear their sound system in action, Zander and I went over.

Again, the moon was high and working its magic on the concrete runways. The circle of trucks was just as mysterious as the night before, but there was still no music. This time, below the wall of speakers was a huge mixing desk that curved around a lone figure. Intrigued, we moved closer. As he hunched over the desk, he was lit from below by hundreds of green LEDs that flickered in rows up and down the desktop. Wing-like, his hands hovered over the knobs and sliders, which he tweaked with delicate little flourishes.

We said hello. He seemed oblivious to our presence, but as we were about to walk away, he looked up with a big grin, the green lights twinkling in his eyes, and, like a conductor signalling an orchestra, waved his hands up and stabbed them down to hit a single button.

Nothing happened.

By Saturday Gastro had fixed their technical problems and The Normals' stage was up and running. Or at least it was kicking music out at full volume. But the music was provided by one of those all-male bands that posture with guitars between their legs, periodically screaming into the mic, while a drummer crashed about in the background. The lads on stage looked like they were enjoying themselves, but not many people in the audience were, mainly because there were only four of us – two of them being Zander and me. The other two were blokes with big, bushy beards. One was wearing a battered top hat, the other a headband. I guessed they were Normals – of the fugitive biker gang type.

Zander and I stood there with our arms crossed, trying to find something to like about the music. But the rock-n-roll strut and thrust of the performance just didn't work for us. It was then that I noticed the other blokes weren't checking out the band – they were checking us. I thought nothing of it until I realised that they were edging closer. At two or three metres distance they began circling – Mr Top Hat to the front, Mr Headband behind.

I turned to face Zander so I could keep an eye on them both. The one in front, though he still had his back to us, positioned himself squarely in the centre of our line of sight of the stage. In an otherwise completely empty space, it felt like a provocative move. The bloke behind, also only two or three metres away, stood facing us, his boots planted firmly apart, his arms slightly away from the sides of his full-length duster.

At that moment the bloke in front of us turned. He swigged

on his beer, came up to us and launched into a rant, which for some reason he directed at Zander.

'You and your puffed-up little DJs, with their faceless-tech-no-bollocks, like it's fuckin' something, you're killing live music!'

Though Zander can have a dangerously short fuse, he can also, on occasion, show a talent for striking up an instant rapport with some of the more intense characters he meets. But it's difficult to know which way the dice will roll.

Zander thought for a second, raised his eyebrows, and with only the hint of a smile in his eyes, said, 'We'll happily put it out of its misery, if there's anything left after this lot have finished with it.'

Mr Top Hat took a deep breath, then laughed. He threw open his arms and, wildly sloshing beer, gave Zander a big hug. The bloke behind us came and stood next to me, reached inside his coat, pulled out a tobacco tin and rolled a spliff. He introduced himself as New Zealand Andy. 'And that,' he said, gesturing towards the other bloke who'd danced off, 'that's Chris. Spider's brother.'

Contact with The Normals had been made. And the chemistry between us appeared to be good. But I still hadn't met their main man, Spider. It was Debbie who arranged the introduction.

On Saturday afternoon, I was putting the finishing touches to one of the Technoglypic flags. 'He's been offsite on some mission, all very mysterious, but he's a nice bloke, wants a chat,' she said.

'Who?'

'Spider!'

'What about?'

'I've absolutely no idea.'

'Where?'

'In his trailer.'

I rinsed my brushes and followed Debbie.

The Normals' stage was closed. The music off. Spider's show-man's trailer stood apart from their main camp. It was long, with shallow bay windows and a gently bowed mollycroft roof. All the paint had been scraped off, making it dark and patchy with what looked like bitumen and grey primer. We climbed the wooden steps to the open door.

'Knock-knock!' called Debbie.

There was a heavy thud, then a clang of metal. Spider appeared at the door, dressed in oily jeans and a black vest that showed off his tattoos.

'Alright, Debz, come in,' he said as he wiped his hands on a rag. 'And you must be Mark.' He gave me a nod. 'Come in, make yourselves at home.' He was softly spoken but his voice was low and gravelly.

We squeezed past him in the narrow doorway and stepped into the trailer. Or at least tried to. It was a little tricky as the floor was completely covered in engine parts. The inside walls of the wagon had also been stripped back to the same tarred wood. There was a smell of engine oil and something like paint thinner. Debbie found a jerry can to sit on.

'Come in, come in!' he encouraged me as I scanned the floor for spaces to step. He perched himself against a half-assembled motorbike. Maybe there was some truth in the biker stories after all, though he also had a punk-style mohawk hanging in curls front and back, with the sides of his head shaved.

'Busy then?' I asked when I'd found enough foot room to comfortably stand.

'Always,' said Spider. 'Takes a lot to keep the show on the road.'

'Yeah, I noticed "Circus" painted on some of your trucks.'

'That's us, "Circus Normal".'

'But you're a sound system?'

'No, we're a circus, not with trapeze and all that, but I'm a clown,' he said with such seriousness that I smiled. He added, 'But I usually save that performance for the Old Bill. They don't know what to make of it.' He chuckled, but then was serious again. 'Talking of plod,' he continued, 'did you have any problems at Stoney Cross?'

Debbie and I glanced at each other. I guessed she was as surprised as me that he knew we'd been there.

'They showed up at the end with some bullshit story that they'd had complaints from *over twelve miles away*,' I answered. 'Guess they were just bored and had nothing else better to do.'

Spider nodded.

Sensing that there was more to Spider's question, I continued, 'But we were surprised that no one else, apart from the horse-drawn, came from Rat's Run. I mean, it was literally thirty minutes away, and Stoney Cross is such a beautiful spot.'

Spider was looking at the floor.

There was a moment of silence. In the distance I could hear the pulse of our sound system.

Spider looked up and asked, 'Why Stoney Cross?'

'It was on the list,' said Debbie. 'The festival list.'

Spider stroked the top of one of his arms as if brushing something off his tattoos. 'We did Stoney Cross in '86 but it wasn't a festival. It was a trap.' He looked up at us. 'That was the year after the Beanfield, and the police roadblocked our convoy at every turn, pushing us onto the old airfield. We didn't know what they'd planned, but a woman – a good woman – who worked with social services drove up in the middle of the night to warn us that 500 coppers were on their way. They planned to take our kids into care and impound our vehicles. We managed to get the kids out, but they got all the vehicles. They took everything. Made us homeless.'

There was another pause, just long enough for us to hear a few more heartbeats of distant bass.

He exhaled. 'Well, fair play to you lot. You must have given them a surprise.'

I was shocked by what I'd heard. *Why, with its recent history and high risk of police action, was Stoney Cross listed as 'a festival'? No wonder we were the only sound system there.*

'Yeah, I suppose we did,' I said.

Spider shifted his weight away from the bike and stood up straight. 'But now they know you, it won't be long before they come for you too.'

'The police?' Debbie asked. 'They keep trying but they have to let us go. They know we're only harmless party people.'

'They'll come,' said Spider quietly, 'and when they do, they'll cover their numbers.'

'But that's illegal!' protested Debbie.

'Illegal?' Spider shook his head. 'Just watch your backs. They'll come. They always do.

I shuddered, remembering that the young punk at the factory had said the same thing.

Spider cupped his hands behind his head and stretched.

'Now, while you're both here, let's talk about Spiral Tribe and Circus Normal teaming up to throw the biggest pirate parties the world has ever seen!'

●

It was with a mixture of outward enthusiasm and inward apprehension that Debbie and I reported back to everyone at the Spiral camp. Enthusiasm for Spider's proposal of working together in the future. And apprehension caused by his warning about the police with no numbers. Apart from the gang-war stabbing, the summer had been joyful. Relations with the cops had been . . . okay-ish. It was hard to imagine anything other than Spiral Tribe continuing to pump out peace, love and harmony – forever!

●

The first week of the festival had been so good that we decided to stay for another. Word was out, and more people and crews came, including Sam Haggerty with his sculptures of enormous rubber ducks and a rotating wheel of giant severed heads made of life-like, moulded fibreglass – surreal, funny and grotesque.

Thomas Schwartz, another sculptor and metal fabricator, arrived in his monstrous, ex-US military, matte-black pickup truck. In the back he had his latest invention – the white-knuckle ride of the rave scene: The Gyrocycle. Three large concentric steel rings bolted into a frame, each individually pivoted around a centrally mounted bucket seat. A person could strap themselves in and, by means of bicycle pedals, spin all three rings – with themselves spinning at the centre. A high-speed ride that delivered an incredible sensation of weightlessness.

We met DJ Atzek for the first time, who blew us all away with his precision mixing of Belgium and German techno. The Spiral DJ crew welcomed him onboard. Then there was the stream of young DJs from all over the country, eager to play a continuous flow of cutting-edge music. It was a great mix of styles, the British breakbeat and the Northern European sounds meshing perfectly.

On the last weekend, I heard Human Resource's track, 'Dominator', for the first time. On either side of the stage truck, we'd set up green-and-red strobes that would flip-flop – green on, red off, red on, green off. Debbie and I were dancing when Automanic Josh slammed the track on. The sliding buzz of a Juno synthesiser electrified the air. The boastful rap – 'I'm-bigger-n-badder-n-rougher-n-tougher' – was perfect for the moment. It wasn't just a boastful rapper givin'-it-the-large – for me, it was the moment techno announced itself with an upfront and fearless confidence.

On the dance floor the flip-flop strobes jerked our bodies between hard shadows and highlights. Red edges. Then darkness. Green edges. Then darkness. Totally messing with any sense of where our bodies were in space. One moment my hand was in front of my face, the next it had jumped away on the end of my extended arm. The same happened with whole people. Like a scene from science fiction, people were beamed up from one position and a second later dropped back in another. The whole dance floor was jumping in and out of space-time, powered by the surging 'Dominator' sound.

Then something inexplicable happened.

I left the dance floor to have a piss. Around us the moor was pitch black. Behind the sound system, in total darkness, completely hidden, just three or four metres from the ground, was a dark, unmarked helicopter. Just hanging there. All its lights off. Unheard above the volume of the music. But this was no LSD hallucination. This was no cosmic joke. This was horribly real. My mind went into overdrive. All kinds of thoughts. All kinds of outcomes – none of them good.

I stood there for a few seconds. Frozen. *How long had it been there crouched behind the rig, lurking in the shadows, watching us?* I ran back around the speakers to the dance floor to warn everyone: *There's a fucking helicopter hiding . . . right there!* It sounded ridiculous. *Who would believe me?* But before I could get there, the helicopter had jumped over the top of the rig and hovered over the dance floor. A blinding searchlight came on, the downdraft blowing dust and dry grass into the air. It made a slow turn, the searchlight pushing into the face of each person. Then it went. Straight up. Disappearing into the night.

Clearly someone was messing with us. Was it the military on exercise, having a laugh with some fancy stealth tactics? Or was it more sinister? We'll never know. But regardless of the intention, the effect added weight to Spider's ominous warning. A warning that suggested that there was a more secretive and malevolent power in play. We might have thought we were doing nothing more than having fun. But then again, perhaps there was some substance to the growing sense that we were disrupting the carefully constructed narrative that had, for centuries, mapped out the balance of power. The power that hides the power.

UPOTTERY AIRBASE AND THE VILLAGE IDIOTS: SEPTEMBER 1991

It was the first week of September when we left Davidstow Airfield. A single police car tailed us for miles. Aztek had the antidote. We pulled into a service station and parked up. The police followed and stopped some distance away. With a little flourish, Aztek produced a potato and, with a furtive glint in his eye, disappeared into the carpark. When we pulled out of the service station the police car stayed stationary, unable to start with the spud shoved up its exhaust.

We drove 100 miles due east to another abandoned airbase at Upottery, near Smeatharpe in Devon. I don't remember much about it except that I slept a lot. Since our Tour Launch Party at Cable Street in June, we'd organised parties more or less non-stop for thirteen weeks. I found a quiet patch of long grass to lie down in the late-summer sun. Looking up through a circle of grass at the feathered wisps of Mares' Tail cloud, I fell asleep.

Is someone shouting my name? I struggled to open my eyes. No one was there. I drifted back into half-sleep. The call came again, long and extended, carried by the wind – somehow distant but right in front of me. *I must be dreaming.*

'Maaark!' I opened my eyes just in time to see Thomas waving at me, his long, black dreadlocks trailing behind him as he flew through the air on a parachute towed by a Land Rover that was speeding up and down the runway. I managed a wave, then rolled over and went back to sleep.

•

The following weekend we travelled to the other side of England to The Village Idiots Festival in Kent. It was pretty non-eventful, except that Ixy and horse-drawn travellers were there.

None of us were particularly inspired to go back to London. The real Spiral magic only seemed to kick in when we were out in the wilds, beyond the capital's sphere of influence. But summer was coming to an end and the weather was changing.

Spider and The Normals were keen to get back to London for the winter. The suggestion that we organise big warehouse parties together was, on the face of it, a great plan. They had a huge sound system and a dwindling crowd. We had a small system and a massive crowd.

DEPTFORD RAILWAY ARCHES: SEPTEMBER 1991

In the months we'd been away, our abandoned Walterton Road squat had been redeveloped and was now dead. It was still empty, but it was watched over by a twenty-four-hour security guard. The Green House was still very much alive, but it was too full to accommodate the entirety of our newly found friends, family and crew.

Big Alex, a friend we'd spent time with at the Davidstow Festival, had offered us alternative accommodation in his railway arch in Deptford, South London, close to the river. With nowhere else to go, we accepted.

The previous occupant had used the arch as a commercial workshop and the sign above the door still read: 'Nu-Trix Electronics'. Big Alex was not a businessman or an electrical engineer, but as a punk who appreciated a bit of poetry and drama, he loved the mischievous symbolism of the Nu-Trix name.

'New-Tricks!' he'd enthusiastically pointed out on our arrival, though he also admitted that he wasn't entirely sure if it was a good omen. 'The question is,' he said as he flung open the door, 'who's the trickster – us or them?'

Walled at either end, the arch enclosed a windowless space, big enough to park several vehicles on the lower level and high enough for a second mezzanine-type floor to have been added. On the second level was a dimly lit living area furnished with old sofas and armchairs that Alex had found on the street. At the back, he had a basic kitchen. I was curled up in an armchair. Around me other members of the crew had also done their best to get comfortable.

That night heavy goods trains slowly rumbled into the sleeping city and into my dreams. An endless night with metal screeching on metal. The weight of the loaded wagons compressing the blackened Victorian brick, compressing the foundations. Foundations built on the mud of the old marshes, the bodies of slaves and the exploited poor. The roots of the city pulling sustenance from the airless tombs of empire and vaults of mouldering gold. There are many places where London's dark history pools. Like a dampness from the river, it permeates everything. A stagnation. A putrefaction. A lifeless haunting that excludes even the ghosts.

I awoke in darkness but was relieved to see white lines of daylight outline the large barn doors. Other people were stirring. Alex was at the back, cheerfully singing to himself while he made tea. Over a breakfast of white bread, out-of-date yoghurt, cheese and ham – all food liberated from a nearby supermarket skip – we discussed our situation.

'What we could do with is a base for the winter,' I suggested.

'Somewhere we can get properly organised.'

'I've still got keys to my old flat on Maygrove Road,' said Debbie. 'I know it's small, but the phone and the leccy are still on, which would be well handy.'

'Why don't we just open another squat in Westbourne Park?' asked Tim.

'We need to get rid of that hire truck and get one of our own,' said Zander.

'Why don't we do a party at the Green House?' said Simone.

'A party at the Green House?' I was unconvinced.

Simone looked at me. 'Why not?'

'I don't think they'd appreciate the idea.' I was thinking of the icy reception we'd received earlier that summer.

'Maybe that's *exactly* the kind of idea they'd appreciate!' Simone said, giving me one of her dazzling smiles.

I didn't answer.

'Any news from Spider about his humongous warehouse?' asked Joe. We all looked at each other blankly. 'Be sooo sorted to use that massive rig! Imagine!' He shook the fingers of his right hand so that they slapped together. 'Gorr! That would be one mental party!' he laughed.

'We need to do some serious maintenance on the rig!' said Big Reggie. We all looked at him expectantly. 'Oh, no.' He shook his head. 'No way! I've been AWOL all summer, and now we're back in town I need to catch up with my own thing.'

'I know a guy,' said Simone. 'Runs a sound and light shop over on Acton Lane. I could ask if he's up for it.'

'Meanwhile you're all welcome to stay here!' said Big Alex, holding up a teapot and doing a surprisingly dainty pirouette for a bloke of his build.

•

For a week Nu-Trix became our temporary HQ while we all headed off on different missions.

Simone, Sanchia and Justin went to chat with the Green House crew.

Big Reggie went to catch up with his home life.

Zander and Tim went scouting for a new squat.

Joe went scouting for 'humongous' warehouses.

Debbie and I went to see if her Maygrove Road flat was worth holding on to.

And Steve stayed on at Nu-Trix overhauling the sound equipment with the help of Simone's sound guy, Adrien. Of course, overhauling the equipment meant that the rig needed to be set up and tested. Properly tested! And after a big bag of unclaimed Red-n-Black Ecstasy capsules was discovered hidden in a crate of cables, one thing led to another and Nu-Trix, as you might expect, got properly raved.

I personally ducked out of that party, as I had other things on my mind. Being back in the city was not where I wanted to be, but it had practical advantages. Nancial had finally given up the ghost. Since then, Hamish's hire truck had been bleeding his business dry, and the ritual of collecting donations introduced by Ixy and Ness barely provided enough money for food and fuel. Zander was right: we needed to get rid of the hire truck and get new transport.

It was also decided that we needed more bass bins. As Tim pointed out when asked if he'd be up for making them, perhaps the word 'decided' was inappropriate.

'Decisions,' he said, 'are not a part of it'. Meaning, of course, that once one begins building a sound system, adding more bass bins is not only predictable but inevitable. And once that genie is out of the bottle, more bass bins need bigger trucks.

The next day, Joe reported back on his search for a warehouse. He'd found one, but on his way out he'd had to climb through an awkwardly small window. As he dropped back down onto the street, a bank of blinding lights went on. Police surrounded him – as did a TV crew. They were filming for an anti-crime show called *Crimewatch*. As he was handcuffed, Joe was shocked to have a camera shoved in his face. He told us that he was momentarily lost for words – but as the police tried to lead him away, he turned back to the camera and shouted, 'You might stop the party – but you can't stop the future!'

Not only was this aired on the show, but his impromptu words became legendary within the free party movement – a phrase I still hear people use today.

He was released without charge, and immediately went to reccy another building.

THE ROAD TO AUTONOMY

It wasn't all about big trucks and bass bins. It was also becoming obvious that we could, if we put our minds to it, open up other independent channels of creative communication. We were all enthusiastic about getting our own record label. If we could somehow achieve economic autonomy, it would make so many more things possible. But the road to autonomy is long. Especially when the world you're living in is encapsulated by the capitalist matrix. We were already giving all of our time and labour for free. Pushing ourselves further would risk burning out. One way or another, we were going to have to dance with the devil.

●

Debbie and I collected our paints together, packed them into a rucksack and went to check on her old flat. After the long drive back from Cornwall, Debbie's little van had also given up the ghost. We didn't have the money to fix it, or to buy a new one, so we walked the two miles from the Green House to Maygrove.

Since we'd been away, she'd not had a chance to clear out her belongings. Her tenancy was about to be terminated, so if we did decide to occupy it, we'd be squatting.

Debbie pressed the front door open against the heap of mail that had accumulated in the hall. Inside, the flat was dark and damp. The air was stale, the walls stained with mildew. All the windows at the back were heavily shaded by greenery. Ivy had wormed its way over the top of the back door, which was difficult to open. Outside, the garden was overgrown, except for the spot where we'd had the big fire a year and a half earlier. A year and a half since I'd first spoken with Katia. Staring into the bald patch of grey sludge and charcoal, I could still feel a flush of heat on my face and the sting of smoke in my eyes.

'You okay?' asked Debbie as she joined me.

'Yeah. Seems like only yesterday we were partying here – while London burned.'

'Debbie thought for a moment. 'And it's a year ago exactly that we did the Skool House!'

'Happy birthday, Spiral Tribe!' I kicked the charred remains of what I imagined had once been part of Tim's wardrobe.

'So, what are we going to do with this place?' Debbie got out her tobacco and started rolling one of her prison-thin cigarettes.

'It's a bit gloomy. But it's here. Be great to have somewhere to work.'

'It needs a good clean!'

'And a lick of paint.'

Debbie tucked her cigarette behind her ear. 'We best crack on then!'

We boxed up all the clutter that Debbie had inherited from her aunt. We took down the faded velvet curtains from the bay window. With a broom we twisted the trailing cobwebs from the ceilings. Then scrubbed the mildew from the walls with hot soapy water.

'Cuppa tea?' Debbie called out the front door as I tried to squash the very last of the rubbish bags into the already full wheelie bin.

We sipped musty-tasting tea while we discussed getting some white emulsion and rollers. We were in the kitchen. Next to the kettle. I didn't know exactly what the small noise was, but it was a kind of creaking. Debbie and I both looked at each other. Whatever it was, it triggered a lightning reflex in both of us. A reflex that transported us from the centre of the room into the hallway – a split-second ahead of the entire kitchen ceiling crashing to the floor.

There we both stood, in the settling dust, shocked by the sudden violence of the collapse and the realisation that if the full weight of all that old plaster and rotten wood had hit us, we'd have been knocked cold – or worse. But what was remarkable was how fast we'd moved. So fast that neither of us had any recollection of how we'd got from A to B. One second we were in the kitchen. An instant later, in the corridor. Both with tea in hand – unspilled.

Luckily the bedroom door had been closed and so escaped the worst of the acrid dust. But not so the rest of the flat. It took us all the next day to shovel the plaster into rubble bags and clean everything – again. Once that was done, we painted the place white. The light and smell of the wet paint – with help from one of Danny B Spooky's hardcore mix tapes, which we played over and over – purged the last of the gloom from the flat. Maygrove Road was temporarily back in action.

THE MOLECULAR MIX

The next morning the radio alarm woke me from a deep sleep with a *BBC News* report. Two tribal elders from Maralinga in Australia were coming to London to file a complaint against the British government. Rubbing gritty sleep from my eyes, I sat up in bed.

Apparently, the British had exploded seven nuclear bombs on their lands in the fifties and sixties, as well as tested over 600 other nuclear devices that had contaminated hundreds of square miles with deadly plutonium. As soon as the report was over, I got up and phoned the BBC to ask where the meeting between the elders and the government was taking place. That done, I got dressed and taped a clean piece of calico to the wall and mixed up some electric blue UV paint.

While still at school I'd read books about Aboriginal 'Dreamtime'. I don't know how accurately the books, which were probably penned by European anthropologists, translated the various beliefs of the First Nations People, but still, the interpretation that made an impression on me was that Dreamtime is the 'ancestral now'. That which embraces past, present, future and connects with the landscape and everything in it. Rocks, plants, animals and people. It was one of the first times I'd read anything about different ways of perceiving the world, or that acknowledged there might be any connection between rocks, living things and consciousness. Even at that early age, intuition told me that the boundaries defined by my science teachers at school were too rigid. Just because science had not yet understood the complexities of these deeper connections didn't mean that we shouldn't be curious about them. This unknown zone fired my imagination. Back beyond primordial history. Back beyond the single-celled extremophiles that partied in the volcanic vents of Earth's first oceans. Back beyond the molecular mix that spawned it all.

THE GREEN HOUSE PARTY: OCTOBER 1991

While Debbie and I had been fixing up Maygrove, Zander and Tim had opened up another empty house one minute's walk from the Green House. Number 23 Grittleton Road.

The rig had its own room by the front door. Aztek had taken the attic. Zander had a room up on the second floor, as did friends Fran and Axel. On the ground floor, Simone and Joe were now together and had a room. Sasha, another new acquaintance, had the room behind them. Across the hall were Hubert and Abi. Tim, another ground-floor room. Debbie the room next door to that. Steve Watson, with his girlfriend Shelly, in the basement. And if you hopped out the window into the back garden, then over the low wall to next door, Kirsty had taken the basement there.

Justin was also in the area, having parked the Techno Bus outside our old address on Walterton Road, which, like the Green House, was just around the corner. Outside the Green House was an old ambulance belonging to Axel. Zander's Landy was parked outside number 23. Our community had literally burst at the seams.

Though Debbie and I were still the best of friends, after being cramped up in the back of her small van all summer we both needed our own space. Debbie having a room at Grittleton Road gave us that possibility, which was good for both of us.

Simone had been right about the Green House crew: 'Of course they wanted a party!' My misgivings had been somewhat, though not entirely, unfounded. Zander put me straight on the subject. Yes, at the beginning of the summer there had been talk at the Green House about us giving up our city living for an itinerant life. The talk had ranged from friendly concern about how we'd survive to rather more negative comments about us being out of control and that *free* parties were a crazy idea.

But after a weekend of thorough tweaking at the Nu-Trix arches, when the rig pulled up outside the Green House, everyone rushed out. This time not to stand and stare but to help unload. Free parties didn't only work – they were now a force of nature.

In the front room, Simone, Sasha and Aztek got busy running cables and plugging in. Steve Watson set up the various lights we'd begged and borrowed. Debbie and I, with the help of Greg, Kerry and Camden, gaffer taped décor around the house. We'd also brought a box of paints over from Maygrove for people to use. A graffiti artist, high on 2C-B and wearing a full-face aspirator, was wildly spraying spirals on the walls while others were, more calmly, using marker pens and paint brushes.

When the power was connected, Aztek was keen to start. But first I wanted to show him the design I'd been painting over at Maygrove. I carefully unrolled the new backdrop. As I did, I explained about the news report and the First Nations elders coming to London to protest about the British nuclear testing. I held the painted calico up.

Aztek took one look at the design and said, 'And I'd love to do them a mix tape!' We had the beginnings of a plan.

·

The party at the Green House defied all my expectations. It blew away my uneasiness about coming back to London. It also opened up a whole new network of friends, which included Didz, Ian Orinoco and Steve and Simon Bedlam (though at that moment they were not calling themselves that, as the Bedlam Sound System would come together a little later). Both Steve and Simon were full of energy, loud and straight-talking. Steve had a relaxed charm and easy laugh, while Simon was more serious, more blunt.

Simon was quizzing me on the significance of the spiral. At first I thought he was being cynical, even suspicious, but once he realised we weren't a New Age cult, he lightened up.

Didz joined our conversation. She too was curious about the spiral. But unlike Simon, she didn't need any persuading – she was already intuitively connected with its symbolism.

She told me that she had a Brian Machine: a set of headphones and goggles that gave sound and light pulses which could induce a state similar to lucid dreaming. I was enthusiastic. She promised to bring it along to our next party. At that moment Ian Orinoco, in a tweed cap, his little dreadlocks dangling out the back, introduced himself.

'Talking of the next party,' he said, 'have I got a venue for you!'

•

In the Deptford area of London, Ian Orinoco and I walked along the busy main road, Lewisham Way. The building he had in mind stood on the corner of Rokeby Road. Though big, from the outside it looked pretty nondescript. Originally, I guessed, it had been designed to look grand and imposing, with its classical portico, pillars and large arched windows. But the architect had got the proportions all wrong. Instead, it appeared squat and heavy. Years of city rain and dirty air had faded the stonework, so it invisibly blended in with all the other grey high-street buildings. It could have been a generic bank building, except that the scrolled stone inscription high up on the portico apex read: 'Deptford Central Library 1914'.

I gave the huge double doors a knock with the ball of my fist. The sound was deadened by the weight of the heavy oak. I pushed and pulled but the doors were locked solid.

'This way,' said Ian, leading me around the corner into Rokeby Road and unlocking a small side door. We slipped inside.

Nothing about the drab exterior of the building had prepared me for the interior. It was a huge rectangular room with a high, glass barrel roof, a polished beech parquet floor, either side of which were arched colonnades, and, at the far end, a stage. The high curve of the glass roof gave the place a light and airy atmosphere. It was beautiful – but for a couple of details.

The place had been abandoned for some time, so pigeons and, I guess, local kids had been in before us. The mess caused by the pigeons was minimal. But the kids had had a field day pushing over all the library shelves, domino-style, into a tangle of twisted metal and papers. Not books but thousands of loose documents and pamphlets. These cascaded from the shelving to form shale slopes around the mountainous wreckage. I was lost for words. *Such an amazing space! But it'll take days to clear up this mess.*

Ian and I decided that we'd meet again midweek. If we could get some help, then perhaps we could get the place cleared before Saturday. I also wanted to make time to design new décor – the space demanded it. It was going to be a busy week as we had another important appointment – with the First Nations elders.

BRINGING THE MESSAGE HOME

As I pushed the squeaking sack barrow along the street, we passed several vans making deliveries to the very grand but anonymous central London addresses. I realised then that we'd made a mistake. Instead of wrapping our cargo in an old bedsheet and rope, we should have packed everything in plain cardboard boxes and brown paper. That way our load would have looked like any other delivery. Mind you, that still wouldn't have explained why one sack barrow needed seven or eight rather scruffy people accompanying it.

'This must be the place!' My cheeriness failed to hide the apprehension in my voice.

After hearing about the elders' visit on the radio, I'd managed to get the phone number of the building where the meeting was taking place. After a short time on hold, I got through to an office where a woman quizzed me about what my interest in attending the meeting was. I replied that I represented a community group called Spiral Tribe that wanted to show support for the elder's cause. She took my details and gave me the time and address of the meeting, which I hoped was as good as an invitation.

With minimal fuss we managed to bump the loaded sack barrow and ourselves in through the huge front door and into the polished marble lobby. A man in an immaculate suit blocked our way. He looked more like a bodyguard than a receptionist, but he smiled and asked how he could help.

'We have an invitation,' I reassured him, and myself.

He asked for our names while he walked over to the desk. As he moved, I noticed we all shuffled around the sack barrow in a vain effort to block it from his view.

'We are Spiral Tribe!' I attempted to announce as I boldly strolled up to the desk, but it came out a bit more mumbled than I'd hoped.

He'd glanced down at his list, then looked up and, to my amazement, said, 'You're expected.' He then very graciously walked us through the building and ushered us and the sack barrow into a room that had an enormous mahogany table at its centre. And like the ubiquitous marble and gilt decorations, it too was polished to a mirror gloss.

We took our places around the table. Opposite us was a group of middle-aged men in dark, pinstriped suits. They appeared to have been drinking at lunch as their faces were flushed – more purple than red – and they didn't speak between themselves, at least not coherently, but rather in snorts and grunts. I got the impression that they were complaining about something. Perhaps it was indigestion. Whatever it was, they seemed to want to make their feelings of discomfort – or was it disapproval? – clear.

There was also a small group of younger people, dressed smartly but not as stiffly as the men. One of the women introduced herself to us as an Oxfam NGO and mentioned quietly that the men in suits opposite were, in fact, government officials.

At the head of the table were the two elders. They sat patiently waiting for us all to settle. Both had white hair and beards and wore scarlet headbands and loose-fitting, dark blue clothes. In between them was a white guy in a beige suit. He didn't give off the same hostile aura as the other officials. He stood up, cleared his throat, and introduced himself as the lawyer representing the elders. He asked that the blinds be drawn as they had a slide show. Being on the side of the table nearest the windows, Aztek and I obliged. He continued that the elders didn't speak English and so he would be making the presentation on their behalf. He pulled down a screen and asked for the lights to be turned off. The government men were nearest the switches, but they didn't move, so instead the woman from Oxfam got up.

Zander and I grew up in the sixties and seventies. And by chance we lived twenty minutes away from Britain's Atomic Weapons Research Establishment (AWRE). As the name suggests, it's where they designed and made atomic bombs. Even when we moved a little further west towards Oxford, we were still surrounded by government nuclear laboratories and US nuclear missile bases, Greenham Common being the most infamous. Our mum was one of the Greenham Women who protested against the cruise missiles there. I went on my first nuclear disarmament protest when I was fourteen. Zander was just twelve.

To us kids, the idea of a nuclear war seemed unthinkable, if not for the fact that only thirty years earlier the US had dropped bombs on Hiroshima and Nagasaki, killing a quarter of a million people – mostly civilians.

Even as conscientious teenagers we still didn't fully realise the extent of the catastrophes unleashed on the world in the name of creating capital and holding power. At school I'd had some classes in economic and social history, and so had a vague idea about the British Enclosures – laws that allowed the wealthy to steal land from the poor – the slave trade and the genocidal programs of colonisation. These histories always positively equated capitalism with civilisation. But when I walked into that opulently decorated room in London with my friends and our sack barrow, I still hadn't connected all the dots.

As the carousel of the slide projector turned and the first image clunked into place, the lawyer began to tell us exactly what the British had been up to.

•

The lights came on. I blinked while my eyes adjusted. The gilded ornaments, polished marble and antique furniture had taken on a heavier, lifeless atmosphere. The same glassy-eyed atmosphere as a room of hunter's trophies.

Slowly people started to get up. I sat where I was. There were a few murmurs, but the mood remained solemn. The elder's presentation had been about their dispossession and the plutonium that now poisoned their lands. With a half-life of 24,000 years, it was topping up the toxic load of all the injustices against the planet and her peoples. And just as plutonium has lasting toxicity, it begged the question: what are the long-term effects of the slow and invisible violence of insidious land appropriation, dispossession and extractive capitalism?

The lawyer was packing his papers away. *Is this the right moment?* The elders were still sitting, talking together. After hearing of such serious crimes against a people and their lands, would our presentation be appropriate? I checked myself. *Just ask.*

I stood up.

'Before you go,' I addressed the elders, 'would it be possible to give you a short presentation of music?' I glanced across at the government men. They scowled at me. The Oxfam woman raised her eyebrows.

Introducing myself and the others, I explained our idea. The lawyer quietly translated my message while the elders gave me a studied look.

The lawyer answered, 'Thank you. Please.'

Not sure if that was a yes or a polite no, I hesitated. The elders stood up, smiled and nodded their encouragement.

Breathing a sigh of relief, I said, 'Well, we just need to hook up some power.' I looked around the room, but the others were already on it. Justin ran a cable to a power point. Simone positioned the UV. Debbie and Zander unfurled my painting. Joe took charge of the smoke machine. Sasha switched the lights off. And Aztek pressed play.

The little guerrilla rig we'd wheeled in on a sack barrow kicked in. The backdrop bounced UV colours into the room, which reflected in every polished surface, transporting us out of the oppressive building and into a new space. The elders were the first to start dancing. Their lawyer politely bobbed his head in time to the beat. The government men immediately left the room.

After our presentation, Aztek and I gave the elders the tape and backdrop. I attempted to say a few words but only managed to say how sorry we were to hear about what had happened to them and their lands. I admitted that we didn't know how to help, but I hoped they'd accept our small offering of art, music and solidarity. Not as people in power, but just people.

In that shared moment of deep eye contact and warm handshakes, the connection between us all was strong, but it didn't solve the problem. That of the government men, and their type, slipping out of the room, no doubt to continue with some other catastrophic scheme.

DEPTFORD LIBRARY: OCTOBER 1991

Back at Maygrove Road, Simone was playing with words and rapping some of her lines to Debbie and me. I was making a flyer for the party at the library. There was a buzz in the room, as was often the case when the three of us were being creative together. But I was still finding it difficult to fully recover my optimism and energy after the revelations of the elders.

Reclaiming space and building a community around parties was clearly important. It certainly had a positive impact on the society we knew – a powerful antidote to the poison of alienation, exclusion and fragmentation caused by Conservative Britain. But putting so much time and energy into non-stop parties felt far removed from the urgent issues caused by the power-crazed nutters running the world. The meeting with the elders showed us that the course set by the idiots in control was not heading away from a destructive past. Quite the contrary. Each and every incidence of environmental and social injustice was part of an ever-expanding program.

Searching for a way out of the gloom, I began sketching ideas for the library's décor. Because it was such a beautiful space, I wanted to integrate the new designs with the architecture. The curve of the barrelled glass roof, the colonnades of arches and the raised stage area all lent themselves to framing just two or three strong motifs.

Simone interrupted my thoughts. 'Did you know that an anagram of Spiral Tribes is Pirate Bliss?'

'Tribes?' asked Debbie, emphasising the plural 'S'.

'Yeah, okay,' said Simone. 'Or without the extra S, you could have Pirate's Lib.'

'As in Woman's Lib?' Debbie thought for a moment. 'Sounds about right!'

'What other words come up?' I asked.

'Well, if we use Tribes in the plural, we have words like pirates, arise, surprise, but spelled s-i-r-p-r-i-s-e, so maybe it counts?'

'Surprise parties,' Debbie laughed, 'our speciality!'

'Bright, spelled b-r-i-t-e. Star. It's kinda like the tarot – you have to decide how things feel to you.' Simone raised her eyebrows and paused. 'Then, there's the dark side! Words like: Rat. Lies. Trial. Split.'

There was a moment of unease in the room. It wasn't paranoia. More a heightened awareness. As if the elder's message had burst our little bubble of fun and we were beginning to get a measure of the casual brutality that the establishment wielded.

Simone and Debbie continued chatting. I put some music on to help blast away the disquiet I felt and tried to focus on the décor designs.

Perhaps, I thought, *I could combine my intuition about the evolutionary energy of the spiral and ideas around Dreamtime.* This train of thought felt positive and even powerful enough to, at least temporarily, resist the creeping shadow of hopelessness and desolation that threatened to suck the life out of everything on the planet.

I imagined myself as a distant, ancestral organism. Living at a time when the Earth was bombarded by killer gamma rays and meteor storms. Perhaps a fish – of the pre-leg variety – that jumped up and saw, for the first time, the world above the surface. Would it have seen a new dimension of possibility? Whether the fish actually had an '*Ah-ha!*' moment may or may not be relevant, but I liked the humour of the image.

Sketching out these thoughts gave me a simple fish shape, slightly curled as if jumping up and about to dive back into the water. Under the fish's tail was a drip. The two shapes together formed a stylised question mark. It was simple, fun and, in a pictogram kind of way, symbolised not only an evolutionary leap but also a leap of consciousness.

The second motif I developed was 'The splash'. The liquid-crown shape that forms when a droplet hits and breaks the surface of the water. These splashes were flat on the bottom edge and semi-circular along the top, and so lent themselves, if scaled up, to fit perfectly into the spaces behind each arch in the library's colonnade. I would paint the smaller fish motifs at the top of each pillar.

Happy with the designs, I packed a sleeping bag, my paints and brushes, and went to camp for the rest of the week on the library floor.

*

Ian Orinoco and I spent long days and nights straightening the twisted metal shelves back into shape. Luckily we had help from people who dropped by or were now permanently squatting the building. A couple of local lads came and helped: MC Techno and Little Reggie (*Little* Reggie so as not to be confused with Big Reggie), Big Alex, Kevin Brewer, who was another friend we'd made at the Davidstow Festival, and his mate Marcus, who ran missions to supermarket skips to keep us all supplied with food.

The repaired shelving was taken out of the main space and put into other empty rooms. We re-stacked them with the files and pamphlets. It was a long and laborious process. Once the main space was cleared, we moved two square sections of the staging out to the middle of the floor. These were professionally constructed rostrums, about half a metre high. Once in position, it was official – we had dance podiums.

Late on Friday, Steve Watson and Darren set off in Darren's van to collect our still very limited collection of lights. In fact, we only had a couple of old projectors with coloured filters, plus the clunky old Moonflower. As usual we got a couple of UV tubes from Rudi. We also splashed out and hired two Terra Strobes. These, along with a Monster Mist smoke machine, were all we needed.

Unfortunately, on their return trip to the library, Darren rolled his van. Fortunately, neither he nor Steve were seriously injured, though Darren was bruised and the van a write-off. But such details weren't going to stop them – they were hardcore – and both made it back to the venue with the lights, which still worked.

On Saturday afternoon the energy was up for the final push to prepare the venue. More help arrived from Grittleton Road, along with DJs Charlie Hall and Automanic Josh.

Sanchia found a large projection screen crumpled in the corner of one of the back rooms, which we smoothed out on the floor.

'What do you want to paint?' I asked her.

'A spiral, of course!' She gave me an exasperated look.

I got some string, tacked it to the centre of the screen and into the floor. On the other end of it, I tied a pencil to form a giant compass. By allowing the string to wind around the pencil we marked out a huge spiral. Starting at the centre, Sanchia and Sasha began to paint.

Balanced on a high ladder, Debbie painted a large spiralled 'S' up in the curve under the glass roof at the opposite end of the building to the stage.

I set myself up with a desk and began cutting stencils for the fish designs and marking out the larger splashes with a cardboard template. Then I got to work on the arched colonnades that ran down either side of the room. Fourteen arches in total, each with a pillar on either side, back and front, making thirty-two pillars altogether. My idea was to 'subtly marble' them with UV colours so that at night, with the UV light, the colonnades would glow. The marbling process involved dipping crumpled pieces of fabric into buckets of watery UV paint, then gently pressing the cloth against the pillars. People were super enthusiastic to help. Within minutes we'd lost sight of the original concept and had instead gone for the 'slapped-about-with-a-wet-rag' look.

It was getting late. Sanchia and Sasha's backdrop had grown from the small tack-hole at the centre to a giant black-and-white spiral that entirely filled the large screen. As we cleaned up the painting stuff, the first party people began to arrive. The giant spiral was hoisted into prime position – behind the decks, centre stage. Even though the paint was, of course, still wet.

•

This party was particularly special. Not only because it was a full house, with incredible DJ sets, but also because all our extended family had come together to prepare and organise the space. It was a lot of hard work, but it strengthened old friendships and cemented new ones. Working as a team, we were not just celebrating what had been achieved, but what we had achieved together.

It had its intense moments, though. Sanchia's skills as a nurse were called into action again when a girl had an epileptic seizure. She made a full recovery.

Aztek had the sound beautifully pumping, though at one point, probably when Automanic Josh was playing, one of the eighteen-inch bass cones ripped and started flapping. Single-handedly, and without stopping the music, Aztek swapped out the damaged but still fiercely kicking speaker and replaced it with a new one.

With printed Indian cotton throws, Didz had tented off a small area under one of the arches in the colonnade. Inside she'd set up the Brain Machine and arranged a mattress with cushions. She asked me to sit down next to her and get comfortable. The machine was a little rectangular box with a couple of simple switches and knobs. It was wired to a set of goggles and headphones. The party was raging outside the tent. She leaned in close to explain that by using a combination of pulsing sounds and flashing lights at certain frequencies, the device altered the brain's Alpha waves, which had a psychedelic effect.

'Just close your eyes and relax,' she helped me put on the headset. I laid back and she switched the machine on.

For the first few seconds I was only aware of the machine's built-in flashing diodes in front of my eyes and some low-pitched bleeps. As I relaxed, the exterior sources of light and sound faded, and colourful geometric patterns began to appear. They were real, as in I perceived them through my optic nerves, but if I opened my eyes, I was back to seeing the interior of the plastic goggles. Closing my eyes again, I decided to see where this machine trip might take me.

After about a minute of watching swirling patterns I became aware of a sensation of floating and could no longer feel the mattress under me. *Nice and relaxing.* The coloured patterns started to fade, and the floating had an upward motion. With surprise, I realised I was looking down at myself, lying against a black background or void. The experience felt and appeared completely real – to the point that my floating self could actually see the apprehension on the face of my other self. It was disconcerting, but my curiosity won over and I kept my eyes closed. My floating self was the only body that was self-aware. As if it was my consciousness that was floating away from my physical body. It took some getting used to, but it was pleasant enough and so I stayed with it. As I rose higher above my body, the sensation of floating included a feeling of acceleration. Slowly at first, but then it quickened. My body shrank away into the darkness. At this point I started to feel a rising panic. It was as if I was headed into oblivion – but an oblivion of darkness, cut off from all the senses of the living world. Too late I realised I'd run out of options. Cut off from my physical body, I couldn't open my eyes, take off the headset, or speak. The sense of acceleration was increasing to the point of becoming unbearable. I was in trouble. I tried to stay calm, but the only reassurance I could offer myself was that a full-on panic attack was not going to help.

Just as the accelerating G-force was about to crush me, it slowed. The darkness started to fade. I was moving through mist, which brightened. Instead of ascending, I was now descending through wispy clouds into daylight. I was flying above a planet's surface. Red-brown, hot, arid, ancient. Somehow, I knew it was early Earth at a moment of transition. I knew other things too – that this transition was from raw mineral elements towards living organisms, that it was a mistake to draw borders between them, that one flows into another. These thoughts were familiar to me – and I already had a predisposition to think along these lines – but regardless of my theorising around the subject, I'd never actually experienced it before.

With an uncomfortable jolt, I was back at the party. Didz
was gently taking the headset from me.

'You okay?' she asked.

I took a moment to answer. 'Yeah ... I suppose I am.'

'Looked pretty intense, so I thought I should pull you out.'

'Yeah ... thanks ... it was a bit of a bumpy ride!'

THE HOUSE-TEKNIC

One of the great advantages of having Maygrove as a temporary office/art space was that we could spread out. The communal spaces of both Grittleton Road and the Green House
were overcrowded. Not just with the people that lived there
but also with endless streams of visitors. I'd tried working at
both addresses, using my lap as my desk to draw and write
on, if I could navigate the constant interruptions of people
making food and tea, wanting a chat, or rolling very sociable
spliffs.

Having found a large desk out on the street, Debbie, Simone and I installed it in the bay window at Maygrove. It was
big enough for three or four people to work without cluttering
each other. In pride of place in the middle of the desk was a
landline telephone and cassette tape answerphone. We'd also
been donated a black-and-white photocopier by a generous
tribe member. And if we needed colour copies, I still had my
contacts at Grove Reprographics.

The black-and-white machine was instrumental not only in
printing our batches of weekly flyers but also in the cut-up
style of those flyers. By chopping up previous flyers, rearrang-

ing the graphics and adding in a few more, our look remained consistently raw.

The colour laser copies were very effective at visually documenting our events. Simone, Debbie and I asked around and managed to get a collection of photos that people had snapped across the summer. It turned out that Paul Brash and Tracey had some beauties.

Back then, before phone cameras, the images were usually printed no bigger than a postcard onto photographic paper. I laser copied the best of them, blew them up to A4 and put them together in the pages of a clear plastic folder. The results were spectacular. Not because the laser copies were larger and brighter than standard photos, but because of the rare subject matter. Vivid images of a secret subculture and the hidden phenomenon of underground dance parties. Pictures that, thanks to Paul and Tracey, captured the elusive magic of those pioneering rave days. 'The Folder', as we called it, became our number-one tool when explaining ourselves to potential allies who hadn't experienced Spiral Tribe first-hand. Sometimes words are just not enough, but slam The Folder down on the table and the only words necessary were 'Check this out!'

While going to the trouble of doing all that photocopying, I also took the opportunity to create another little pamphlet, or zine. Like my original Butterfly Flyer, it was made of two A4 pages folded together. On the front cover was a colour photo, taken by Paul Brash up on Exmoor, of Hubert raving against a heavenly blue sky. Above him was the zine's title, 'Tribal Warriors'. On the back cover, I laid out nine full-colour examples of my flyer artwork, along with a few photos of our biggest crowds. Inside, it featured an account of the Maralinga land's fate at the hands of the British government. A long list of all our DJs to date – at least all those that I could remember. And on the centre pages was a collection of statements, some quite tame, others a little more provocative.

The centre spread was titled in blocky, pixelated letters, 'Living By The House-Teknic' – a rather clumsy wordplay on house music and the Technics decks. Here's a sample of a few of those statements:

'We are here to reconnect the Earth.'

'We are all part of one big family, one tribe, the human race. We are part of life and a way of life. It is called living by the House-Teknic.'

'Wherever we park up the trucks – we party!'

And, of course, I found it irresistible to add what the police sergeant at Stoney Cross had said, untrue as it clearly was: 'We have had complaints – some from over twelve miles away!'

Flipping negative comments from coppers or the press into points of merit gave us some resilience. They called us outlaws to try and diminish us. To neutralise this, we proudly celebrated that outlaw status.

•

Back at Grittleton Road, Ian Orinoco showed me a copy of the local newspaper from South London. The article suggested that we were some kind of cult. One line particularly caught my eye. It said that the walls were daubed with 'pseudo-mystic symbols'.

'Wicked,' I said to Ian, 'at least they got it half right!'

'What do you mean?'

'Well, the décor must have meant something to the journalist – at least enough to describe them as mystic symbols.'

'Pseudo-mystic symbols!' said Ian laughing.

'Exactly – they got it half right!'

SAMHAIN

Despite the chocolate-box image of bow-top wagons and beautiful horses, the horse-drawn travellers were a hardcore bunch. And they loved techno.

Debbie and Simone were in touch with Ixy and Ness. They'd invited us and the sound system to join them for Samhain – Celtic Halloween.

Steve Watson had bought Axel's old ambulance and got it back on the road. Keen to reccy the horse-drawn travellers' site and take 'The Ambience', as Steve now called it, out for a spin, Steve, Shelly, Debbie, Little Reggie and Joe all piled onboard and headed down to Tunbridge Wells, a couple of days ahead of the planned party.

Once they'd arrived, Steve reported back from a phone box with directions.

'Go through High Brooms Industrial Estate. The track that leads into the woodland is behind the big green building, with the illuminated sign, DSL". You can't miss it – it's LSD backwards.'

It was completely dark when I arrived. Even with the work lights blazing, their dazzle only darkened the night beyond. As far as I could make out, we were in a clearing or paddock in a valley surrounded by woodland. The ground was wet from recent rain. The smell of damp earth and leaf mould hung in the air. Just as we got the rig on, it started to rain again. We covered everything with tarps, hoping that the weather would clear. It got worse. So bad, in fact, that very few people came.

Justin's bus had no passenger seats, and so the interior, which was decked out with bright pink fun-fur, had just about enough space for everyone, the decks and a small speaker stack. Someone placed the strobe against the windscreen facing outward. What had been miserably wet weather was immediately transformed into a slow-motion lightshow of silver raindrops.

'Mother nature provides!' said Simone as the music came on and she plugged in a mic. The bus bounced on its springs as she started to rap.

But the warmth and shelter of the bus was not to everyone's taste. Toney (not to be confused with Dance Party Tony) was a chef by trade and one of the residents of the Green House. He was out in the woodland with a torch foraging for mushrooms. When it came to food, he had the sensibilities of an artist. It was his passion. Back in London, I'd had some interesting conversations with him around his ideas of cooking with edible elements – even earth. He wanted to include gold leaf in one of his recipes, not because it was swanky but because, he said, 'Gold is a pure element, created in the heart of stars.'

After hours out in the rain, Toney reappeared back on the bus. He was soaking wet but glowing with smiles. With the pride of a triumphant hunter, he held up a half-full black bin liner. Water puddled around him as he loudly announced that Samhain was the time when the membrane between this world and that of the spirits was at its most transparent. And that fungi, the agents of decay, grow through the veil and connect this world to the other. I was the only person listening. Mainly because he was standing right next to me and no one else could hear him over the music. What he was saying may or may not have been 100 per cent scientific, but to me it made perfect sense.

'What gourmet delights did you find?' I shouted.

He opened the black sack. There was a heavy smell, like unrefrigerated red meat. He reached inside.

'These!' he said, thrusting a fleshy mushroom towards me, his glowing smile now appearing impish and his eyes shining with a dark light. The mushroom was blood red with white spots. A fine specimen of Amanita Muscaria.

'Oh . . . I see,' I said.

'This one is for you, Mark!' he grinned. 'Eat it!'

The impishness in his eyes made me wary. But there was something compelling about the sight of him holding up the perfect fairytale mushroom on a bus lined with pink fun-fur with that mischievous look on his face.

'Thanks,' I said, 'I'll save it for later.'

'Yes, whenever. But don't forget!' He hurriedly looked around. Everyone else was dancing. 'I must get back to the forest – I must get back.' He turned and started down the bus steps to go.

'Toney – stay! Get dry!' I called after him. But he'd gone.

I looked at the mushroom. It felt . . . alive. It was unnerving. Not sure what to do with it, I gently wrapped it in tissues and put it in my jacket pocket.

•

By morning the rain had stopped.

The autumn sun was slow to clear the eastern lip of the wooded valley. The horse-drawn's field was towards the top end of the land, so we had a good view across open ground, down towards more woodland below. As the valley warmed, mist drifted across the top of the trees.

Ixy got a fire going. From a metal milk churn, she ladled clean water into a large sooty kettle. The kettle went over the fire, suspended from a hook on an iron tripod. A circle of us had gathered around the hearth to warm up. When the tea came, it was very welcome. Debbie told Simone, Zander and me about the couple of days she'd spent with the horse-drawn before we'd arrived. Her, Little Reggie and Joe had been riding with Ixy, galloping around the fields bareback.

'I'd love to get horses,' said Debbie.

'I'd love to get decks!' said Ixy.

•

By the afternoon, more people had arrived and the party was in full swing. Then the police showed up. Ten of them. Eight constables in uniform. A sergeant in uniform. And a chief. *But what is he wearing?*

I have no knowledge of official police outfits, but I'd never seen this combo before. His top half was what you might expect. Flat hat, white shirt, tie and cop jacket, with fancy epaulettes. His bottom half, though, was rather unusual. He had skin-tight beige trousers and knee-high black boots. And just to set off the whole outfit, tucked under his armpit, was an officer's swagger stick.

He strutted across the dance floor, up to the decks, trailed by his men. He demanded that the music went off – immediately. We turned it down. Apparently satisfied with the volume, he strutted back across the dance floor, not to leave but to stand where the ground was slightly higher. His men filed in behind him. On his little grass pedestal, legs astride, arms behind his back holding both ends of his swagger stick, which he flexed across his arse, he had the attention of the whole dance floor.

'This is an illegal gathering!' he announced, waving his stick in front of him in a large sweeping movement that was meant to implicate us all.

'No, it's not!' someone shouted from the crowd.

He continued. 'By the power vested in me by Her Majesty Queen Elizabeth II, I instruct you all to pack up and vacate this land!'

'Why?' came the reply.

He turned towards the section of the crowd where the question had come from. 'To prevent a breach of the peace!' He tucked his stick under his armpit and stuck his chest out.

Another person to his right shouted, 'Breaching whose peace?'

He turned. 'This is a respectable, law-abiding community. We do not appreciate this . . .' He searched for the word. 'This anarchy! You are in clear breach of the peace. You are trespassing, and I believe you have caused damage to private property. Disperse immediately or you will be charged!'

'With what?'

Instead of replying he took his stick out again, jerked his chin up, and stepped down from his grassy hillock into the crowd. The sergeant followed two paces behind. The constables, uncertain what to do, shuffled about but stayed where they were. The crowd parted to give him space.

'Who's the organiser of this . . . this chaos?' he demanded.

There was a moment's pause.

Then someone called, 'Chaos is self-organising!'

As he approached me, I could see he wasn't ruffled by the heckling – he was enjoying himself.

'Just look at you!' He stopped and tapped his stick on the chest of the bloke standing next to me. 'I don't expect you've ever done an honest day's work in your life,' he sneered, 'have you?' The bloke didn't answer but his body swelled with anger. The sneer became a smug smile. 'Just as I thought!' He took a couple more steps and turned to a girl with facial piercings. 'And what on Earth have we got here? A ring in your nose – are you a savage?' He looked around at us all. 'Have you no self-respect?'

As his insults became more personal, so his enjoyment became more visible. The crowd around him tightened. He strutted back towards the decks, and as he passed, people spat on his back. He was oblivious, too enthralled in his own self-importance. But his sergeant was far from oblivious. A stout, broad-shouldered man, he saw each and every person who spat on his boss.

'Alright, lads,' he said quietly as he followed behind. 'Easy now, please.'

His half-hearted appeal for restraint was ignored. Understanding that the chief was headed towards the decks again, the crowd flowed around him and headed him off. Standing shoulder to shoulder we surrounded the tarpaulin DJ booth in a solid wall.

'Now turn that infernal racket off, or my men will turn it off forcibly!'

As he'd moved towards the decks, so his constables had drifted along behind him. When the chief uttered the word 'forcibly', his men responded. But not by standing to attention, drawing their batons and squaring up. Instead, some screwed up their faces and shook their heads. One lifted his hands and shrugged with a gesture of helplessness. Another was blushing bright red before he hung his head and stared at his feet.

Unperturbed the chief edged around the crowd and up onto the steps of the Techno Bus. Having found himself another pulpit to preach from, he continued his rant.

'Have you not got anything else better to do than waste your lives away living like vagabonds?' He noticed a twig mobile dangling above him in the bus doorway. 'And what's all this pagan nonsense!' He tapped it with his stick to make it spin.

'It's Halloween, you knob!' someone called.

'Halloween!' he smiled. 'So that explains why you're all dressed as gypsies and tramps.'

This sparked a chorus of catcalls.

'What are you dressed as, dickhead?'

'Where's your trousers, copper?'

He held up his hand as if modestly asking applause to end.

'I'm wondering,' he said, tapping the Techno Bus with his stick, 'if these vehicles are taxed and insured.' He turned and took a couple of steps up into the bus, but immediately came back to his pulpit.

'Pink fun-fur!' he announced, as if his brilliant detective work confirmed his suspicions. Smiling and gently slapping his stick onto the flat of his hand, he issued us with an ultimatum: 'You have until six o'clock to leave! If you don't, we'll be back!' He gave his hand one final whack, stepped down off the bus and marched across the dance floor. His men scurried after him. The sergeant stayed a moment.

'Just keep it down a bit, eh?' he asked. He stood there, solid, unafraid – and reasonable.

One of the lads answered, 'No worries, mate. But your boss is a total wanker!'

The sergeant shrugged. 'Please. Just keep it down.' And they left.

Of course, we turned the music up to a reasonable level. The cops didn't come back, and the party went on – all day and all night.

GANGSTERS

We were desperately short of money. Every penny that we had we spent on food, fuel and maintaining the sound system. We barely had enough money to survive, let alone fund any more projects. Our hopes of doing a big benefit party with Spider and Circus Normal were beginning to fade.

Then news came. Not from Spider but from Stikka. He wanted a meeting.

Debbie and I went to see him at the Green House. We all arrived at the same time on the street outside. Stikka was with a couple of other blokes who I didn't recognise. Stikka made the introductions. His mates had a venue. A big venue, for a collaboration between Fundamental and Spiral Tribe. I shook hands with his friends, then Stikka. The spark in his eyes was back. I smiled. He nodded some kind of acknowledgement. And in that moment all my misgivings about our previous encounter – coincidently in exactly the same spot outside the Green House – were dispelled. I was very glad that we had another opportunity to work together again.

•

In a local charity shop I'd found a long piece of straw-coloured, heavy-duty satin. Around ten metres in length and a metre and a half wide, the sheen on the fabric created a metallic gold effect.

'How about this for a crop circle backdrop?' I asked Debbie.

'In silver and gold!' she answered.

'Absolutely! I'll go to Brodie and Middleton this afternoon and grab some gold – maybe more silver!'

We decided on a sun disk as the central motif. Radiating horizontally from it would be circuitry-style wings which included concentric circles along their span. This gave the design not only a Technoglyphic shape but also the look of an alien mothership with engines mounted along its wings.

•

When we went along to view the venue with Stikka and his new crew, we were blown away. The Alperton Community Centre in Wembley, just five miles west of the Green House and Grittleton Road. There were two big rooms. Stikka would have one, we'd have the other – a gymnasium. Not dissimilar to Zander's 'bedroom' at the Skool House, but four times bigger. Polished beech parquet floors, painted with the markings for basketball and tennis courts. Varnished wooden frames of climbing bars that folded flat against the walls. Wooden gymnastic benches around the walls. All the light-coloured wood gave the room a natural glow.

'What do you reckon?' Stikka asked.

'It's beautiful!' I said.

'It's golden!' said Debbie.

'So it's still used as a community centre?' I asked.

'Yeah, kinda. My mate works here sometimes.'

'So we have permission?'

Stikka's eyes twinkled. 'Let's just say my mate has a key!'

We worked out the business deal. It would be a benefit party for both our sound systems. Five pounds in. Equal splits. We'd organise shifts on the door from both crews to look after things.

•

On the night everything was going to plan. The door was busy. The place was kicking – two full rooms of very happy people. The Spiral rig sounded gorgeous. As did Fundamental. The new mothership backdrop looked awesome. Gold and silver wings welcoming the world to techno.

The first I heard of the trouble was from Joe. I found him sitting in a back room, visibly shocked.

'Gangsters!' His voice was weak.

'Joe? What do you mean – what's going on?'

'Fuckin' gangsters! They steamed the door!'

'What do you mean "steamed"?'

'They said this was their manor – this was their party. They've taken the door.'

'Fuck that, man! Let's sort this out. Where's Stikka?'

'No, Mark – really, no! They've got fuckin' guns. I grew up round here. I know them. An Irish firm you really don't wanna mess with – believe mate, believe!'

'Fuck . . . what we gonna do?'

'Nothing we can do. Roll with it.'

'I'm gonna look . . . Does Stikka know?'

'Yeah, he knows.'

'You coming?'

'No way, man. I need a spliff – serious!'

I went out into the foyer. Without stopping, or staring, I walked past the door. The crowds were still flowing in, waving fivers. But none of ours or Stikka's crew were there. Instead, a large group of young blokes were pocketing the money. I arrived at the other end of the foyer and the doorway into Stikka's room. He was standing just inside.

'You heard?' I asked.

'I heard,' he said.

'What we gonna do?'

'What can we do?' He stroked the top of his shaved head. 'They're fully tooled up.'

The party in his room was rocking. The crowd oblivious to who was running the door.

'Any other problems with them?'

'Nah, they're just interested in the door. If we leave them alone, they'll probably leave us alone.'

'You think?'

'It's the party pulling in the cash.'

'So if we stop they'll kill us?'

Stikka managed a wry smile. 'Something like that.'

I went back into the crowded foyer, taking the opportunity to get a closer look at the gang. There wasn't any real need for me to be clandestine, as they were completely fixated on the job in hand – plucking the fivers from people's hands as they squeezed in through the doors. All the blokes taking money looked like brothers, with the same short back and sides and with a preference for clothes with Burberry or Aquascutum checks. Standing close to me was an unusual character. An older bloke on his own. Away from the door, against the opposite wall, but watching it like a hawk. Middle-aged. Clean shaven. Dark hair. Balding. Nothing unusual about that, but he was wearing a yellow ochre roll-neck sweater under a tweed jacket. Smart trousers and polished brown brogues. His hands were in his trouser pockets. His chin held high. Even before one of the younger blokes came over and leaned into his ear to speak with him, I knew he was the big daddy – presiding over his boys. His manor. His door. His party.

•

A pattern was emerging. Whether it was the corrupt leaders of local government pushing people out of public housing, international governments stealing land of indigenous people, jumped-up police chiefs thinking they could dictate the correct way to live, or hooligans with guns, they were all playing the same game. Making the same bogus claim: 'Because I have power over you, I am superior. And as a superior, I have the rights to this territory, and everything in it.'

Later that night, when the queue had subsided, the gang left with all the money, but without further incident. We relaxed and the party continued into Sunday morning.

But there was more trouble brewing. A middle-aged woman

appeared in the doorway of the gymnasium with Debbie. From across the room, Debbie was frantically waving and pulling pleading faces at me, while the woman at her side stood aghast. Realising that some emergency diplomacy was being called for, I pushed through the crowd to join them.

The women, dressed in her Sunday best, was outraged.

'Upon my word – what is this ruckus! What're you doing here?' Her jaw was slack with disbelief, her eyes furious.

I introduced myself and explained that this . . . was a party.

'I can see it's a party! But you can't do this! Not here!'

She said she was the manager of the community centre and had just come from church.

'The manager?'

'Yes, the manager!' After an awkward pause, she said, 'I need to sit myself down.'

Debbie and I took her to one of the gymnasium benches at the back of the hall where we could talk. We sat either side of her. Perhaps overenthusiastically, I then tried to explain who we were and what we were all about.

'Don't you try and sweet talk me, young man! I have eyes and ears!'

There was another long pause.

'What do you call all this commotion?'

Debbie answered, 'Acid – techno – just dance music really.'

'Dance music?' she said, surveying the hundreds of people busting their moves in the sunshine that was streaming in through the windows.

'Not my kind of dance music.' Her head was gently bobbing to the beat. 'But this has some soul!' she laughed.

Debbie and I caught each other's eye.

She continued. 'It certainly livens up the place!'

'Perhaps . . .' I started, but I lost my nerve.

Debbie picked up the baton 'Perhaps we could do some other events here, for young people?'

The woman turned to Debbie, then to me with a frown. 'What do you mean?' she demanded.

Sensing we'd overstepped the mark, I said, 'Well, maybe some DJ workshops?'

'Art and dance workshops?' Debbie added.

The woman looked at us with suspicion. 'I'm no fool! You'd have yourselves a big bashment!'

'Well . . .' I looked at Debbie.

'Perhaps that's not such a good idea then,' said Debbie.

The woman turned to me with a stern look.

'Yeah . . . maybe not,' I agreed. 'But still – it's a beautiful venue.'

'Indeed, it is a beautiful venue!' There was anger in her eyes. 'And I'm thinking that might be exactly what this place needs.'

I'm sure Debbie's look of surprise and confusion mirrored my own.

'Really?' said Debbie.

I didn't understand. 'You want us to come back and do more?'

'Maybe, just maybe,' she smiled, but shook her head and shrugged. 'But this place is closing down. Government cuts.'

'Closing down?' said Debbie.

'When?' I asked.

'The truth is,' she said, turning to each of us, 'it's already happened.'

Mine and Debbie's eyes locked. Eyebrows arched.

'Look at this! This is what youngsters round here need!' she continued. 'This is what's missing!'

'Well . . .' Debbie began. I was pretty sure I knew what she was going to suggest, and I nodded encouragement. 'We could, perhaps . . . squat it. You know, as a community-run-youth-centre-thing?'

The woman tapped a knuckle on her lips as she thought.

'Now that would certainly kick up a rumpus!' she laughed.

'Oh yeah,' I said, 'we're good at that!'

●

After the party, crammed into the tiny kitchen at Grittleton Road, Debbie, Simone, Joe, Zander and I were discussing all that had happened over the weekend. It was a lot to take in.

Our hopes for making a little money were in ruins. But the party, despite the gangsters, had been exceptional. The big silver and gold backdrop had looked stunning. When the sun flooded into the room, there was a palpable synergy between it, the music and the hundreds who continued to dance across the day. It was as if the new winged sun disc backdrop embraced all the warmth, harmony and love in the room.

After our chat on the bench, Clara, the Community Centre manager, had taken Debbie on a tour of the whole building. She had sat Debbie down in her office and made it clear that she was totally up for us squatting the building. It was an amazing opportunity. Debbie, who was sitting at the small kitchen table with Joe, was enthusiastically telling us about the tour.

'There's space for studios, workshops, a massive kitchen.'

'The Spiral Centre.' Simone moved her hands in a slow arch as she envisaged the new name in lights above the door.

'And that rave room!' I said. 'One of the best yet!'

'But who wants to be in London?' said Zander.

'We're here for the winter whatever,' said Simone. 'It could be perfect.'

'But it's not,' said Joe, crumbling hash into a spliff. 'Seriously, I know that family. They wouldn't stop at just robbing the door. No way could we do anything there without them holding guns to our heads. It would be pure madness!'

Joe was right. Holding a squat against eviction was one thing. Dealing with extortion and violence from a local firm was another level. It was heartbreaking because it was the perfect place for us to realise so many of our ideas. But those ideas could wait. We still had space enough to function and resources and skills to share.

'What are you all looking so glum about?' said Aztek as he squeezed into the kitchen. 'Budge up.' He tried opening the fridge door. We squashed up just enough for him to reach in. He took out an empty bowl, a spoon and a carton of milk.

'Chilled milk, spoon and bowl?' I was curious.

'Oh yeah, you should try it,' he replied. 'Just remember to chill the bowl and spoon overnight and it takes your cornflakes to a whole new level!'

Joe tucked a roach into his spliff, stood up and gave his place at the table to Aztek.

Aztek put the bowl down and arranged the spoon to be perfectly positioned next to it. Then he centred the milk on the table, sides at ninety degrees to the tabletop and did the same with the cornflakes box.

'Mr Organised!' said Debbie.

'Well, I gotta be living with you lot!'

A couple of days later, Ixy showed up at Grittleton Road. She'd left her horse with Ness and the rest of the horse-drawn on the outskirts of London and hitchhiked in to have a go on the decks. Sanchia and Sasha lent her some records and Aztek showed her how to mix.

GATECRASHERS

There are not many dates I remember from the history of the kings and queens of England. But I do remember 1649. The year King Charles I had his head chopped off. It was during the Wars of the Three Kingdoms, which may have provided an opportunity for revolutionary ideas to be discussed: questioning the divine right of kings, a parliament free of the dictates of a monarchy, regular elections, a fair legal system, extended suffrage, religious tolerance. But by the end of the bloody reshuffle, it was still an elite of landowning men in control.

The year 1649 was also the date that a bunch of squatters occupied a place near Weybridge, on the south-west edge of London, called St George's Hill.

The group, led by Gerrard Winstanley, became known as the Diggers because they dug the land, removed the boundary hedges and planted crops to feed themselves and all who joined them. St George's Hill had been common land. Many commons were being taken away from the people and privatised under the Enclosures Acts – 'legal property rights' that changed the law and allowed the property-owning class to take land into private ownership. The Diggers directly challenged this, arguing for the rights of access to land. They acknowledged the connections between people and the environment; they argued for a synergetic relationship between humans and nature, non-hierarchical ownership and communal living. Even though their ideas resonated with many, including the Levellers within the army, their homestead was repeatedly attacked by thugs in the pay of the landowning classes. After only five months, they were forced to leave. But their efforts sent ripples across history and their legacy is still influential today.

What we didn't know was that the hill was now the site of one of the most expensive gated estates in Britain. Perimeter fences, security firms and closed-circuit cameras guarded the 420 private mansions within. The estate had its own golf course and tennis courts for the exclusive use of the millionaire residents, which included pop stars, footballers, oligarchs and judges. All we knew was what Ian Orinoco told us on the phone.

'It's an abandoned mansion on St George's Hill – yes, the Diggers' St George's Hill!'

How could we say no?

Ian and the Weybridge posse had discovered an unmanned security gate. We arrived that evening at a prearranged time, the barrier gate was opened, and we drove in past the empty sentry box, up the tree-lined road into the estate and onto the driveway of a large house. A very large house, standing alone in an acre of overgrown garden. It was built, I guess, in the seventies in a mock-Georgian style in pale brick, with a large white portico and balcony above the front door. Around the back was a swimming pool of black stagnant sludge and green algae.

Inside, ten bedrooms and seven bathrooms, but the quality of the construction was noticeably cheap. The fittings, bannisters, kitchen units were all thin and flimsy. The only remarkable feature in the house was a ridiculously oversized chandelier hanging in the foyer. Probably three metres across, with thousands of clear plastic crystals hanging within concentric metal hoops, anodised in fake gold.

In fact, the whole 'Millionaire's Mansion' felt fake. Little more than a cardboard cut-out, as if it's claim to existence, there on the historic Diggers' site, was as flimsy and cheap as its construction. The Diggers' legacy had only grown stronger over the last three centuries. This mansion would not outlast them, even if it did survive our bass bins. Which of course it did – but only just.

Luckily for us, our zero-strategy plan of leaving the directions to the party on our answerphone outwitted the estate's security just long enough for us to get a full house. And a beautiful party – made all the merrier because everyone there knew the history of the hill. The sense of reclaiming what had been taken was enhanced when some nefarious character went up into the attic and cut a cartoon-style hole in the ceiling where the chandelier hung. The great crystal crown crashed to the floor – fortunately without injuring anyone. Immediately, people repurposed the tangled chains of plastic diamonds into necklaces, bracelets and tiaras. Two or three hundred people adorned in sparkles. Each bead a worthless bauble to a millionaire, but a priceless talisman to everyone sharing that moment.

•

The party continued on Sunday. We had no complaints. Until Monday. The music was off, the sound system 'Spirited away by mysterious figures', as one newspaper put it. Of course there was absolutely nothing mysterious about it – we'd simply loaded it into the van and drove it back to London. A few of us stayed behind discussing if we should extend our occupation. It was freezing cold but there were open fireplaces in the house and we could collect wood from the huge overgrown garden. That afternoon, huddled around the fire, we had no food, no bedding, no money. But a very posh postcode.

The fact that the common had now been secured as one of the most exclusive and expensive addresses on the planet was, to me, no more than an ironic twist. Our real excitement, while warming ourselves around the fire, came from being on the Diggers' land. Not by conscious intention, but by an unplanned set of circumstances. Circumstances that, in that moment, felt magnetic.

While in deep conversation about the Diggers, someone found a small leatherbound book lying around. It was a bible. I've no idea where it came from, but for fun we took turns reading parts of it out loud. Of course, we skipped all the boring stuff and cut straight to the apocalyptic prophecies of the *Book of Revelation*. Armageddon. Pestilence. Plagues of scorpion-tail locusts. Bottomless pits. Lakes of fire. Seas of blood. The white rider of death. The whore of Babylon. 666. And the red dragon.

While enjoying the drama, it became clear how coercive the stories were. And to top it all, the ascension of the chosen few! It made me angry to think of all the millions of people who'd been taught to believe that all human hope and salvation lies in unquestioning obedience to an imposed authority.

Wacky, a good friend of Didz, was with us at the fire while we read. He was small in stature, with scraggly beard and hair, scruffy denims, a front tooth missing and a very particular way of viewing the world.

'St George's Hill!' he growled. 'St George never killed the dragon! It's a lie! The dragon is alive! The dragon *is* life!'

As Wacky said this, a shadow crossed the small window at the side of the house, and there was a flash.

Thinking it was an approaching storm, I joked, 'God didn't like that!'

There was another flash. I got up from the fire and went over to take a look. As I stood on tiptoe, trying to peer through the high narrow window into the garden, there was another.

'It's a fucking photographer!' I yelled. Holding his camera above his head, he was shooting blind into the house.

Everyone jumped up and peeped out from behind the curtains that hung at the front windows. To our shock and amazement, the woodland road, outside the gate, was full of photographers, TV crews and their vehicles. Seeing movement at the windows, the paparazzi sprang into action. Swarming up the drive. Knocking on the door. Tapping on the windows. Catcalling for pictures and interviews. We were trapped.

•

I was exhausted. I'd been up all weekend. I stared into the fire watching little red dragons in the flames. The fire was the only comfort, our only sustenance, our lifeline. Aztek came and sat with me.

'There's someone I'd like you meet,' he said. 'Come and have a quick word.'

I was puzzled. 'Who? Where?'

'I've been chatting with him at the door.'

'No way, Aztek! I'm not talking to any of that lot!'

'Nah, but this one's different, really. Come and listen to what he's gotta say.'

We went to the front door. Aztek drew the brass bolts. I checked that the chain was in place. The door opened a crack.

A tall bloke in a dark suit and smart black Crombie-style coat was waiting there. 'We don't have much time,' he explained. 'We go live in . . .' he looked at his watch, 'One hour and fifty-one minutes. I have a car waiting.'

'Hang on.' I was confused. 'What are we talking about?'

Aztek answered, '*The Jonathan Ross Show!*'

Jonathan Ross hosted a very popular, primetime TV chat show in Britain.

'No way!' I shook my head and pushed the door to close it.

But the bloke's foot was in the way. 'Let me just say one thing. We're an independent production company. Channel X. Owned by Jonathan. We're not connected with this lot.' He gave a small nod in the direction of the crowd blocking the gate. 'We're not here to stitch you up, I promise.' He moved his foot.

'No, sorry.' I closed the door.

'Why not, man?' Aztek protested. 'This is our opportunity to go live – to millions!'

'Yeah! Exactly! Live TV! Millions! No fucking way!'

There was a polite knock at the door. Aztek opened it.

'One hour forty-eight minutes,' said the bloke.

'Give us a minute.' Aztek closed the door again. 'Look, the

opportunity to tell people, on live TV, about Spiral Tribe, without all the shite the papers say. We'd be crazy not to!'

Aztek had a point. The newspapers would make up a whole load of bullshit anyway. They already had. Live independent TV might be different.

'But,' I said to Aztek, 'we haven't slept for days. How we gonna handle it?'

Aztek opened the door. The bloke tapped his watch. Aztek nodded and closed the door.

'We're bloomin' hardcore!'

It was serendipity that had brought about this situation. We had not, nor did we want to, court controversy. But now that we'd be in all the national newspapers, this could be an opportunity to tell people who we really were.

I took a deep breath. 'Okay, Aztek,' my mouth said as my entire nervous system silently screamed, *No!*

•

When the bloke had said, 'I have a car waiting', what he actually meant was that he had a chauffeur-driven limo. He sat in the back with Aztek and me with an expensive looking attaché case on his lap.

'I don't think you realise how big this story is in the papers.' He opened the case. 'It's a national scandal.'

'What, that we're squatting a millionaire's mansion?' I asked. 'Or that mansions are standing empty while people are being made homeless?'

'That's exactly my point,' he said, 'Most newspapers ignore the real issues, but Jonathan and our producers have a lot of sympathy for your cause.'

'Really?' Aztek sounded more convinced than me.

The bloke took out some documents from the case. 'Did you know that there are actually forty empty properties on the St George's Estate?' He spoke calmly in a measured, practical tone – which made me even more suspicious of him.

'Forty? Blimey!' said Aztek.

'So you're a researcher for Channel X?' I asked.

'I do some of that,' he replied, and gave me a little smile. 'Research, finding, fixing.' He pulled out another document to show us. 'Did you know the property has been repossessed by the Halifax Building Society and has been empty now for two years?'

'And where exactly is the TV studio?' I asked as he handed me another document.

'Riverside Studios, next to Hammersmith Bridge,' he answered. 'I just need to get your signatures.'

'What's this for?' I asked.

'Release forms. Your consent to filming.' He produced a gold pen. 'Just here, and here.'

My brain was racing, trying to make some sense of all the information.

•

We turned off the small, wooded roads in suburban Cobham, and onto the motorway towards London. With an effortless purr the limo slipped into the fast lane.

'Are we gonna be in time?' asked Aztek as the acceleration pressed us deeper into the plush leather seats.

'It'll be close.' The bloke looked at his watch. 'When we arrive, you'll go straight into makeup.'

'Makeup?' Aztek laughed.

'The girls will do a great job. Clean you up for the cameras.'

I felt that we were speeding towards an interrogation in close-up. A public inquisition carrying the judgement of millions. Questioned by a professional tormentor. A matador, who, behind his showbiz cloak of jokes and geniality, hid a sword and the intention to give the crowd the bloody sacrifice it craved. The acceleration of the car, pressed into the pit of my stomach, and the closer we got to London, the more difficult it was to breathe.

DOWN BY THE RIVERSIDE

The River Thames has always been important in my life. Throughout my childhood and teenage years, it's always been there. It's a place where I can find inner tranquillity. Just standing on the bank and watching the river flow for a few minutes was usually enough to clear my mind and wash away any worries. That night, as we approached Hammersmith, I was extremely nervous, but the river didn't fail me. As we crossed the Victorian suspension bridge, the lights of London mirrored in the water, my thoughts calmed and everything came into sharp focus. The mission was clear.

We were out of the car. Running into the building. Along office corridors. Sat down in a mirrored room by a couple of women who dabbed our faces with powder. The presenter, Jonathan Ross – in a swanky purple suit and silk tie to match – appeared, shook our hands and introduced himself.

'The segment with you guys is just six minutes,' he said. 'Remember this is a family entertainment show. I've got two jokes scripted, so please don't let them throw you. They're not meant to be personal – I actually think what you're doing is great!' He then told us the jokes. Both were silly. 'Great!' he said again and smiled, without waiting for any response from us. 'And er . . . what's all this?' He motioned to the coils of chandelier crystals that hung heavily across our chests.

'Spiral bling,' Aztek said with pride and rolled back his shoulders.

Mr Ross laughed. 'Beautiful as it is, probably best to lose it – you don't want people to think you've just robbed the crown jewels!' He winked and left the room.

The women helped to unwind us from our ill-gotten gains, then guided us into the backstage greenroom where we could watch the live audience laughing and clapping on TV monitors. Another woman, with a headset and clipboard, said, 'You're on', and hurried us out into a haze of blinding stage lights, applause and whistles. Johnathan Ross sat at his chatshow desk and introduced us.

'Squatting is back in vogue as the none too subtle art of occupying homes without the permission of the owner. Is property theft – or is this the theft of property? Here to dispute the rights and wrongs of the issue are two of the squatters you've been reading about in all the papers this week: Aztek and Mark from Spiral Tribe . . .'

Aztek had wanted to talk about his music. I'd wanted to talk more generally about free party culture. But with the fast-paced intro and scripted questions, that clearly wasn't going to happen. It was probably true that the independent TV company liked us and loved that we were challenging the status quo. It made a great story. But other than those few moments of airtime, they had no skin in the game. No further responsibility or consideration outside of that little bubble. One clumsy answer from me or Aztek, one wobble on the diplomatic tightrope, and we'd put everything we stood for at risk. If we were going to challenge the status quo, it had to be worthy of our cause. In those six, indelible, unforgiving minutes, every question was loaded and each of our answers would have consequences.

The questions, though light-hearted, all centred around issues of private property and, more specifically, the implication that squatters were invaders, taking homes away from people. I argued that squatting was the exact opposite, a community organising itself to create new homes in unused buildings. Though there was a bias to the questioning, Mr Ross certainly wasn't hostile to the idea. We were pretty relaxed, and thanks to the 'fixer' in the limo, I had all the right stats to back up my arguments.

The final question was, 'How do you get on with the police?'

I didn't want to be antagonistic, so my answer was diplomatic. I said that they didn't have a problem with us. I think this answer came across as trivialising their authority. My intention was to reassure anyone interested that Spiral Tribe were a friendly, peace-loving bunch. But denying that there was any problem could be seen as signalling my contempt for their authority. If I thought they had no problem with us, then, by implication, they had no power over us. We did not fear them, or their masters.

In that moment, I was oblivious that there was an active and extremely predatory echelon of the establishment that didn't want there to be 'no problem'. Its raison d'être is to generate and maintain a certain level of fear, doubt and division. For us to go on live TV and articulate a case against homelessness was one thing. Squatting a millionaire's mansion was another. But the real thorn in the establishment's side was that we, as squatters, were given a voice – and it turned out, contrary to the relentless efforts of the mainstream press, that we were not mindless invaders of the sanctity of home and hearth. We were cheerful, approachable, reasonable people, who liked to party. And yes, we did gleefully stick it to the rich who'd appropriated the common land on St George's Hill. But then, what's the harm in that?

ASCOT: DECEMBER 1991

When we arrived, Circus Warp had already pitched their blue-and-red striped marquee. They, like us, where a free party and festival collective. Though we didn't know them well, they were always very welcoming.

The place had been an old junkyard for aeroplanes situated in a large area of woodland. It had long been cleared of any planes and was now abandoned, although the council seemed to be using the place to store gravel. Mountains of the stuff. What we hadn't realised was that the woodland around us adjoined Royal Ascot Racecourse on one side, which in turn adjoined Royal Ascot Golf Club, which in turn adjoined Windsor Great Park. 'The Queen's Back Garden', just fifteen minutes away, and the site of the legendary Windsor Free Festival of the 1970s. Fifteen minutes in the other direction, the woodland adjoined the Royal Military Academy at Sandhurst, where all British Army officers were trained. Above us, another golf club. Below us, the National Rifle Association's firing ranges at Bisley. You get the idea. No wonder, then, for such an apparently unpopulated area of woodland, the national newspapers made the most of it:

'Prince Andrew was caught up in the chaos as police tried to break up a 5,000-strong acid house party, it was revealed last night.' (*The Sun*)

'More than 600 people, among them Prince Andrew, protested to police, jamming the 999 emergency line as the party raved on for 24 hours [. . .] A police 999 operator was telling callers that if nothing could be done to help Prince Andrew, nothing could be done to help them.' (*News of the World*)

To the newspapers we were a demonic spirit haunting the rich and powerful's woodland and, very possibly, souring their milk. Outraging the likes of Prince Andrew and his aristo neighbours fired up the scandalmonger machine. Of course, we saw pissing off the royals for one night as a little feather in the cap for the free party movement. Unaware that, just up the road, back in 1974, the Windsor Free Festival had ended in extreme police violence against men, women (some obviously pregnant) and children (some as young as nine). That attack had caused a public outcry, radicalised many young people, and was one of the seeds from which the Stonehenge Free Festival had grown.

We set up at the opposite end of the site, away from Circus Warp, next to the huge heaps of gravel. It was icy cold, which may have put some people off coming, but for those that did, the reward was magical. The night was clear. At least the sky was, as a mysterious mist hovered in the bare trees all around us.

We built a roaring log fire in the middle of our dance floor. Beyond its glow the cold bit through even my thickest jacket. Our light show was the stream of hot orange sparks against the frosty stars.

As dawn broke, we found ourselves in a different world. The mist had frozen on every tree, branch and twig to form long, spiked ice crystals that sparkled in the morning sun. Winter had arrived in all her beauty.

Meanwhile, no doubt, Prince Andrew and his neighbours were frothing down their phones to the police and the newspapers. *Polite society* needed to be rescued from the rabble!

THE COMMER 04

Back in London we got a call from Spider. He and New Zealand Andy had found a truck that Zander might like.

•

The abandoned warehouse was squatted by a crew calling themselves Conspiracy. Parked up inside was a beautiful collection of vintage trucks and showman's circus trailers. Some of which were for sale. Among them was the pit bull-of-all-pit bull trucks. A dark green, ex-military, 1957 Commer Q4. With a handsome snout and streamlined front wheel arches that tapered back towards the step up to the cab. Wide wheelbase. Flatbed. Solid steel bumpers. Towing hitches front and back. And chunky tires – the wheels half the height of the entire vehicle.

Spider introduced us to Matt and Giles. Matt, dressed in overalls and with round wire-rimmed glasses, opened negotiations.

'She's old but solid.' He patted the top of the curved wheel arch. 'And MOT exempt.'

Giles added, 'She's slow but powerful, could tow any one of these showman's.' He gestured towards several vintage circus trailers. 'Perhaps you'd be interested in one of them too?'

'Not now,' Zander answered, 'but maybe another time.' I could see Zander was already in love with the truck – he just wanted to drive.

'Give it a go,' Matt said as he handed Zander the key.

Gilles removed a couple of blocks of wood that were choking the front wheel. 'Handbrake needs adjusting,' he explained.

Zander climbed up into the high cockpit, a rounded bump, just big enough for two seats, and small compared with the heavy-set bulk of the beast. It started first time with a roar. Zander went for a spin around the interior of the warehouse. It looked and sounded awesome.

Hands were shaken. Cash was paid. And the beast had joined the Tribe.

I climbed up into the passenger seat, marvelling at the utilitarian design. The seats were original, as was everything else, not built for comfort, but built to last. Every detail was curvy and heavy duty. Even the bodywork appeared to have been sculpted from quarter-inch steel.

Zander revved the engine in farewell to the Conspiracy lads. I wound down the window and waved goodbye. Giles came running up alongside and hopped up onto the passenger-side step.

'Don't forget these!' He handed me the two big blocks of wood.

We followed Spider and New Zealand Andy out. They were in one of Spider's red and yellow circus trucks and were taking us to see a 'beautiful' new warehouse they'd found.

Everything was fine at the first set of traffic lights. But at the second stop, which was on a slight slope, we started rolling backwards.

'Fuck!' Zander yelled. 'Quick, the . . .'

I jumped out and slipped one of the blocks under the front wheel, just before we crunched into the car behind.

It happened every time we stopped on a slope. Zander cussed and cursed the entire journey, but we managed to get across town without destroying anything.

•

The site was on an industrial estate by the Blackwall Tunnel in Greenwich, South London. An enormous warehouse. The gates were open, and we drove straight in.

'Don't mind the smell,' said Spider as he jumped out of his cab. 'That's just the dog meat factory.' He nodded towards the steaming stainless-steel chimneys of the building next door.

'What's important is that it's on the Greenwich meridian!'

He winked and tapped a finger against the side of his nose. 'The zero line of longitude. The point that all space and time are measured from! We do a party here and we'll be messing with their grid and sending our own signals!'

'Seriously, on the Meridian?' I was impressed. Again, I wasn't in complete agreement with the science behind Spider's thinking, but a party on the meridian – that would be a potent piece of poetry.

Spider was an imaginative thinker, very able to step away from the background noise of mainstream reality to view the world through different eyes. The same was true of Wacky. Some people may have thought that their take on things was non-applicable, or just plain weird. But their insight often drew on a deeper sensitivity of the world. It was imaginative, and artistic, often symbolic – and always shamanic.

I'd left Zander with Spider and New Zealand Andy talking trucks and caught the train back across London to meet Seb.

RAILWAY CONNECTIONS

Station Road in Harleston sat on top of one and a half square miles of railway junctions and sidings. A huge area that stretched west to Acton Lane, east to Scrubs Lane and all the way south to Old Oak Common. That's a lot of iron railway track to have in your back yard.

Even without the bird's eye view of Google Earth or drone footage, in my mind's eye I pictured these great intersections from above as large Technoglyphic forms. The original purpose of them was clear, but for me they also held a mysterious energy beyond their intended function. And it wasn't only me who was intrigued by the layout of these industrial conduits. Seb was too.

I met him at the Station Road house, where he'd lived before going up to Leeds to study music. As it was a beautiful day, and I had a new design to show him, we decided to walk over to Maygrove Road.

The most direct route was to follow the overground railway north-west towards West Hampstead. It's about half an hour on foot.

'Had you ever noticed,' Seb asked me, 'that in just this small distance this railway connects some of the key Spiral hotspots? Station Road, Chris's house, your old place at Brondesbury, the Skool House, and Maygrove? All connected by this one curved line.'

'Yeah, it's weird,' I said. 'And of course Parliament Hill, where we all got to know each other that night running around blind under that tarpaulin on Red Dragons!

'And crashed into Boudica's grave!'

'And Parliament Hill was the place where the name Spiral Tribe came into being.'

'Hmm, strange.' Seb slowed down as he thought. 'Perhaps the vibe is like electricity, and travels down the metal of the railway lines?' He stopped and looked at the railway next to us.

'Or how about: the railway banks are undisturbed havens for nature,' I suggested, putting my hand through the railings to touch the long grass growing along the embankment. 'And it's a continuous living bio-vibe?'

'Ah yeah, that's a good one. But maybe it's a combination of the two?'

'Or three?' I suggested.

'What's the third?'

'Our consciousness. We make connections. We make maps. We *are* connectors.'

•

At Maygrove I made tea, then Seb and I sat down at the desk in the bay window. I got out my sketchbook and told him about a train journey I'd recently made on the mainline coming into London Paddington.

Onboard were several families with young kids, no doubt having a special day out in the capital. The train slowed as it made its final approach into Paddington. That last section of railway is overshadowed by deep cuttings, bridges and tunnels, and one gets a sense of the layered substructures of the city. Riveted iron girders and brickwork blackened with ancient soot. Runs of bitumen-coated cable and rusted pipework. Liquid seeping through the heavily buttressed walls designed to contain the guts of the city behind. A subterranean world. A world that is only experienced in the few seconds that it takes the train to pass. Inhabited at night by graffiti artists who set their visual traps then disappear back into anonymity. Ambushing that brief moment when someone on a passing train catches a glimpse of their artwork.

The overexcited children of the visiting families, noses pressed to the windows, were spellbound by the energy of the graffiti. Pointing out with delight the vivid colours and dynamic shapes. The parents sat in silent apprehension, as if they were entering bandit country – surrounded on all sides by lawless symbolism and gangland codes.

One little boy, who was particularly excited by the urban vibes, noticed that his breath had misted the window. He started to design his own graffiti with his little finger on the glass.

'Stop that at once!' snapped his mother, as if the wobbly little face he'd drawn was vandalising the whole carriage.

As the train came under the six-lane sweep of the Westway, I noticed that its concrete piers, closest to the rail tracks, were free of any artwork. I was surprised – of all the spots I'd seen, that was the absolute best.

Just as empty urban spaces had helped shape Spiral Tribe, so now this raw concrete pier conjured an image. An image that, for me, invoked the spirit of subculture: graffiti, free parties, pirate radio and independent records.

I showed Seb my first sketches.

'It looks like . . .' He tilted his head, then my sketchbook, one way and then the other. 'A jester. A grinning skull. A Jack-in-the-box?'

'Yeah, it's all those things – but can you see the hidden message?'

It slowly dawned on him. 'Aahhh . . . it's a face made from the number twenty-three!'

'You got it!'

A 23 formed the features of the face (as on the cover of this book). But it was inspired by the skeletal warriors with plumed headdresses that had jumped out of the sand at me, the reversible grinning face I'd originally created for our party in Cable Street, and the scribbled little face in the child's breath on the train window that had caused such an upset. What I found intriguing about this impish entity was how it immediately felt independent of me, with a life – and destiny – all of its own.

Our record label had a logo. A face. Now we needed some music. And money.

•

Seb's studies in Leeds were not specifically about electronic music, but he'd discovered a small, unused electronic music studio hidden away in the basement. He had his Roland 303 and had also recently swapped four Es for a funny little yellow-and-black synthesiser called a Wasp.

A massive fan of acid house and techno, he was enthusiastic to experiment with making tracks. Charlie Hall had expressed an interest too. If we could pull off a big party, we might be able to raise the funds we needed to press a record. Raising funds at the shebeen to buy the sound system had been intense. But in theory, if we found another good venue, we could do it again.

MAKING CONNECTIONS

Sadly, that venue did not turn out to be the Greenwich warehouse. I'd had high hopes of working with Spider and The Normals. Plus, I was excited by Spider's idea that we'd send vibrations out along the zero line of the world's meridian. But the party at the warehouse was a disappointment. The place was a hellhole. The stench of putrefying meat from the pet food factory didn't help, plus it was bitterly cold. To stave off hypothermia we built a fire on the concrete floor, just inside the hanger doors. The only available wood was pallets from the surrounding industrial zone. When they burned, even smoke-lessly, they gave off some kind of vapour from the chemicals they'd been treated with. This may have helped cover the smell of rotting flesh, but it irritated my lungs, and in combination with the cold, I got the beginnings of a heavy bronchial infection.

One small consequence of squatting the Greenwich meridian came when *iD* magazine arrived to take photos and interviewed us. *iD* was an alternative fashion and culture magazine famous for its street photography of real people with unique style. The photos they took of us – cold, hungry and dirty, huddled around a fire in a kitchen sink that had been dumped outside the warehouse gates – were perhaps a little more real and rather less stylish than the magazine's readers were used to. But the article was very supportive, calling us 'Revolutionary ravers, utopian dreamers and the force behind some very good parties.' But more importantly, they also made the point that I'd raised on TV about rising property prices, homelessness, and the need to allow people to squat disused buildings. Not only as residential shelter but also as a space where non-commercial community cultures could flourish.

•

Mine and Seb's game of connecting the dots of our experience in the urban landscape was infectious. The 'Spiral Vibe Line' became a thing. Other people had also given thought to similar ideas. There were the hippies and Ley lines, Situationists and psychogeography, beliefs in geomancy, and my favourite: the Songlines of the Australian First Nations People. One of the reasons that the Songlines seem more relevant to me was because, in my understanding of them, it is not an imposed system of control over the world, but more a conscious acknowledgement of it and one's own integral and ancestral part within it.

It's interesting to me how overlaying one's own synaptic maps onto the world can reveal patterns that may never have been noticed without the extra, and possibly random, input. The number 23 is a good example of this. To the mind searching for power and control, the magic – if that's what it is – will be missed. I'm not disputing that human curiosity and its quest for power and control, especially as channelled in the West, has not added some scientific understanding of the world. Isaac Newton was an alchemist, his curiosity aroused by pursuing the goal of turning lead into gold. A clear indication of what incentivised him. That's not to downplay his intelligence or achievements. But the reductionist and power-seeking path that a lot of science follows is wilfully excluding. And as the atomic bombs and global warming have shown, it can lead us towards apocalypse.

Firing up the pattern-recognition department of the brain can take one to some interesting places. But if the observer is searching to hold power over the patterns in nature, then perhaps the bigger opportunity is overlooked. Playing the game of 'spot the number 23' is much more fun when the object of the game is not to try and impose human-centric ideas of meaning and rationality. But instead, by allowing the two-way interaction between the world around us and our perceptions to flow freely, it can be a cognitive exercise to widen perception beyond habitual boundaries.

The game of making connections from Seb's place at Station Road all along the railway line was about to prove more fruitful than the rather optimistic plan to fuck with the meridian.

THE ROUNDHOUSE

It was Ian Orinoco who made first contact.

On a large triangle of wasteland, sandwiched between the corner of Regent's Park Road, Haverstock Hill and an area of railway sidings, was one of London's most iconic buildings. A hub of early industrialisation. One of the main nodes in the synaptic map of history. A great Victorian mothership. A temple to technology.

The Roundhouse. The vast locomotive turning shed. Still empty from when Katia and I had been drawn to it the year before.

That afternoon I stood on the edge of the wasteland with Ian and Zander.

Ian was explaining how he'd met a group of squatters from Camden who'd asked us to come and organise a rave – or two.

Zander examined the deep trench and bank that had been excavated all around the perimeter. Clearly it had been dug by the owners with the purpose of keeping people like us out. I stood there speechless, amazed by the building on so many levels: a historic landmark, legendary underground music venue of the sixties and seventies, and on the Spiral Vibe Line right in the centre of trendy London. And with Christmas and New Year's Eve around the corner, perhaps even the dream venue that would provide us with enough money to bring us one step closer to the Spiral Tribe record label.

'That roof is like a massive speaker cone!' I exclaimed.

'And,' Ian added, 'it was built as a giant turntable – but not your Technics!'

'This is going to take some doing,' said Zander climbing up out of the ditch onto the bank. 'But with a few of us on it, we can backfill it.'

'We could come back tonight and make a start,' I suggested.

Zander shook his head. 'We'd look like a bunch of grave robbers. Best to do it during the day, sometime this week. We can wear our hi-vis.'

With that decided we walked across the flat wasteland towards the back of the building, although it didn't really have a back, or a front, just several arched doors of steel all the way around, each big enough to drive a steam locomotive though. As we approached, the magnetism of the building became palpable.

'This door's open,' Ian said.

We arrived at a small door welded into one of the bigger doors. 'And later,' he added, pointing to a set of stone steps to the left, 'if you're feeling adventurous you should check out the basement. But don't get lost – it's dark down there!' We followed him though the small metal door into the main building.

Stepping over the threshold into the windowless twilight, everything seemed amplified. Stretching before us was a floor of some 2,000 square metres. Around the curved walls, a high gallery. Halfway between the exterior wall and the centre, a ring of twenty-four pillars supported ironwork arches and the coned roof.

Outside, you could only see one aspect of the building at a time – and then only at some distance. Inside, you felt the impact of the whole, all in one expansive jolt. Outside, the world was chaotic and random. Inside, it was geometric and organised. The simplicity of the architecture was calming, clear and elegant.

In the exact centre of the floor was a campfire. Within its small circle of yellow-orange light was a group of four figures. A couple of excitable dogs were chasing each other in and out of the gigantic shadows. We went over to them to have a chat. They were all quite young and seemed tired. All except Willie X.

Willie X had a bubbly personality. In his early thirties, he was dressed in a white boiler suit, now smudged with oil and ingrained ash. On his head sat a trapper's hat with earflaps sticking out sideways. He was hugely enthusiastic about having a party, involved as he was in the Stonehenge Walk – an annual pilgrimage to the stones every summer solstice. Part protest at the government's opposition to the free festival, part spiritual homage to the stones themselves.

I left Zander and Ian chatting round the fire with Willie, not only because the smoke was irritating my lungs but also because I was curious to check out the basement.

At the bottom of the steps the low door was unlocked. I switched on my torch and, feeling a mix of apprehension and excitement, went underground.

Inside, the roof was low. The ground uneven. The air stale. As I wound my way around the network of short walls that were supporting the building above, I was surprised that the foundations were not neatly symmetrical. Not as elegantly geometric as the engine room above. Some of the brick piers were angled along radial lines, others seemed to follow a concentric pattern. It was a haphazard labyrinth. Going deeper, the gaps between the piers got smaller. Space tightened. The air grew heavy. The darkness more pressing.

I don't know what drove my curiosity. Perhaps it was my own obsession with shapes and symmetry. But it felt like the pull towards the centre was coming from the building. A pull towards the core that I couldn't resist.

Finally, I came to a central chamber. It was small, round and claustrophobic. I guess I'd hoped for some ancient machine room that housed the workings of the giant locomotive's turntable. The direct drive. The central spindle around which everything turned. But it was empty. I sat at its centre on a pile of rubble. I dared myself to turn off my torch.

In total darkness and silence I waited for some kind of insight. Something that would suit the sanctity of the building. Some greater connection or deeper understanding of this temple to technology. Nothing occurred to me. In fact, the only thing I was aware of was the oppressive weight of my surroundings, as if I were experiencing the exact opposite of the sense of expansiveness that I'd felt in the engine room above. Bored and disappointed, I switched my torch on and headed back.

I didn't get lost, but I'm not sure how many wrong turns I took before I saw the rectangle of light in the doorway. The further I moved away from the middle of the labyrinth, the lighter my body felt. My mind cleared and I realised that at the core of this historic hub was not only technology, global industrialisation, transport and communication, but that it also stood at the heart of the imperial power that has, and continues to, oppress so many.

MILITANT

A couple of weeks previously, Simone, Sanchia and Justin had gone on a little adventure together on the Techno Bus. After driving south across Europe, they arrived at Justin's gran's empty holiday home in Spain. Justin had popped out for a moment while Simone and Sanchia showered and borrowed a couple of Justin's gran's dressing gowns and a pair of slippers each. Moments later the door crashed in and the house was flooded with armed police. Unfortunately, they discovered Justin's stash of acid. Simone and Sanchia were arrested – still wearing dressing gowns and slippers – and joined Justin in the police cells. He had apparently tried to swap some acid with an undercover cop. He took full responsibility and, after two days, the girls were let go. Justin went to prison awaiting trial. Penniless, Simone and Sanchia had to abandon the Techno Bus and hitchhike back to England.

We were all devastated to hear the news. Justin was a rebellious kid who could be reckless just for kicks. But he was kind, gentle and generous. He didn't deserve prison.

•

Spider had a seemingly infinite collection of incredible vintage trucks. But the word vintage may at times be misleading. For sure, modern haulage trucks are faster, more energy efficient, easier to drive and more comfortable. But nobody can deny that trucks of a certain era win hands down when it comes to sheer awesomeness. One such truck in Spider's collection was a beast among beasts. The AEC Militant. A 1950s, six-wheel drive, artillery tractor. It had the general appearance of a military lorry with drop-sides, tailgate and a canvas bow-top canopy. But it was a monster, designed to tow heavy field guns in rough terrain. With a top speed around 25mph, it was slow but unstoppable.

The plan was simple. The plan was Militant.

That night Spider pulled up outside 23 Grittleton Road. The gigantic truck completely blocked the quiet residential street. Spider was buzzing. As we carried our speaker cabs out of the house to load into the roaring beast, he revved the engine and shouted encouragement down from the driver's window. Each of the six wheels of the Militant was at least one and a half metres in diameter, and the top of the tailgate was well above my reach. It took me several attempts to jump up and pull myself into the back. Inside the truck was The Normals' sound system, but there was space for a little more. After a struggle I managed to unbolt the tailgate, which dropped open with a crash. The bed of the Militant was still a good two metres above the road. Spider revved the engine again.

Everyone from Grittleton helped, getting under each speaker cab and pushing up, while I pulled. One by one we got each onboard. The lads went back in the house to get the amp rack. It would be a bastard to load. Our largest W-bins were heavy but manageable. But the amplifiers bolted one above the other in their racked flight case were a dead weight – difficult for four strong bodies to lift, even up normally spaced steps. I scratched my head. *Perhaps Zander could rig a block and tackle to hoist it up.* I examined the metal struts that supported the canvas roof. *Too thin, they'd never take the weight.*

Spider called, 'Come on!' and revved the engine again, which didn't help. It was going to take some careful planning to get the amps safely in – or some time to unbolt them from the rack and load them one by one. I waited for the others to come back out of the house to ask what they thought was best. *But they're taking their time!*

After a few more minutes, Hubert came out. He looked up and down the street, then came to the back of the truck and called up to me. 'We didn't bring the amps out, did we?'

'No,' I answered, rather puzzled at the question.

''Cause they're not in the house.'

'What?'

'They're not in the house.'

'But . . . where are they then?' My mind couldn't grasp the possibility of the amps, in their super-heavy flight case, just disappearing.

'Well, they're not there!' Hubert looked around the sides of the truck, clearly as confused as me.

From inside the house, I heard Zander going ballistic. With the force of his curses behind them, the household exploded out onto the street. The amps were nowhere to be seen. They'd gone. Stolen. But when? By whom? We were all in shock.

'Who the fuck left the rig room unlocked!' Zander shouted at all of us. 'How many times have I told you to keep that fucking door locked!'

Everyone was silent while Zander relentlessly vented his fury at no one in particular. Lights in nearby houses were switching on. A neighbour opened a bedroom window and called for us to 'Keep it down!' A car drove into Grittleton Road and started beeping us to move. The Militant roared. But

Zander's fury rose above it all.

The truck lurched forward then stopped. A speaker cab nearly knocked me out the back. With help from Hubert, I managed to pull the tailgate up and bolt it shut.

'Let's go!' called Spider.

Hubert jumped in with me.

We had no choice. We had to leave, with or without the amps.

•

The short trip from Grittleton to Chalk Farm was one of the most intense twenty-minute journeys of my life. It wasn't just that my head was reeling from the disappearance of the amps. The 1950s Militant might have six huge wheels, but it had no smooth suspension. Spider hadn't given us time to secure the speaker cabs, so everything was sliding about. We had to simultaneously try and hold them in place without getting squashed or thrown out the back.

It was about to get worse. In his rush to leave, Spider hadn't mentioned the spectacular entrance he'd planned. Rather than waste time backfilling the trench and levelling the bank that protected the Roundhouse, he was going for a ram-raid approach. As we neared Chalk Farm, he got up speed, slammed the beast into six-wheel drive and powered up and over the trench and bank. It worked. We were in. The equipment survived the crash back down to Earth. As did Hubert and me – with only minor cuts and bruises.

WINTER SOLSTICE: DECEMBER 1991

With no amps of our own, we were dependent on The Normals' equipment, which was unfamiliar to the Spiral crew. Gastro was the only person who had any notion of how it all worked.

Our business deal with The Normals was a straight 50/50 split. Not only were we in desperate need of money to survive, but now that the Techno Bus had gone, we needed another vehicle. But because our amps had been stolen, we were now more or less back at square one. If we did make any money, buying amps would take priority over our dreams of a pirate radio transmitter and creating the Spiral Tribe record label.

Working together, we knew we had the ability to make the Roundhouse parties a success. It would be long hard hours for us all, but we were fired up and had the resolve. The central London location, the iconic status of the building and the holiday dates meant we could expect big crowds. To be safe, the consensus was that we needed as many responsible people as possible to be in key positions all night. With Simone and Sanchia still stuck in Europe and Justin in prison, our numbers were depleted, so we hired in some extra help in the shape of a nightclub security firm. It was their job to take care of the carpark and help manage the queue. They seemed like nice lads, and all went smoothly – to start with.

The first party was the winter solstice.

Back in 1991, all disco lights were pretty basic, either just flashing on and off or motorised with spinning mirrors and prisms. Just like the clunky old Moonflower we had. That was not the case with the lights we hired for the winter solstice party.

Strobeflowers were a game-changer. They could be set to respond to the beat or fired by a controller. Still based on the spinning mirror principle but with several major differences. They were agile and fast, able to spin in any direction, or remain stationary. The multicoloured beams strobed at any speed or intensity. They could narrow or widen their focus and the area that the beams covered – from a piercing pin-spot to an exploding radial blossom. We had six rigged to rotate together, or independently. When they 'flowered' the splayed beams of each unit overlapped and interlocked.

The radial geometry of the flowers meshed perfectly with the radial architecture of the Roundhouse. The roof struts, the metalwork within the circle of arched columns, the sweeping curve of the wall and the upper balconies. Strobeflowers, whether the manufacturers realised it or not, were purpose built for the Roundhouse parties. And the Roundhouse, whether the Victorian designers realised it or not, was built with Strobeflowers embedded somewhere in its future.

•

And there we were – dancing. Thousands of people orbiting the winter sun. At that historic hub of transportation and communication. In the circle of The Normals' heavy haulage trucks. In the interlocking vortex of the Strobeflowers. In the spiral groove of spinning vinyl.

That night the old rulebook of history was overwritten, along with its archaic attitudes and hierarchies. Replaced with something more valid, more inclusive, more equal. That night we broke free from the course preordained by the traditions of the establishment – we even defied linear logic. But it was logical because there was no denying it: all the technological inventiveness that spanned the centuries was now re-routed into and through that place with new purpose and new direction. We danced on the edge of transformation. A technological transformation, heralded in by techno.

•

It had been hard work staffing the door all night. The queues had been enormous and backed up along the street. The party had gone so well that Kevin Brewer, who'd helped feed us all at the library, suggested we donate a chunk of the takings to organise a thousand free Christmas dinners for the homeless. It was a great idea and Kev sorted it all with a local cafe.

It was in the Roundhouse carpark that I first met Jeff. Dressed in denim dungarees, he was loading his records into the back of his white Renault 5. We started chatting and he told me he'd just got back from Corfu where he'd been DJing. I was hugely impressed with his expansive knowledge of dance music, and we had a great conversation about Belgian new beat. He said he was keen to get involved with us, not only as a DJ but with organising too.

'You are more than welcome!' was my reply.

•

On the afternoon before the Christmas Eve party, the police arrived, 'Just to ask a few questions.'

We explained we were having a party and hosting Christmas

dinner for the homeless, so they seemed quite happy and left us to it. But not before confiscating the cranked starter handle for Big Lizzie, our large Lister diesel generator. This left us powerless, except for a tiny little petrol gennie that didn't have enough output for the building and all our hardware.

Luckily, Spider knew a bloke who could lend us another large gennie, which was hurriedly delivered that afternoon on the back of a recovery truck. It was huge and difficult to handle. Unfortunately, it slipped off the truck during unloading and was badly damaged. Spider and his crew managed to botch a repair and get it running again just in time for the party.

NEW YEAR'S EVE: 91/92

The Christmas eve party and the Christmas dinner all went well. But after Christmas a bout of flu went around. Tim was the first to catch it. Fortunately, Maygrove was close by, so when the fever struck he was able to get offsite and recover in bed. The non-stop intensity of holding down the mega parties, the sleepless nights and the cold didn't help my cough, which got worse. Then, on top of that, I too got the flu. By New Year's Eve, Tim had made a full recovery and I was out of action with the fever. Meaning that, while the New Year was being celebrated at the Roundhouse, I was shivering under the bedcovers at Maygrove.

But they weren't celebrating the New Year at the Roundhouse. Nobody there knew what the hell was happening. The following is pieced together from the testimonies of others.

Early in the evening, before the party was due to start, Gastro had been rushed to hospital with suspected blood poisoning. He had wired the rig for a live band, which had played earlier. The configuration, with the mixing desk out in the dance floor, did not work for DJs, and nobody understood the set-up.

There was a glimmer of hope. Over the previous few weeks, Steve Watson had been helping with the sound and hanging out with Gastro. He was perhaps the only person, in Gastro's absence, who might have any clue. But where was he? The hunt was on. The poor bloke had been on it for days. He'd finally escaped the endless shift he'd been working and hidden himself away to get some well-deserved sleep. Debbie tracked him down, huddled in a trailer. After some difficult persuading, he stumbled through the gathering crowds to try and get his head around the mess of cables that ran between the mixing desk, stage, decks and sound system. Single-handedly, and one by one, he managed, in a semi-delirious state, to get the speakers running. The party was on. The dance floor kicked.

Then just before midnight, the repair on the big generator failed. The crowd of thousands was plunged into darkness.

Ironically, the police arrived and, rather unhelpfully, demanded that the power be restored, though they didn't bring Big Lizzie's starting handle with them. Zander and Hamish left the door to help with the power. It was then that the security firm showed their true colours. Instead of holding the huge queue back, they continued letting people in – and taking the money for themselves.

By torchlight, Zander and Hamish opened up the other doors around the building to allow people out the back. Spider tried to repair the faulty generator. Thomas began modifying an electric drill chuck to work as a replacement crank handle for Big Lizzie. A troop of performers kept the atmosphere chilled with some spectacular fire breathing. Gastro returned from hospital, cured of his ills. He and Zander, armed with a long coil of cable, snuck over into the neighbouring yard, took the base plate off a lamppost, and connected to the live wire. Zander remembers he and Gastro had a guess at what time the streetlights across London would turn off, which would cut the power again. They both reckoned around 8 a.m. Not ideal – but better than nothing.

With the lamppost connected, for the second time that night the party was back on. Zander then went to help Thomas with his electric drill conversion.

At 8 a.m. sharp, the streetlights went out and the party ground to a halt. Gastro and Zander gave each other a knowing nod. Thomas started up the tiny petrol gennie to supply just enough power to the electric drill, which then turned Big Lizzie's engine over and – to everyone's delight – fired up. Third time lucky, the power was back on, and this time it stayed on.

As soon as it had got light the police disappeared. As did security, pockets stuffed with cash.

Though our decision to hire in more help had been based on a sense of responsibility, we learned that even when we were few, with our backs against the wall, it wasn't muscle – state sanctioned or private – that had won over. What had made the difference was everyone's solidarity and community spirit.

SNOWDONIA: JANUARY 1992

Simone and Sanchia made it back from Spain a couple of days after the last Roundhouse party. They were still in shock at the ordeal they'd been through, and that Justin was facing years in a Spanish jail.

My fever had gone but my cough was getting worse. Debbie, Simone, Hamish, Tim, Zander and Joe came round to Maygrove. As they filled me in on the details of the New Year's Eve party, they looked as ill and exhausted as I felt.

The Normals had decided to stay on at the Roundhouse in their trucks and trailers. The rest of our crew had gone off in various directions to chill. Without the Techno Bus, we had no onsite accommodation. After the relentless intensity of the past two weeks, we needed to make plans. To do that, we needed contact with nature.

'Let's go to Wales!' suggested Debbie. 'Connect with the dragon!'

Connection with the dragon, everyone agreed, was exactly what was needed.

'How we gonna get there?' asked Hamish.

He had a point. Zander's Q4 only had room for two in the cab. With no more Nancial, post office van or Techno Bus we were trapped.

'Buy another van?' Zander suggested. 'We need something practical.'

Simone nipped out to the corner shop and came back with an assortment of local vehicle trading magazines and newspapers. Hamish handed out a few beers and passed around a spliff. I drank tea, huddled close to the gas fire with a duvet over my shoulders. The smoke in the room felt acrid in my lungs. But I cheered up as Hamish and Simone started reading out various small ads and everyone warmed to the possibility of escaping the city.

'Check this out!' said Simone, 'Ford Transit minibus, 400 quid! "Has unique and unusual paintwork", bla-bla-bla, "Good runner".'

'Gotta be worth a look,.' said Hamish. He phoned the number, took the address, got up and said, 'On the fucking case, maties!'

Two hours later he was back with the van. We all rushed into the street to check it out. Originally it had been white, but at some point in its long life it had belonged to another group of squatters. How did we know? The 'unique and unusual paintwork' was not shy about announcing it. Writ large on the bonnet, each door and on the back, in bold red-and-black brushstrokes, was the international symbol of squatters: a circle diagonally crossed with a lightning-flash arrow.

'Not massively undercover though, is it?' said Debbie.

'But 400 quid for a Squatmobile,' said Simone. 'Can't argue with that!'

Hamish did a little celebratory dance in the street, turned his baseball cap backwards and jumped in the driver's seat.

While Hamish had been buying the van, Simone and Debbie had found a cheap deal on a rented cottage in Wales in the newspaper. We had no idea where it was, though the advert mentioned the Snowdonian mountains. After a quick shop for food supplies, we loaded up the minibus and left that night.

•

The rhythm of the road had changed. I opened my eyes. Everyone was asleep except Hamish, who was driving, and Simone in the passenger seat reading the map. Wiping away the condensation from my window, I peered out into a green, misty morning. We were traveling a narrow road, along the edge of a lake. Either side of us mountains pushed up and disappeared into low cloud.

After an hour of winding deeper into the mountains we arrived at a solitary, slated-roofed, stone house. No neighbours. No nearby village. Nothing but mist, mountains and a comforting silence.

Inside, the house was modern and warm. As soon as we found our beds we slept. I can't be certain, but I think it was two days before we resurfaced, refreshed and re-energised. The clean air seemed to have helped my cough. Over a big breakfast thrown together from our supplies and leftover packets of biscuits and crisps from motorway service stations, we discussed our situation.

•

Despite the chaos of New Year's Eve, our two weeks of hard graft had paid off. After the business with The Normals, we had enough to allocate funds for new amps, a radio transmitter and a record label. We'd pulled it off! It was time to celebrate. And so it was with a sense of relief and achievement, combined with a feeling of freedom, that we burst out of the front door and into the Squatmobile to explore the mountains.

Hamish was in the driving seat taking any random direction that felt right. A sheet of Strawberry blotters got passed around. We drove until the LSD kicked in. Hamish pulled over at the side of the road. We jumped out into the mist, climbed the fence next to the van and, laughing like maniacs, ran up the mountain.

Half an hour later we stopped for breath near a ridge of exposed slate or shale. We were up in the clouds. Literally. The wet mist and surrounding mountains felt welcoming, enveloping and protective. Though it was January the weather was mild, with a spring-like freshness in the air. A dormant fertility in the ground. A sense of anticipation, as if the Earth itself was about to bud.

Zander had wandered up to the shale ridge. He called down to us.

'You've got to see this, but watch your step!'

It turned out that the ridge was actually the lip of a large hole. A perfectly round hole about fifteen metres in diameter, with vertical sides. Five or six metres down it was flooded with dark water.

Joe threw in a flat piece of shale. Ripples moved across the black surface, not as concentric circles but as interlacing Celtic knots. Below these, the shale didn't sink in a straight line, it moved sideways, first one way, then the other, in smooth gliding curves. Like a falling leaf on a windless day. The grey stone catching the light on the high points of each curved motion. We all watched spellbound as the shale zigzagged down, and down, and down, glinting as it went. The water was not dark. It was crystal clear – and fathomless.

'Oh my gosh!' said Joe, taking a step back from the edge. 'That's deep!'

'Gaze into the abyss,' I quoted from somewhere, 'and the abyss will gaze back.' I shuddered.

'Unless you got rocks to chuck at it!' laughed Joe as he threw in a larger slab. Again, with hypnotic attention, we watched the Celtic knotwork flower on the surface while the rock below spiralled down into the underworld.

Then we all joined in.

The angle of entry gave each stone a slightly different twist. If we got it just right, some even did a loop the loop.

•

We'd been playing like children for more than an hour when the mist began to lift from the landscape, but the cloud was still dense above us. Below we could now see a lake and, above its most distant shore, another range of mountains. Curiously there was a vertical slot cut through the blue-grey peaks. But the symmetry didn't fit the natural shape of the skyline. It was man-made. Then, as the mist shifted, I could see the remnants of a causeway across the lake's surface. Built of rock in a straight line from the cutting in the distant mountains and, I realised with surprise, in a direct line to where we stood.

I pointed out the connection between us and the slot on the horizon. 'Looks like the route of an old railway. I suppose this was a mine. I wonder what they were after?'

'Must have been important,' said Debbie.

'Valuable,' said Zander.

Rather than just seeing the course of the old railway and mineshaft as historical artefacts, I became aware of the human effort involved in digging the mine and building the railway.

Not from the perspective of the rich mine owners, or the endeavours of industrialists, but of the workers. Of the hardship. Of the exploitation of people and place. The line, dynamited through the distant mountains, across the lake and down into the mineshaft, resonated with all the force and violence that had created it.

•

The LSD experience is never shallow. Below the surface patterning there is always a more profound connection. I can understand how the chemical shift within one's own head can be deeply insightful and open up new ways of perceiving the world. What I still find mysterious about the experience is how it seems to be connected with external events and the timing of those events. This could be a trick of the mind, just as deja-vu can be neurologically explained. But acid gives the impression of simultaneous space-time. Because, at that moment, standing at the brink of the mineshaft, experiencing the raw and unfiltered pain of both the labourers and the landscape, my emotions opened up completely. Crossing time. Compressing past and present together. Feeling overwhelmed by the question of *what is so valuable to merit such a deep and painful wound?* I tried to explain this to Zander. And as I did, we were pushed to the ground by the sudden shock of a helicopter dropping down out of the cloud.

Like the one on Bodmin Moor it hovered only metres over our heads. The rotas chopping up the air. A dazzling searchlight pushing into our faces. Terrified, we ran for cover. Zander and I jumped behind a boulder.

What the fuck is going on? The timing of the thing, dropping into that emotionally charged moment, was too much to bear. *What is so important? What is the cause of this connection between the past and this moment?* Crouching behind the boulder I felt a pain in my knee. In the run for cover I'd landed on a rock. Looking down to rub the bruise, I found the culprit. A large chunk of white quartz. I picked it up. Its shattered crystalline structure was shot through with blue-green veins of verdigris. Holding it up, tears of disbelief streamed down my face. *Copper! All this pain for copper! Copper the connector! The conduit. The conductor of electricity in our technological tools. Including the machine pushing down on us from above.*

The helicopter shot back up into the cloud and was gone. One by one, Zander, Debbie, Hamish, Simone, Tim and Joe reappeared from their hiding places. I was left standing with the copper-veined quartz in my hands, looking up at the swirling cloud above the mine.

Shaken by the weirdness of the encounter we walked to the Squatmobile and drove back towards the cottage.

Why would a helicopter, in all the vast wilderness of Snowdonia, randomly drop out of the clouds to exactly where we were, then aggressively buzz us in the same way as the other helicopter had done? It was beyond explanation or rational thinking. Or was it? Because as our little van, dwarfed by the emptiness and scale of the mountains, drove down the valley to the next junction, our road was blocked by a waiting police car.

They wanted to see the documents for the van. We didn't have any. They gave us a producer. The next day, feeling that the open spaces were exposing us to invisible, hostile eyes, we headed back to what we hoped would be anonymity in London.

•

As Seb and I made our usual walk between Station Road and Maygrove, I told him about the strange incident in Wales. As is often the case, even when recounting a difficult or intense moment, I was laughing at myself for the comic scenario of being buzzed by a helicopter, all of us running for cover, and me left standing there in tears, holding a rock.

Both Seb and I had a similar opinion. It probably wasn't that the police were tracking our every move, nor was it paranoid delusion. It was more probably a case of 'Cosmic-Co-Incidence'.

This was a term that had crept into the Spiral's everyday speech. It related to all the weird and wonderful synchronicities that seemed to be occurring ever more frequently. It was a fun and playful term. A word that made no claim to being an explanation, but a word that at least questioned how reality presented itself. The etymology was pretty self-explanatory. *Cosmic,* as in the totality of everything, and *Coincidence,* not as in *a chance connection,* but with the emphasis on the word *coincide,* as in mutually sharing the same space and position in time. The humour in such moments was always important. As if the playfulness was inherent, or even an elemental force, in the underlying structure of the universe. After all, playfulness is fundamental to human curiosity, learning and creativity, and is clearly visible as an energy on the dance floor.

The same playfulness was present in my finished record label design. The grimacing face that could be seen as both smiling and growling. Its face a hidden number 23.

Seb and I were on our way to Maygrove to look at the final inked-in version. Charlie Hall and his mate, Lol Hammond, whom I'd not yet met, were making one of the four tracks, while Seb had been busy in his Leeds basement with the little Wasp synth and was finishing the last of three.

The remaining question was: how did we want to present Spiral Tribe and the individual artists on the record label? The atmosphere at our parties was one of anonymity. An anonymity that refused to place anyone on a pedestal – unless they were brave enough to dance (like Jeff) on top of the speaker stacks. For Charlie, Seb and I, it was important to keep the record anonymous for the simple reason that so many people behind the scenes had worked hard to bring the project into being.

Though a network of individuals, Spiral Tribe had evolved as a synergetic community. Living by the code of anonymity, we rejected top-down hierarchies and actively created other ways of working together. Some were more successful than others, but the ongoing process of exploration was key.

KINGS CROSS: FEBRUARY 1992

In the warehouse space we'd found behind Kings Cross Station, Thomas was working in a pool of halogen light. Outside, the little petrol gennie surged then steadied each time his welder spat blinding white light, fusing metal to metal. Hard shadows strobed across the undulating curves of the cast concrete roof. The smell of hot steel hung in layers on the cold night air.

The warehouse on Battle Bridge Road backed onto a large expanse of railway sidings at the northern end of Kings Cross Station. Built in 1852, around the same time as the Roundhouse, Kings Cross was, and still is, one of Britain's biggest railway stations. Below the Regent's Canal, it was one of the city's main points of entry for coal. Around us were still many of the old railway buildings and gasworks. Considering its central London location, the area was rundown and abandoned. The busy public areas around the front of the station had a reputation for prostitutes and drug dealers, but the old industrial area lay hidden behind. An island cut off from the bustle of the city by railway sidings to the east and west, the canal to the north and the mainline station blocking any access from the south. Walking the dark, cobbled streets behind the station and past the gasometers, one could have been in Victorian London.

What made the warehouse unique was that it was open along the entire length of the side that backed onto the railway. Instead of a wall, it had supporting pillars running along a platform. Clearly it had originally been a depot where freight was loaded on and off waiting trains. Standing on this open loading area, looking to the right, you were in full view of people using the mainline station's platforms, which were literally next door.

Thomas was working with square section steel tubing, constructing a ribcage to support a new canopy for Zander's Q4. Dressed in black with leather chaps, gauntlets and a welder's helmet, he was busy bending, cutting and welding the frame he'd designed to slot into place on the truck's flatbed. His work was precise and skilled, and not only did the shaping fit the military style of the Q4, but he'd designed the cover so that either side of the canvas could be rolled up to instantly create a mobile stage.

When he'd finished, Zander, Debbie and I helped him tidy up. As we loaded his tools into the back of his Dodge Ram pickup, he told us that the reason the street outside was called Battle Bridge Road was that it was the site of the famous battle between Boudica and the Romans around AD 60.

Boudica was the daughter of an Iceni tribal chief. After her father died, the Romans sacked the Iceni lands, raped Boudica's two daughters and beat her. In revenge, Boudica amassed an army and marched on London, burning it to the ground and killing 80,000 Romans and their supporters. She was killed in the battle, and one version of the legend says that she was buried between platforms 9 and 10 on Kings Cross Station. The other version says she was buried on Hampstead Heath. The actual site wasn't important to us. But the symbolism was.

'So,' said Debbie as she picked up the offcuts of steel from the floor, 'if this really is the site of Boudica's battle, why on Earth is it called Kings Cross?'

Thomas took off his welder's helmet. 'They changed the name from Battle Bridge in the 1800s when one of your fat English Kings died of gout, George IV, I think.' He wiped his brow with his forearm and smoothed back his dreadlocks, 'They built a statue to him and renamed the area Kings Cross.'

'You know a lot about British history,' said Debbie.

'Not so much about history,' replied Thomas, 'but I'm pretty good on statues and sculptures.'

'He wasn't English,' said Zander as he coiled a cable. 'He was German.'

'Actually, he was Hanoverian,' laughed Thomas, who was originally from the Black Forest region of Germany.

'Wasn't he the philanderer who built the Brighton Pavilion?' I asked, remembering a visit to his opulent party palace as a child.

'The same.' Thomas jumped up onto the back of his pickup.

'Now that place really is crawling with dragons.' I passed Thomas his disc cutter. 'Dragon design wallpaper, dragon lamps, dragon carpets!'

'Probably more to do with his opium consumption than his connection with nature.' Zander put the neatly coiled cable on the back of the pickup.

'But Kings Cross?' Debbie tapped a length of steel up and down on the concrete floor. 'It conjures images of a crusader's broadsword.'

'Exactly,' said Thomas. 'Because you know what, before the king died they had planned to build the monument to St George!'

'Not him again!' said Zander as he and I grabbed either end of the welder and passed it up to Thomas.

'They were determined to obscure the Boudica legend with the same old macho fantasy then?' said Debbie.

'You're not wrong there!' Thomas chained his welder to the pickup's rollbars.

'But hang on, there's that massive statue of Boudica in her chariot down in Westminster.' Debbie bundled the odd lengths of steel together.

'Queen Victoria commissioned that,' replied Thomas, 'though probably for all the wrong reasons!'

Debbie passed him the steel tubes. 'Careful, they're sharp.'

'You gotta give it to these power freaks,' I said, sliding a heavy toolbox onto the pickup's tailgate. 'They do take their fairy tales seriously!'

One of the lengths of steel slipped from the bundle Thomas had taken from Debbie. It hit the floor with a loud clang and a flash of tiny orange sparks.

•

There was another more recent piece of history connected to the warehouse. Painted in large green and red lettering on the opposite wall to the open platform were the words 'Mutoid Waste'. As a metal fabricator and sculptor, again it was Thomas who knew all the details. He told to us that The Mutoid Waste Company were a travelling group of artists who constructed large scrap metal installations and Mad Max-style vehicles. Apparently, they'd squatted the exact same warehouse a few years earlier and were now travelling in Europe. But that didn't explain why, under the words 'Mutoid Waste', in the same green and red paint, was a large number 23.

The warehouse was at least the size of a football pitch. Circus Normal parked their fleet of vehicles end-to-end across the middle to create a wall that divided the space into two. The idea was that they would stage live bands in their section, and we'd take care of the techno in ours. We tried it for the first weekend, but it didn't really work as half the time no bands were playing. The Spiral side of the warehouse was full night and day.

Ixy and Ness suggested that we use the big party to collect donations to fund a trip to Spain to visit Justin. They worked hard all night taking round their decorated buckets. Someone, who shall remain nameless, helped them, and had charge of the money at the end of the party. A few days later, Ixy and Ness were ready to leave. The plan was to fly down to Seville and see Justin and, if possible, rescue his stuff that was still on the abandoned Techno Bus. But there was a problem. The bloke who had charge of the donated funds had taken it upon himself to 'reinvest' the money in some dodgy deal, meaning that he didn't have the money. We scraped together what we could and Ixy and Ness bought their flights.

•

At that first party we had a few problems with a gang of local youngsters, some of whom had mugged people. When we confronted them they scarpered. Talking to some of those who'd been robbed, I couldn't help but notice that they all appeared to be the people dressed in the more colourful outfits. Daft hats. White gloves. Flowery face paint. It got me thinking. I looked at our collection of backdrops. They too were all brightly coloured and psychedelic. *Perhaps we look like easy targets because of our loved-up vibe?*

•

We'd had no complaints or visits from the police, so we decided to stay on at the warehouse for another weekend. The Normals abandoned their idea of staging live bands, and they moved all their trucks down to one end. Debbie and I had spread out our backdrops on the floor to make repairs and touch them up with paint where necessary. Thomas had gone out in his pickup to collect the Gyrocycle from his Hackney workshop. A few minutes after leaving, the throaty V8 pickup roared back into the warehouse and stopped with a screech of tyres.

Thomas jumped out and called over to me and Debbie. 'Come and see what I just found!'

Paintbrushes in hand, Debbie and I went over. Thomas was unloading bucket-sized metal cans.

'What you got there?' I asked.

'Paint, gallons of it, brand new – from a skip outside!'

'What colour?' asked Debbie.

Thomas checked the labels.

'Industrial ... Rubberised ... Matte black!'

He looked up at me and Debbie.

Debbie and I looked at each other.

As Tim had once said: 'Decisions were not a part of it.' It was, of course, inevitable that we then spent the rest of the week painting all our vehicles industrial, rubberised, matte black.

Seeing how the paint transformed the vehicles got me thinking again about our fluffy fluorescent colour scheme. The elements were already in place. The newly painted vehicles could be arranged to form a wall of shadow. Not quite the entire width of the warehouse, but if I designed a couple of extra-large black backdrops to go either side of the stage, the wall of darkness would be complete. The design I decided upon was two huge, winged pentagram stars, each with a number 23 at its centre. To increase the shadow behind and energise the dance floor, we hired six Terra Strobes and mounted them in a straight line across the top of the vehicles.

The big trucks, speaker stacks and the winged symmetry of the number 23s didn't just look awesome – it looked fuckin' hardcore. And that following Saturday I recognised some of the local kids from the previous weekend. We kept a close eye on them, and this time they didn't cause any problems – they were too busy dancing. I like to think it was because they not only understood that we were not to be messed with, but that the new tough image didn't alienate them – they felt included.

•

We stayed in the warehouse the following week. One evening while we were chilling, the police swarmed in, shouting at us to line up. We had to face the wall with our hands up against it, legs wide, while they frisked us. That done, they questioned us about a bloke named Paul, not to be confused with either of Stikka's Pauls or Paul Brash. This was Poole Paul, who apparently came from Poole. The thing is, Poole Paul had been hanging out with us, but he wasn't with us on that particular night, and the man was an enigma to us all. The police seemed satisfied that he'd slipped through their net and left. But the big question was: how did the police know Paul was hanging around our camp? That information came from somewhere.

NUMBERS FARM: FEBRUARY 1992

After Kings Cross it was good to escape into the countryside, even if it was just outside the perimeter of the M25. Empty and boarded-up, the hilltop buildings of Numbers Farm were constructed in a symmetrical U-shape around a courtyard, in the centre of which was a well. The buildings looked old, almost mediaeval, with low, widely pitched roofs and timber frames. But the style was odd: it didn't fit in with the architecture of that part of England, or any part of England. As if the buildings were part of an abandoned theme park.

Looking out from the courtyard on top of the hill, the view below was dominated by the immense Ovaltine Factory, some 500 metres away across open fields, and a mainline railway track. The Factory, built in 1929, was an Art Deco masterpiece of industrial architecture. Long, low and layered, it was three storeys high with great stepped wings spread symmetrically either side of a huge, and anachronistic, digital clock. Watching the electronic numbers flash each second, it was impossible not to notice the exact alignment of the farm with the factory opposite. The gingerbread style of the farmhouse, the name 'Numbers Farm', the flashing square digits of the clock, and the centring of both buildings on the same line of symmetry all came together to create a surreal atmosphere. An atmosphere that over the course of the weekend would help propagate a bizarre sequence of events.

Owned by the Swiss food company Wander, Ovaltine was an early adopter of Bernays-style propaganda, promoting their malted chocolate drink mix as beneficial to health. We didn't realise it at the time, but the farmhouse was actually built by the company as a showcase dairy, complete with milkmaids and pedigree Jersey cows, to bolster the wholesome and no doubt trademarked company image of a radiantly smiling, buxom blond girl in a low-cut milkmaid's dress, carrying a golden sheath of corn with a basket of eggs on her arm. Mother Earth, fertility and the abundance of nature, rebranded as a powdered milk drink.

Though the factory was still in production, the showcase farm had been empty for years. Many of our close friends and crew originated from the area and had often mentioned the site as a possible venue.

Around the back of the farmhouse was an abandoned orchard. It was there, hidden from view, that we decided to put the sound system. The only snag was that there was a wooded box on bricks in the middle of the dance floor which looked suspiciously like a beehive. We couldn't see any bees flying in or out, so presumed it too was empty.

At twilight Zander lit a campfire in the orchard. We were setting up the speakers when, from around the front of the buildings, against the evening sky, the silhouette of a familiar bus appeared, honking its horn.

'I don't believe it!' said Debbie. 'Its Ixy and Ness!'

That night around the fire they told us about their adventures in Spain. Having had to hitchhike from the airport to where Justin was held, they'd arrived outside the prison late at night. With nowhere to stay they'd made a bed inside some large cardboard boxes, on wasteland, outside the prison walls. In the night they'd been woken by sirens and gunfire. Terrified that if they moved they might get gunned down, they stayed huddled under their boxes.

They survived but had a sleepless night. In the morning they went to see Justin, who was still awaiting an appeal against his sentence. He told them that there had been an escape and they were lucky not to have been caught in the crossfire or arrested as accomplices. He was well, and optimistic that he could get moved back to Britain. Meanwhile he suggested that the girls take the Techno Bus back with them, as it was just sitting on the beach rotting in the salt air.

Easier said than done. The Techno Bus' brakes didn't work, so they had to use the gearbox to slow down – and avoid as many mountains as possible. With no money for fuel – the bus was petrol and thirsty – they'd syphoned as they went. On one occasion, Ixy had been overcome with petrol fumes and, in her altered state, told Ness that she'd stumbled upon the answer to the mysteries of the universe. Unfortunately, before Ixy was able to tell Ness any of the details, the effect of the fumes wore off and with it went all memory of the answer.

It had been a long journey, but against the odds they were back in time for the party, with the Techno bus – and all the secrets of the universe – still intact.

●

And what a party it was. A celebration of many things. The return of Ixy and Ness. The hope that Justin would be able to come back to England. We had new amps to replace what had been stolen. Tim had done a beautiful job of finishing his two new bass bins. And, of course, every time the number 23 flashed up on the factory clock, a cheer went up. Then at some point during the celebrations, someone tripped over the beehive.

It was full of bees, but they seemed to be sleeping, or perhaps hibernating. Zander stood the hive back up and covered it with a tarpaulin for extra protection, being careful to leave a gap for the bees to come and go if they pleased. Despite all the fuss, no one was stung – until Sunday afternoon, when the black Mercedes arrived.

•

The entrance to the party was under a railway bridge, then up a narrow lane. During the night, the police – in their heroic quest to protect the public – had blocked the tunnel under the railway, so ravers were finding alternative routes. One was a two-mile hike in the dark across the fields from the back, the other a quick dash across the four tracks of the mainline railway. So to see that a Mercedes limo had got through the roadblock was a bit of a surprise. To then see four blokes in business suits get out was just plain weird. They had German accents and told us to get off their land.

We ignored them. But harder to ignore were the police with dogs that followed. On short leashes the handlers were using the two snarling animals to try and clear the dance floor. Some people danced further back into the orchard, and some danced up in the apple trees. The boss cop got increasingly angry and threatened to unleash the dogs. The businessmen stood smugly behind him.

Then the miracles began. Or maybe not miracles, just a run of bad luck – for the cops. Because it was then that the bees buzzed into action. Stinging the dogs on their noses and attacking the police. The dogs were put back into their van and the police and businessmen, with panicked swatting motions, ran for cover and drove away. No ravers were stung.

We thought we'd seen the last of the police, but an hour later they were back. And this time they'd brought their champion, dressed in shining white armour – of sorts. In fact, it was a bloke dressed from head to toe in a white beekeeper's outfit, complete with a wide-brimmed hat, veil, boots and thick gloves. He looked like an alien spaceman as he hovered around the edge of the dance floor awaiting orders. The dogs were back out and, poor creatures, were immediately stung again by the patrolling bees. Flanked by the dogs and their handlers, the beekeeper approached the tarpaulin-covered hive.

The irony of the police aggression, pitted against the tiny insects was not lost on the crowd who watched in disbelief as a bee got inside the beekeeper's veil and stung him. He had an allergic reaction and had to be rushed to hospital. The police, very wisely, took this as their cue to leave. Job done, the bees went back to sleep, and the party around their hive in the old apple orchard continued without further ado.

Note: The beekeeper, we were told, made a full recovery.

MONSTER MOVES

It was dawn as I walked towards the Unigate building in West London. Part-warehouse and part-factory, it had been a depot for Unigate, a large meat and dairy corporation. The building was big and ugly, made of steel girders, covered with correlated sheet metal. Walking towards it, across the surrounding industrial estate, I could feel the basslines under my feet. Parked in the front yard were trucks and buses, including a bright red London double decker. A circle of people stood outside warming themselves around a fire of pallets. Climbing the metal-grill stairs to the entrance, I could see the bass vibrations flaking paint from the building's corroded exterior.

The music was a transformative force. Not just a psychological force that had attracted me and a thousand other people from all over London, but a physical force. A force that could cause an entire building to shed its old skin. The empty shell of a cruel industry, freed of its ghosts, mutated by the music into a pulsing techno chrysalis.

Inside, I was on a metal gantry. Steel stairs led down into a mass of heaving shadows. I couldn't see, but I could feel the sound system, liquifying every molecule of the darkness. Fusing metal and flesh into a new life form. A monster sound, making monster moves. This was Bedlam.

•

Steve and Simon Bedlam were behind the new collective. I'd met them a few months earlier at our Green House parties along with Didz and Ian Orinoco. Back then they didn't have a sound system. Now they did, and in February and March 1992 they put on a series of wicked parties. Two at the Unigate building, another in a warehouse in Hayes, and another in an abandoned Second World War bunker – originally a secret anti-aircraft gun factory – in Tubney Wood near Oxford. We went to all of them. With Bedlam we were always among friends.

Before Bedlam was born, we'd obsessively organised parties every weekend. Rightly or wrongly, there'd been a sense that, if we didn't, the fragile new reality we were creating might evaporate into nothing. There were other free party sound systems.

But there was a very particular vibe at Spiral and Bedlam parties. Perhaps it was the music – we both knew and worked with many of the same DJs. Perhaps our frontline antiauthoritarian attitude – we both reclaimed space that had been taken from the community. Or perhaps it was that we were both sound systems created by the people, for the people.

Now, instead of Spiral Tribe being an isolated blip in history, the era of big, pirate, nonstop, travelling, techno rigs had arrived. And on a personal level I felt that we were no longer the outsiders, the nutters who dreamed of a culture that was not based on competition, but cooperation, not on profit but creativity.

Our friendship circles widened. The community bonds strengthened. The new free party techno scene was solid.

·

The difficult birthing period that had brought Spiral Tribe into existence was, I thought, over. Especially now that Bedlam was broadening and strengthening the foundations of the movement. Personally, I never felt comfortable with my role as one of the main organisers of Spiral Tribe, though I often found myself roped into it. Probably because I'd initiated much of the earlier ideas and projects.

It was also true that when the police or press turned up, I was usually the person asked to deal with the situation. Which was fine, because I was pretty level-headed and diplomatic, but after eighteen months of being on the frontline, I could see that by automatically stepping into that role, I was often seen as 'the organiser', or even worse, 'the main man'. Nothing was further from the truth, but in order to change that perception I needed to make an effort to keep Spiral Tribe non-hierarchical.

Hierarchies have an annoying habit of creeping into communities, even when you're actively trying to make sure they don't. There's no doubt that at times Spiral Tribe functioned as a meritocracy, where the people who put in the most work got more say in what happened. While we were a small group, focused on just one mission, we had no issues with our structure. But as the group got bigger, we needed to try and keep relationships level. I felt that my new role – now that the midwifery phase was over – was to open up and facilitate creative opportunities for as many people as possible. I also had to look after my health and give myself more time to focus on my art. It was with all these things in mind that I decided to take a back seat on the organisational front.

SWINDON: MARCH 1992

Debbie and Simone had had news that Ixy, Ness and the horse-drawn were on a new site near Swindon. Of course, a party was planned and everyone, apart from me, piled down there. I was submerged in designing the label artwork for the flip side of our first record.

It was late Sunday night. I'd just finished inking-in my latest pencil sketch when Zander and Debbie got back to Maygrove. They looked tired. I made a pot of tea. Debbie went out to smoke a rollie (she was mindful that smoke hurt my lungs) while Zander and I went and sat at the big desk in the bay window.

'How was the weekend?' I asked, moving my artwork out of harm's way.

'There were plainclothes onsite even before we started.'

'Shit.'

'We all got arrested, apart from Ixy who galloped off on her horse! They towed and impounded the vehicles, and we spent the night in the cells.'

'What were the charges?'

'None – we hadn't done anything! But they ripped the front of the bus off with their tow truck!'

'What!'

'Yeah, the bumper and grill!'

'Twats! So they let you go in the morning?'

'Well, no,' said Debbie as she came back into the room and sat with us. 'It was a bit more complicated than that. They let us go, but not the vehicles – the pound was closed till Monday!' Debbie smiled and placed her hand on her heart. 'But luckily, I persuaded the chief to give us all a lift back to the horses, otherwise we'd have had to walk miles!'

'But the three arseholes that took us weren't happy.' Zander shook his head. 'We were in the back of the police van –'

'– With hard wooden benches and no seat belts!' added Debbie.

'The cops in the front were laughing, driving like maniacs so we'd get thrown about in the back.'

'Fuck!' I shook my head in disbelief.

'Yeah! Then they dropped us off in a layby on a dual carriageway,' said Debbie, 'and told us we had to walk a mile across muddy fields to get back to site.'

Zander laughed. 'We were halfway across the first field

when we heard them shouting at us to come back. It was only then that Kev showed us he had all their hats under his jacket!'

'Great idea!' Debbie rolled her eyes. 'So then we had to run across the fields and hide the hats in a hedge before the police caught up with us!'

'Did they?'

'No,' Debbie smiled, 'they were too busy rummaging around in the undergrowth!'

'So what about the vehicles?' I asked.

Debbie made an exasperated face. 'Well, obviously, we had nowhere to sleep, so the lads got on a mission to get them back.'

'The police pound wasn't that far away,' said Zander, 'so me and some of the others paid it a little visit.'

'But it was guarded and locked?' I asked.

'No! No one around. But yeah, big steel-mesh gates, chained and padlocked, but we slipped them off their hinges. It took some lifting! The gates came down with an almighty crash! Everything was there: the bus, Thomas's Dodge and workshop trailer, the Q4 and showman's!'

'Wicked!' I was impressed.

'Drove out in convoy over the top of the gates, back to site!'

'So did they come back,' I asked, 'and give you more grief?'

He shook his head. 'Nah, it was fair dos. They were well out of order – and they knew it.' He took a sip of tea. 'Anyway, what have you been up to?' He nodded towards the chaotic pile of papers at the other end of the desk.

'Nothing as energetic as galloping around on horses or crashing the convoy out of the pound!' I reached over to the pile of sketches. 'A design for the flip side of the record. Hang on . . .' I shuffled through to find the inked version. 'Ta-da!' I held up a A3 sheet.

'Nice!' said Debbie, 'Same style as the 23 Face.'

'Cheers. Yeah, I think I'm happy with it.'

'What is it?' asked Zander.

'Obviously it's a hand, Zander!' replied Debbie.

'I can see that – but what's it doing?'

'It's another secret twenty-three sign.' I raised my right hand with just my index, middle finger and thumb extended 'You see, two digits down and three digits up. Two and three!'

'I think you'll find,' said Zander, 'that's actually the Girl Guide's salute.'

Debbie made a double clicking sound with her tongue and raised both hands as if they were cocked guns. 'Not anymore!'

WELWYN GARDEN CITY: MARCH 1992

Heather had sold Rose Farm, which was a shame because it had been at Heather's parties where many of the friendships between us had their roots. But the good news was that she'd moved two minutes' walk away from Maygrove. And even though it was a small, terraced house, Heather had been sure to bring the all-important, big kitchen table. The very same table where the plans to go to Amsterdam had been made, if acid-inspired impulses count as 'plans'. Next to the kitchen was the basement, where she had decks set up and music was always playing.

Curls of smoke were backlit by the sunshine from the double glass doors that faced out into the garden. Not all of us had been out partying, so we were squeezed around the table to hear about the weekend's events.

Jeff started, 'Well, that was . . .' He glanced around the room. '. . . an experience.'

'Jeffry? What happened?' asked Heather, who was sitting at the head of the table smoking a cigarette.

'You remember me telling you about that wicked place I found over in Welwyn Garden City, behind the Shredded Wheat Factory?'

Heather narrowed her eyes. 'Yes.'

'Turned out it wasn't actually an abandoned industrial estate.' Jeff had both elbows on the table, propping his head up with a hand on each cheek. 'It was a riot cop training facility.' His head sank lower into his hands.

There was a pause.

'A what?' Heather's bright blue eyes widened.

Zander, who was perched by the kitchen sink, took up the story. 'A bunch of police turned up in full body armour. But armour like I've never seen before, like costumes from the film *Tron* – all black apart from the chief, who was all in white. It was weird.'

'Me and Kev were on the gate when they arrived,' said Simone. 'We were immediately arrest . . .'

'Taken hostage!' interrupted Kev. 'No, really! Everyone else had barricaded themselves into the building, and the police said they'd only give us back if they all surrendered.'

'What did you do?' asked Heather.

'We told the cops they could keep Kev!' Zander laughed. Kev punched him on the shoulder.

Thomas, who'd been sitting quietly next to me, said, 'They

herded us out of the building and down the road, banging their shields with their batons. Like robot chess men.'

I shuddered. 'Sounds horrible.'

Thomas didn't answer, but he turned to me with a solemn look and nodded.

ACTON LANE: APRIL 1992

In the nineties, industry was collapsing – or moving out of the country in search of cheaper labour markets – leaving the factory and warehouse buildings to the pigeons, graffiti artists and us. Park Royal was, and still is, the biggest industrial zone in London. The north-eastern side is bordered by the vast Willesden railway junction, which the Station Road house sits on top of, and the south-east side by the even bigger railway sidings of Old Oak Common. The other two sides are diagonally bordered by arterial motorways, Western Avenue and the North Circular. Through the middle of this abandoned industrial wasteland ran Acton Lane. It was here that we found the perfect building.

Looking from the front, it was a long, two-storey office building of glass and brick, with a large roller-shutter door on the left-hand side. Above the offices was the company name, 'Unichem' – a pharmaceutical distribution company – and its logo, a circle with an arrowhead pointing to the right, the symbol usually used to signify the masculine.

The roller-shutter doors were big enough to drive trucks through, which was handy. We drove all our vehicles into the large warehouse behind and set up camp at the back. There wasn't just one space. A metal door in the wall led into an even bigger warehouse behind the offices. It was a sliding door, only slightly bigger than a standard domestic door, but it was heavy and over-engineered, and took some effort to open. It became a running joke with us, while rolling the door along on its rusty tracked wheels, to imitate the techno-swoosh of the doors opening on the old *Star Trek* TV series.

Exploring the building on the first afternoon, I noticed that there were access ladders on the walls which led to service gantries in the zigzag pitch of the roof. Perfect for positioning lights. In one of the front offices, I found Wacky looking through the draws of a dusty old desk.

'Found anything interesting?' I asked.

'If you mean pharmaceuticals, no. If you mean *omens,* then yeah.'

'Omens? What kind of omens?'

'It's a warning.' He stood an overturned chair back on its feet and sat behind the desk in front of me. 'I found this in one of the filing cabinets.' He placed a large roll of tape on the table.

'So what's so ominous about tape?'

'It's not tape, it's stickers. Spiral stickers.' He unrolled a short length to show me. I leaned over the desk to take a closer look. The design, outlined in black on a white background, was of a ram's head in profile. The horn had been over-emphasised and took up most of the design. And the horn was, of course, a spiral.

'But what makes you think it's a warning?'

'Because,' he said, taking in a deep breath, 'it says so!'

Around the edge of the design I read: 'Beware the rams!'

I laughed. 'Ahh . . . you mean Aries!' Zander and Debbie were not only Aries but also shared the same birthday, which was only a week away.

'No! Not Debbie and Zander! This!' Wacky stood up and, with a finger on the dusty desktop, wrote RAMS. 'And if I rearrange the letters.' Under the first word he wrote ARMS. And under that he wrote MARS. He looked up at me. 'Are you following this?'

'Yeah.'

Then he drew a circle with an arrowhead pointing away to the right. 'And this?'

'The Unichem logo – and the male symbol.'

He blew the dust of the tip of his finger. 'But it's also the alchemical symbol for iron and Mars – the god of war!'

'I'm still not sure I . . .'

He tore a sticker from the roll and walked around the desk to me. He peeled off the backing paper. 'Beware of the RAMS, ARMS, MARS!' he said and slapped it on my chest. 'Understand?' He walked towards the door. 'I'm going to make sure everyone gets one of these – it's important they know.'

The rumblings of the first sound check came from the warehouse behind. Turning away from the runic signs on the table, I walked towards the exit. Only then did I see the small, coloured poster above the door. It was a cartoon depicting a group of happy little lambs, dancing and playing electronic instruments – complete with amps and speakers. They were performing on a table, in a room of smiling wolves. *Beware the rams*, I mused as I left the room and went to help set up.

•

The party that night was incredible. Many elements connected. We'd replaced all our lost amps, and, just to be sure, hired a little extra from Rudi. The upgraded system ran super smoothly and sounded the best it ever had. All the DJs had been on form, and the mix of styles across the weekend was perfect. Acid, British breakbeat and European techno were as one. The music was united, as was the community.

After his set, Danny B Spooky and I had a chat at the back of the warehouse, close to the sliding Star Trek door.

'Great set, Danny! Totally blew me away – literally! What's that track with the rolling breakbeat and explosions?'

'Cheers, Mark. You mean "Bomb Scare", 2 Bad Mice. Blinding track!'

'And no squeaky cartoon voices – just pure sub-bass, beats and bombs! What was the other track – kinda similar hip-hop feel but without the explosions?'

'Probably "Ware Mouse", 2 Bad Mice again, on the same EP! There's four blinding tracks all on the same vinyl, but the other two are more ravey.'

'I prefer the darkness!'

'That's the way it's going – darker, much darker!'

EASTER WEEKEND

On a high from the successes of the first party we decided to ride the wave and stay at the Unichem warehouse – just for one more weekend. It would be Debbie and Zander's shared birthday – and Easter weekend. Everyone was enthusiastic. Everyone except Wacky.

The Easter party continued all day Sunday and into the early hours of Monday morning. We'd been taking it in turns to keep an eye on things. I was doing my shift on the main entrance – the large, slatted-steel, roller-shutter door. When someone arrived, I could see them through a crack in between the metal frame and the brickwork. The door was rolled up and down manually, by means of a heavy chain that hung down on the inside. This main entrance led into the first warehouse space, which we were using as car parking. To keep the area well-lit and secure, we'd installed halogen work lamps on the metal gantries that led up onto the roof.

Bedlam had also done a party that Saturday. When that ended on Sunday afternoon, all their hardcore ravers came to us. So, for a Sunday night there was a big crowd on the dance floor, plus a lot of people hanging out in the car parking area.

I was chatting to Lol Hammond, Charlie Hall's mate who'd made one of the tracks for the up-and-coming Spiral EP. We'd only recently met but immediately hit it off. He was a gentle and softly spoken bloke who was always helpful when it came to advising us about where to go to master, cut and press records. While we talked enthusiastically about the record there was a tap on the metal roller shutter. I peered through the crack and rolled up the door.

'Cheers, mate!' said a clean-shaven bloke dressed in jeans and denim jacket.

'No worries. Party's through there.' I pointed him to the Star Trek door. 'Have a good-un!'

I wound the roller-shutter down again. Lol and I continued talking about when we might receive the test pressing of the EP. He reckoned it would be at least two or three weeks.

There was a heavy thud and crash from the back of the warehouse. The Star Trek door slid open, and a group of blokes rushed out and ran down towards the back of the car parking warehouse.

'What's going on?' I shouted after them.

'Police! Trying to get in at the back!'

Lol and I looked at each other. There was another crash. Without saying anything we both ran towards the commotion.

Halfway down the length of the warehouse I realised we'd left the main entrance unguarded. On instinct I sprinted back to the roller-shutter door. Sure enough, the clean-shaven bloke I'd just let in was running towards the door. He got to the chain a second before me.

'Don't even think about it!' I shouted. He turned, looked me up and down, then ran back into the other room. My heart was in my mouth. I had a horrible feeling that I knew exactly what I'd see through the crack in the door.

The orange glow of the streetlights highlighted the shine on the helmets of a squad of riot police. Fifty or more in a tight square formation just two or three metres away.

A moment later, Lol was back.

'They're barricading a hole where the cops are trying to get in!'

I put my finger to my lips and pointed to the crack in the doorframe.

Lol took a look, turned to me, and silently mouthed, 'Fuck!'

We took a few steps away. I explained in an urgent whisper that I'd just caught the bloke trying to open the door.

'What are they playing at?' I was puzzled. I always spoke to the police if there was any complaint, and nine times out of ten there were no problems. 'Why haven't they said anything to us? I'll give it a go now.' I went back to the door and called out. 'What's going on? What do you want?' I peered through the crack. There was no answer, no break in the silent formation. I turned back to Lol. 'Something's not right . . . And why send in that undercover guy when they could knock and we could chat?'

'How long have you been on this door?' asked Lol.

'At least two hours.'

'And no cops have been to talk?'

'No, none. Just ravers.' I cautiously approached the door and took another peep. The solid block of police was still there.

At that moment the bottom of the door shook under multiple blows. Both Lol and I jumped against the door, expecting it to move. It stayed down, but in between each crash against the metal we could hear screams. With horror we realised that the police were beating people to the ground and kicking them against the door. For a split second I was in a dilemma. Risk the cops getting in or raise the door to rescue the people.

I wound the chain round to lift the door, just enough to allow people to roll inside. Girls and boys covered in blood, crying and screaming as they scrambled in. Those that couldn't move were dragged in by Lol and some other lads who'd come to help. I shut the door. Looking out of the crack again, all the police were back in formation. No way could anyone have gotten near the door unless they'd let them through. It was a trap. Let a few kids through. Close ranks. Beat the shit out of them, knowing that we'd let them in, shocked, bloodied and bruised. A calculated plan to spread panic in the building.

Lol and I were shaken. And then it happened again. In

exactly same way. Again, I pulled up the door to let the injured people escape. As they ran inside the building, so the level of shouting and screaming within rose.

'You okay on your own just for a minute?' said Lol. I shrugged. 'It's just that one of those blokes was a bit too clean and tidy.'

'Sure, check him out – but don't be too long!'

Lol gave chase.

Ten minutes later he was back.

'Mark, I would never say this unless I was 100 percent sure, but I followed that bloke on to the roof. I saw him shouting down information to the police – how many people are here, the layout of the place. Here he is now! That's him!'

The bloke, dressed in clean beige trousers and a brown sports jacket, was walking towards us through the parked cars.

'Fuck! I said. 'What we gonna do?'

'I don't know.' Lol took a deep breath. 'If people find out he's undercover he'll get battered.'

'Let's see what he's got to say.' As he approached, I squared up to him with my back to the door chain. 'Where you going?'

'Just going home now.' His eyes flicked back and forth between me and Lol.

'But you only just arrived,' said Lol.

'I lost my keys.'

'You lost your keys, so now you're going home?'

'Yeah, I just had to nip in and try and find my mate who had my car keys, and I couldn't find him, so I was just looking.' There was a tremor in the bloke's voice.

'Did you find your mate?' asked Lol.

'No. I mean yeah, not at first, I looked everywhere.'

'On the roof?' I asked.

'Yeah. No. No, I mean, I looked there but no, he wasn't anywhere.'

'But you did find him?' asked Lol.

'Yeah, I found him. Somewhere else. In there.' He glanced nervously behind him.

'So you've got your keys now?' I asked.

'Yeah, I got my keys now and I'm just going home.' He started fumbling as if trying to get his fingers into his tight trouser pockets, but his hands were uncontrollably twitching.

'If you're not a copper and I let you go, the police will batter you,' I said. 'You know that, right?'

'But I found my keys now, so it's okay – it's okay, I just want to go home.'

Lol and I looked at each other. We'd both heard enough. I turned, peeped through the crack. The solid wall of police was still there. I nodded to Lol and hoisted the door high enough for the bloke to crawl out. He walked through the police line untouched. As I watched him go, I knew that if his mates got in, they wouldn't be so nice to us.

There was another almighty crash from the back of the building. People started running back towards us and piling back into the party through the Star Trek door.

'They're in!' someone shouted.

Lol went to investigate. I stood with my back to the chain, every muscle tensed.

Another group of people ran to the sliding door, but it had been barricaded from the inside. People were running from the far end of the warehouse through the parked trucks and cars. Behind them, like armoured insects, stalked a squad of baton-wielding riot police. There was nothing I could do but wait for them to get to me and the door. Those few moments seeing people clubbed to the ground felt eternal. I backed up into the corner in a futile attempt to protect the door chain. A tall, thick-set copper, masked in black, with piercing blue eyes, stood over me, his baton raised high.

'Move!' he shouted. I ducked out of the corner and under his raised arm. The slatted steel door screeched as he started to hoist it open. I braced myself for a deluge of baton blows from all directions. I closed my eyes and covered my head with my arms. To escape the sound of screaming I tuned into the music that was still playing in the other room. An MC was on the mic, adding his own words to the track 'The Bouncer' by Kicks Like A Mule. He was chanting: 'If your name's Old Bill, you're not coming in!'

The screech of the roller-shutter door stopped. A chill of night air blew in behind me. Shoulders hunched, I turned expecting to be beaten to the ground by the cops that had been waiting to storm the door. They'd gone.

Instead, steel pedestrian barriers had been set up to form a path along the front of the building. Cops in normal uniform were directing people out and away from the warehouse, as if they were doing nothing more than directing traffic.

'Move along, this way please, move along.'

Behind me the armoured insect-men were pushing people from the car parking area towards me and the open door. If anyone hesitated, they were hit. Another group of riot police were attempting to force the Star Trek door open. Rooted to the spot, I was unable to leave while I could hear the screaming coming from inside.

'Fuck off!' A riot cop stood over me, baton raised. I jumped away from him, out over the threshold and into the street.

The police outside politely directed us along the barrier, funnelling us towards a point of exit. This, I was sure, would be where they'd arrest us. But it didn't happen. Instead we were paraded past three chiefs with big hats, shiny buttons and braid on their jackets. All three were smiling. The middle one was dressed in a uniform I didn't recognise.

As I walked past, I heard him boast, 'Back home we'd have cleared the building in twenty minutes.' He had an American accent.

On the street more uniformed constables kept us moving. From the opposite side of the road, I looked back at the open roller-shutter door. Framed in the cold brittle blue of flashing police lights, the doorway was a rectangle of yellow. Inside I could see the insect-men hunting down the stragglers. A heavy thudding, out of time with the muffled beat of the music, punctuated the crash of breaking glass and the screaming. I had to do something. There was a phone box. *Who could I phone? Who could help?*

'Keep it moving.' A copper ushered me away from the phone and further down the road. Away from their crime scene.

CORDONED

Our dance floor was now at ground zero of a brutal siege. The first shockwave of the attack had flung me, and everyone who'd been outside the second warehouse, 100 metres down Acton Lane. Here, on the perimeter of police operations, was a line of frightened people. Some concussed. All confused.

I found Jeff looking pale and exhausted.

'You okay?' I asked.

'I can't believe they're doing this.' He was staring towards the building.

'Jeff?' I repeated. 'You okay?'

'Yeah.' He pulled his gaze away from the police lights. 'And you?'

'No injuries – but fuck . . . what we gonna do?'

Jeff looked as lost as me. 'What can you do when it's the police attacking you?' His gaze went back towards the warehouse.

'We need witnesses,' I said. 'We need a phone!'

A tall, lean bloke with dark skin and long dreadlocks stepped out of the shadows. 'I live round the corner – you can use mine.'

'Leroy! How you doing?' I knew Leroy as a regular at our parties.

'Been better . . . But serious, if we're gonna stop this madness, we need to move.'

•

Together with Leroy and a girl named Sue, Jeff and I walked away from the police cordon. My legs were heavy, my head swimming, and my cough had come back with a vengeance. It took all of my remaining energy to push through a suffocating sense of powerlessness. By the time we got to the house, even though I'd no physical injuries, I felt as if my lifeforce was draining away.

Jeff and I sat on Leroy's sofa with the phone book. We called solicitors, newspapers, and even a priest. Either the phone rang unanswered, or the answer was an indignant, 'I can't help you!'

In one last desperate bid to find someone who might give a fuck, I phoned the Samaritans. A woman answered. She was sympathetic, but explained they were a helpline for people at risk of suicide. When I told her that innocent people were being beaten and no one else could help, she took Leroy's number.

By this point I was having difficulty breathing. A week of camping on the floor of the cold, dusty warehouse offices had not done me any favours. That combined with a long sleepless weekend and a crushing sense of hopelessness.

The phone rang. It was a solicitor. He gently explained to me, 'What you have to understand Mark, is that once the police have cordoned an area, it's only the police that have access. Even a judge would have difficulty getting in. And just as the police have complete control of who gets in, so they also have control of who, and what, gets out. That includes information. The only official information that comes out from inside a cordon is police information. I'm so sorry.'

Leroy helped me to his spare room. 'You need to rest, Mark. Serious, just chill. You've done everything you can.'

I lay on a small single bed in the dark. Wheezing and coughing. I felt too weak to breathe and slipped into unconsciousness.

•

It was light when I woke. A small girl, about six or seven, I guessed Leroy's daughter, was holding my hand. 'Are you okay?' she asked.

'Yes. Thank you,' I smiled. 'I'm okay.' I was surprised to be alive and that there was kindness and hope in the world.

I drank a cup of tea with Leroy, Jeff and Sue and went back to the warehouse.

AFTERMATH

The police had gone, apart from a helicopter that hovered overhead. The building looked as if it had been targeted by a missile strike. All the glass at the front of the building was smashed. Large holes knocked through walls. Doors wrenched from their frames. Water poured from broken pipes in the roof. Rubble strewn across the floor. The sun coming through the skylights, reflected back up off the water and projected rippled patterns under the zigzagged roof.

Zander was on the far side of the warehouse, sorting through wreckage next to a toppled pile of speakers and flight cases. Sasha and Ixy were sitting on another jumbled pile of speaker cabs. Wacky was searching for something on the floor. Seb was sat cross-legged in his orange jacket on an island of pallets in the middle of the flooded dance floor. I splashed over to him.

'You okay?' I asked.

'Wet and cold, but nothing broken.'

Wacky came over. 'Pharmaceuticals!' he announced as he held open the pouched bottom of his T-shirt to show us a collection of small plastic bags and foil wraps.

'Find anything to smoke?' asked Seb.

'Take your pick!' He stretched his T-shirt towards Seb. 'I warned you about the rams!' he said without looking at me.

I didn't know how to answer. The multiple co-incidences, the symbolism, the dates and the warzone. I left him and Seb on their island trying to make a spliff with damp weed.

'How you doing, Zand?' We gave each other a hug.

'You missed my birthday party!'

'Looks like you had a right old knees-up!'

'Fun and games all night! Two and a half hours of running around barricading holes that the police were knocking through the walls – and when the music stopped, we all had to lie face down in a puddle. A bit like musical bumps, except the bumps were twats round the head if you moved – and the prize at the end was a smashed-up sound system.'

'Smashed?'

'Everything. Decks included.'

'Fuck! And you're okay?'

'Never been better!' He gave me a little smile.

I helped him sift through the wreckage and salvage what we could while he filled me in on the details of what happened.

'They were using sledgehammers and battering rams to break through the walls. When a new hole appeared, everyone barricaded it with pallets.'

Debbie appeared through the twisted frame of the Star Trek door. She skirted the worst of the flood and came to join us. After an exchange of hugs, and more birthday jokes, she told us that she'd just see an *ITN News* crew sniffing about.

'I showed them the damage the police did, but they weren't interested.'

'Why not?' I asked. 'This is a major incident!'

'No idea. I explained what happened and the TV geezer just said, "I'm outta here" and left!'

'They're gonna pretend this never happened,' said Zander.

'No one gives a shit.' I told Zander and Debbie about the phone calls Jeff and I had made during the attack.

'No arrests,' said Zander. 'No one charged. They just wanted to fuck us up.'

'They might stop the party . . .' I started to quote Joe's infamous line.

' . . . but they can't stop the future!' Debbie finished. The phrase felt hollow.

THE YSTWYTH VALLEY

Horror stories about some of the injuries inflicted by the police began to circulate. A pregnant woman, kicked in the belly while on the ground. A raver thrown off the roof breaking his arms and legs. With the sound system destroyed – and in such violent circumstances – morale was at an all-time low. It took a huge effort of will to try and keep positive, about anything.

We wanted to leave London and didn't need any further encouragement from the police, though they gave it to us anyway in the form of the helicopter that escorted our convoy out of the city.

•

In a bid to stay strong we decided to collaborate with Bedlam. But with little or no functioning equipment, it was more of a collaboration of DJs. The biggest of these parties was two weeks later on 1 May. The pagan festival of Beltane.

Bedlam and Circus Warp had a site. Apparently, it was a disued quarry. Suffering from worsening bronchitis, I'd arrived on the Sunday when the party was already in full swing. It was not in a quarry – it was next to the village of Lechlade, in a meadow that backed onto the houses.

For the 10,000 ravers at Lechlade, the party was sublime. But the choice of site, next to the village, meant that a few days later Sir David Mitchell, the Conservative MP for North West Hampshire, made a speech in the House of Commons citing the event at Lechlade as a problem. He called for the Public Order Act to be tightened, to prevent such events happening in, or close to, populated areas.

Shortly after that we headed back to Wales. Spiral Tribe needed to rebuild its sound system, nurse its wounds – and rethink its strategy.

•

The single-tracked road wound along the bottom of the Ystwyth valley. Either side of the small, glittering river, steep treeless hills rose. Moss green, with patches of rust-coloured bracken.

Further up the valley and deeper in the hills of the Cambrian Mountains we came upon an area of abandoned workings. High terraces built of rock spoil lined the road. Camouflaged against the wasteland of grey shale were the remains of buildings, stone ruins reclaimed by the hills that they'd been built from. To our right, a thin waterfall cut into the hill behind. Halfway up the hillside was a fortress, heavily walled with double aches, above which were two square towers. We pulled over to explore.

The fortress turned out not to be a military installation. In fact, it was the foundation platform of an industrial building. The towers were perhaps supports for machinery or sluices that had long gone. What had looked like windows in the towers were alcoves that might have housed beams or axles. Immediately in front of the wall, hidden from the road, was a flat cement floor – a dance floor, twenty metres by twenty metres square. Standing at the centre of this space, drinking in the emptiness and isolation, I could breathe again.

•

We had three different info lines to let people know where our parties were. One was the answerphone at Maygrove, one was run by a friend named Debbie Staunton (not to be confused with Debbie Spiral), and another was via announcements by the Ruff Crew (two doctors who moonlighted as DJ G and DJ TC) on the pirate radio station Touchdown FM. It was through these channels that a couple of hundred people found their way to our remote Welsh fortress for the weekend.

On Saturday night a huge full moon lit up the valley. When the sun rose, at the east end of the valley, the moon was setting at the opposite end. The river, in the shadows below us, made a shimmering ribbon of light between the two.

We'd had to borrow and hire in a fair bit of equipment as our rig was still in pieces after the Acton Lane attack. People brought what they could from London, including new decks and a hotchpotch of speakers. Also from London came the first test pressing of the new Spiral Tribe EP: *Hidden Forces*. Seb had made three of the tracks, Lol and Charlie the fourth. That morning, when it was played for the first time, Seb and I stood nervously at the edge of the dance floor trying to gauge the crowd's reaction.

Unfamiliar with the record, the DJ didn't mix it in. The abrupt change in tempo cooled the crowd. Everyone stood still. Seb and I looked at each other. At that moment Mitch – a tall, slim figure, his head shaved bald, wearing a black, ankle-length leather coat – stood motionless at the centre of the crowd. Arms above his head, hands together, fingertips to fingertips. After a moment he spread his arms wide and began to turn. His long black coat flowed around him, like a techno-shaman working a spell. As he spun, the crowd began to melt back into the groove.

While the EP was playing, I'd noticed someone, or something, moving in the rocks, some fifty metres above the dance floor. At first, I'd presumed it was ravers exploring the hills and paid no attention. But then, just for a fleeting second, I caught sight of a face, deathly white with dark eyes. It peered around a rock, then dropped out of sight. Whoever it was didn't want to be seen. I watched the rocks for a few more minutes. The face popped up again, this time in a different place, and was joined by a second – with the same anaemic complexion and deeply shadowed eyes.

•

Thomas was down where we'd parked the vehicles, outside his workshop trailer, shaping a piece of metal bar over a small anvil. Zander held one end of the bar while Thomas swung the hammer.

'Great sound,' I said, 'you should sample that!'

'Already have!' said Thomas, giving it another whack.

I walked around the anvil. 'I don't want to sound paranoid, but I think we're being spied on.'

'The ghost-people?' Thomas asked.

'You've seen them?' I looked back towards the hill. 'Who are they?'

He struck the bar. 'Dunno. By the time I'd got up there, they'd gone.'

'You want to try again?' I asked.

'Give us a minute.' Thomas nodded to Zander, who lifted the bar from the anvil.

'What's that for?' I asked.

'Strengthening the canopy on the Q4,' said Zander. 'I can't keep the ravers from dancing on the roof!'

Thomas packed up his gear and the three of us walked a short distance down the road, then circled back up the hill. That way we hoped to get behind whoever was watching us. We turned off the road at a small stream and followed it up between the spoil tips. There we came upon a tunnel that disappeared into the hillside. Clearly the entrance to a mine, which explained the huge terraces of broken rock contouring the valley. We peered inside and made a few experimental low-pitched calls. There was no echo, the blackhole swallowing all sound and light. We resolved to come back later with our torches.

I picked up a piece of rock and examined it, but it gave no clue about what minerals might have been mined there. I told Thomas the story about the flooded mine shaft we'd found in

Snowdonia, the helicopter and the white quartz shot through with the blue-green verdigris of copper. While I recounted the tale we circled up and back down towards the party. As we went, we occasionally stopped to pick up stones that caught our attention. But whatever the treasure in the hills had been, now there was no trace.

Zander climbed up a little further and stopped to watch a pair of circling buzzards, while Thomas and I sat on the edge of a rocky outcrop and looked out over the valley. Below us was the party and, hidden among the terraces of spoil, the ruins of other buildings. On a dull day they might have been difficult to see, made as they were of the same weathered stone as their surroundings, but in the morning sunshine their walls cast hard, angular shadows that spiked the skin of the otherwise rolling landscape.

'Interesting that it was quartz and copper you found when that helicopter buzzed you.' Thomas shaded his eyes and looked up at the buzzards.

'It was an intense moment!' I laughed. 'As if that rock held all the codes for tools and technology!'

'That's one of the reasons I love working with metal. I feel a mutual magnetism between me and the elements.'

'Mutual magnetism – that's it! Technology feels like part of the evolution. Evolution – exploring all possible routes.'

'Or perhaps it's nothing to do with evolution.' Zander jumped down from the rock he'd been standing on. 'Perhaps all this destruction is just about power and money.'

'But isn't it the middlemen fucking everything up?' I asked. 'Our relationship with nature and technology doesn't have to be this destructive.'

Thomas threw a small pebble at a nearby rock. 'I suppose getting rid of the middlemen is what we're all about.'

There was a trickle of loose stones from the slopes behind. We turned to see a man standing a short distance away from us, dressed in rags, the same worn-out grey as the hillside. His face translucent white. Sunken cheeks. Dark, glassy eyes. Startled by his appearance, nobody said anything. After a moment he began to take a hesitant step towards us.

'I heard what you said . . . about the rocks,' he said slowly, then seemed to change his mind about coming closer. He took a step back and looked down at his scuffed boots.

Thomas, Zander and I exchanged glances. *Had this bloke been listening to everything we'd said?*

'We've been watching . . . but we don't know if we can trust you.' His head was bowed, hands clasped.

Talking on top of each other, Zander, Thomas and I threw questions at him.

'Trust us with what?'

'Who's we?'

'What do you want?'

He looked up at me. 'We don't want anything . . . just to welcome you to this place – our home. We can't trust most people.' He turned to Thomas. 'We live hidden lives.' He turned to Zander. 'I'm with my wife.'

A woman who looked as grey and fragile as him emerged from the rocks behind.

We invited them to sit with us. They explained that many years ago their van had broken down next to the mine. Unable to leave, they'd bedded down for the evening. During the night, they'd been woken by the sounds of a raging battle. Apparently, supernatural echoes of a historic massacre of Romans, ambushed by the hill tribes. The experience had been so profound that they decided to stay and live in the hills.

'The Romans,' said the woman very slowly, 'wanted the wealth of the mines, but to the tribes the Earth was sacred.'

'And what was mined here?' I asked.

'Silver,' the man replied, 'and lead.'

'Lead?' I looked around at the shattered landscape in a new light. 'That's totally toxic!'

The man made small up and down moments with his hands as if weighing up the truth of my words. 'Don't drink the water . . . but if you want to understand this place . . .' He turned to his wife. 'We can show you.'

'We know these mines,' she nodded. 'The old forgotten tunnels.'

'You can give us a tour?' asked Thomas.

She leaned forward and said softly, 'Into the heart of the hill.'

Zander and Thomas continued chatting with them. I nipped back to the trucks to get them some food before we set off into the mines.

•

Seb and Mitch were sitting on the steps of the showman's, deep in conversation about the new EP. Seb was explaining how he had no MIDI on his Wasp synth and so had to sync everything on the go.

'In another words,' he laughed, 'my tracks were pretty improvised and live!'

'Scuse me.' I squeezed between them and into the showman's. It was a mess. Heaps of bedding, cables, flight cases, broken speaker cones and a couple of cardboard boxes with some basic supplies. I picked out a couple of cans and a bag of pasta.

'We need to sort out this trailer,' I said, carefully stepping out between them. 'It's a tat-pile on wheels!'

I started back up the hill.

'Yeah, if we cleaned it out, it'd make a nice studio!' Seb called after me.

'And if the EP does well,' I called back, 'perhaps we should buy some MIDI equipment!'

On the way past the dance floor, I bumped into Debbie.

'Where you off to with those snacks?'

'Just some food for the hill-people.' I told her about our strange encounter.

'I couldn't live here,' she said. 'I mean, totally techno, but no way! Too cold and bleak!'

'Yeah, you're right – we need trees. Somewhere hidden where we can have a fire, fix the rig, and not get harassed!'

'Back into the undergrowth!' She narrowed her eyes, looked from side to side and, with her hands in front of her, made the movements of a cat carefully padding through the forest.

'We should do it soon – I got a nasty feeling that this land-scape isn't just a relic from the past.'

'How do mean? She stopped her little dance.

'It's part of an unfolding future. Barren, contaminated, exhausted.'

'But that's why we're here, isn't it? To heal these places. To reconnect the Earth!'

'Yeah. Yeah, you're right. I'm just tired.'

'Get some sleep! You'll feel fine after some rest!'

'If only! The showman's is full of tat, everyone's partying on the bus, there's now a dance platform on the roof of the Q4 – it's a hard life!'

'Find a nice spot in the sunshine.'

'Or maybe, I'll just curl up in a cave! Anyway, must get this over to the hill-tribe, don't want to miss them.'

Debbie slipped back into cat-mode and danced back towards the sound system.

By the time I got back to the mine entrance, I had missed them. So I took Debbie's advice and laid down in the sunshine.

•

I woke to the sound of excited voices. Zander, Thomas and the others were back above ground.

'How was it?' I stood up and brushed dust off myself.

'Amazing!' Drops of water flew from Thomas's dreadlocks as he flicked his head backwards.

'Dangerous!' Zander pulled off his head-torch and wiped water from his forehead.

'The underworld!' Thomas laughed.

'Nearly was too!' said Zander seriously. 'My fucking torch had a dodgy connection.' He clicked it on and off. 'I was ahead of everyone, and it went out – just for a second. When it came back on, I stopped to wait for this lot, and there behind me in the floor was a mineshaft!'

'Bloody hell. Lucky you stopped. One more step and . . .'

'No! No, the shaft was behind me! I'd already stepped over it! Fucking torch!'

'Fuck!' I shuddered.

'Yeah – Fuck!'

I gave the hill-people the food. They were shy about coming back with us to the party, so said their goodbyes and disappeared back into the rocks. As we made our way back down along the edge of the stream, Thomas stopped me and Zander.

'Look what I found.' Cupped in his palm was a geometric noddle of sharp-edged metal cubes. From the polished surfaces emerged smaller cubes. Some in perfect alignment with each other's right angles, others piercing the surfaces on a diagonal tilt.

'Whoa!' I blinked in wonder at the techno-rock. 'What is that?'

'Galena,' said Thomas. 'A mix of silver and lead!'

'And you just found it in the mine?'

'Yah, deep-deep inside.'

'Why would anyone want to smash up and melt down such a beautiful thing?' I asked.

'Silver and lead?' Zander stroked the top edge of the crystal. 'It's gonna be money and bullets.'

Thomas held the crystal up to eye level. 'And if you look closely – can you see the square patterning on each facet?'

I peered into the gunmetal shine. 'It's kinda fractal.'

'It's still growing.' Thomas's eyes shone. 'The mines might be dead, but the rock is alive!'

IN THE FOREST

After the party most of our visitors headed back to their homes in the cities. Except for Mitch, who stayed with us in Wales. Although we'd all loved the mines, we felt that it was unwise to stay too long in such a contaminated place. The water contaminated with lead, the Earth contaminated with the violence of relentless extraction. We needed some greenery. A friend told us about an isolated place in a forest that would make a good park-up.

•

In the valley we were in shadow but above the spiked tops of the conifers, the mountain peaks were sunlit. Blocks of commercially planted pine enclosed the forestry track that we'd parked along. If there were any birds, we couldn't hear them. The dense woodland deadened all sound. It wasn't the kind of woodland we'd hoped for, but it was remote and hidden.

Zander was chopping the wood we'd collected. I cleared a flat area next to the track and made a pile of dried pine needles and cones for kindling. In the distance the purr of the little gennie powered the decks and monitors on the bus. Mickey was helping Ixy, Sanchia and Sasha practise their mixing skills. Joe, Hamish and Little Reggie were trying to teach an overexcited puppy to 'Sit!'

A few months earlier the UK government had introduced the Dangerous Dogs Act. This little pup had been on death row, accused of being a pit bull. Friends of friends liberated him from the pound and thought he should live as an outlaw with us. Joe named him Terra – as in the Earth – which suited the rich, red-brown colour of his coat.

Under the trees, twilight came early. I got the fire going. As the shadows closed in, we all came together around the res-in-scented fire and cooked a big pot of pasta with tins of baked beans stirred in. It was delicious.

After we'd eaten, everyone went back to the bus to listen to music, leaving Zander, Debbie, Simone, Mitch and me sitting round the fire drinking tea.

'That Lechlade site was on top!' I poked the fire with a stick.

'In what way?' asked Simone.

I put the stick onto the fire to burn. 'Right next to the village.'

'But still,' said Mitch, shrugging and smiling, 'a wicked party!'

'Not massively undercover though, was it?' said Debbie.

'Acton Lane, then that.' I stared into the fire. 'Spider was right, they've got us in their sights.'

'So what do we do? Just give up?' Simone's voice was defiant.

'No surrender!' Mitch raised a fist.

There was a moment's silence. 'Perhaps,' said Zander, 'we just need to do things differently?'

'Ninja style!' Mitch covered the bottom of his face with his forearm and narrowed his eyes.

'Let's get horses!' said Debbie. 'Live on the moors and up in the mountains!'

'Black horses?' I perked up at the thought.

She laughed. 'Well, obviously!'

'With silver pentagram stars, just here, on their bridles!' Mitch tapped a finger to his brow.

'And black plume headdresses!' I could see it.

'Bow-top wagons, painted with silver Technoglyphs!' Debbie mimed a design in the air.

I gulped a mouthful of tea. 'And a string of mules to carry the massive bass bins!'

'That's a lot of new kit. Horses, mules, wagons. A lot of money and time.' Zander stood up to get more wood from the stack behind him.

The rest of us exchanged glances.

'We've already got what we need,' he said as he stepped back into the firelight with an armful of logs. Carefully he fed the fire. The dry pine spat orange sparks.

'Okay,' I said, breaking the silence, 'forget the horses. We could leave the country and travel Europe?'

THE MYTH

It was a few days later when we got the phone call.

Outside the bus, on the forestry track, Terra was being gently swung around on the end of a stick by Joe. With the other hand, Joe was holding the phone to his ear. Zander was perched on a Jerrycan and having his head shaved by Sasha. Ixy and Mickey were now together and were probably cosying up in Mickey's truck.

Little Reggie was on the decks, which we'd set up outside. He was playing two duplicate copies of The Brothers Grimm's track 'Exodus (The Lion Awakes)'. The section he chose to loop back-to-back had a dark melancholic atmosphere, a reverb on the breakbeat giving it a remote and lonely feel. The reggae-style voice sample went something like, 'When the lion awakes, when the lion awakes, there'll be war, trouble and war', then a stronger, defiant beat kicked in. Repeated over and over it felt like a call to arms, but it was tinged with the sadness and sacrifice necessary to defend against oppression, racism and injustice.

On the bus, Hamish was in the driver's seat rolling a spliff and chatting to Simone. Debbie and I were sitting at the top of the steps, looking through some sketches, though I was distracted by the sight of Joe on the phone as he spun, slowly raising Terra up off the ground and gently landing him.

Moments later, Joe jumped up the steps into the bus.

'Aww mate! That was Bedlam! They're at the front of a thirty-six-mile convoy heading to Worcestershire!'

'Thirty-six-mile convoy?' asked Debbie.

'The Avon Free Festival was roadblocked so everyone's heading down to Castlemorton Common, in the Malvern Hills, and . . .' Joe caught his breath '. . . the Old Bill have given them a site!'

'In the area!' Hamish bounced up and down in the driver's seat.

Debbie and I exchanged doubtful looks.

'Believe!' Joe waved the phone in the direction of Terra, who was outside staring at the now motionless stick. 'That was Bedlam – it's for real!'

'Come on!' Hamish tucked his finished spliff behind his ear and grabbed the steering wheel with both hands, 'Let's 'ave yah!'

'The police have given them a site?' Simone turned round in the passenger seat to face Joe. 'Sounds well dodgy to me.'

'A thirty-six-mile convoy! It's unstoppable! It's gonna be humongous!' Joe bounced down the steps.

Simone got up and called after him. 'But the rig is still fucked from Acton.'

'So? We borrow some more bits and bobs – or just go and chill. Anything's better than staying here.' Joe picked up Terra's stick.

'Just go and chill?' Simone followed Joe out.

'Yeah – just chill!' Joe laughed. Terra growled as he locked back onto his stick.

CASTLEMORTON COMMON: MAY 1992

An hour later our matte-black convoy was heading south-east towards the Malvern Hills. From another direction, channelled across country by strategically placed police roadblocks, the displaced Avon Free Festival snaked its way north-west to the same location.

The Malvern Hills are not rounded but rise abruptly from the surrounding countryside like a ridge of mini mountains. Geologically they were formed by some of Britain's most ancient rock, but their sharp, conical shape made them look out of place – odd, unusual, almost unbelievable. As were the smiling policemen that directed us on to the site.

Coincidences are often dismissed as chance. But some fit a narrative so beautifully that they acquire a deeper significance, whether or not that significance is relevant. At the entrance to Castlemorton Common two currents of improbability met and seamlessly flowed together. As we arrived from one direction, so too did the lead vehicles of the Avon convoy from the other. The smiling policemen filtered our vehicles into the head of the queue, and we drove along the narrow track leading onto the site.

The timing was perfect. Perhaps too perfect – because if *someone* were to have taken note that we were among the first vehicles on site, then it could be construed that we were leaders of the festival convoy and therefore organisers of the event. Even though it was clear to the thousands of witnesses in the convoy that it was the police who'd relocated everyone to Castlemorton.

But, of course, as our convoy bumped off the track and bounced across the springy green turf, thoughts of such an implausible stitch up didn't cross my mind. Nor anyone else's. The glorious sunshine and smiling policemen had us all fooled.

•

The common backed onto the steep slopes of the Malvern Hills. Dug into the hillside at the top of the track was an old quarry, now a deep lake of sparkling turquoise. After a quick reccy we found a flat area and swung our vehicles into a circle. The canopy on Zander's Q4 was flung back, and the DJ desk installed. On the ground, either side, the speaker stacks were secured with ratchet straps. In the middle, Thomas bolted together the spinning steel hoops of his Gyrocycle. Black and silver flags were unfurled. The rig powered up, and the first record dropped.

New arrivals, bursting with smiles, exploded out of their vehicles. All around us tents and marquees went up. Sound systems switched on – Bedlam, DiY, Adrenalin, Circus Warp, LSDiesel and more. The air buzzed with excitement, heat haze and basslines. As the sun went down the endless convoy became a twinkling river of headlights flowing onto the common.

By dawn the landscape had changed. We were now at the centre of a festival-village populated by thousands. I went for a walk.

The festival stretched for over a mile along the single track that came in off the road and gently climbed up the common towards the base of the hills. Either side, the land was rough pasture dotted with marsh grass, bracken and thickets of gorse. We were lucky to have arrived early enough to get a flat spot. Walking up towards the quarry, I passed Bedlam erecting a huge, white marquee. Further up was Adrenalin – Big Reggie's new sound system. The crowds, criss-crossing in all directions, were a vibrant mix of urban ravers in soft, bouncy sportswear and spikey punks in rags and big boots. Despite the superficial fashions, there was a shared excitement and camaraderie.

Continuing up towards the quarry, I passed the police. They were in their shirt sleeves and enjoying a game of rounders, their helmets in the grass marking the bases of the game. I stopped to watch. They were super-relaxed and genuinely having fun. Looking back down across the colour that the festival had splashed across England, I couldn't help but think how archetypal it felt.

As kids, Zander and I had grown up in a small village. In the summer, games of cricket and village fetes were held on the church green. As an innocent child, those endless summers worked a particular charm – an idyllic scene of stability, decency and fair play. But in the formative years of adolescence, it became clear how those home county rituals were cornerstones of a grand denial. Those 'jolly decent folk' played along with the status quo. Psychotic in their polite refusal to acknowledge the oppressive roots of the comforts they so enjoyed.

In contrast, the village greens of Castlemorton tapped into a deeper current. People being people. No ritual. No messing about. Feet back in contact with their common land. The punks, travellers, ravers and cyber-spirals were an integral part of the landscape from before the myths of Britain began. A village fete of minstrels, jesters and revellers from a timeless techno-dimension.

The police, flushed in the summer heat, were now enjoying a picnic. I continued up to the foot of the hills and the flooded quarry. Some people were skinny dipping. Others were hurling themselves off the surrounding cliffs, busting as many silly dance moves as possible before plunging into the cool blue depths.

•

Back at the Spiral circle, the dance floor was full of people exploring every possible space between themselves and the outside word. The roof of Zander's Q4 was crammed with ecstatic dancers reaching up into the sky to collect armfuls of sunshine and then, as if casting spells, zapping cosmic rays down into the crowd below.

We'd still not fully repaired the damage caused by the riot police at Acton Lane. Steve Watson arrived from London with a friend, Tom, who'd helped build the pyramid with Billy at Stoney Cross. They'd brought with them a little more sound equipment, but we were still running far below full capacity.

Seb also arrived with boxes of our newly pressed record. However, the initial jubilation of finally having the fruits of our labour was soured when people took them on the promise of selling them to raise funds for the sound system, but instead pocketed the money or swapped them for drugs.

Then there was the idiot that fired distress flares at the ever-present police helicopter. It was this act of stupidity that caused the mood to flip. The police playing rounders vanished, and the media went into a frenzy.

The festival was no longer just an annoyance to a few neighbours. Now it was an abomination. One of the traveller's horses that was being nursed, after having been injured on the road en route to the festival by a speeding car, was now reported in the newspapers as a local animal that had been butchered and eaten by monsters. The site was now 'knee deep in needles, used tampons and excrement', which it wasn't. The joyful free party people were now murderous rogues revelling in a hellhole of blood sacrifice, filth and drug-induced hysteria. And inexplicably, Spiral Tribe were the 'Techno-pagans' behind it all.

Someone had brought copies of all the national newspapers to show us. After reading through them, Debbie and I sat together on the hillside looking out over the festival. It still looked gorgeous. Thousands of people enjoying one of the best weekends of their lives. But even in the full spring sunshine an ominous mood darkened our day. Acton Lane. Lechlade. And now this.

'We're being stitched up,' said Debbie.

The circling police helicopter passed overhead, the warlike rhythm of its rotors overpowering the gentle heartbeat of the dance music.

We walked back down the hill. Debbie went to check out Bedlam, I headed back to the Spiral circle. Sitting alone I found Sazz, a young woman we'd met across the summer. Hugging her knees she gently rocked back and forth. Her long fair hair covering her face.

'You okay?' I asked.

She looked up, tears streaming down her face.

'My family, my friends, terrible things are happening back home . . .'

Fighting the tears, she told me that the violence was escalating in her city, Sarajevo, in former Yugoslavia.

I knew nothing about the situation, only her anguish in that moment. Lost for words I sat down next to her.

'I must go!' She got up.

'Sazz?' I called after her.

She turned and raised both her hands and shook her head. She wanted to be alone. I felt her grief, and I felt stupid not knowing more about what was going on. I was uncomfortably aware that the Castlemorton Festival was splashed across the frontpages of all the national newspapers. The headlines screamed about 'the unholy alliance between ravers and travellers'. And yet behind that manufactured outrage, the warmongers were going about their business.

•

By the end of the festival an atmosphere of paranoia was spreading. Not helped by several individuals, none of whom we recognised, running around inciting panic. It was unusual because, of all the festivals I'd been to, Castlemorton was the only one where there was this level of agitation. The exception being Acton Lane, where I'd witnessed the dirty tricks the police had used to induce panic.

We held our nerve, determined not to leave until we'd bagged every last piece of rubbish left by those who'd shirked their responsibilities. Not because we wanted to make a good impression on the authorities, but because we always cleaned up, out of respect for our planet.

FRIDAY 29/5/1992

With the site tidy and the equipment packed away, it was time to leave.

To be on the safe side we packed Terra and Joe off in a friend's car, just in case the police did any spot checks. Getting stopped and searched was one thing. Terra getting the death sentence was another.

With a sense of trepidation we pulled our vehicles into a straight line, the engines idling. Each of us wished each other luck and exchanged hugs before we left. Something that we'd not done before.

Zander was driving the Q4, I was in the passenger seat. We were towing the showman's. Within minutes of driving off the common, plainclothes coppers leaped out of the hedgerows on either side of the lane. They jumped up onto the steps of the moving truck, their heads in through the open windows, demanding that we pull over. We did as they asked.

They arrested Zander and me. In the bus and the other vehicles, they arrested Debbie, Kevin, Thomas and Darren. They confiscated the Q4 and the showman's. The Techno Bus and Darren's van. Thomas's pickup and workshop trailer. They held, as evidence, all our sound equipment and lights. Our personal possessions. DJ's records, plus the remaining boxes of our new EP. The bucket of donations we'd collected and all the bagged-up rubbish.

We were taken to Worcestershire police station and locked up overnight. In the morning we were charged with 'Conspiracy to cause a public nuisance' and bailed, awaiting trial.

We walked out of the police station with nothing but the clothes we had on and a ravenous hunger. We raided the local supermarket's skips for food, collected as many large cardboard boxes as we could find and took them back to the police station, where we used them to make a shelter – on the station steps.

All night the police had to step around our makeshift camp. When they complained, we pointed out that the problem was of their making. If they returned our vehicles and all our stuff, we'd be happy to leave. The more irate they got, the more we insisted. In the morning their chief, Inspector Ian Imray, came and had words. He told us that he didn't have a problem with us protesting our innocence – but could we please do it in the public garden in front of the police station. After realising that we could build a bigger camp on the lawns in between the municipal flowerbeds, we agreed. Later that day he gave an interview to the *Independent* newspaper and said, 'They have been a nuisance, but they have not caused any problems as such. This morning they even asked for a brush and swept the footpath.'

Debbie Staunton, who ran one of our info lines in London, started a campaign to raise awareness about what was happening and launched an appeal for people to come and support us.

Locals and people from all over, brought us supplies: polythene sheeting, ropes, blankets and food. As well as paint and brushes. People joined us and the camp grew. In the trees we strung ropes and hung all the scrap metal we could find: short pieces of scaffolding, steel sheet, suspension springs, angle-iron. We made a drum kit with plastic barrels and buckets. We painted protest banners but refused to use the language of victimhood. Our banners were defiant and satirical: 'Illegal Music in the area!' For nine days and nights we feverishly bashed away at our improvised instruments, playing 'Industrial Hardcore'.

Despite our anger at being singled out as 'criminals', the protest was a good-natured affair and we got no further harassment from the police.

One evening Hamish and I were standing on the curb in front of our camp. A white car pulled up. A Rover SD1 3500. A car popular with police, though this one was plain white and lacked the usual 'Jam Sandwich' fluorescent orange strip along the body. The interior light went on and the passenger window wound down. I couldn't see the man's face, but he wore dark trousers and a white shirt. I presumed he was a copper. *Here we go!* I thought as he leaned over and handed Hamish a sheet of paper.

'I want you to have this,' he said.

Hamish took it. I guessed it was an eviction notice or threat of further legal action.

The car drove off. Hamish's expression was one of shock.

'What the fuck?' He handed it to me.

It was a pencil drawing of a woman lying on the ground. A heavily pregnant woman. Standing over her, kicking her in the belly, was a riot cop. Underneath were the words 'What have we done?'

It's hard to imagine why anyone would have drawn and hand-delivered such a picture. Unless, of course, the person doing so really was a copper who had some knowledge of the horror stories from Acton Lane and felt compelled to express remorse about the brutality of his colleagues. This small gesture was a hint that perhaps the police were not united in their views.

•

Stuck outside the police station with next to nothing, we focused on what little we had – our ever-growing set of trash-built drums and percussion. As the days passed, our rhythmic jams became more shamanic. They may have taken everything from us, but free from all material possessions our creative energy burned ever bright.

But while we'd been protesting, the police had been busy in London. Nine days later we returned to find that Maygrove and Heather's house had been raided, searched and 'evidence' taken. Not only my notebooks and artwork but also Heather's computer and various personal documents. Worse still, they'd arrested Simone.

Simone, along with a few others – Joe, Little Reggie, Hamish, Mickey, Ixy, Steve, Jeff, Sanchia and Sasha – had slipped through the net on the way out of Castlemorton. From the raid on the London addresses, it was clear there was an ongoing investigation. No one was safe.

Debbie and I sat either side of Heather, who was on the

phone trying to find where they'd taken Simone. A few of the lads were skinning up and drinking tea. The mood was sombre.

There was a loud knocking at the door. I got up and went down the hallway to answer.

'Who is it?' I called without opening.

'Police!' Followed by another three blows.

My outrage erupted. 'What the fuck do you think you're doing!' I screamed at the back of the door. 'Arresting us for having a party is totally out of order, but arresting us for quietly sitting at home drinking tea is . . . is . . . fucking fascist!'

I heard muffled voices, but I just continued shouting. *They had overstepped the line – No, they couldn't come in, and no, I didn't want to talk to them!* This very one-sided exchange went on for over twenty minutes. As my anger vented, I realised that all the feelings of paranoia which had built up over the past months stemmed from uncertainty. It felt like we were being watched, but we hadn't known for sure. Now the hidden forces behind the door had faces. And I wanted to see them.

I put the security chain on and peered through the crack.

'Mark *Angelo* Harrison?' asked one of the two plainclothes officers. He had a beard, but I still couldn't see his features. 'Mark, please. Can we just come in and chat? It's raining.'

I expected myself to reply: *Good! I hope you get fucking soaked.* But I didn't. Instead, I closed the door and went back into the kitchen and asked the others. 'They want to come in, it's raining – shall I make them a cup of tea?'

Everyone stared at me blankly.

•

It was Lol who first suggested that we should try and get some kind of record deal as a creative way to fight back. The proposal met with a fair bit of resistance from members of the crew. Not least from Zander, Simone, Debbie, Seb and me. The problem, as we saw it, was one of assimilation. We regarded 'the music industry' as an integral part of the capitalist system. A show business entity that defused rebellious creatives by putting them on the payroll. That, of course, was an oversimplification which ignored that there are good people who, like us, were blocked on all sides by the same exploitative economy. We just had to find those people. If the system could send police to investigate us, then we could investigate the system. Seb, Simone, Lol and I, got on the case.

•

Before the internet, TV and newspapers controlled the conversation. Generally, these institutions existed to preserve the status quo. There were a few exceptions: some freelance journalists at the *Guardian* newspaper, the street culture magazine *iD*, and the music press, who perhaps weren't massive fans of electronic music but were excited by the anarcho-punk attitude of Spiral Tribe. This small pocket of rebel writers could not balance the torrent of anti-free party and anti-techno propaganda that the mainstream media generated. But the establishment was missing a trick – we knew it, the music press knew it – and so did a bloke called Youth, bass player with Killing Joke, music producer and founder of Butterfly Records.

It was an Easter egg hunt. Lol knew a woman who had a job at a big record company. They weren't interested in us and we weren't interested in them, but she knew a bloke who worked at Polygram. Lol and I went to an unofficial meeting in his office overlooking the river at Hammersmith. He was very helpful, but clearly over-worked. He buzzed about his office while answering Lol's questions. Polygram man suggested we chat with Youth at Butterfly over in Brixton. In his studio, Youth, sitting on a pile of coloured cushions smoking a chillum, said he loved the free party vibe and reckoned there might be some kind of deal to be had. But we'd first need to chat with his business partners, Jazz Summers and Tim Parry over at Big Life Records on Regent Street. He made a call, and a date was set.

•

Around Heather's kitchen table we wrote out a list of stuff we needed. It was a short list: 'Studio equipment'.

Si (aka Simon Carter), who'd recently joined us, had some experience working with independent record labels.

'Remember,' he said to Simone, Seb and me as we got up to leave for the meeting, 'big business is to the underground what the Death Star was to the Rebel Alliance!'

'Yeah, thanks for the encouragement,' replied Simone.

'And every Death Star has its thermal exhaust port!' Si's raucous laughing at his Star Wars joke made me feel less nervous.

'Proton torpedoes locked and loaded!' I replied, patting the record bag I had over my shoulder. Inside was 'The Folder', fat with A4 colour photos of our parties, examples of my artwork, newspaper cuttings and a newly written text. Seb patted the breast pocket of his big orange coat and gave the cocked-guns salute. He had the tape safe.

We got off the tube at Oxford Circus and walked four blocks north to the top end of Regent Street. In front of us was Broadcasting House, headquarters of the BBC. Its rounded, Art Deco style, stepped storeys and radio mast made it look like the stern of a 1930s ocean liner.

The BBC effectively controlled the music industry with their national pop music station *Radio 1*, their weekly teen TV show *Top of the Pops*, and their administration of the national charts. This meant that a state institution chose which music got airtime, plus it defined the industry template of what a 'pop song' should or could be. That's not to say all commercial music was bad music – but as far as acid, techno and breakbeat-type tunes were concerned, the BBC imposed a radio silence. We, and I'm sure many millions of others, didn't care about this Machiavellian policy. As far as we were concerned, the state-sanctioned silence amplified the presence of the underground and destroyed whatever street cred the BBC might have had.

'Blimey! We really are in music-control central!' said Simone as the BBC's building came into view.

Our meeting that day was not at the BBC. We were on another mission, in a building just a stone's throw away.

We continued walking, glancing up at the door numbers.

'I think the only time I've ever listened to *Radio 1* was when it was blasted at me at full volume in the factory where I worked.' I stopped to check the address. 'That really was mind-numbing – but, of course, none of those bastards got arrested. Oh look, here it is: the thermal exhaust port!'

Seb paused before he opened the door. 'Are we ready for this?' His voice was low and unusually serious.

'Bring it on!' Simone chirped.

I patted my record bag reassuringly.

He swung the door open, and we stepped into the Regent Street offices of Big Life Records.

•

Being slightly early for our appointment we were sitting in Big Life's cosy little waiting area. Around us the open-plan office was buzzing. It was small but not pokey, taking up a single floor of the building, with about eight or nine employees, including the bosses: Jazz Summers and Tim Parry, who were in one of the four enclosed offices around the central space.

Seb, Simone and I were fidgeting. I was nervous, not of the meeting with the bosses but of the details, the legalese, the small print – we had zero experience or understanding of such matters. All we knew was we didn't want to get ripped off, compromised or assimilated into commercial pop culture. We had our own agenda. But still no clue about how to get what we needed.

Simone's phone rang. It was her stepdad. While she chatted, Seb and I tried to rehearse our pitch. But we didn't get far. Simone had stood up and was dancing about, her voice getting louder.

She finished the call. 'Ohhh-my-gosh! You'll never guess what!' She continued her dance while explaining that her dad was painting some offices around the corner, at a big legal firm. In fact, Princess Diana's lawyers. He'd mentioned to the staff there that his daughter and her mates were fishing for a record deal. The lawyers immediately offered their services.

•

Moments later we were ushered into Jazz's office.

'Spiral Tribe!' Jazz stood up and leaned across his desk to shake our hands. 'The new Sex Pistols!' He wore a light-yellow linen shirt and cream trousers. His rosy face was open, and his blue eyes, even in the dimly lit office, glittered with enthusiasm. Tim Parry sat in the corner. The younger of the two men, he stood up, feet together, shook our hands and returned to his seat.

We talked them through each of the images in the folder, pointing out with particular relish our 'bad' press. Jazz took time to turn each page, smiling at the more ridiculous newspaper headlines.

'So tell me, what is Spiral Tribe to you?' he asked, elbows on his desk, pointing in turn to each of us.

'We're a collective,' I said.

'Of artists, musicians and DJs,' said Seb.

Simone puckered her lips in thought, then said, 'We're fuckin' hardcore!'

Jazz laughed.

'But why *Spiral* Tribe?' He looked at me.

'It's the all-connecting shape of nature,' I replied.

'The source,' said Seb.

Simone thought again for a moment. 'We're the sound system. It's the groove.'

'Okay. Yeah, I get it,' Jazz said. 'It's the spiral energy.' For a second, he looked wistful, then slammed the folder shut. 'I don't think we've ever seen such a comprehensive press pack! Impressive!' He looked over at Tim, who remained expressionless.

Tim asked, 'You got something for us to listen to?'

Seb reached inside his jacket and handed over the tape. Tim took it to a rack of machines on the wall. There was a gentle pop from two large speakers as he switched on the power. The cassette slotted into the machine and the carriage clicked shut. Tim sat back down. He stared at the floor, waiting, as we all were, for the first track to come on.

•

After our meeting, Seb, Simone and I went to an Italian espresso bar in nearby Soho. It was narrow, with a lot of polished glass and chrome. The blue Formica countertops looked original 1950s, as did the Gaggia coffee machine. With its pressure gauges, hissing steam and rich-roast aromas, it was the engine driving that intense Soho moment. We squeezed onto the barstools in the window.

'Well!' I said 'That was . . .'

'Very positive!' said Seb, stirring his coffee.

Simone laughed. 'You mean totally fucking sorted!'

•

We now had two firms of lawyers. One was working on our record deal, the other – Peter Silver and associates – were getting our defence together for Castlemorton. Peter had told us that he could get our equipment back, but we'd have to wait until it had been photographed and forensically tested. There was no chance of that happening before solstice. Whoever was masterminding the ongoing police investigation was going to make damn sure of that. And, as an extra precaution, Debbie, Simone and I had received court injunctions banning us from Stonehenge.

•

'So, how did it go?' Debbie had to raise her voice over the excited chitchat back in Heather's kitchen. The atmosphere was buzzing with weed smoke and anticipation.

Simone told everyone about her stepdad painting the offices of Princess Di's lawyers.

'And what about the record company?' asked Debbie. 'Were they sorted?'

'Youth was pretty laid back,' I replied. 'Shades, Indian printed cotton – smoking charas.'

Debbie feigned outrage. 'And I thought he was a hardcore-punk-motha-fucka!'

'Well, yeah, I'm sure he is . . .' I said, 'inwardly.'

'And what about the others?'

'Jazz was very enthusiastic, straight-talking, loved the unstoppable-techno-pagan-vibe. But he's a shrewd one. And Tim Parry . . .' I thought for a moment.

'Straight-laced,' said Simone.

'Yeah,' I agreed. 'I got the feeling he disapproved of us.'

'So a good result then!' Debbie laughed.

'Couldn't have been better!' said Simone.

Debbie got out her baccy. 'What happens next? Rizlas anyone?'

Simone passed Debbie her cigarette papers. 'We'll let the lawyers battle it out.'

Seb, who'd been chatting to Joe, came down to our end of the table. 'We're pushing for an advance. Enough to kit out the showman's as a mobile studio.'

'You're probably gonna want to soundproof it,' said Tim.

'Can you do that?' asked Seb.

Tim leaned back in his chair and stretched. 'I reckon!'

Thomas, who had been sitting quietly next to me, said, 'As soon as we get our stuff back, we should get out of Britain. I left Germany because it was ultra-conservative. But no way was it this bad.'

'That would be living the dream,' Seb nodded, 'on the road in Europe!'

'Dancing on the beaches in the sunshine!' Debbie closed her eyes and wiggled her fingers next to her cheeks.

Seb looked doubtful. 'But I'd need to leave music college.'

'I can show you more in one day than you'd learn at that college in a lifetime!' Si called across the room. Seb went over to talk with him.

'If we're really on the vibe,' said Jeff, 'we shouldn't go anywhere until we've checked out Ireland. Lots of bad shit's happening over there.' He had a point. In England we only heard the government's propaganda about The Troubles, so we had no idea what was actually going on.

'Awh-mate!' Joe sounded despairing, 'How we gonna hold down all these different angles?'

'For fuck's sake.' Simone took a deep breath. 'We don't all need to be together in one place. We're not just decks and a stack of speakers! We're *Spiral* Tribe! We're an attitude!'

'Hang on a moment!' Debbie stood up and raised her voice over all the excitement. 'Hang on!' The hubbub quietened. 'It's solstice in a week and we still don't have any money.' She looked around the room at everyone standing. 'Or transport.' She looked at each of us around the table. 'And no sound system – we need a plan!'

'I need a faster truck,' mumbled Zander.

•

Our record contract had been drafted. As the main instigators of the project, the job of checking it was entrusted to Simone, Seb and me. It was an honour to represent the collective, but at the same time it was a heavy responsibility. We had to study the small print and really understand what was being proposed by Youth, Big Life, their lawyers – and ours.

With a copy of the contract each, we again sat in the window of the Soho espresso bar. The smell of dark roast mingled with the vanilla of cakes and pastries. Steam shrieked from the coffee machine before muffling into milky foam. Empty coffee cups in front of us, we ignored the clamour and searched the small print for devilry.

'Looks pretty solid,' said Seb. 'The use of Youth's studio, two EPs, an album – and we get the advance we need.'

I tuned back into the clink and hiss of the coffee bar. 'Can we add conditions?' I asked. 'Before we sign?'

'We could,' Seb replied, 'but it might mean paying for a new draft.'

'No, not to add to the contract,' I said, 'but as an extra condition *before* we agree to sign.'

'Are you thinking what I'm thinking?' Seb laughed.

'A 23K suicide rig.' I raised my eyebrows.

'Yeah!' Seb's face it up. 'A fuck-off big hire rig!'

'On the back,' I continued, 'of a curtain-sided truck.'

'For solstice!' Simone clapped her hands.

'Let's ask!' Seb smiled.

'Ask?' Simone looked serious. 'You mean negotiate?'

'Okay,' Seb laughed, 'but it is a bit cheeky!'

Simone opened her clasped hands. 'And that is why they like us!'

SOLSTICE 1992

As solstice approached, the government put the whole country on alert. National newspapers and TV channels warned that extra police were on standby to enforce a four-mile exclusion zone around Stonehenge. With injunctions banning us from the stones, an unmarked police car sitting outside Maygrove, and with the ever-present danger that more Spirals might be arrested, we guessed our phone lines were tapped. But that wasn't going to stop us.

Our plan for solstice was not to align with a traditional monument. Our plan was to *un-align* a new monument in the centre of London. A monolithic structure which had the single purpose of amplifying the power of the elites.

•

London's West India Docks were a vast, abandoned area of warehouses and quays in a loop in the River Thames known as the Isle of Dogs. Built in 1802, the docks controlled imports from the slave economies of Jamaica and the Caribbean. While in power, Margaret Thatcher got together with a group of bankers and property developers. They decided it would be the perfect spot for London's new financial district and the centre of their neoliberal global economy. At its core they built the tallest skyscraper in Europe. A lone, stainless-steel tower, its fifty-five storeys crowned with the symbol of immortal dynastic power – a pyramid. Officially named One Canada Place, Canary Wharf – but better known as 'Thatcher's Cock'.

After four years of construction, it had recently opened and now dominated the London skyline. From the top of the pyramid, a white strobe flashed, and at night all the lights on every floor were kept on. But it was empty. Empty while thousands were homeless or struggled with their rents and energy bills.

It also happened to be dead opposite the Greenwich meridian. The zero line of longitude – the British Empire's way of synchronising space-time, measuring its territory and navigating its global power.

Security within and around the tower was tight. But in its shadow was an area of parkland known as Mudchute, so named because it was where the river mud from the docks, which needed to be dredged regularly, had been pumped. When the docks closed, local residents resisted attempts to develop the land and it was now a grassy public space.

Trying to coordinate a party at Mudchute in complete secrecy was tricky. We couldn't just roll up in our trucks and plug in our rig as we'd always done. We didn't have a rig or trucks. Plus, we couldn't use any of our usual phone lines.

'What about the Big Life office?' Simone suggested. 'That's empty at the weekends.'

'How we going to blag that?' asked Seb.

'No need to blag,' I replied. 'They've been happy for us to use their photocopier. Why not their telephone too?'

The plan was coming together on multiple levels. A solstice celebration. An act of resistance against our arrest and the crackdown on free festivals. A symbolic statement against corporate power. And somewhere, amongst all that, was a test of Big Life's attitude. If there was a fence – which side were they on? We refused to sign the contract until we had an answer.

·

Jazz was up for it. All of it. Using their office, the curtain-sided truck and hiring a 23K sound system for the occasion. The suicide rig.

It was a high-risk manoeuvre. Even if we could set up undetected, there was another potential problem. Being in a tight loop of the Thames meant that the tower was encircled, moat-like, except for a narrow spit of land on its northern edge. If the police blocked these access roads, they would be pulling up the drawbridge and Canary Wharf would be impenetrable. But there was a chink in its armour: a pedestrian tunnel under the river from the south bank – The Greenwich Foot Tunnel.

Our plan was to ask ravers to park discreetly south of the river and walk the 400 metres through the tunnel to the party. In this way, we could secretly amass a full dance floor before switching on.

Simone and I were left answering the phone lines in the office while the others went with bolt croppers to rendezvous with the 40-ton truck and sound system. The plan was to keep the phone lines open till 2 a.m, then hand them over to our friends running our usual info lines and get to the party ourselves.

The first hour, from midnight to 1 a.m., went as planned.

Around 1 a.m. there was a problem. Word had got out on the pirate radio stations about the party's location, not the meeting point. Police had started blocking the roads at the entrance to the river loop. Two helicopters had been mobilised. The phone lines went crazy. Until 2 a.m. we were still able to direct people through the tunnel. But around 3 a.m. a private security firm sussed the secret entrance. The drawbridge was up. The tunnel, and the chink in the armour, were sealed.

Over a thousand people had made it in. But by 3.30 a.m. the police had surrounded the sound system, and by 4 a.m. they'd persuaded the truck driver that he should pack up and leave – or face the consequences. I don't think he'd fully understood the concept of a 'suicide rig'. He switched off, packed up and left.

The phones continued ringing. We redirected everyone to another party in Leicester with DiY, Armageddon and Circus Warp.

In the early hours, about thirty of the crew, along with some ravers, piled back to our undercover HQ at Big Life. After all the cat-and-mouse antics, spirits were high. But I felt low. Despite our best efforts we'd been let down again by not having our own kit and not being in full control of how we ran the party. Seeing that I was not enjoying the moment, a lad I didn't recognise came over to my desk.

'Alright there, bruv?'

'Yeah, but been stuck here all night on the phones.'

'No? Geeza! It was mental! That Tunnel! That rig! Those helicopters! Fair fuckin' play!'

I didn't mention that the helicopters weren't part of our plan. Instead, I just said, 'It got stopped.'

'It happens! But tell you what – you lot proper stuck it to that pyramid!'

'Yeah?'

'Yeah! Wherever I was in town, there it was, in my face with that fuck-off flashing light. Making everyone feel small . . . unimportant. Know what I mean?'

'Totally.'

'And now – well, now I don't feel it no more!'

'The spell's been broken?'

'The spell's been broken! That's it! Talking of pyramids, you lot doing Pilton next week?'

'Glastonbury? Nah. There's no Traveller's Field – and a fifteen-mile exclusion zone if you haven't got a ticket!'

'What?'

'Yeah.'

'So what you gonna do about it?'

Before I could answer, Simone, hand over the mouthpiece of her phone, shouted, 'Everyone! The police are outside!' She indicated with her eyes that it was them on the phone. 'They're coming up!'

The switch from everyone dancing, shouting and skinning up was balletic in its transition. Two coppers burst in to find an office of record label employees working the nightshift. Leaning back in swivel chairs, feet on desks, negotiating deals and deadlines. The photocopier was scanning documents and people were rushing around with piles of records.

Simone, on reception, smiled brightly. 'Good morning! How can I help?'

Wide-eyed the police took in their surroundings. Posey posters of pop stars on the wall. Gold discs. Freaky people. Vibey girls with shaved heads. Strange music and the smell of something exotic in the air. Simone offered them coffee.

They politely declined and explained that they'd thought that this was the info line HQ of an illegal rave. Simone totally understood the confusion. 'Yes, there was a video shoot earlier in the evening, and as you can see, we're on a tight deadline to finish it in time for this week's *Top of the Pops*.' She hoped they understood.

Of course they did. And after a few more seconds of standing in the middle of the room in stunned amazement, they left.

Still wanting to party, most people decided to leave the office and made the trip up to Leicester. I wasn't in the mood. My mind was elsewhere. *Had we really stuck it to the pyramid?*

•

It was two years since Tonka and DiY had played in the Traveller's Field at Glastonbury. That moment was central to the conception of Spiral Tribe and inspired a huge underground scene. Unfortunately, this important cultural moment had been overshadowed by the trouble at the end of the festival between the security and the travellers. In response, Glastonbury's organiser Michael Eavis had banned the travelling community.

Glastonbury had its roots in the creative chaos and rebellious attitude of the free festival movement, the same attitude that played an important role in the electronic music scene in the Traveller's Field. Michael Eavis had hosted the travellers for years. He was respected. If the riot hadn't happened, or if the travellers had not been cast as the only villains involved, then he would have been seen as one of the enablers of early techno culture. But instead, he'd denounced the travelling community, closed the free space and shunned techno. *What had happened?* I felt compelled to speak with him. *But how?*

We were back at Heather's place.

'Phone him up!' said Simone.

'Yeah. Right. I don't know his number, he doesn't know me, and we're three days away from the festival – he's going to have more important things to do than chat with some ranting randomer.'

'Phone their office number,' Simone said slowly. 'Tell them who you are and ask to speak with him.'

I did as I was told. I was put on hold. A few minutes later, Michael came to the phone.

It took me a moment to shake the surprise from my voice and get properly into righteous indignation mode. Michael spoke softly. He knew who I was and what I represented. He listened attentively. He didn't interrupt any of my points, all of which centred around how important it was that Glastonbury continued to have free space. He let me finish and said that he agreed. That's why he'd always supported the travellers and provided that space. But the pressures from the authorities, police and insurance companies meant that his hand had been forced. If he hadn't closed the Traveller's Field, it would have been the end of the festival.

We spoke for over half an hour. I was struck by how kind and empathetic he sounded. He seemed to really care. But it wasn't him who had control. He and the festival organisation had become enclosed within nested boxes of bureaucratic power. Festival-goers were fenced in for a weekend, but the festival organisers were permanently fenced in.

THE DONGAS FULL MOON RITUAL: JULY 1992

Debbie Staunton had something elfin about her. Not only her long, blond hair and delicate features but also in the quiet, gentle manner that masked a determination and passion for social and environmental justice. Initially she'd volunteered to run our info line, but she quickly saw the benefits of pulling everyone together by growing the info line into a shared communications network.

It was via this network that she'd heard of a meeting with a group calling themselves the Dongas. They were part of a protest against a new motorway that was planned near Winchester. The M3 was to be extended and would excavate a deep cutting through Twyford Down, next to St Cathrine's Hill – an ancient hillfort and burial ground as well as an area of habitat for endangered wildlife.

That same evening, together with her partner Ian (not Ian Orinoco), we drove down to St Catherine's Hill to find out more. We parked at the bottom of the hill and climbed up the steep, grassy slope. Halfway up I stopped to catch my breath. Behind me were the city lights of Winchester, and in front, bats flitted across the full moon. At the top, the hill was crowned with giant beech trees. At their centre, in a clearing, was a large fire. The encircling trees formed a cavernous space of vaulted shadow and flickering light. There were perhaps fifty people gathering there.

A large figure, dressed in animal furs and wearing a horned mask, strode into the circle and stood, arms raised, by the fire. In a booming voice he called for us all to form a circle and hold hands. Normally I would have walked away muttering something insulting about hippies, but it didn't feel like silly theatrics. The hill beneath our feet, the encircling trees, the golden dome of firelight, the full moon – it all felt very real. I reached out and took the hand of the strangers either side of me. As the circle connected, so too did the clarity of the moment.

The figure started a monologue. Poetic yet powerful. Pagan yet political. He spoke of the beauty of our planet, of the dissociation from nature. Of how this destruction would unleash an uprising. Of the poison that polluted the Earth and our minds. He started to spit into the fire.

'Spit out the poison! Spit out the poison! Spit out the poison!' he chanted.

•

The next day, back in London, I told Debbie Spiral about the unexpected 'meeting' with the Dongas.

She was enthusiastic. 'Perhaps they'd like a party?'

'It's the perfect place – and a great cause!'

'I'll see if Heather will lend us her van.'

•

Debbie and I drove all the way back to St Cathrine's Hill. We found a small group of young, white people with dreadlocks. They were sitting around the cold ash of the campfire from the previous night. Their clothes were lived-in, multi-layered and ingrained with ash, earth and woodsmoke. Debbie was dressed head-to-toe in silver. I was all in black. We both had shaved heads and wore mirror shades.

They said they were the Donga Tribe. We introduced ourselves as representing Spiral Tribe. We explained that we'd been reclaiming ancient sites, the commons and abandoned buildings. How we'd been up against the law, uniting urban youth and building community with a mix of breakbeat, acid and techno. And how important it was to us to reconnect people, especially city kids, with nature.

They said no. They didn't like *that* kind of music.

Although frustrated that they didn't see the benefits of such an alliance, Debbie and I still supported their cause. We wanted to help in any way we could. I had an idea. One that avoided all personal taste in music but still gave them access to our huge dance music crowd. The next Torpedo Town was coming up. I could make flyers to give out, asking people to come and support the protest at Twyford Down. After some discussion amongst themselves, they agreed.

As Debbie and I walked back down the hill to the van, Debbie asked, 'So what did you make of that lot?'

I thought for a moment. 'Maybe, just a teensy bit too – *cliquey?*'

TORPEDO TOWN AGAIN: AUGUST 1992

For many people, I imagine signing a record deal is a dream come true. But we weren't seduced by the fantasy. We signed, but without compromise. Our contract was rock solid.

We got the first instalment of the advance. A chunk went to Tim to soundproof the showman's, some we saved for maintaining the equipment and décor, and the rest we handed over to Seb and Si.

Si was a member of Earth Leakage Trip, along with Neil Sanford and Rob Playford. The group who'd created one of our all-time favourite dance floor anthems: 'No Idea'. This was the tune that, back in 1991 at the picnic site, had helped shape the future mood of Spiral Tribe.

Back in November, Debbie and Joe were at Camden Lock. Enthusing about the track as they navigated the crowds. Despite the push and shove of the market and the hubbub of excited bargain hunters, as they passed a lone figure sitting on a wall, they heard him say, 'I made that tune!'

It was Simon Carter. The cosmic co-incidence had brought our orbits into sync, and from that moment on, Si became a close friend to us all. Already working with Moving Shadow Records as a studio engineer, Si was deeply immersed in 'all things machine'. With an insatiable appetite for the latest developments in music technology, equalled only by his appetite for partying hard, he immediately gravitated to the spiral's creative core.

He wrote a list:

Allen+Heath 16:8:2 mixer

Atari STACY portable computer running C-Lab Notator

Akai S1100 Sampler

Alesis QuadraVerb multi fx

Boss DR660 drum machine

Roland JD800 synthesizer

JBL monitors

Yamaha amp.

And a fuck-ton of cables!

And then went shopping with Seb.

They came back buzzing. Wildly ripping open cardboard boxes. Effing and blinding at fiddly sticky tape and covering Heather's basement in statically charged pieces of polystyrene.

Heather had kindly invited us to set up the new equipment in her basement, which gave Seb and Si a chance to figure out how everything worked. Meanwhile, Tim was finishing off the showman's, as well as doing up another bus that he and Thomas planned to take to Europe.

Things were looking up, but the police still had our sound system. I was persuaded to go and talk to Jazz and Tim Parry – again.

We didn't stand a hope in hell of persuading them into hiring us another suicide rig. Not after last time – the police operation, the helicopters, the raid on their offices. But despite being shut down by 3.30 a.m., the media seemed to have understood the spirit of the party. Symbolically at least, the event had garnered support – it seemed that everyone hated Canary Wharf.

Because of this, Jazz and Tim were only too happy to lend us another rig. This time smaller, so that we could transport it and set it up ourselves. Keen to get back to the festivals, we loaded up and headed off to that year's Torpedo Town.

Unfortunately for us, and many thousands of others, the police were having none of it. They set up roadblocks to split up the convoys. This was a ridiculous strategy because, of course, it just created more problems – and more festivals. Instead of one, there were now three. Luckily, Zander, who was travelling with Ness in her bow-top wagon, managed to get onto site by galloping full tilt through all the roadblocks.

I was on the Romsey site, on top of a steep, grassy hill overlooking lush green countryside. The vehicle with the decks had not managed to get in. Steve Watson, as inventive as ever, rigged up a ghetto blaster and the whole party was run off mix tapes. It kicked!

I handed out hundreds of info flyers about Twyford Down. It did rain a little, but the strobes took care of that. People dancing with tongues out, drinking in the strobing sparkles. All was good, until Sunday morning.

I was standing at the edge of the dance floor on the lip of the hilltop. Riot police swarmed around the foot of the hill, encircling us. They tried to beat their shields in rhythm with each other. Though unable to keep time, the sight and sound was still daunting. Keeping the circle unbroken, they started to climb towards us. The ever-tightening wall of doom panicked people. Facing the police, I had my back to the sound system.

The music went off. I glanced over my shoulder to see a crowd of people rescuing the equipment from imminent destruction. Box by box it was hurriedly dismantled. The police pushed on and up. Other people had joined me along the top of the slope. We were surrounded, we had nowhere to go. I glanced back over my shoulder. The rig was almost packed away. But not quite. The police reached the top. I was confronted by a tall bloke in full body armour – shield, baton and helmet. His face masked with a black scarf.

I was incensed at the aggression, the injustice – *and that face mask!* With no other defence, fists clenched, I found myself screaming at him.

'Take that fucking mask off! You fucking coward! Take that fucking mask off!'

To my astonishment, he stopped in his tracks, lowered his baton and shield and awkwardly stood there, uncertain what to do. I glanced around. The rig was gone. It was safe.

The police had broken formation and appeared to have no idea what to do next.

Still furious, I continued to shout at the copper in front of me. 'Show me your face!'

To my astonishment, he put away his baton, dropped his shield and pulled down his scarf.

I was now speaking with another human being. 'Why'd you wear a mask?' I demanded.

He replied, 'So you can't see that we're scared too.'

•

Our troubles were not over. At least mine weren't.

Although the police had broken up a good party, I was glad there'd been no violence and the rig was safe. Again it had been 'spirited away by mysterious figures'.

The problem was: it *had* been spirited away – permanently.

I felt betrayed. While me and others had risked a beating

by defending the sound system, it had vanished into thin air.

Back at the Big Life office it was me who had to face the music. We had only just signed the deal and had only received part of our advance. The vanishing rig put everything on a knife-edge. Jazz summoned me into his office. Tim Parry sat in the corner scowling. Knowing how serious the situation was and how much was at stake, I told them what I knew.

At the moment in the story when the police came marching up the hill, Jazz stopped me.

'Look,' he said, fixing me with his intense eyes, 'I need a signed statement about how the equipment got stolen.'

Again, I tried to explain.

Jazz held up a hand. 'A signed statement – for the insurance company.'

I felt helpless. 'But I don't know what happened.'

'Then find someone who does, get them to sign a statement so the insurance can take care of it.' Jazz pointed a stern finger at me. 'Okay?'

I understood. 'Ah, okay.' The meeting was over.

The next day I came back to the office with someone who was happy to sign all the necessary documentation. I never did find out who was responsible for the equipment disappearing, but coincidentally it was around that time that several new sound systems appeared on the scene.

DEMOLITION SYSTEM: AUGUST 1992

Big Life's rig getting stolen hadn't only incriminated me, Seb, Simone and Lol, but it'd also jeopardized everyone's hard work.

Our priority was getting the communal studio together so that anyone who wanted to could produce their own music. The last thing we needed was our creative and economic autonomy being sabotaged.

Despite this wobble, Jazz didn't hold it against us. My reading was that he understood that we were on the frontline, where shit happens. But when I pushed my luck a third time to get a rig for Notting Hill Carnival, the answer was 'No! You cheeky fucker!'

All was not lost. A friend-of-a-friend had a rig and was up for us using it. Now all we needed was a venue.

●

Kim lived on Uxbridge Road in a shared house. She was a young woman of few words and a passion for dark techno. It was she who'd first played me The Mover's 'Nightflight (Nonstop 2 Kaos)'. Spiral Tribe played a diverse range of music, but no one was playing what Kim was playing. It was through our shared love of this darker style that we became friends.

One day we were out exploring wasteland five minutes away from her house. Rising up out of the rubble, in the middle of a flattered industrial site, was the remains of a tall, rectangular building. Perhaps six storeys high. The front of the tower block was missing, no windows, no walls, just a concrete shell with the interior floors and rooms exposed to the elements. On the right-hand side was a rubble-choked stairwell.

Picking our way over the broken bricks at the foot of the building, we noticed a hole which, after heaving a few pieces of concrete out the way, dropped into the basement. Torch in hand, Kim and I squeezed inside to find a room that had been sealed since the collapse of the façade. We found boxes of pamphlets from the 1950s which gave the history of the building.

'Callender's high-voltage research laboratories'. Built on the site of one of London's first power stations. When the power station closed in 1928, it became Callender's Cables. A company that was key in the electrification of Britain and the world, manufacturing all types of power lines and telegraph communications. Reading through the pamphlets by torchlight, I got a tingle of electricity coming up out of the damp earth and darkness.

The Notting Hill Carnival weekend was coming up. Callander's laboratories were only twenty minutes' walk from the carnival route. It all made sense.

The friend-of-a-friend's rig was installed in the building two storeys up with the speaker stacks facing out into space. We blocked the only door from the stairwell with as much junk as we could find. To get to the decks, DJs had to climb onto a ledge on the outside of the building, skirt around the stairwell wall, and climb back into the room where the turntables were. No way would the police be able to attack us or break up the party.

But that didn't stop them having a go.

Later that night, when the party was in full swing, hundreds surrounded us. But our tower block fortifications were impenetrable.

The next morning, the chief of police showed up wanting to talk to 'whoever's in charge'. As did an MTV film crew.

The chief was alone. He was civil to us, as we were to him. He complained that three of his officers had been hurt in the night. I said that I hoped they didn't have serious injuries but added that it was them who'd viciously attacked us and tried to incite a riot. Surprisingly, he agreed. We then chatted about the carnival, which he thought was an important cultural event. On leaving, he turned and congratulated us on being 'the longest running carnival sound system of 1992'.

There could be many reasons why he turned up alone and was so amicable. I'd like to think it had something to do with the atmosphere of the party. A real community event put together with the local kids, with local DJs playing the tunes of the moment. Whether this was the proto-jungle of British breakbeat hardcore, or the darker techno sounds, the unity of the crowd was clear.

While the police chief had been chatting, Kim had been playing her set. She was a distant figure, high above the dance floor in a white summer dress, her bob of thick, black ringlets catching the breeze. The concrete structure of the derelict building dwarfed everything, except the sounds of X-101's 'Sonic Destroyer', Mescalinum United's 'We Have Arrived' and Underground Resistance's 'The Seawolf'. At one moment a vortex of dust, and even someone's hat, whirled around the concrete tower. It was probably a gust of wind, but in that moment it appeared Kim's music was conjuring an elemental force that rose up from the ruins.

•

While packing up after the carnival party, it occurred to me that Zander and I had come full circle from volunteering to drive that dodgy old truck around Notting Hill two years previously. There we'd been heavily inspired by the energy of sound system culture. A culture that, regardless of who tries to control of it, remains a free and unifying spirit.

Callender's Cables, at one of the world's historic epicentres of electrification, was a good place to start our advance into the wider world. Or, as I printed on the flyers: 'The Earth is reconnected – the signal is ready to be sent!'

The crew preparing to reccy Europe were almost ready to go. The police had been releasing some of the vehicles, but not the rig.

Thomas had managed to get his pickup truck back, and Zander, Debbie and I went to see him before he left. He and Tim were still working on their bus. They'd parked up on an abandoned garden centre near Watford. Also staying there were Ixy and Mickey. And Ben, the bloke who'd originally sold us the sound system, he was now back in the area and keen to get involved.

That evening we arrived to find Thomas holding the fort by himself, sitting by the campfire making coffee.

'You know,' he said, wearing welder's gauntlets to pour coffee from a handleless saucepan into jam jars, 'I used to make cowboy coffee by heating a knife, red hot, then plunging it into the coffee to clear the grounds. It worked.'

Zander sucked in a sharp breath. 'Ruined your knife though!'

'Completely! Thomas laughed. 'And, as it turned out, unnecessarily.' He took off one of his gloves. 'Just disturbing the surface, with a spoon or your finger, works just as well!'

'I'll stick to tea thanks,' said Debbie, waving away the jar that Thomas handed her. 'So, when you off to Europe?'

'Soon as possible.' Thomas handed the jar to me. 'I left Germany because it was so uptight, but now . . .' he shrugged.

I took the jar by the rim and quickly put it down to cool. 'You reckon you'll visit Germany this time round? It's the Black Forest, right?' I blew on my fingers.

'Schwarzwald, maybe.' He shook his head. 'We'll see.'

'It's s'posed to be beautiful,' said Debbie.

'Yah, the mountains, the forest.' Thomas handed Zander a coffee and sat down.

'The chocolate cake, the cuckoo clocks,' Zander grinned.

'Not so much! But I tell you what.' He took off the other glove. 'In the autumn the forest floor is red with Fly Agaric mushrooms!'

'Ah, last Halloween!' I winced. 'I haven't seen Toney since!'

'You got to be careful,' Thomas nodded. 'Get the right dose.'

'Don't you have to scrape off the white dots and cook them?' asked Debbie.

'Feed 'em to ya reindeer.' Zander's tone was matter-of-fact. 'And then,' he said, pausing and grinning. 'Drink their piss!'

'You could do that,' laughed Thomas, 'or you could just eat a piece no bigger than the palm of your hand.'

'What do you mean?' asked Debbie.

Thomas opened his hand, and with his forefinger described a small circle at the centre of his palm. 'It's only a rough estimate, but the idea is that this is an approximation of your body mass and the dose best suited to your size.'

'Hmm, I'll have to give it a go sometime,' I said, having remembered that, dried and pressed between the pages of my notebooks, I still had the mushroom Toney had given me.

•

With one group going east to check out Europe, Jeff, Auto-manic Josh, Mitch and I thought it only right to go west and check out Ireland. Everything we'd heard about The Troubles was filtered through the British media. We had no first-hand experience of what was actually going on. Our idea was to go and meet the people to find out for ourselves.

Ignoring all the scare stories disguised as friendly advice, we squeezed into Jeff's tiny Renault 5 and headed over to Dublin on the ferry. Jeff had recently shaved off his mane of curls, Automanic wore his signature red tartan bondage trousers, Mitch shaved his head bald and wore his full-length black leather coat, and I was in my paint-splattered hoodie and com-bat fatigues.

The plan was typically Spiral – as in, we had no plan, knew no one there, and had nowhere to stay. Arriving in Dublin we turned left and drove clockwise around the country. Cork, Limerick, Galway.

With very little money we stopped off at village stores to buy food: sliced white bread, cheese, and packets of crisps and biscuits. The car was a mess.

On more than one occasion we slept in country lanes, the car nosed into a hedge, the doors flung wide, with us variously draped, stretched or squashed in, on, or around the vehicle.

Lost in the folds of the meadowed landscape we followed the lanes, often slowed by horse-drawn wagons on the roads. The tranquillity was enveloping. The warmth and friendliness of the people, disarming. We were in another world.

At first the change was difficult to spot. Heavily camou-flaged British soldiers squatted by the roadside, guns aimed at oncoming traffic. Aimed at us. The closer to Belfast we got the less camouflaged the occupation became. Coils of barbed wire. Nests of sandbags. Roadblocks. Chicanes. Troops pressed into every nook and cranny. And, overhead, the constant war-drum of the helicopters.

TO LEDBURY

Despite the police giving back our vehicles and equipment in dribs and drabs, our reputation for being a solid crew preceded us, and we were never short of a sound system.

The first reccy out to Europe took some rig, in part donated by Ben. Rudi was still a core supporter and supplier of equipment in the UK. Steve Watson and friends had formed a new crew in South London called Circus Lunatic. Bedlam also stayed in the UK, and together with Kim's crew we did some huge Spiral Tribe raves. The Ireland reccy had also been a success and we went back to do a party amongst the haunted ruins of the Hellfire Club, high on a hill overlooking Dublin.

•

As soon as Seb and Si had got their heads around the new equipment, they were inviting anyone who was interested to join in. With commitments to Big Life, there was always a crew making music. Sometimes in Heather's basement, at Kim's place, or at Youth's studio. We were mobile.

These were lean times. None of us personally profited from any of the money we'd generated. I lived off porridge oats and water. Crashed where I could, often in the corridor at Kim's where, with help from the household, I painted a huge set of new backdrops.

Automanic Josh had a contact for T-shirt printing, so I designed our first real piece of 'merch', with the idea of making some extra money to fund our growing need for materials. On the front I had the 23 Face circled by the words 'Spiral Tribe Breach the Peace', in reference to our first EP released with Big Life, and underneath, 'Illegal Music In The Area!' On the back, big and bold, Spiral's call to action: 'Make Some Fuckin' Noise!'

The very first batch of shirts was never distributed. Kevin had offered to deliver the freshly printed shirts to a buyer in South London. He returned empty handed – no T-shirts and no cash. Apparently, he'd taken the bend at the bottom of The Mall too fast. Rolled the van. The box of shirts was thrown out the back doors, bursting in front of the gates of Buckingham Palace. With no documentation for the vehicle, he'd done a runner.

As unlikely as this story is, I believed him, and perhaps deep down we all wanted this poetic bombing of the palace gates to be true. If so, I can't help but wonder what the security services made of Spiral Tribe's message delivered to the Queen's front door.

The second batch of T-shirts had much more impact on the establishment. And possibly helped change the course of our destiny.

All the time we'd been busy being creative, making original music, networking across Europe and putting on huge events in Paris, there was an ever-looming cloud on the horizon. At least for those of us who'd been charged with conspiring to organise Castlemorton Common – and that was our first court date. A committal hearing before a district judge in the small mediaeval town of Ledbury in Herefordshire. Just six miles west of Castlemorton Common.

Peter Silver and our team of barristers said it was important that we got our case moved to a Crown Court. As far away from Castlemorton as possible, with a jury, rather than being tried by local magistrates who, no doubt, would be influenced by the conservative attitudes of the area.

The judge needed to be convinced that we were a lawless bunch of ne'er-do-wells who deserved the higher penalties that a Crown Court could impose. We didn't have to try too hard. We arrived outside the court in Thomas's black monster pickup truck. The roar of its V8 engine pulled onlookers to the courthouse windows and caused the coppers standing sentry to shake their heads in disbelief. Around fifteen of us piled out of the back wearing 'Make Some Fuckin' Noise!' T-shirts.

The courtroom was full of our supporters, every one of them wearing the new shirts. As we entered, Zander pointed out several display boards of police photos. Photos of our stuff. The boards were titled 'Vehicles', 'Disco Equipment', and 'Weapons', which showed a selection of kitchen knives, axes and crowbars.

Before we took our seats, Zander and I asked Peter Silver about this skewed labelling.

'Don't worry about it,' he said. 'These are just the kind of prejudices that will help you to get to Crown Court.'

The district judge entered the room. He was wearing a dark blue tailored suit. His posture and range of motion apparently limited by his starched white shirt. His face was crimson, either because his collar was too tight or because he didn't want to breathe the same oxygen as us. Curtly he called the room to order with the clipped accent of an upper-class military man.

Ten minutes into proceedings, he noticed the T-shirts. The vulgarity and insubordination enraged him.

'Take those T-shirts off now!' His face contorted. 'I order you! Take those T-shirts off!' Spittle flew from his purple lips.

The assembled crowd were in turn bemused by his sudden outburst and, on realising the idiotic nature of his command, delighted to oblige. Everyone, including the women, took off their shirts. The room was bare chested. Realising his mistake, he almost choked on his own froth.

'Put those shirts back on! I order you to put those shirts back on!'

The crowd was in stitches.

'Order! Order!' he screamed into the naked chaos.

•

From day one we were confident that this man's prejudice would get us our ticket to Crown Court. But still, we had to sit through two weeks of his authoritarian posturing. On different days, different witnesses were called.

One morning I found myself waiting for the courtroom to open with a police chief superintendent. As the gowned clerk slid the bolts and swung the doors wide, the chief and I walked up the steps together. Just before entering, he leaned into my ear and said, 'I just want you to know, this is nothing to do with us. This is a political stitch-up. You,' he said, looking me in the eye, 'are being stitched up!'

•

I don't know how people cope with being summoned to court, in the middle of nowhere, for weeks on end. The courts make no provision. The accused are expected to find their own accommodation. We'd done our time sheltering in cardboard boxes, under polythene sheets, or under the stars. This time we squatted an abandoned house on top of a hill, a couple of miles outside Ledbury.

The place had clearly been empty for years. A thick layer of dust covered the remaining furniture, curtains and bedding. Thomas got the water back on and fixed a leak that was spraying from the kitchen ceiling. There was no leccy, so we used candles. The garden was large and overgrown with old fruit trees choked with brambles, and a small chapel smothered in ivy.

On the first evening we had a visitor. His name was Fridge-man. Fridge-man because he was an independent entrepreneur who showed up at some of our parties with a fridge full of beers to sell. He'd come on his motorbike, bringing with him a large slab of hashish – as a gift. While he sat on the dusty old sofa smoking, we all gathered around as he demonstrated his new toy: a police radio scanner.

With the static, bleeps and Alpha-Charlie-Alpha-Bravo babble, I couldn't make any sense of what was being said. But Fridge-man was well versed in the lingo.

'In my line of work,' he laughed, 'it's a useful bit of kit, but sometimes I get a bit para – thinking they're on to me!'

The little device flashed and prattled away on the coffee table.

'Hang on!' Fridge-man picked it up and held it closer to his ear. 'I'm not being para!' He looked around the room, his voice now a whisper. 'They *are* outside!'

The room fell silent.

Having explored the garden earlier, I volunteered to take a peep. I crept out the backdoor, into the night, looping my way around the garden to the side of the chapel. There, silhouetted against the night sky, were a number of parked vehicles. Engines and lights off. Some were police cars, some pickup trucks. Within earshot were a group of men. What I understood from the conversation was that the police were explaining to the men that they should not storm the building and beat the shit out of us because we were due in court the next morning.

Having managed to sneak undetected to within a few feet of the vigilantes, I was now terrified of being discovered. Very slowly I crawled backwards, while silently praying to the spirits of overgrown gardens to help me escape. But after only a metre or so, brambles caught my skin. While unhooking a clawed thorn from my hand, I noticed something glint in the under-growth. I moved closer. It was the spoked wheel of a car, so overgrown as to be almost invisible. At the centre of the wheel hub was a small enamel badge. It was loose. It unscrewed. I slid it into my pocket.

Free of the brambles, I looped back around the garden into the house to report what I'd heard. Realising the danger, we were on alert all night. But by morning the thugs and the police had gone.

In the courtroom, while the judge deliberated over our fate, I remembered the badge I'd found. I took it out of my pocket. It was a round, slightly domed circle, about six centimetres in diameter. The enamelled design was a stylised world map complete with a grid of latitude and longitude lines. The landmass in red enamel, the sea in blue. Across the globe, in a chrome script, was a single word: Triumph.

I squeezed my planet Earth talisman tight while the judge, from behind his dark wood podium, glared down at us.

He ruled that our 'crimes' were serious enough to warrant a Crown Court trial. The date was set. A whole year away. Which was fine, but we were on bail and told not to leave the country or organise any more parties. A ruling we ignored.

•

We'd finally got all our vehicles and sound equipment back from the police. Tim had finished fitting the studio into the showman's. Zander borrowed a truck from Tree Co and towed it, fully loaded, with the studio equipment, plus Tim's motorbike, to the port at Dover. The dockland tractor unit took over the towing on the quay and loaded our precious cargo onto the ferry. Hamish met the showman's at the docks in Calais with a Unic haulage truck. With all our sound system, trucks – with a few more editions, including the Unic – and a beautiful new studio trailer, we were now fully autonomous. Collectively we owned the means of our production.

•

The crew in Europe had teamed up with a bunch of squatters in Rotterdam. They had a venue known as 'The Storm Gallery'. It was a multi-storied Art Deco building, each floor a huge theatre space, complete with balconies and stage. With our first court appearance out the way, those of us who'd been arrested escaped over to Holland.

With help from Sanchia and Sasha, Debbie and I spent two

weeks decorating the huge space with crop circle-type wings embracing the space. Ben and Sasha went out on a midnight mission and came back with bin liners full of car hubcaps. These we hung around the theatre, like the shields in a Viking hall.

The afternoon before the party, the chief of police appeared. As usual I was volunteered by the crew to be Mr Diplomat.

The copper spoke quietly in perfect English. But as we sat down with a cup of tea, he placed his gun in the centre of the table facing me. He said, in between sips, that he was quite happy for us to have a party. 'But,' he said, putting his cup down, 'keep the chaos off the streets! Otherwise . . .' He tapped his gun and peered at me over the top of his gold-rimmed spectacles.

At a loss of how to react to the gentlest threat of violence I'd ever heard, I said nothing. He got up, re-holstered his pistol, thanked me for the tea and walked towards the exit. Half-way across the dance floor, which now sported a huge spiral, painted by Sanchia and Sasha, he stopped to admire our decorations. He nodded approvingly, but then caught sight of the silver hubcaps lining the walls. He turned and wagged gun-shaped fingers at me. I shrugged apologetically. He turned and left us to it.

•

After the Rotterdam parties, Debbie and some of the crew went to France and parked up at a squat on the River Seine, at a place called Riz Orangis, just south of Paris. I went back to England to help organise parties with Bedlam and Circus Lunatic.

Back in London, I went to a particularly crazy party in an anonymous Victorian brick building just off the Elephant and Castle. Four storeys high, with a sub-basement. It was here, underground, in two cavernous arches, that the sound systems were installed. A spiralled roadway wound up through the floors, which were also served by a fully functioning vehicle lift.

It wasn't only the lift that was fully functioning. So too were all the workshops, compressors and paint booths. Industrial racks were full of brand-new vehicle components. Strewn around the place were large wooden crates full of the same. It appeared the previous tenants were still in the process of moving out.

Sets of vehicle window caging, blue flashing lights and royal crests inscribed with the words 'Metropolitan Police' were clues as to whose porridge was being eaten. Both dance floors were packed. But so too were the other floors, not that the people there were dancing – they were far too busy helping the absent tenants pack up and move out their stuff.

In the morning we were all chased out of the building by a squad of very angry riot police. Angry for several reasons. One being our sheer brass-neckedness of partying a police building. Two, because they spent ten minutes trying to kick down their own front door, only to find it was unlocked, and opened outwards. And three, because someone had eaten all their porridge.

Before I went back to Paris, I had to finish the artwork for our album cover. The original concept had been 'Know Your Enemy'. I'd already done all the design work, used it on T-shirts and as the artwork for a huge party we did with Bedlam, Circus Lunatic and others in an abandoned government laboratory on Oxgate Lane, north-west London. The concept was strong, as was the artwork, the 23 Face crowned with missiles, bullets for teeth and a gun sight crosshair as one of the eyes. But Youth didn't like it. He said it was too confrontational. He was very polite about it, but it was clear that contractually it was his decision to make. Rather than argue, I decided to be more subtle.

In those days I didn't have a computer. Everything I did was in pen and ink. But I did know Perry. He worked at a graphic design studio in Brixton, and they had *Apple Macs!*

I took my new designs to Perry and asked him to lay out the new album cover for me. I sat with him, in awe of the power of a thing called *Photoshop*, while he cleaned up and arranged my artwork. The new concept was 'Techno Terra', the design, a grid of grey blocks with industrial hazard stripes in yellow. Youth and Big Life approved the new cover, and it went into production. What nobody knew, apart from Perry and me, was that camouflaged within the grid were big, block-style letters that spelled out, 'FUCK THE LAW'.

•

I went back to France, where Debbie and the crew had made friends fast.

Rachel was a quiet and unassuming woman who adopted Debbie and the Spirals as part of her family. She also took on the all-important job of running the Paris info line. The success of the sound system in Paris was in no small part down to her help and generosity.

The Paris parties were huge. No matter the size of the warehouses, they were always rammed.

The very first party there set the tone for the rest that followed. In convoy we'd been cruising around a large industrial zone on the edge of the city. It was Saturday, early evening. Flyers had already gone out and we still hadn't found a venue. We pulled our convoy over to the side of the road in front of a large warehouse that was for sale. Windows at the front of the building were boarded up. Next door to it was another abandoned warehouse. The problem was, the empty warehouse had a manned security office on the front gate, and the other housed a large Romani camp. It would be dark soon. We needed to find somewhere quickly.

'If only we could get around that security guard.' Hamish looked longingly towards the small, brick gatehouse and metal barrier. From where we were, looking out the windscreen of the bus, we could see the guard silhouetted in the gatehouse window. Next door, the hangar doors of the other warehouse stood wide open. Two Romani women, in traditional dresses and headscarves, were filling plastic buckets from a standpipe in the street. Behind them, in the shadows, we could see a group of Romani men watching us.

'We could always ask,' I said.

Hamish and I got off the bus and walked over to the camp. With little command of French, we had both adopted the same strategy. Big, open, friendly gestures, peppered with Bonsoir-Madame-Bonsoir-Monsieur. The women taking water stared blankly as we passed. The men came out to meet us. Hamish and I sketched diagrams in the air. The blokes seemed to get the gist of what we were asking and, with expressions of amused curiosity, escorted us into their camp.

We walked through their village of caravans to the end of the warehouse. We stopped against the concrete wall that backed on to the building next door. The Romani men crowded around us. I then went into an animated mime of wall-bashing. Hamish pointed towards our vehicles and made long, snaking arm movements back towards me as I hammered the wall with my fists. Hamish then started a kind of beat boxing rhythm through his nose and started dancing. The men laughed. They understood the language we were speaking. Within minutes, two sledgehammers had appeared and work began.

How a rave of thousands magically materialised in his warehouse must have left the poor security guard scratching his head. In the morning, the Romani people joined the party: whole families, kids, parents, grandmas and grandpas. Everyone dancing together.

•

I was bouncing back and forth between France and England. While I was away, Debbie was on the bus, parked inside a large concrete bunker, somewhere in the woods outside Paris. It was here that she came up with the concept, and the word, 'Teknival'. Not only did the word convey the style of music we played, but also the carnival spirit of the boundless dance floor that spontaneously materialises wherever people dance.

Debbie explained that it wasn't just the poetry of putting

these two words together that had inspired her. It was because no matter how long our parties lasted, there was never enough time for all the new music. Music that was rarely played anywhere other than underground clubs, pirate radio stations or illegal raves. Teknivals were the next step in making space for that music, plus the burgeoning new sound systems and the tens of thousands of people that would imminently join sound system culture.

The first Teknival was on the 23 July 1993, near the town of Beauvais, two hours' drive north of Paris. In a flower meadow in woodland, it was small. With the atmosphere of a village picnic, albeit with an ever-fresh bowl of fruit punch laced with acid – and a big rig.

Being autonomous could have made us more insular. But our attitude of experimentation and continually moving across borders helped us, and the new underground culture, flourish. Rather than a fixed group of individuals, or even a single collective, we'd become an energetic flow. Our openness to new people and new ideas meshed perfectly with the direction of the music and Debbie's vision of what a Teknival was.

•

After months in France, we drove north to Holland. There we met up with the Blauwe Aanslag (Blue Attack) crew. This was a large squat in the centre of Den Haag, in the city's old tax office. The collective had had a long history of struggle against the municipality, the police and right-wing hooligans. But they'd won every battle they'd fought. The Blauwe Aanslag had a large residential community upstairs. A cafe and bar on the ground floor – they brewed their own beer and grew their own weed – and, in the basement, a nightclub. Siuli was our main point of contact. She was super enthusiastic for us to stage parties with them, plus she introduced us to Jan and Richard of Unit Moebius. The connection in Holland was strong. The mobile studio in full effect. As was the supply of purple microdots.

Seb, Si and I were totally focused on getting the mobile studio functioning, not only as a studio but also as a hub of co-creation. Working with Unit Moebius was the first of many such projects. Inspired by our new friendships, born out of the Blauwe Aanslag, I came up with the concept name for our collaboration: 'Out of the Blue'. Unit Moebius did two tracks, Seb and Si the other two. I designed the record label and took a box of promos back to England. John Peel played the EP on his radio show – twice.

We weren't just bouncing around in the sound system convoy. We were continually ping-ponging back and forth to England on various trafficking missions. Not drugs – vinyl. London had high quality cuts and pressing plants. But it wasn't only us getting excited about deliveries of new records. Sniffer dogs on the borders – trained to detect plastic explosives – also loved the smell of fresh vinyl. Back then there were no trade restrictions, so getting a pull from an overly excited sniffer dog was not a problem. Nor did we have chips in our passports, so breaking bail travel restrictions also went under the radar.

Debbie and Hamish had gone on a reccy to Berlin. They'd met up with Joe Rush and a faction of the Mutoid Waste Company calling themselves The Lost Tribe of MiG. The call went out. Spirals from all directions plotted a course to the Lost Tribe's city centre wasteland.

Zander now had a faster truck, a white Isuzu pickup which was smaller than the Q4 and the Land Rover. With just three seats in front, our journey with Scouse Paul and Seb from London to Berlin was organised on a strict rotation. Every few hours, Zander would stop and the person huddled in the back, cocooned in blankets and a tarpaulin, would swap places with one of the people in the cab. But not Zander – it was his pickup, he was the driver, there was no argument.

I don't know exactly what I'd expected. In my mind I'd pictured Germany as a super-rich, super-organised country. But instead, the nearer we got to Berlin, the bumpier the ride got. The concrete motorway had not been repaired or maintained. It wasn't potholes that were the problem. In parts, large chunks were missing. Wrecked cars had been left to burn out where they'd crashed. The news reported that, since the Wall had come down, a crime wave had swept Germany from the east. A cynical lie, designed to draw attention from the biggest crime wave: the plundering of businesses, property and resources of the east by the triumphant capitalist class.

Broke, hungry and tired we pulled over at a Turkish bar. Scouse Paul counted out our money in little stacks of copper coins, hoping we had enough to buy some chips to share. The proprietor watched us as we dreamily gazed up at his photo menu. He shook his head with what I'd thought was disdain and left us stacking the small coins in columns of ten. A moment later, he returned with a bottle of raki and shot glasses. He waved away our money. Poured us drinks, and one for himself. He invited us with smiles and gestures, to choose what we wanted from the menu. After eating our fill, he insisted that we had one more raki for the road.

Replenished, we finished the last leg of our journey into central Berlin. The wreckage along the roadside had foreshadowed what we found: a city centre that looked as if the bomb damage of Berlin had only recently been cleared away by bulldozers. But it wasn't only the municipality that had been tidying up and rebuilding. In the wasteland, slap bang in front of the Reichstag, were two military tanks upended, with another horizontally across the top. This was Tankhenge, built by the Mutoid Waste Company. Painted in fluorescent colours and dabbed with graffiti, the absurdity of the monument challenged the power that it confronted. We were nearing our final destination.

•

In 1989 the Mutoids had their squat in Battle Bridge Road, Kings Cross raided by the police. This was the same warehouse we'd found empty three years later, still with their painting on the wall. Since Thomas had first told us about them, we'd been intrigued and inspired by their post-apocalyptic sculptures, outlandish vehicles and audacious attitude. After the police raid at Kings Cross, they moved to Berlin. That had been in June 1989, a few months before the Wall came down. We arrived almost exactly four years after the historic moment. But still much of central Berlin was a ruin, its old Nazi centre laid waste in the closing moments of the war.

Staying in trucks, surrounded by their scrap metal sculptures, were Joe Rush, Frank, Tamsin and Kolja. This particular incarnation of the Mutoids called themselves The Lost Tribe of MiG, after the two MiG-21 jet fighters they'd 'liberated' from the Soviets. They welcomed us with open arms, and we parked up next to them.

In the city's hollowed core, on no man's land between the doubled walls, we'd found our new home, at least for next few months.

Rather than do huge warehouse parties as we'd done in Paris, we mainly worked with other groups of squatters. It was a pivotal moment in history. The asset stripping of the east by western interests was in full swing. The Berlin squatters understood this. After the destruction of the war and the collectivism of the communist bloc, the question of ownership was a hot topic. And it was made all the more urgent as powerful business interests were hungry to exploit the opportunity. Those interests asserting that their ideology and money gave them rights over and above the people. No man's land was worth fighting for.

•

Within three months of being there, we'd got to know the crews at many of the squats – Tacheles, The Kopi, IM Eimer, Rigaer Strasse 94 and Linienstrasse 206 – and done some great parties together. Meanwhile, we'd been working on paint stripping and polishing one of the MiG fighter jets. The idea was to have it rise up at midnight at the up-and-coming New Year's Eve party.

•

As I made my coffee in the campfire the way Thomas had taught me, the government man sitting opposite closed his briefcase. He'd made his offer: 'Leave Potsdamer Platz peacefully and we'll give you an abandoned Soviet base.' As he spoke, a swirl of snow crossed between us. It picked up ash from the fire and caused a defiant red glow to flicker among the embers. As I watched the glow waver, I realised the old walls of crude, brutal control may have come down, but new perimeters were under construction, this time mirror-polished. As the government man trudged away through the snow, I thought about his proposal.

Tempting as it was, I had more pressing things on my mind. Should I return to England to fight the case against us, or evade the British authorities and stay in Europe? If we did the deal with the Germans, we could settle down on an abandoned military base.

The bouncing pulse of a 909 kick drum disturbed my thoughts. Seb and Si were awake and powering up the studio. The door to the showman's burst open.

'I know who I am!' announced Si to the world, standing on the steps. He stretched and came over to the fire.

'Any coffee?' He rubbed his hands together.

'I've just put some on. So, who are you?'

'Ahhh!' His face, though still creased from sleeping – and with indentations from the knobs and sliders of the mixing desk – lit up. 'From now on, I'm . . . Crystal Distortion!' He laughed. 'What do ya think?'

'Suits your style!'

There was a hollow twang of strings as Seb manoeuvred himself and his guitar out of the studio.

'Any coffee?' he asked as he sat down on a beer crate next to Si.

'Off busking?' I passed them both a tin mug.

'Yeah, saving up for an 808,' replied Seb. 'Almost there!'

'What song earns you the most?' I asked.

Without hesitation, he answered, 'Imagine. John Lennon.' He picked up his guitar.

'Don't you dare!' growled Si, aka Crystal Distortion.

•

I wasn't sure if I could believe what the government man had told me about Mercedes and Sony planning to build their European HQs on the land we occupied. It wasn't that I doubted him personally, but the desolation of Potsdamer Platz was so total that it was hard to imagine anything else. It was clear that parts of Berlin were being rebuilt. Clusters of tower cranes were visible on the horizons. There was one small clue that the toxic sand we were camped on was about to be remoulded into the new city centre. Next to our Wagonplatz, looking very out of place, was the entrance to a new S Bahn Metro station. Like the tentacle of a subterranean entity, it had pushed up through the rubble. It seemed to serve no purpose. Who would want to catch a train to the centre of oblivion? But it was convenient for us, especially Seb as an S Bahn busker.

After I told them about the government man's visit, we finished our coffee. The rest of the crew started to appear. Some a little worse for wear. The previous evening we'd had another episode of macho posturing.

Dennis, the drug dealer who'd tried to force his bag of pills on Debbie when we'd been confronted with a police roadblock two years earlier, had reappeared. He was popular with some members of the crew. A crew that was forever getting bigger.

Our lack of money and the bitter winter was hard for us all. We each had our own vices that made life a little more bearable. For some it was alcohol or weed, or for others just a nice cup of tea. My preferred poison was coffee. When you're living a precarious existence, the importance of these small pleasures is dramatically amplified. It was Dennis' supply of hash and weed that gave him kudos within our group, or as they called themselves, The Puff Posse. Of course, he also sold every other drug you can imagine. Nothing wrong with a bit of black marketeering, and I'm certainly not against people taking drugs. But his business was extractive. He profited from the sound system and everyone's hard work. Once Dennis had got his foot in the door and understood that his wealth gave him power within the group, things got twisted.

As was usual, the previous day me and Paula, a young woman who'd joined us in Rotterdam, had cleaned the kitchen trailer, done the washing up, gone shopping – or as was more often the case, liberating – and prepared the food. The crew were sitting down to eat the evening meal we'd cooked at the long trestle table in the trailer.

Dennis came to the door and announced he was going to a restaurant. He invited a handful of people – those he'd groomed to sell his drugs. They got up and left, leaving a bad taste in the mouth of everyone else.

This wasn't the first time he'd done this. Another trick he and his gang would pull was to conspicuously give little gifts to members of the crew they were trying to curry favour with. Tobacco, chocolate, coffee and red meat was their currency. Accumulating private wealth from a collective project is bad enough. But accumulating power and then dividing that community in such a calculated way was hugely problematic for all of us.

Debbie, Paula and Sanchia worked hard to keep our community together. Hamish had taken on managing the crew to strip and polish the MiG. His energetic personality motivated us, even on the coldest days. Seb and Si were 100 percent dedicated to making music and training people up as co-creators. I also spent many long hours in the studio working on tracks with them. Ixy too was keen to learn how to use the equipment and make her own music. Zander had found work as a climber with a local arborist. Tim and Darren maintained the rig. Thomas had left because of work commitments as a metal fabricator and set builder for a film company in the UK. Simone and Joe were back in London as they were expecting a baby. And Mickey and Ixy were also expecting a baby but had decided to stay in Berlin.

All of us were bouncing around on a million missions trying to hold things down. The last thing we needed was to be infiltrated by a group of divisive drug dealers.

•

The snow that had been falling thickened. Si took his coffee back into the showman's. Seb zipped his guitar into its case and slung it over his shoulder. I walked with him to the S Bahn.

'What we gonna do about Dennis?' he asked.

'Not much we can do without starting a war.' I answered.

'I just don't get it. Why does he treat people like that? What's the point? Power, control?'

'I think he's trying to take control of something he doesn't understand.'

'And we gotta put up with his head-fuckery.'

We stopped outside the doors of the S Bahn. Seb unslung his guitar and brushed off the snow.

'We've survived worse attacks from the capitalist system!' I held the glass doors open.

'True!' he laughed as we walked into the warmth. 'Talking of which, you decided if you're going back to England for the court case?'

We stopped at the top of the stairs. 'We're gonna have to fight them on every level. Can't have these power-tripping arseholes pushing us around – so yeah! Yeah, I'm going back. Zander's going back in a couple of weeks for a job in London, so I'll jump in with him.'

Seb gave me the cocked-gun salute and started down the stairs.

I returned the salute and turned to go. Walking back towards the doors I heard Seb singing, 'Imagine there's no heaven . . .'

I went back to the Wagonplatz and told everyone about the government man's offer of a Soviet base. No one was interested.

OUR BIG DAY IN COURT

Our big day in court was not a day. It was ten weeks. It had taken two years for the prosecution to compile their case against us. In that time, we'd spent countless days and nights in police custody, been on bail and had injunctions imposed upon us. According to our barristers, our trial was to be one of the biggest and most expensive in British legal history. And for what?

The Conspiracy charge had been dropped. Now we were facing charges of 'Causing a Public Nuisance'. A mediaeval catch-all law that would ensure, if found guilty, we'd get between two to four years in prison. To lighten the mood, whenever the opportunity arose, we pronounced it 'Causing a Public New-Sense'. The judge didn't think it was funny.

Originally twelve people had been arrested and charged, though Thomas and Kev absconded and Simone was excused from appearing in person, as she was pregnant. That left Zander, Debbie, Darren and me representing Spiral Tribe. The other unlucky defendants had just been caught up in the mass arrest. These included two lads who'd simply been raving. Two lads who'd gone to the festival to sell pancakes. And one lad who'd delivered a marquee to one of the other sound systems.

Peter Silver and our defence team had pushed to get our hearing as far away from Castlemorton as possible, as local gossip would prejudice our case.

Wolverhampton was fifty miles north of the common and in a different county. A large town with a long industrial history, known for its coal mines, abundance of iron ore and famous for the manufacture of high-quality locks.

The Crown Court had recently been built and stood alone on an area of wasteland that was still under development. It was a long rectangle of a building, horizontally banded with yellow and brown bricks. Over the main entrance, in the shape of a Roman portico, was an open structure of blue metal girders. Typical of the architectural fashion of the early nineties, the roofless design served no purpose other than to look arty. Which it didn't – just cheap, and a constant reminder to the citizens of Wolverhampton that their public funds had been misspent. As were the £4 million of taxpayers' money spent by the state to prosecute us.

We'd squatted the piece of land behind the court and parked up in an assortment of vehicles. The judge was not happy, but the police pointed out that it was probably best to have us close at hand for the smooth running of the trial. The judge begrudgingly agreed as the only other option was to keep us in the cells. That said, we did spend an hour of each day locked up, at lunchtime.

The guards, who were all out of work miners, put us in separate cells and brought us tea in plastic cups and food in disposable trays. The cells, like the rest of the building, were brand new. The heavy metal doors were twenty centimetres thick. On the first day we discovered that the locks Wolverhampton was famous for could be slipped with our plastic tea-stirrers. For a week we messed with the guards' heads by swapping cells and locking the doors behind us. When the guards came back after lunch to take us into court, they sensed something was wrong, but couldn't quite put a finger on it. On the last day of the week, they found us all together in one cell. They couldn't figure it out, but from that moment on, they gave up and just left all the cell doors open.

Our courtroom was the biggest in the building. It had rows of blue, cinema-style seats facing the bench. The floor, in between us and the judge's lofty podium, was filled with the desks of our council and the prosecutor. On each of the desks was a tower of documents. All the legal people wore black gowns and white wigs. The judge had an extra big wig. Behind him, a large royal crest, complete with lion, unicorn, shield and the scrolled lettering *'Dieu et mon droit'* (God and my right) – an archaic but apparently still relevant reference to the divine right of kings.

It was the same crest I'd seen on the Theatre Royal every time I'd gone to buy paints. And this too was a theatre. The nine of us sat in our plush velveteen seats to watch our real-life selves rewritten as pantomime scoundrels. Having sketched out our villainous characters, the prosecutor went on to invent us each a narrative that demonstrated that our heresy had been committed 'knowingly'. We had not gone to Castlemorton to 'knowingly' rave. Nor to 'knowingly' make pancakes. The truth was, we'd 'knowingly' gone to Castlemorton just to piss everyone off.

Because we were innately evil and had annoyed every right-minded person in Britain – minus the 50,000 that were there enjoying themselves – he then made the point that our sins were amplified, not only by the loud music but by the number of everyone in attendance. A somewhat tenuous metric of magnitude. But if one were to believe that it was our wickedness that had conjured the beast of Castlemorton, then all the pagan souls participating should be weighed on the scales of justice – along with our hearts.

His claims that we were the masterminds behind Castlemorton, and that I was the ringleader, were flattering but not true. We had witnesses that were willing to testify on our behalf.

Debbie Staunton came and took the witness stand and explained, as the expert witness who ran one of the main party info lines, how the Avon and Somerset police had pushed the festival off its usual site and successive police authorities had kept the convoy moving out of their jurisdiction. The festival had not been organised by anyone, and if it had, then the police themselves should also be held accountable.

Willie X, one of the Roundhouse squatters and a Stonehenge Free Festival campaigner, took the stand and told the court that he was furious that we were getting all the credit – because it was actually him who'd organised Castlemorton!

And the defence's star witness, from his hospital bed, was Chief Superintendent Clift – the copper who, on the steps of the committal court, had warned me that we were being politically stitched up. He sent a statement taking responsibility for his role in allowing the festival to settle on the common 'for humanitarian reasons'.

Even the video footage from the police helicopter that had hovered ominously over the festival showed us cleaning up the common and leaving it spotless.

The prosecutor called several witnesses. One was a very young WPC who had been sent in undercover. She was shaking in the witness box and blushed every time she spoke. She told the court how terrified she'd been at the festival. Her sworn testimony about the arrival of the lad transporting the marquee was found to be false when the helicopter footage, with date and time flashing onscreen, showed said truck arriving on a day that contradicted her statement. The accused was immediately set free. She left the witness stand in tears.

Other undercover police statements were read out in court. One said that he'd witnessed a man roll a spliff a metre long, take one puff, fall backwards and proclaim he'd seen God!

•

As the end of the trial and the day of judgement grew closer, the tension began to build. With so many defendants, the legalese, and the prosecutor's strategy of obfuscation, it was difficult to follow all the threads. The success of the prosecution depended on us not knowing what their final angle of attack would be. If I could guess that angle, I'd be better prepared to address the jury.

The past two years of stress and uncertainty concentrated into these closing moments. The state had spent two years gathering evidence. Phone taps. Intercepted mail. Photographs. Fingerprints. We didn't have those technical resources.

Then I remembered the dry mushroom I had squashed in the back of my notebook.

Amanita Muscaria, the mushroom of the Siberian shamans. Thomas's words came back to me. *Just eat a piece no bigger than your palm.* If, as Toney had suggested, the magic of the mushroom lifted the veil between worlds, then perhaps I'd get some insight into what the prosecutor was planning.

On the evening before the final day, parked up on the wasteland behind the court, I took the mushroom and gave myself to nature.

It started well, with lucidity and a brightening of colours. A closer merging of the inner with the outer. The case's key points floated free from the background confusion. One of the prosecution's star witnesses had been a handwriting expert. He'd analysed my sketchbooks and identified my pencilled notes. On another occasion, the prosecutor pointed out that my pencil scribblings matched the text in our newsletters. The police had recovered a box that contained hundreds of printed zines with the title 'Bad News'. This included a collection of some of the most outraged newspaper headlines that I'd copied out. The prosecutor was keen to draw the jury's attention to the gleeful tone of my writing. There was one line that particularly irked him: 'We have had complaints, some from over twelve miles away!'

The handwriting expert confirmed that I was the author. He had the pencil note. He had the typed-up version. He had a box of multiple copies, ready for distribution at Castlemorton. Clearly, I knew that my actions were going to cause 'A Public New-Sense!'

All of this was a guess. But with the help of the Amanita, I was pretty sure this would be the trap the prosecutor would spring on me. I needed a counter-argument. If I didn't have one ready, his cherry-picked sequence of logic would stand as unchallenged fact.

As the mushroom's effect grew, I started hearing voices. Perhaps taking psychedelics on the eve of an important date with destiny had not been such a good idea. Initially, the trip helped me collect my thoughts and model possible outcomes. Now my thoughts were interrupted by an impish voice that repeated over and over, 'Spin it around! Spin it around!' It was driving me crazy. Then I noticed that it only agitated me when I tried to construct a logical counter-argument for the court. What I needed to do was listen.

'Spin it around! Spin it around! Spin it around!'

Listening relaxed me, and the voice softened then faded away. In that quiet moment, it struck me. *The little squeaky voice was right!*

•

The day of reckoning. The mood in the court was heavy. This was the only moment that the jury heard us speak as individuals. We needed to make a good impression. Or did we? The impish voice, from the night before, suggested otherwise.

I was called to the stand. In a righteous frenzy, the prosecutor began his attack. 'This court has proof of handwriting and authorship!' He peered over the top of his half-moon glasses and held up my sketchbook. 'Proof of printing!' With his other hand, he picked up a copy of my zine. Holding the two exhibits he turned full circle to be sure we could all could see the hard evidence. He put the sketchbook back on his desk. He slapped the top of the cardboard box that contained all the copies. 'Proof of intent to distribute *this* document!' He shook the photocopied zine, then held the page as if he was going to read a royal decree. '*The* document that contains the line.' With eyebrows raised, he glared at me over the top of the page. "We have had complaints, some from over twelve miles away!" He turned to the jury and puffed out his chest, jabbing a finger in my direction. 'Proof that the accused went to Castlemorton Common *knowing* that by doing so he would cause a public nuisance!'

Then it was my turn. I wasn't going to try and hide that part of my personality that irked the prosecutor. The gleeful tone that he recognised in my writing. The irreverence with which I regarded the ruling elites. Yes, in his eyes, I was a cheeky fucker. But he was not on the jury.

I asked the court, 'What evidence is there that this complaint was because the music was too loud?' I shrugged. 'Perhaps the complaint was that the music was not loud enough?'

It took a second for the jury to register what I'd just said.

The prosecutor went rigid, his mouth opening, then closing. Too entangled in his own self-importance to see the humour. Too uptight to understand what it was to have a joke – to have a party – to have a dance. Some members of the jury started to laugh.

The case against me had been based on the negative hyperbole of the newspapers and the words I'd reframed, copied and printed. In my story, I'd used satire to twist the establishment's negatives into our positives. In the prosecutor's story, he'd tried to twist my positives back into the negatives I was ridiculing.

The judge leaned towards me from his perch, white with anger, eyes full of menace. The prosecutor thumped his desk, the veins in his neck swollen.

One by one the rest of the crew took the stand. The case against each of them was equally fanciful. It was clear to the jury we'd been stitched up. It was clear to the jury that they *too* had been stitched up. Led down the garden path by the prosecution. When the state fabricates tales of folk devils and heretics to validate its illegitimate dominion, it corrupts justice. A joyless justice in which peaceful (but lively) gatherings, dancing and creative expression are prohibited – unless, of course, you can pay for the privilege.

When the foreman returned the not-guilty verdicts for all of us, the rush of elation was like nothing I'd felt before. A physical rush from the tips of my toes and up out the top of my head. A torrent of joy streaming through me. Our relief was mirrored in the faces of the jury members. They returned our smiles and graciously acknowledged the 'thank-yous' that we mouthed to them across the courtroom. One woman even returned the kisses we blew.

I didn't see the judge leave. Perhaps he disappeared through a secret panel back into the corridors of power, hidden behind the Royal Coat of Arms. Or perhaps, consumed by his contempt for us – and now the jury – the rage that had drained all the colour from his face had bled him dry. Deprived of his hope to send us to prison, translucent and wraith-like, he'd faded away.

The prosecutor remained at his desk. A livid shade of purple. Hot thermals of rage scattering his papers as he hurriedly tried to put them back in order.

EPILOGUE

Our trial had been an opportunity for me to see behind the establishment's façade and had given some clear insights into how it conducted its business.

The prison guards at lunchtime had complained bitterly to us about Margaret Thatcher's destruction of their communities and livelihoods as miners. The investigating police officers, who'd asked to be let into Heather's when it'd started to rain, had sat with us all afternoon drinking tea and moaning about their bosses. The police helicopter pilot and videographer had shown the court that we'd cleaned the site and that the newspaper reports and undercover police statements – as with the chap delivering a marquee – were untrue. And then there was Superintendent Clift, who'd taken it upon himself – apparently against the wishes of his superiors – to allow the festival convoy onto the common. Rare little glimpses of the human beings under their uniforms. Too rare, as across my lifetime I've witnessed far more injustice, brutality and prejudice from the police than anything they've done in support of the community or to protect the interests of the people.

During the trial there had been another sworn statement delivered to the court. A statement from another undercover cop. He'd said he couldn't get onto the Spiral Tribe dance floor at night because it was guarded by a ring of black security guards with pit bulls. In reality, what he'd seen was nothing more than some of the Spiral lads playing with little Terra.

The fact that this statement was allowed to be presented in court as evidence against us speaks volumes about the true purpose of the prosecution. The statement's racism goes to the core of the strategy of divide and rule. What everyone failed to mention – other than Debbie Staunton when she gave her evidence – was just how integrated the free party scene was. A fact that was clear from the beautiful images of the dance floors that appeared on TV and in the newspapers.

Beyond doubt, the two-year police investigation and epic court case proved that we were not arrested for disturbing the neighbours around the common. We were arrested because of our ability to unify thousands of people.

Many of the big free party sound systems, including Spiral Tribe, had created open-access platforms, and in doing so had built coalitions of people from all backgrounds and cultures.

Castlemorton is sighted as the last great free festival. The end of an era. But this overshadows the fact that it was a great moment of unity. A high point in the history of community culture. A culture that should, and could, be nurtured – not criminalised.

After the trial, having failed in their attempts to portray us as the villains, the spectres that haunt the bowels of Whitehall changed the law. Not to accommodate free festivals, but to try and destroy them – forever. They introduced The Criminal Justice Bill that legislates against every aspect of freedom of movement and freedom of gathering. And to this day they continue to 'knowingly' create new laws that 'legitimise' their catastrophic economy while stripping away legislation that protects the rights of the people and the environment.

The establishment, apparently without shame, showed us that it relies on spies, lies and violence to bolster its fragile existence. It cannot tell the truth. It is so far removed from the needs of the people that it has no relatable truth to tell.

This story has traced many of the tributaries and underground currents that brought Spiral Tribe into being. For me this was both a personal journey and a collective experience.

Many people who lived through the early years of acid house, techno and breakbeat celebrate that time as special. A magical moment when a portal opened into a dimension of new possibilities. That's true. But it wasn't a mystic portal that enlightened the chosen few. It was a moment when everyone was physically able to gather together. To find our feet on common ground. To connect with it and each other. An opportunity to recognise and explore ideas of cooperation and creativity.

Nostalgia is a dead-end emotion. To dwell on 'how good it was back in the day' is to relegate our history to the trash. A history that has shown us that these great swirling portals of creativity, imagination and innovation can be accessed. But just like any great wealth of minerals, fertility or labour, they are quickly cordoned off and privately plundered.

Forward the Revolution!

Truth in the new-sense,
No pretence,
The book is now open,
Think it,
Feel it,
Put it into motion,
No Nu-Trix from the masters of illusion!

(Lyrics from 'Forward the Revolution', Spiral Tribe, 1992. Words, Simone Sim Simmer. Hubert Humphrey, aka MC Scallywag. Music, Seb Vaughan, aka 69DB)

BIG UPS

A massive shout-out to all the free party sound systems, past, present and future!

I'd like to thank all the people who encouraged me to start writing and get this book finished:

Wendy and Tony Harrison. Barbara Trapido. Caroline Brothers. Francis Deutsch. Debbie Spiral. Ixy. Julien Ipno. Aaron Trinder. Colin Steven. Vera Marques.

All the fantastic (and very patient) friends, family and crew, who've given me interviews, answered my endless questions and helped me fact-check.

Zander. Debbie. Simone Sim Simmer. Seb, 69DB. Si, Crystal Distortion. Ixy, Ixindamix. Jeff23. Mickey Meltdown. Hubert, MC Scallywag. Tim, Noise Control. Sanchia. Sacha. DJ Aztek. Steve Watson. Ian Young. Aaron Trinder. Jezz Lewis. Steve Bubble.

Special thanks to Colin Steven at Velocity Press. Paul Baillie-Lane, editor and typesetter. Seana Gavin for the foreword. Beta readers and blurb writers: Aaron Trinder, Matthew Collin, Sam Batra and Ed Gillett.

I hope by keeping this origin story close to the people involved in the beginning, I've given some insight into the bigger picture. A picture that included so many more people than I was able to squeeze into this one book!

Everyone mentioned by name, in the story and here in the credits, has a place in my heart. Without the enthusiasm, inspiration and support of these friends, none of this would have been possible. This list is not definitive, but:

Josy Fullvibes, Sandrine, Gabba, Ivana, Beate, Bibby, Mel, Nigel, Rosie (Normals), Tom, Jasper, Denzel, Ian Rushton, The bloke who gave us the blue truck! Roshie, Gary DS, Kath, Sonny, Reno Gay, Shnok, Frikkyo, Charlotte, Stephen, Curly, Sacha, Chris T, Jane Howard, Kayla, Keira, Colin Faver, JP, Willyman, Johan, Sean and Tommy, Huggie and Jay (Persons Unknown), Tony (Dance Party), Tony Marcus, Joy, Seal, Whitney, Pete (Techno Travellers), RJ, Sara Sender, Alex Oldfield, Dan (Rose Farm), JJ and Graham (Chip Nam Posse), Darrel, Alison Hussey, Gráinne, Geoff, Kieren, Chris L, Peter Rampazzo, Alan (UFO), Pete, Simon, Fran, Sam, Paola, Paula, Jibber Jake, Karim, Jake, Jessie, Ed, Ben, Jonno, Robin, Emily Whittle, Monique, Jay, Abi, Sara Sender, Roger Raver, Christophe Fringeli, Colin Faver, Kris Needs, Andy (Big Life), Jon (Tekno Terrorist), Ian (Debbie Staunton infoline), James (Debbie Staunton infoline), Glen (Exodus), Edge, Cliffy and Dom, Renaat Vandepapeliere (R&S) Frank (Acid Orange), Gordon (Rabbit City), Neil Sanford, Seb, Ceely, Jim, Anna, Rob, Eve, Shawn, Shawny, John Jones, Dom, Si, Botty, Matt Day, Warren Grassi, Phil Underwood, Clive Kempster, Ellen Kilchman, Cath Haymes, Eddie S, Billy Boots, Nick E, Alex L, Tim W, Tom A, Jos P, Sarah, Beka, Mel P, Ness P Andy S, Dave H, Phil H, Mikee, Little Al, Patrick P, Suzz, Siobhan, Berin, Lex, Simon L, Nick Y, Blodders, Nick L, Andy B, Ade, Georgina, Andy, Henry, Chris, Aaron, Radha, Dangerous Dave, Eddie Bridges, Alex Parsely, Gary Coaches, Bill,

Madge, Bonnie, Maya, Fat Matt, Neil and Karen, Geri and Kelvin, Mr Fish, Mewenn (Marvin), Benoir, Gwar, MC Ta Mere, Chateau Marc, Sid & Zilliah, Fabrice (Tekno Tanz), Bernard (Tekno Tanz), Bernard (Invaders), Jeff Mills, Lisa n Elias, LTJ Bukem, Colin Dale, Easy Groove, Ramjack, T23, Terra Eyes – and all the other crews and people I may have left out! (If you joined us later in our journey around Europe, perhaps you'll be in the next book!)

PRE-ORDER THANKS

This book would not have been possible without everyone who bought it on pre-order. Your faith in this project enabled me to get this story down. Power to the people!

Marco Abate, Sally Abraham, Acid Steve, Stan Adamec, Nikola Adamovská, Simone Alderliesten, Jason Allen, Jon Allen, David Ameixa, Boyer Alexandre, Claverie Alexandre, Nicolas Alexandre, Mark Allbrighton, Alessandro Allegri, Mathieu Alline, Marine Alluchon, Clément Alziari, François Ame, Karl Andrews, Paul Andrews, Serena Annibali, Ben Antrobus, Lucy Antrobus, Leanne Archer, Sigrid Arlen, Ffion Armour-Brown, Koan Arth, Noel Ashley, Richard Ashrowan, Tom Askew, Sara Askey, Christopher Astin, Patxi Aubé, Anthony Augereau, Jimbellina Austin, Richard Austin, Martin Avenell, Adrian Axe, Warren D Babylon, Badger (Oorpi), Kevin Baggus, Jason Bailey, Ruth Baird, Roger Ballance, Joost Bamossy, Zsolt Bangha, David Banham-Hughes, Jules Banzept, Grant Barber, Elena Barlesi, Peter Barnes, Ruth Barnett, Virginie Barré, Janni Barrett, Luca Bartolini, Andrew Barton, Sophie Baruchel, Alberto Bassotto, Juan Pérez Bastida, Claire Bates, Nicolas Bats, Carla Battisti, Thomas Baumann, Tristan Baussan, Anna Baylis, Julian Bayliss, Sebastien Bazin, Paul Beales, Andrew Beaumont, Jayney Bedding, Chris Beer, Nina Beinwachs, David Bell, Suzz Bell, Laetitia Bellet, Zoe Benfield, Crantelle Benjamin, Dylan Bennett, Jon Bennett, Enrico Benini, Anissa Bernard, Grimes Berno, Sébastien Bertelli, Eva Bergamin, Florian Berthet, Gaelle Berton, Adrien Bertrand, Cellier Bertrand, Damien Bertucat, Aurélie Besson, Bert Beukeleirs, Adrian Bev-Bebbington, Sarbjit Bharj, Bibz, Ewan Biclet, Cédric Biennassis, Dorian Bienveignant, Cedric Bigot, Ophelie Bigot, Denis Bilajac, Greg Bint, Angela Biondo, Guillaume Biotteau, Ben Biscoe, Clive Bishop, CR Bishop, John Bittles, Chris Black, Keith Blackie, Tomáš Bláha, GR3G BLAME, Christopher Blohm, Xavier Blondel, Pierre Blondet, Paydon Blow, Emma Bodman, Jelle Bollen, Dom Bond, Sheila Borrella Mendo, Nicola Bortolami, Simone Boschi, Alix Bostock, Nils Bouaziz, Nicolas Boucherot, Julien Boudier, Raphael Boudin, Raphaël Bouffette, Roly Boughton, Matthieu Boulard, Geraldine Bourgogne, David Bourrel,

Lina Boutin, Simon Bowker Heighes, Ben Boyce, Nicola Bradshaw, Alan Braine, Emma Bramley, Gweltaz Brandeho, Emmanuel Brault, George Brett, Daniel Brightmore, Julien Brillet, Craig A Broadbent, Daniella Bronzi, David Brookes, Mr Brooks, Celia Brooks, Nasser Brosseau, Maxime Brouhot, Ashley Brown, Gordon Brown, Mark Brown, Den Browne, Gordon Brown, Susannah Browning, Jenny Bruce, Rupert Bruce, Stephanie Brunelle, Jean-Baptiste Brunerie, Patrick Brunmüller, Nathalie Brunner, Rob Bryant, James Bryson, Marlene Büchler, Edward Buck, Bruce Buckmaster, Mat Bulba, John Bulman, Olivier Buquet, Mike Burn, Mazy Burns, Anna Buven, Stefano Busachi, Jonathan Buttolph, Michael Byrne, Rob Calcutt, Megan Caley, Octavio Calleya Garcia, Lara Calus, Yohann Camp, Marco Cangiano, Frédéric Canon, Milo Cantarelli, John Capel, Sedira Capucine, Brice Carbonel, Alina Carbune, Michael Carding, Kevin Carley, Erik Carlson, Debbie Carney, Sinead Carroll, Barry Carter, Fiona Cartledge, Pablo Castellano, Oriana Catino, Giles Cattle, Alex Caulder, Florence Cazillac, Timeo Chaigne, Bertrand Chaigneau, Jill Chant, Aurélien Chapelain, Eddy Charrier, Julien Chaudiere, Roger Chedgey, Simon Chedzey, Marta Cherrill, Sean Chester, Timothy Child, Dorian A Childs-Prophet, Michael Chiles, Christophe Chommeloux, Kylian Choul, Nicholas Chown, Christy, Robert Chrz, Maria Churchill, Michael Cirnigliaro, Agnes Cioffi, Anna Clark, Alice Clark, Tristram Clark, Daniel Clayfield, Clegg from Barton, Civeyrac Clement, Perez Clement, Marcus Clements, Dominic Clifton, Nick Coakley, Sarah Codling, Jonas Coen, Peter Cohen, Iain Coiley, Roger Cole, Maite Colinas, Will Colley, Nellie Collins, Fabio Colombo, Joel Colover, Dale Conlon, Will Conn, Shane Connolly, Alessandro Conrad, Julien Convert, Andrew Conway, Simon Conway, Stephen Cooke, Matt Cooksley, Chris Coomer, Damon Cooper, Jason Cooper, Paul Cooper, Willow Corrado, Marcus Cortese, Kim Cosmik, Orphée Cottret, Julien Cottret, Thierry Coulet, Paul Courtney, Emilie Coutret, Sue Cox, Wendy Craig, Garth Cranston, Johnny Crash, Chris Crate, Mark Craven, Allan Crawford, Jon Crawley, Emma Cree, Simon Creemers, Jean-Baptiste Crenn, Mathew Critchell, David Croll, Amanda Crook, Clémence Cros, Oran Cross, Jack Crotty, Sébastien Crouzil, Paul Cullen, Peter Cunningham, Darran Curant, Roger Curran, Tatsu Curtis, Tiago da Silva Henriques, Amanda Dackombe, Tim Dann, Olivier Dapremont, Marco Darrigo, Marc Davidson, Nick Davidson, Deiniol Davies, Liam Davies, Micheal Davis, Mick Davis, Leite silva Davud, Matthew Dawes, Bart de Balbiaan, Phil De Barros, Edward Degg, Jo Degregorio, Cynthia de Graaf, Senne de Jong, Federico De Marinis, Arnaud De Rocquigny, Tommy de Roos, Andres Declercq, Giulia Della Nera, Saïna Deniau, Mathieu Desré, Ashish Dhru, Holly Dicker, Ben Dorling, Anna Degli Esposti, Franck Dehède, Philippe Delachavonnery, Nicolas Dellea, Galadriel Demeurisse, Jane Deri, Olivier Deschacht, Patrick Devereux,

Fergus Dick, Matthew Dickinson, Stuart Dickinson, Dennis Dietz, Enrico Dionisio, Nicola Dirnberger, Sasha Dixon, Dave Dobson, Marc Dolley, Dave Donders, Sarah Donnelly, Matthieu Dourlent, Aaron (P71) Dowds, Patrycja Drebszok, Freddy Drop, Benoit Drouet, Andrei Drumea, Elliot Drummond, Marcin Druzkowski, Sam Dudman, Koen Duivenvoorde, Thomas Dumke, Luke Dunbar,Thibaut Dunoyer, Nicolas Dupaigne, Théo Dupontavice, Judith Durrmeyer, Alessio D'Urso, Virginie Duval theGlint, Antonin Duviol, John Dwyer, Nicholas Earnshaw, Nick Eatock, Justi Echeles, Abigail Edwards, Lee Elcock, Luisa Element, Ludovic Elie, Radek Eliáš, DJ Miss Ellie, Diane Elliot-Gurney, Ihab Elnaccash, Bruno Eluard, Mathieu Enfrun, Gemma England, Barbara Erber, Peter Ertl, Ben Ervine, Jerome Evanno, Dave Evans, Gareth Evans, Glenn Evans, Fran Evans, Jan Evans, Louise Evans, Sean Evans, Simon Evans, Steven Evans, Terence Evans, Thibaut Exelmans, Jonathan Fabri, Chris Fairbrother, Nicoletta Fallerini, Karlos Fandango, Steve Faraone, Martin Farino, Deborah Farrelly, Taha Fatih, Andy Faulkner, Jeremy Favier, Henning Fehr, Laurenz Feichtner, Christoph Fellner, Clair Felton, Ana Filipa Ferreira, Ester Fester, Romain Feuillet, Sebastien Fillinger, Frederic Fillon, Steff Finn, Gary Finnegan, FiST, Vita FitzSimons, Toby Fletcher, Jos Flinn, Richard Fogarty, Mirko Foglietti, Collette Ford, Tim Forrester, Chris Fowlie, Richard Fradgley, Paul Francombe, Chiska Franco, Vin Franco, Fred Francois, Paul Franklin, Martin Frederic, Meissonnier Frédéric, Charis Frederickx, Oli Freke, Cesa Frenckie, Lorenzo Fresh, Naomi Friend, Matthew Frost, Simon Fullerton, Julian Fyson, Lluis Gabriel, Turpaud Gaetan, Didier Gainot, Claire Gale, Marco Gallerani, Giulia Gallotta, Marco Gamboa, Carlos Seda Gambin, David Garcia, Clément Garcin, Jim Gardner, Garfee, Gaëtan Le Gargasson, Lynne Garnett, Jasmine Garside, Ben Garnham, Simon Garside, Sean Garwood, Marc Gaset, Andrew Gaston, Scott Gaule, Francesca Gavin, Seana Gavin, Nicolas Gayet, Simon Geddes, James Gemmell, Gabriella Gentile, Ricardo Geraldes, Tom Geyer, Tanguy Ghesquiere, Rachel Ghezail, Alexandre Gibert, Fabien Girardi, Colin Gilchrist, Philip Gill, Pauline Gillet, Victor Gillot, Fred Gitton, Duncan Glassman, Mario Gluvers, Edouard Goasdoue, Ben Godfrey, Edward Godrich, Helen Godwin, Matt Gold, Raoul Gomes, Aurélien Gonnet, Tania Gonzalez, William Goodey, Chester Goodhew, Jake Goodwin & DORF N KIDZ, Andrea Goring, Paul Gorman, Tony Goubault, Eric Goudet, Trish Goudy, Lauren Graber, Jaylson Graça, Andy Grace, Morgane Granier, Caroline Grannec, Florian Granger, Gary Grant, Warren Grassi, Simone Grau, Roby Greco, Susie Green, Alexandre Gresset, Debbie Griffith, Guy Griffiths, Sally Griffiths, Matt Grimes, Katerina Grlák, Alexandre Grondeau, Rachael Groom, Claudio Guerrieri, Caroline Gug, François Guilhaumon, Goraieb Guillaume, Frederic Guillemaut, Adrien Guinebault, Romain Guiot, Gosse Gunther, Meirion Guyon, Daniel Gyolcs, Tomáš Haberland, HackneyZed (Major), Kirk Haggerty, Tanja Halasz, Vashti Hale, Chris Hall, Rik Hall, Stuart Hall,

Jed Hallam, Ian Halliday, Julius Halme, Kathryn Hames, Bryan Hamilton, Lol Hammond, David Hampson, Nigel Hancock, Thomas Hanley, Keven Hann, Nigel Hannam, Glenn Hardouin, Claire Hardy, Craig Harlock, Phil Harris, Alexander Harrison, Joel Harrison, Rob Harrison, Harry Harsant, Natalie Hart, Tony Hart, Rory Hartley, Victoria Hartley, Miranda Hawtrey, Néo Hayat, Kevin Hayden, Matthew Hayes, Emma Hazelton, Duncan Heath, David Hedley Jones, Sami Heiman, Edgar Heimedinger, Amanda Helleur, Connor Helms, Octave Henry, Charles Heranval, Nathan Hernando, Darren Herridge, Audrey Hervé, Jochen Herz, Benjamin Hess, Fabien Heudes, DJ Hexxen, Ales Hildebrand, Mark Hill, Christian Hirmann, Rob Hives, Austin Hobson, Elise Hodent, Joseph Hodgkinson, Florian Hofer, James Hoggarth, Stephen Holder, Alan Holding, John Holland, Lucie Holland, Kate Holloway, Lucas Holmes, Martin Holy, Mathias Honoré, Graeme Hopper, Jodie House, Ben Howells, Stacey Hoya, Ian Hughes, Maus Huijsmans, David Hume, Samantha Humphries, Arry Hunt, James Hunt, Stephen Hunt, Matthew Huntingford, Ergin Hussein, Alison Hussey, Marinka Huxtable, Viktor Hvizdak, Wolskie Hylander, Michele Iannello, Horatiu-Dan Ilea, Primlchen Indamix, Roberto Infede, Markus Markus Ipomoea, Francois Issalys, Ivalaalien, Ixy, Martin Izat, Katarzyna Jachowicz, Christopher Jackson, James Jackson, Pierre Etienne Jacob, Just Jaeckin, Alexandre Jalali, Gavin James, Václav Jančařík, Mechell Janes, Damian Jaracz, Colin Jarvie, Philip Jeffries, Krystof Jelinek, Lee Jenkins, Stephen Jenkins, Bronwen Jenner, John Jennings, Max Jevaudan, Jura Jindra, Quentin Johns, Lucy Johnson, Matthew Johnson, Melanie Johnson, Alex Johnston, Robert Johnston, George Jolliffe, Elinor Jones, Leila Jones, Lester Jones, Mike Jones, Paul Jones, Phil Jones, Rob Jones, Tristan Joulain, Pawel Jozefacki, Stefan Julizar, Michal Juszczak, Pavla Kalinová, Wladimir Kamieniak, Tomas Karasek, Olivier Kast, C Kaufman, Neil Keating, Tom Keene, Andrew Kelley, Eamon Kelly, John Kelly, Simon Kelly, Simon Kemp, Nina Kemppainen, Richard Kenny, Peter Kent, Nicolas Kerangueven, Stephanie Kernizan, Mael Kerouedan, Karim Khelil, Marylouise Kidd, Corentin Kieffer, Darren Kilchmann, Ellen Kilchmann, Ian Kimber, Isabel King, Martin King, Laurence King, Erna Kleinfercher, Haydn Knight, Tim Knight, Nicholas Knott, Heather Knowland, Filip Kocik, Jiří Kohout, Karel Kolar, Miloslav Kolář, Sydney Koke, Jakub Kopecky, Monika Krawczykowska, Bart Kremer, Josef Kučera, Nikolai Kugler, Michał Kurcwald, Martin Kutenič, Bosco Kuttner, Matus Kysel, Jade Laborde, Matthew Laffey, Guilhem Lalande, Daniela Lakatošová, Marcin Laksa, Bertrand Lancien, Paul Landreau, Philippe Langleur, Taus Larsen, Gay Lawlor, Joanna Lawrence, Chris Latina, Coudour Laurent, Franck Lavieville, Romain Le Bihan, Fabrice Le Blanc, Arnaud Le Borgne, Elisa Le Corre, Kevin Le Corre, Guillaume le Devedec, Yann Le Duff, Yann Le Levier, Florian Le Mentec, Norwen Le Pors, Olivier Le Saout, Alexis Le-Tan, James Lea, Rich Lea, Chris Leamy, Julia Leary, Jamie Leask, Gertje Lebesque,

Valérie Lecomte, Clement Lefebvre, David-Alexandre Lefranc, Jeannique L'Hour, Vanessa Leigh, Mickael Leininger, Virginie Lejeune, Yann Lemercier, James Lenoel, Lenaïc Leroux, Scott Leslie, Dagmara Levene, Shaun Lewis, Chud Li, Susanna Libonati, Sam Licence, Paul Lichtenstern, Celie Lilja, Jay Lilley, Iz Liney, Mark Linfield, Martin Linford, Francesco Lippi, Andi Liszt, Gerard Llopart, Jonathan Lock, Anthony Locke, Ben Locke, Vladimir Lolo, Keith Long, Federico Longhini, Cai Longman, Mário Lopes, Juan Lopez, Damien Lordier, Alexandra Lort Phillips, Edwin Love, Antony Lovell, Toby Lowe, Ben Lowes, Kevin Lowrie, Michaela Lukaskova, Jerome Lyraud, Harry Macdonald, Neil MacGregor, Andrew MacKay, Ian Mackie, Conor Mackin, Caleb Maclot, Maxime Maes, David Magowan, Paul Maidment, DJ Maiko, Tennae Maki, Markku Mälkki, James Malone, Christophe Manaud, Alvaro Manjarrez, Christopher Mann, John Mansell, Kévin Maquet, Dauja Mara, David Marc, Edoardo Marcato, Steven Marchive, Jérôme Marical, Luca Marongiu, Vera Marques, Oliver Marsden, Kevin Marsh, Nick Marsh, Luigi Martella, R Martens, Beki Martin, Florian Martin, Geoffre Martin, Robert Martin, Richard Martin, Tom Massey, Garf Masters, Marius Matesan, Emily May, Tommy Meyer, Graham McAll, Fynn Mcbratney, James McCormack, Alex McCulloch, Bogart McDonagh, Noah McFarlane, Ian McGee, Andy McGowan, Al McGregor, Fergus McHugh, Gerrard McKillen, Ben Mcknight, Debbie Mclure, Gary McMaster, Colin McShane, Dom Medler, Saskia Meijer, Philip Melzer, Massimiliano Menniti, Jean-Marie Merle, Uja Merkle, Regnier Meryll, Cláudio Mestre, Qix Metek, Association Metemphase, Frederic Meynie, Jean François Michel, Rob Miller, David Milliken, Cyril Miralles, Carl Mitchell, Daniel Mitchell, Jonathan Mitchell, Marius Alexandru Mitran, Alessio Monaco, Killian Monier, Raphaël Monnin, Alexander Montagnani, Joaquin Montes, Sarah Mooney, Christelle Morel, Chris Morgan, Romain Morillon, Joel Morin, Raphaël Morinière, Matt Morley, Justin Morris, Martin Moser, Christopher Moss, Christopher Mott, Pip Mountain, Joerg Mueller-Kindt, Tom Mullens, Bridgette Murphy, Jane Murphy, Marc Murphy, Alistair Murray, Ian Nadin, Simon Nadin, Andreea Neag, Manuel Nechansky, Mike Neufeld, Andre Neves, Duncan Newland, Graham Newlands, Dave Newman, James Newton, Jamie Neylan, Vanessa Ni Chonduin, Lee Niblock, Jane Nicholson, Eduard Adrian Nichitenco, Anita Niklas, Alisdair Nimmo, Mike Nix, Maël Noise, Dan Nolan, Johan Norberg, Gareth Norman, Ian Norris, Rowan Norris, Samantha Northey, Tomas Novak, Mark Nunn, Richard Nurcombe, Kharis O'Connell, Barry O'Donoghue, Allan O'Hare, Alex Oldfield, William Oliver, Laganne Olivier, Valeria Oltean, David O'Malley, Ellie O'Malley, Alex O'Neal, Eoghan O'Reilly, Alex O'Sullivan, Josef Ondriga, Dan Ooops!, Neil Organ, Yoh Ornorm, Miriam Orr, Ricky O'Shea, Scott O'Sullivan, Tyler Overall, Karolina Paceviciute, Nicolas Page, Estelle Païs, Roberto Paparella, Aurelien Parede, Michael Parfitt, Ian Park, Benjamin Parker, Emma Parkinson, James Parkinson,

Mack Parnell, Mel Parr, Matthew Parry, Liina Päss, Craig Paterson, Ian Paterson, Martin Pavey, Dave Payling, Sam Peachment, Christopher Pearce, Philip Pearce, Jamie Pearson, John Peart, Steve Peckham, Shanna Pedersen, James Peel, Jennifer Peers, Mika Peeters, Tommaso Pegurri, Johann Pellé, Mark Pepper, Neil Pepperrell, Julian Percy, Claude Perdriolle, Yvan Perez, Pavel Peřina, Chris Perks, Abigail Perrett, James Perrin, Stevann Perrin, James Peters, Simone Peters, Rohan Peters, Tim Peters, Yann Pfinder, Thomas Pflügler, Franck Pham-Van, Ryan David Edward Phillips, Patryk Piatkowski, Marco Piccoli, Pamela Pichler, Cédric Piktoroff, Julien Pigneux, David Pineau, Jerome Pintori, Pavel Píš, Tamara Plank, Julien Plutta, Gary Polson, Jake Pond, Remus Popa, John Poppleton, Vincent Pornin, Felix Porter, James Potter, Symon Potter, Grégory Pottier, Lars Poulussen, Anthony Pouzoulet, Maya Sala Povedano, Antony Price, Matt Price, Alexis Prost, Stefan Pruski, Joe Public, Mathias Puech, Steve Puleston, Walter Puyet, Calum Rackham, Alex Radiobomb, Adrian Ramsey, Sarah Rand, David Rann, Hunold Raphael, Karl Raydius, Mark Rayworth, Mark Reed, Refugees on Dance Floor, Stije Regeling, Harmel Remy, Bruno Renard, Rob Renton, Paul Revell, David Richards, Jonathan Richards, Ben Richardson, John Richardson, Mark Richardson, Oliver Riley-Smith, Simon Riordan, Nicholas Riva, Marco Rivolta, Simone Rizzo, Large Rob, Sam Roberson, Vincent Robert, Jay Roberts, Joe Roberts, Daniel Robertson, Reuben Robertson, Kimberley Robinson, Jude Robson, Norman Roche, Catarina Rodrigues, Scott Rogers, Greg Rollet, James Rollo, Aymeric Rombaut, Lefebvre Romuald, Fabien Rondeleux, Nick Ronin, Sarah Rootham, Tiago Rosário, František Roubíček, Roue2velo, Ian Round, Félix Rousseau, Nicolas Rousset, Nick Royles, Marina Núñez Rubio, Ian Rushton, Wil Russell, Jean Marc Rutot, Sahinkaya Sahinkaya, Thomas Salah, Simon Salgado, Julien Salies, Natalia Hosie Samper, Raymond Samuel, Kenneth Sandberg, Jon Sanchez-Garcia, William Sant, Eva Sard, Gaëtan Sauvain, François Savoureux, Mark Sawyer, Andrea Scagliotti, Laura Scanavacca, Simon Scane, Daan Schagen, Maximilian Schebek, Tamaro Schmetter, Coralie Schneider, Tijl Schneider, Christoph Schol, Rita Schwarz, Mark Scorah, Emily Scott, Steve Scott, Martin Schroecker, Jonathan Seal, Rob Searl, Ondra Dedmik, Mario Sefrin, Jürgen Seitner, Kevin Sellin, Riccardo Serblin, Guilherme Serodio, Jean-Christophe Sevin, Thomas Seux, Alexander Sharp, Eilean Shearer, Michael Sheppard, Simon Shields, Mana Shigeki, JM Siaud, Simon Siddle, Maria Sikora, Carolina Silva, Raquel Silveira, Will Silverwood-Cope, Pavel Simacek, Alex Sime, Debord Simon, Mark Simpkins, Donald Sisson, Frédéric Siti, Skacid, Christopher Skinner, Christophe Jean Skrzek, Katarzyna Skulimowska, Tyron Slack, Joe Slater, Aka Slater, Michael Smaczylo, Pablo Smet, Andy Smith, Benjamin Smith, Danny Smith, Heidi Smith, Matt Smith, Simon Smith, Rachel Smith-Blair, Poppy Sofocleous, El Pedro Cartel Sonor, David Sorfa, Pablo Soria, Jonathan Soucasse, Coline Sourice, Katerina Spejchalova, Sara Speroni, Dan Spier, Ben Sporton,

Stuart Spring, Nicola Staffolani, Andreea-Alexandra Stan, Moz Stanton, Jason Stapleton, Steve Stavrinides, Rob Staynings, Matthew Steadman, Andreas Stellatos, Rebecca Stephens, Claire Stephenson, Matt Stephenson, Dan Stewart, Ian Stewart, John Stewart, Ezra Stitch, Kieran Stimpson, Craig Stock, Peter Stokes, Simon Stokoe, Sarah Stranks, Emma Street, Giuseppe Strippoli, Dom Strong, Leigh Strydom, Zoe Sudworth, Matthew Summers, Paul Surdulescu, Geoffrey Susman, Ryan Swainson, Ivor Sweeney, Anna Swift, Tbs soundsystem Velema, Kamil Tabor, Roy Talbot, Maria Talboys, Heather Tanith, Shane Tansey, Aurelie Tarlowski, Martin Tausner, Richard Tawn, Joe Taylor, Luke Taylor, Neil Taylor, Sebastian Taylor, Zak Taylor, Johnny Tekno, Terapeutek, Steve Terry, Ian Thacker, Eric The, Scar Thee, Jennifer Theves, Dianne Thomas, Michael Thomas, Caroline Thompson, Julie Thompson, Lily Thompson, Jake Thornton, Daniel Thurley, Ilaria Tore, Nic Townsend, Trauma, John Trevains, Aaron Trinder, Alexandre Tripet, Andrea Trovò, Philip Trueman, Paul Trunks, Alexander Tsimbalist, Erwan Tual, Raul Perez Tuda, Nicolas Turek, Viktor Turecký, Sam Turner, Scott Turner, Lucia Udvardyova, Austin Underhill, Jamie Upton, Alessandro Vallese, Pieter van den Akker, Julie Vanderdoodt, Tim van Akkerveeken, Albert Van Abbe, Blaise van Celst, Harley van Halder, Raquel van Swieten, Corina Van Der Meijs, Jan Vanek, Julien Vasseux, Martin Valero Vera, Raz Van, Jan Vaněk, Guillaume Varin, Linzie Vasisht, Gary Vaughan, Guillaume Vaugoin, Sebastien Vecrin, Zyler Vega, Joshua Velody, Saskia Verhoeff, Marco Vermeulen, Maikel Verwiel, Otakar Vesely, Mónica Daza Viafara, Emma Vickers, Matteo Vignati, Julien Vignial, Juha Vikkula, Francesc Vila Oliveras, Clement Vincent, Jodan Vingerhoets, Jon Virgo, Michael Vlasaty, Lisa Vles, Clement Voisin, Peter Waddingham, Amos Wakefield, Maximilian Waldbauer, Mark Walker, Richard Walker, Mark Wall, Alex Wallace, John Walls, Daryl Walmsley, Ria Walton, Jez Ward, McKenzie Wark, Tician Wasley, Chris Wassan, Heidi Watson, Steven Watson, Renata Wayre, Etilik Wear, Dan Webb, John Webb, Arnold Weber, Susanne Wehlisch, Daniel Weigl, Jonathan Weinel, Charlie Weisfeld, Cyril Weissler, A Wells, Craig Wells, Steve Wells, Rick Wenzel, Karl West, Teo Westerlaken, Carey Westley, Lorna Weston, James Wheatcroft, David Wheten, Allison White, Jason White, Matt Whitfield, Ben Whittle, Ryan Wilmott, Adam Williams, Jake Williams, Mark Williams, Neil Williams, Simon Williams, Luke Wilkins, Matthew Wilkins, Laura Wilson, James Wilson, Rhys Wilson, Kelly Winfield, Si Wingfield, Philip Wise, Fixx Wittek, Stuart Witts, Łukasz Wojnarowski, Stephanie Woods, Matthew Wright, Vanessa Wright, Julien Wyzlan, Yamoy & The Little Freaks society, Pete Yates, Margot Yntema, Barry Young, Ian Young, Istvan Zachar, Z-Bomb Soundsystem, Eric Zampoli, Dario Zani, Acid Zeeman, Lorenzo Ziccolella, Ste (Doc) Proc, Mark K, Paul F, Louise G - Animal House Kru, Worthing Techno Militia, Paul & Finsent